FLORIDA STATE
UNIVERSITY LIBRARIES

MAR 5 1997

TALLAHASSEE, FLORIDA

Transforming Societies, Transforming Anthropology

Linking Levels of Analysis
Emilio F. Moran, Series Editor

Covering Ground: Communal Water Management and the State in the Peruvian Highlands
David W. Guillet

The Coca Boom and Rural Social Change in Bolivia
Harry Sanabria

Diagnosing America: Anthropology and Public Engagement
Shepard Forman, editor

The Social Causes of Environmental Destruction in Latin America
Michael Painter and William H. Durham, editors

Culture and Global Change: Social Perceptions of Deforestation in the Lacandona Rain Forest in Mexico
Lourdes Arizpe, Fernanda Paz, and Margarita Velázquez

Transforming Societies, Transforming Anthropology
Emilio F. Moran, editor

Transforming Societies, Transforming Anthropology

Edited by Emilio F. Moran

Ann Arbor
THE UNIVERSITY OF MICHIGAN PRESS

Copyright © by the University of Michigan 1996
All rights reserved
Published in the United States of America by
The University of Michigan Press
Manufactured in the United States of America
⊗ Printed on acid-free paper

1999 1998 1997 1996   4 3 2 1

No part of this publication may be reproduced, stored in a retrieval system, or transmitted in any form or by any means, electronic, mechanical, or otherwise without the written permission of the publisher.

A CIP catalog record for this book is available from the British Library.

Library of Congress Cataloging-in-Publication Data

Transforming societies, transforming anthropology / edited by Emilio F. Moran.
    p. cm. — (Linking levels of analysis)
  Includes bibliographical references and index.
  ISBN 0-472-10574-4 (alk. paper)
  1. Social change. 2. Social problems. 3. Applied anthropology.
I. Moran, Emilio F. II. Series.
GN358.T73   1996
303.4—dc20   96-25396
                                                                    CIP

*Dedicated to the Memory of
Demitri B. Shimkin
(1916–92)*

Acknowledgments

This volume is derived from discussions carried out over a two-year period by a panel of anthropologists selected by the American Anthropological Association. The panel benefited from the participation during the first year of C. Redman, W. Torry, and I. Karp. To ensure coverage of some of the topics that came out of the discussions during the first year, a couple of scholars were invited to join in the second year—and one was invited to write the final chapter because of his important role in the engagement of anthropology with social change. The idea of the panel came from Roy Rappaport, then president of the American Anthropological Association. The work of the panel was made possible by a grant from the Wenner-Gren Foundation for Anthropological Research. Our charge was to explore ways to revitalize and strengthen anthropology's commitment to the study of social problems in preindustrial and industrializing societies. The panelists benefited from interaction with members of another Wenner-Gren panel that met concurrently with ours. That panel, studying the Disorders of Industrial Societies, was chaired by Shepard Forman, and its report appeared in 1994 (*Diagnosing America: Anthropology and Public Engagement,* University of Michigan Press). Like the authors of *Diagnosing America,* the authors of this volume are making a call for a committed and engaged anthropology, an anthropology concerned with constructing a partnership with the communities in industrializing societies so that social justice, human rights, and effective participation can be achieved in every corner of the planet despite the many forces acting to marginalize these societies from social, political, and economic equality. We want to thank Judith Lisansky, then with the American Anthropological Association, and James McDonald, rapporteur, for their assistance during the meetings. A very special thanks goes to Anne Woosley and her staff at the Amerind Foundation, who graciously hosted our meetings and made our stay in Dragoon, Arizona, an experience we all looked forward to each year. We have dedicated this volume to the most senior member of our panel, Demitri Shimkin, who passed away in 1992 after a long struggle with cancer.

Series Introduction

The series Linking Levels of Analysis focuses on studies that deal with the relationships between local-level systems and larger, more inclusive systems. While we know a great deal about how local and larger systems operate, we know a great deal less about how these levels articulate with one another. It is this kind of research, in all its variety, that Linking Levels of Analysis is designed to publish. Works should contribute to the theoretical understanding of such articulations, create or refine methods appropriate to interlevel analysis, and represent substantive contributions to the social sciences.

The volume before you, *Transforming Societies, Transforming Anthropology,* is the product of more than two years of regularly scheduled meetings by an expert panel of anthropologists. They were called together by Roy Rappaport, then president of the American Anthropological Association (AAA). The meetings were funded by grants from the Wenner-Gren Foundation for Anthropological Research. Emilio Moran was selected by the AAA to chair the panel on Social Transformations in Pre-Industrial and Industrializing Societies. The book fits into the series in that most of the essays, and the overall scope of the book, deal with the ways in which local communities are affected by global and national-scale processes and with how anthropologists have contributed to positive change in these communities. Several of the contributions address theoretical and methodological issues in linking levels of analysis.

The book presents an agenda for anthropology that, if not wholly new, is at least an expanded version of the work of many anthropologists already engaged in these transformative processes. Carol Smith has been working in Guatemala for years, but she now seeks to empower local people with a capacity to collect data that they can use to present their needs to the state. Julie Fisher identifies the richness and variety of nongovernmental organizations that are currently the most important agents of change in developing societies. Conrad Kottak identifies the media as one of the most potent agents of change and presents an anthropological methodology for addressing the impact of television on human communities. Ellen Messer, currently director of the World Hunger Center at Brown University, provides a thorough exegesis of the role of anthropology in the struggle for human rights, seeking to define the processes by which people gain or lose access to food. Demitri Shimkin and Dennis Frate show how community participation has been achieved in Mississippi and Tanzania and how health needs have been met. Emilio Moran questions the value of GNP per capita as a measure of well-being and suggests other, better indices to determine if people are benefiting from economic development. Tim Finan shows how local people in Portugal and Cape Verde have participated in the assessment of their needs and in research and policy making and how this requires different training for anthropologists. Michael Horowitz gives rich details of his twenty years of experience in development anthropology and the tremendous progress and contributions that have been achieved despite the hesitancy of the discipline and the academy. This volume is a call to those portions of the discipline that have remained disengaged from the profound problems faced by people everywhere—hunger, discrimination, disease, poverty. Engagement with these problems, and with the people who suffer these conditions, is a greater moral imperative than cultural relativism and offers exciting possibilities for an anthropology capable of generating theories about societies still in the making.

This volume shows that anthropology can be a policy science and that it brings to the understanding of these problems a capacity to speak to different temporal and spatial levels of analysis. It is my hope that this volume will inspire more anthropologists to favor study of issues that affect people in profound, transformative ways and that they be moved to try to ameliorate the condition of our fellow human beings.

Contents

Chapter

1. An Agenda for Anthropology 1
   Emilio F. Moran

2. Development and the State: Issues for Anthropologists 25
   Carol A. Smith

3. Grassroots Organizations and Grassroots Support Organizations: Patterns of Interaction 57
   Julie Fisher

4. Linkages Methodology for the Study of Sociocultural Transformations 103
   Elizabeth Colson and Conrad Phillip Kottak

5. The Media, Development, and Social Change 135
   Conrad Phillip Kottak

6. Anthropology, Human Rights, and Social Transformation 165
   Ellen Messer

7. Goals and Indices of Development: An Anthropological Perspective 211
   Emilio F. Moran

8. Hunger Vulnerability from an Anthropologist's Food Systems Perspective 241
   Ellen Messer

9. Culture Change and Health: Third World Perspectives 265
   Demitri B. Shimkin, with an addendum by Dennis A. Frate

10. Anthropological Research Methods in a
    Changing World   301
    Timothy J. Finan

11. Thoughts on Development Anthropology after
    Twenty Years   325
    Michael M. Horowitz

Contributors   353

Index   357

Chapter 1

An Agenda for Anthropology

Emilio F. Moran

Today we are participants and observers of major global political and economic transformations caused, and undoubtedly exacerbated, by our growing interconnectedness (Slater, Schutz, and Dorr 1993). New hegemonic centers are emerging, the cold war is over, regional free trade associations seek to buffer themselves in an increasingly global economy (North American Free Trade Association (NAFTA), European Union (EU), South American Free Trade Market (MERCOSUL)). In the Amazon Basin we witness the destruction of vast areas of rain forest and are informed of devastating rates of mortality among native peoples operating until recently by a combination of extensive horticulture, hunting, gathering, and fishing. Overnight they have been confronted with neighbors representing the eighth largest economy in the planet (Brazil), while corporations from the other top seven economies seek to exploit the region's resources. Dozens of environmental organizations visit the region and make suggestions about how to manage it. Missionaries and food aid organizations send delegations to assess the degree of need of local populations. World-renowned artists lend their name, and concert funds, in support of native peoples' struggle for land. These resources have permitted some indigenous leaders to have the capacity to fly over their territories, in their own planes, to monitor invasion of their lands by gold prospectors, timber companies, and cattle ranchers.

Across the Atlantic we observe Asian and African populations being dislocated by oil production, war, famine, and dam construction. In so doing, previously intensive cultivators have joined the already large urban populations in cities hoping to rebuild their lives now that access to traditional lands has been lost. In Namibia populations that have long been characterized as hunter-gatherers have in a short period of time become not only sedentary horticulturalists, but they have joined either armies of liberation or counterrevolutionary ones. The former Yugoslavia and the republics of the former Soviet Union fragment more each year into polities wherein human rights, cultural rights, and even human life is given little value by predatory neighbors.

In this vast world of flux what does anthropology have to contribute? The neat evolutionary stages so useful in looking at past changes do not adequately deal with the contemporary transformations being experienced by "traditional peoples." Warlike New Guinea clansmen of a generation ago now exhibit their paintings and carvings in Sidney, Paris, and New York. Eskimos and Amazonian Native Americans use video and other modern technologies to intensify their traditional social relations and to resist loss of their traditional values and territories. Electronic mass media play a key role in preserving ethnic and national identities in the global village—yet how many anthropologists are studying the impacts of media on human communities? Are anthropologists simply observers of an exotic world that is passing? Is anthropology merely recording the remaining traditional customs of people now transformed into our own image by "development"? Or have these transformations in the world system transformed anthropology itself?

Anthropology's engagement with the critical problems of the contemporary world (poverty, powerlessness, environmental degradation, oppression, urban growth, explosive population growth) is to be understood by examining not its institutional forms (departments, professional societies) but in *how anthropologists practice their craft.* This practice reflects the many forces to which anthropologists have responded. From a relatively small group twenty years ago, development anthropologists may now be found not only in universities but also in the World Bank, nongovernmental organizations (NGOs), and institutions worldwide charged with assisting people in their efforts to change or to cope with change.

For many years the idea of a value-free social science so permeated the discipline that it was judged unscientific to act in behalf of native peoples in their struggle with the state or the forces that were changing their lives (Wright 1988:365). This view is particularly surprising given that even Franz Boas, one of the figures responsible for modern anthropology, felt that it was not possible, nor desirable, to be objective about one's own culture—while preaching that such objectivity was possible in studying other cultures (Mead 1973). He felt that a responsible anthropologist, like any responsible citizen, should take sides in matters of social justice. This view has over the years given way to one in which one's social and moral responsibility encompasses not only our own culture but also those people all over the globe who cry for freedom, justice, adequate health, and food.

Anthropology and the Problems of Transforming Societies

Before World War II, anthropology devoted itself to the study of pre-industrial societies. This focus carved an academic identity and a public image for anthropology as a discipline concerned largely with small-scale, sometimes exotic, and often rural societies. This preference for relatively pristine societies marked the discipline's early years. It was sometimes justified as necessary to have a record of these societies before they were forever changed by contact with the West. Anthropological theory and method were shaped by this focus. Anthropology's widely acknowledged greatest contribution to social science methodology, the method of participant-observation, is a product of a focus on scarcely known, small-scale societies requiring extended residence to make sense out of their languages and customs. Studies of African societies' political and social organization shaped British functionalist and structuralist theories. In the United States, studying North American Indians influenced the development of anthropological linguistics, archeology, and theories of kinship. Historical particularist and culture-and-personality approaches are associated with studies that tried to explain the character of these societies. In both cases, these were societies undergoing transformation from relatively autonomous to societies subsumed under larger states which reduced the autonomy of action of these populations. Despite this situation, many of the theories invoked to make sense out of these societies assumed them to be relatively pristine, existing in relative equilibrium, with members who shared values and interests, representing well-integrated cultures.

In retrospect, it is remarkable that these assumptions were made, given the historical context of some of these studies (e.g., recall the situation of the Nuer at the time Evans-Pritchard came to study them), in which the population had only recently lost the war against the external dominant society and was in the process of facing loss of autonomy and an uncertain future. These theories say a great deal more about the anthropologists and British and North American social order than about the fit between the theory and the experience of changed circumstances of those studied.

After World War II the process of worldwide transformation accelerated in the First, Second, and Third Worlds. Societies which had earlier been colonially ruled began to be given (or had won) their independence—while other still autonomous societies in peripheral places experienced pacification, sedentarization, and incorporation into state-level polities. Many of the newly independent states, as well as those who lost this war, found economic assistance offered by the First and Second World nations. This assistance was seen as a necessary part of the postwar reconstruction of devastated regions such as Germany and Japan, but also as necessary to strengthening the existence of Third World states as economically viable and politically stable entities. Their ability to provide economic opportunity was seen as necessary for their political legitimacy. The economic development of preindustrial economies into industrializing ones became a major thrust of international economic assistance that led to the creation of greater global interdependence. Not surprisingly, this assistance became connected in many cases to the cold war sides and political alliances to either the First or Second World. Nevertheless, the result was increased internationalization of economic systems.

Notable advances since World War II in the control of ancient infectious scourges of humankind, such as smallpox, plague, cholera, yellow fever, syphilis, and tuberculosis reduced mortality worldwide—and fueled population growth rates in economies not always prepared for them. Reduced mortality was not matched by reduced fertility, in no small part due not only to the lag in changing cultural expectations of survivability of newborns, but as an outcome of missionization and other ideologies that often promoted maximum reproductive rates rather than its control among people previously unexposed to the views of fundamentalist Christianity and other expansionist religions.

These changes in Third World societies became commonly associated with a number of processes: rural-to-urban migration, urban growth, expansion of transportation networks, import-substitution capital-intensive industrialization, greater access to national and international media, greater internal stratification, and episodic reliance on military rule to control the political process when the larger population, or elites, found it useful. The economic and political precariousness of many Third World states often resulted in gender, ethnic, religious, and racial oppression. One need only to recall the earlier ethnic conflicts in Nigeria, the episodic massacres between Hutus and

Tutsis in Rwanda and Burundi, the recent Balkan ethnic cleansings, and many other incidents of terror like the Holocaust to realize that the struggle for control of the state apparatus is tied to differential access to resources and to revindication of real and imagined oppression by ethnic, racial, and economic segments.

The anthropological response to the problems of "developing" societies was to decry the passing of traditional culture and blaming development agents and the state for the negative impacts felt by these societies. This was an important and often timely contribution that exposed the unwarranted assumptions made in the model of industrialization exported to many Third World nations. The many cases of poverty, oppression, and violation of the human rights of peoples in many countries were reported. Remarkably, efforts by international institutions, such as the United Nations, to define the universal rights of individuals were resisted by the anthropological establishment. The legacy of cultural relativism seemed to demand that the discipline speak for the relativity of those rights in different cultures and for the primacy of their cultural expression. As a result, anthropology had a lesser voice than it might have had in the definition of universal human rights and in the mechanisms by which international watchdogs monitor those rights worldwide.

Ethnohistorical studies have revealed how native peoples have actively resisted the imposition of colonial rule and the commoditization of their labor (Smith 1984; Hill 1989; Wright 1981). Ecological studies have examined systems of resource management in parts of the world whose level of sophistication has not been equaled to this day. Instances of intensification that have occurred without environmental degradation provide a sound basis today for research to develop sustainable production systems (Denevan 1970; Turner and Harrison 1981; Posey and Balée 1989). Economic studies by anthropologists have revealed tribal and peasant societies' decision making as being neither more nor less conservative than our own behavior (Cancian 1972; Barlett 1981; Cashdan 1989). Historical comparative studies have pointed out that the little community has always been connected to a larger world system (Wolf 1982), which deeply affected its internal functioning and structural relations. Studies of ethnicity (e.g., Cohen 1969) engaged in a critique of the assumptions of the past and sought to explain the politicization of native peoples in various parts of the globe (Wright 1988:367). After World War II, the many economic development schemes implemented throughout the world by multinational lending institutions and developing countries led anthropologists to pay a great deal more attention than in the past to peasantries.

Although the study of peasantries was not new, its growing volume indicated a shift in the condition of many of the world's indigenous peoples. This attention was also expressed in important debates over the nature of preindustrial economies and whether they used the logic of classical or neoclassical economics (i.e., were based on concepts of maximization of individual utility) or were a product of a cultural logic expressing social obligation, community values, and other noneconomic criteria (compare the formalist-substantivist debate in economic anthropology, Dalton 1962, Schneider 1970). Outside of—but influential in—anthropology, dependency theory (Frank 1962) and world systems theory (Wallerstein 1976) offered explanations for the growing problems experienced by these transforming societies. These theories observed that efforts to push preindustrial economies into an industrial condition were expanding the number of urban and rural poor, as well as sinking a growing number of nations into ever deeper debt crisis to international and private commercial lending institutions. This seemed to be a result of heavy borrowing to finance large-scale, capital-intensive development projects such as roads, dams, and irrigation projects. These projects, noted critics, gave the appearance of development and legitimated governments undertaking them. But they also increased dependency of these nations on certain kinds of export-oriented production susceptible to unpredictable price fluctuations and often unfavorable balance of trade. In some cases even staple food production was neglected as prime land became devoted to cash crops for export rather than production to meet food needs of the country's population. The result was increased concentration of wealth in already industrial nations, and growing poverty and powerlessness in developing ones.

Beginning in the 1970s, the world experienced an explosion of nongovernmental organizations (NGOs) to meet the growing crisis of the state. For example, more than 4,000 NGOs are listed by the Organization for Economic Cooperation (OECD), and they have more than doubled since 1980 (Technoserve 1989:3). The state began to be seen as unable to address the endemic problems of the contemporary world: poverty, environmental degradation, population growth, debt crisis, AIDS, ethnic conflict, and urban violence. NGOs and other forms of grassroots self-help organizations in both the First and Third Worlds began to be created. Their explosive growth seems to be related to the failure of the state's top-down approach to dealing with these problems. In contrast, NGOs took a participatory, low-cost, small-scale, labor rather than capital-intensive, bottom-up approach to dealing with locally meaningful problems.

The remarkable proliferation of NGOs was not predicted by social scientists, but interest in understanding them has grown, with anthropology lagging far behind other social science disciplines in this regard (see Fisher, chapter 3). This is all the more surprising in that anthropologists could have been predicted to have the best feel for these locally produced grassroots organizations. Only in the past 5 years is there evidence of some young anthropologists starting to examine the role of NGOs, their impact on local problems, the relationship of local to external NGOs, and the long-term impact of these groups on local and state capacity to meet human needs in culturally appropriate terms. The persistent and continued growth of NGOs says a great deal about the failure of the state in addressing local needs. The sometime pharaonic capital-intensive development schemes often chosen by national governments have rarely produced enough employment or economic returns to help local people, much less pay for themselves and the debt that made them possible.

Anthropology's oversight of NGOs as a transformative kind of institution in the contemporary world has not been the only missed opportunity to date. Another major driving force of these transformations has been the ever growing impact of media on local, national, and global society. Television, radio, newspapers, audio and video, fax, cellular communications, personal computers, and other forms of transmitting information and values have had a revolutionary impact. Audio and videotapes have been used not just to expand the cultural hegemony of Euroamerican society, but they have been used to strengthen traditional rituals and kinship ties, to keep emigrants in close contact with families back home, and to provide alternative interpretation of events affecting them. Radio and television vary in their impact depending on whether the state controls programming and on whether private groups and individuals are able to find space and stations to transmit opposing views and values. Fax, cellular, and internet communications empower individuals and groups with the capacity to communicate instantly with distant allies and mobilize world opinion against acts of oppression, human rights violations, and other acts of terror. They also serve to bond groups previously separated by distance, poor infrastructure, and bureaucratic intermediaries.

Except for a few exceptions, such as the work of Kottak (chap. 5, this volume), few anthropologists have seen the study of media as the contemporary equivalent of the discipline's earlier fascination with indigenous languages and ritual. The latter were the means of communicating cultural information in small-scale societies, now transformed in a globalized village through electronic media. A large-scale research program to understand these complex media needs to be an anthropological priority. The contemporary forms of media are powerful driving forces in people's participation in their own transformation, in how and what they will preserve of their past in a global culture.

A struggle is clearly under way over the shape of global culture. Major multinational broadcasting corporations see an opportunity to create a more homogenous global culture directed at promoting the consumption of the products that make their existence possible. On the other hand, to appeal to the largest possible audience, broadcasters often make spaces for alternative programming that appeals to a variety of ethnic, religious, and cultural groups, thereby promoting unintentionally heterogeneity in values, ideology, and consumption. The arrival of digital communications has further facilitated the proliferation of alternative stations promoting specific religious and cultural values, environmentalism, alternative economics, and critiques of global culture brokers.

This new struggle for the values and behaviors of the next century—for the *content* of global culture—is an exciting challenge for anthropology. It is a struggle that runs from small, preindustrial rural villages to the centers of power in the First World. The Cold War has been replaced by the Global Culture Wars. Like the numerous ethnic conflicts characterizing the post–Cold War period to date, it is a series of small wars playing on a global stage. It is a struggle over whether global culture will value human cultural diversity, and if so, over whether global cultural diversity can peacefully coexist with respect for human rights, health care, freedom from hunger, freedom from discrimination, and differences in cultural expression.

This is not entirely new ground for anthropology, but one that requires major transformation in how anthropology trains the next generation. To engage the problems raised above requires a set of theories different from, but grounded in, the approaches of the past. Above all, it requires increasingly rigorous multidisciplinary skills, team-based rather than individually based research, and flexibility in conceptualizing units and levels of analysis. For example, engaging the study of media requires familiarity with a vast literature from the field of communications. This literature embodies not only findings of research but a set of well-tested methods and research designs that ensure that future findings can be grounded to this body of literature, that the instruments of data collection and analysis are state-of-the-art, and that the whole community of persons interested in communications (a very interdisciplinary lot) can judge and accept/reject the findings based upon their reliability and verifiability. It requires that anthropologists work with colleagues in this field in a joint enterprise to the mutual enrichment of the research. Likewise, serious research on environmental problems, like tropical deforestation, can lead to Anthropologists' traditional decrying of deforestation, or they can engage the issue by bringing to bear upon it tools such as remote sensing, geographic information systems, botany, soil science and tools of the social sciences to understand the complex driving forces, the impact of different kinds of deforestation and land use practices, and ways in which natural and managed restoration efforts occur or may become widely practiced. In short, to figure out ways to balance conservation and use at various scales by linking local actors, NGOs, government and private groups, and the characteristics of the environment into realistic systems of use that consider local people's needs, and global impacts like carbon emission and sequestration (Moran et al. 1994; Brondizio et al. 1994; Skole et al. 1994).

A research strategy to understand transforming societies needs to be concerned with process, with history, with the role of political and economic power as it influences social relations in time and space at a number of scales from local to global. This is a research strategy that must not become an artifact of rhetoric. It requires rigorous attention to combining qualitative and quantitative methods, to large sample sizes, to precisely defining what each sample represents at different scales (both temporal and spatial), and concerned with engaging the problems of contemporary society rather than remaining detached from them.

Anthropology cannot remain disengaged from the changes that contemporary populations are undergoing without expecting others to find the field trivial and its theory increasingly banal. How can an anthropologist, in conscience, go to study the kinship system of an Amazonian population and proceed to do so while ignoring that children and adults are dying from epidemic disease and that their lands are being invaded? To return and write a monograph of a kinship system that is rapidly becoming but a memory, while failing to collect mortality data and to document the failure of national institutions and local representatives to deal with the lives (and deaths) of those people, is nothing short of criminal. Although ethical choices are individually made, rather than by a whole discipline, it is quite possible that cases such as this occur, at least in part, because graduate training does not prepare anthropologists to deal with processes such as increased mortality, fertility decline, epidemiology, and changes in labor composition as well as it prepares them to expound on Eskimo kinship terminology and praxis theory. Nor do anthropological academic training or typical academic accolades reward those who deal with the changing lives of people as much as those who claim to find exotic peoples, "frozen in time," in some part of the world—even when such isolation may be a result of the researcher's ignoring their history. As soon as major social transformations begin, anthropologists often join the chorus of those who decry such changes and rush to study and salvage the shreds of the past while paying little attention to how local people construct their future through new political and economic arrangements. What anthropologists sometimes decry are the painful transitions and transformations people must undertake to cope in a changing world. It is these efforts to deal with change that constitute the empirical realities for an engaged anthropology.

Among the sciences anthropology has a particularly valuable lens through which to diagnose the human condition. Archaeology brings a perspective of longtime change in which transformations result from change in one or more components of an environmental or social system. Archaeological studies have been among those that alerted us to the sophisticated systems of resource use in so-called traditional societies, some of them adopted by contemporary resource managers (Evenari et al. 1971). Through bioanthropology one gains a population-level view of how changes in society can lead to altered rates of growth and development, altered fertility and morbidity, and other biological measures of well-being. These studies have played key roles in bringing anthropology into close cooperative research with scientists in the biological and medical sciences and, jointly, addressing basic issues such as international growth standards, monitoring of health and nutritional status, and the biological impact of different kinds and magnitudes of change on populations. Cultural anthropology and linguistics have contributed to an understanding of the historical, social, economic, and political dimensions of human action and thought. From these areas have come contributions adopted by many other disciplines: the ethnographic method of data collecting, a recognition of folk knowledge embedded in language that has been important in fields such as ethnobotany and ethnobiology, and an appreciation of the decision-making processes of traditional peoples.

Finan, in this volume, brings to our attention the need to reform the methodological training of anthropologists. The mystification of "the year in the field" has led some to ignore the appropriate role for short- and long-term field research, respectively. In fact, research methods need to be adjusted to the scope of work and the purpose of the study and be cumulative in nature. Rapid rural assessment and other rapid assessment procedures are becoming increasingly common and ever more systematic. Practicums in field research, as part of large research teams, is one of the best ways to learn the craft of research—and its development constitutes a major transformation in the methods of cultural anthropology—long enamored with the image of the lone anthropologist among exotic peoples. The new anthropology is one of anthropologists working side by side with other scientists, local participants in the research, and NGOs seeking to improve knowledge of, say, biodiversity in a watershed, in order to draw up a sustainable development plan for an area.

Because institutions in contemporary societies play such a critical role in ameliorating or exacerbating the consequences of transformations in production systems, diet, housing, demography, religion, and marriage practices, it is all the more imperative that anthropology engage the study of both traditional and novel institutions and the conditions under which they relieve or magnify the difficulties faced by human populations. What is surprising is that anthropology has ignored the emergence of new social forms as objects of study, even in academic terms.

The financially, politically, and morally compromised state, particularly in many Third World countries, has become a contested arena. Powerful elites, often with the support of military forces, impose their will despite precarious popular support. To legitimate their rule, they promote development schemes of high visibility but often poor trickle-down benefit. High external debt has been the result of many of these development efforts—further impoverishing the poorest in society. The failure to meet local needs has prompted a virtual explosion of grassroots organizing and a favorable environment for nongovernmental organizations of all kinds, an explosion in entrepreneurship in the informal economy, and other creative responses such as peri-urban gardens and microfarms on unoccupied or public lands along railroad tracks to meet household and urban poor's needs. It is in these settings that the transformations of Third World societies are taking place.

This is but one example of the numerous social phenomena that exist in the contemporary world that are important to the development of robust new social theories. They have been ignored by many in academic anthropology because they do not fit neatly into the objects of study that are characteristically anthropological. They are not communities bounded in space and time. Instead, they operate within other social systems, deal directly with those they "serve" rather than through existing institutions, and some may even subvert the role of local organizations and weaken the authority of the state (see Smith, chap. 2). Out of anthropological engagement with the study of these new kinds of institutions and organizations, one might expect, in due time, to derive an anthropological theory less concerned with structure and function than with process, committed to the preservation and further development of indigenous knowledge systems, committed to development through participation and empowerment of local people in their communities' fate—a transformed anthropology indeed.

Changes in the Study of Health and Disease

The study of human transformations can involve the study of ritual, religion, mythology, production and exchange, environment, politics, and institutions. Any good anthropologist, at some time, will devote his or her time to each of these dimensions in order to arrive at the comprehensive understanding of society that lies at the heart of anthropology. Less often heeded has been attention to the biological dimensions of change.

Social transformations leave "signatures," or biological marks, upon individuals in a population. This means that events such as mortality, fertility, growth, disease prevalence, and nutritional stress leave permanent marks that can be used to diagnose the extent of the change and its consequences upon members of a society (Goodman et al. 1988). These biologically felt events have consequences for ". . . social relations, ideological constructs and evolutionary trajectories" (ibid. 169–70). For example, nutritional stunting is a biological signature for the experience of disease and/or chronic dietary insufficiency. It is also believed that such stunting, in turn, decreases immune response, intellectual skills, and visual perception (Martorell 1989). The use of health indices for human well-being has been a notable contribution, one that continues to advance and that has not advanced further only because of the lack of attention and funds given to local-level data collection.

An example of just such a development is the recent anthropological critique of the "small but healthy" hypothesis, which suggests that reduction in stature does not provoke any functional, psychological, or other forms of impairment (Seckler 1980). According to the hypothesis, nutritionally stunted populations are well proportioned, therefore not malnourished. As a result, they do not require food aid. What such a hypothesis suggests is that food aid should be reserved for the acutely malnourished, or wasted, and withheld from the chronically malnourished, or stunted, since the end result is simply a lesser height. Anthropological engagement in this issue, jointly with nutritionists, has led to the rejection of this hypothesis based upon its tendency to ignore the negative consequences of chronic malnutrition to human populations. Maternal size is a strong predictor of child mortality (Martorell et al. 1981). In addition, the relationship between lower birth weight and higher infant mortality is well-known (Mata 1978; Victora et al. 1987). Chronically malnourished children are not only shorter, but they may have reduced work capacity due to reduced muscle mass, which may be important in physically demanding occupations (Spurr 1983). They may have impaired immune system responses, which has been associated with increased child morbidity and mortality (James 1972; Kielman et al. 1976; and Barros et al. 1987), and both learning and perceptual difficulties (Klein et al. 1972; Pollitt and Thomson 1987). In this, as in many of the other new directions taking place in a transforming anthropology, longitudinal studies are fundamental, since they allow for the evaluation of incremental changes of growth performance that can be correlated to dietary intake, parasitism, and other variables.

Empowering local communities with the skills to monitor their health and nutritional status would be an important contribution of an engaged, transformed anthropology. A number of anthropologists have already demonstrated the feasibility of low-cost anthropometric methods and other forms of community medicine executed by local people (see Shimkin and Frate, chap. 9). This kind of engagement needs to become far more commonplace in anthropological praxis. Communities would gain a greater awareness of their situation and have a basis for community action. The data could be used also to make a case for assistance from government and nongovernmental groups. It could also improve the quality of health data at regional and national scale over the less frequent surveys carried out from the top-down. More importantly, the engagement of the community in monitoring its own health and nutritional status could very well lead to increased community-based participation in many other activities of common concern. Health is one of the most basic and widely regarded needs of a population. It is a particularly effective way to engage a population in their own empowerment.

Anthropologists throughout the globe today work with health providers to improve the quality of the data that is generated and that will permit a more refined development of monitoring indices of human vulnerability (Hansluwka 1985; Wallace and Taha 1988). The late Demitri Shimkin, in chapter 9, discusses the positive contributions of anthropologists working in Africa to the delivery of health services and warns us of the upcoming crisis of chronic diseases in the Third World with all the high costs that any chronic condition entails. An agenda for anthropology must be engaged with their transformation and how local, regional and national economists prepare to deal with it.

Anthropology brings important insights to the study of health and the delivery of health services. Health problems and health status are often arbitrarily defined by providers, to fit into priorities other than the health of those affected. Health is an environmentally conditioned phenomenon that reflects cultural values and social order (Shimkin, chap. 9). Schizophrenia, for example, is far less disabling in Nigeria than in the United States (Hoben 1985). The severely disabled are able to survive and function in the United States at rates inconceivable in Africa (ibid.).

Donor organizations engaged in providing health assistance are often more concerned with their own priorities and ways of doing business than with adjusting their resources to the needs of a population. Cooperation between international donors is generally poor and deteriorates further among national system providers. Local-level health statistics are poor and make delivery of health services difficult.

Anthropology's engagement with health has emphasized the development of local capacity—a capacity that can be oriented not only to preventive health but also to the collection of data and the monitoring of outbreaks of various epidemic and transmissible diseases. This effort requires valuing people, but it requires the assurance that resources will be forthcoming when needs are documented. A transformed anthropology needs to work with governmental and nongovernmental organizations to empower local communities in mobilizing to provide for their health needs. Decrying the poor state of health of the poor is necessary but not sufficient. Engagement in solving these problems needs to accompany academic analysis.

Studying Human Rights

The best of anthropological studies through time have dealt with the experience of people in comprehensive ways. The classic study of the Bemba by Audrey Richards (1939) looked at both seasonal and chronic hunger and examined the ecology of food production, the social rules for consumption and distribution, and the nutritional consequences of existing ideologies, behaviors, and productive potential. Hunger, disease, and out-migration are consequences of local-level processes, which are, in turn, embedded, in larger political and economic structures that influence local behaviors and institutions (Millman and Kates 1989).

Human societies regulate through social and cultural mechanisms access to resources, such as food (see Messer, chap. 8). When reduced access to food occurs, a range of actions may be undertaken to alleviate the predicted food deficits. Some of these actions may be short-term adjustments, while others may be long-term adaptations. Short-term adjustments may include replanting a crop, changing from drought-susceptible to drought-resistant cultivars, consuming less preferred foods, and transforming stocks of wealth into cash to guarantee access to food. Some will hoard food, before the food deficit is felt, while others may shift from food production to wage labor to ensure themselves access to the means to acquire imported food.

Long-term adaptations have been implemented as well. Most important has been the effort to locate production in ecologically favorable sites, the storage of portions of production from good years to ensure sufficiency in bad years, and the linking of distant production systems through trade to guarantee access to different resource areas (Millman and Kates 1989).

Because human communities are linked with one another in ever more inclusive systems, they may be more or less vulnerable to fluctuations in basic needs depending on their relations with those other entities. Thus, villages may be able to produce food in one region of a country, but whether portions of that food supply reach other regions of the same country or not may be affected by internal strife between ethnic groups, how the vulnerable area relates to the central government, what price or distributional mechanisms are implemented to entitle one to food, and whether the vulnerable population has access to remittances or not.

It has become increasingly clear that famines do not occur because there is a lack of food but, rather, because the mechanisms for food distribution fail to guarantee the rights of some people to food. Those rights are influenced by political, social, cultural, and economic criteria (Sen 1989:774). Countries like postindependence India, with considerable less food per capita than many countries in sub-Saharan Africa, have been able to avoid famines because of the political inadmissibility of famine, the creation of administrative systems that provide employment in times of calamities and sufficient freedom of information to mobilize the population in support of early implementation of famine relief (775).

Other human rights, too, are under attack constantly (see Messer, chap. 6), and the collapse of hegemony in the Second World has led to genocide and levels of violence unheard of since World War II. The violation of human rights in the former Yugoslavia, the continued ethnic conflicts in Somalia and Iran, and the growing number of refugees worldwide demand anthropological engagement. Anthropology has a great deal to contribute by monitoring, reporting, and advocating the protection of basic human rights in a global village that at times seems to be returning to the chronic warfare common before the rise of states. This promise has, so far, been rarely fulfilled. Anthropology's traditional high valuation of ethnicity becomes uncomfortable when ethnic groups practice "ethnic cleansing." The horror at such practices has not led to vigorous engagement that could lead to its end; a theoretical reassessment of ethnicity, moral norms, and civil standards in different cultural contexts need to be examined, particularly to clarify how human rights are protected or not below the state level. The extension of human rights not only to political rights (as is currently the case) but to socioeconomic and indigenous cultural rights will require complex negotiations. Despite its difficulties, it is important for anthropology to work toward making congruent the rights and duties of distinct cultures with those specified as universal rights and duties. For example, Islamic law and the United Nations' Declaration agree on the importance of protecting people from hunger, but the way each would protect people may vary. How might NGOs assist in finding a middle path between the top-down approach of the UN and the bottom-up approach of Islamic law? How might food aid be provided by outsiders without thereby weakening the existing institutions that respond to food shortages?

A growing number of anthropologists are engaged in the study of "people on the move," the large flows of peoples across international boundaries as both laborers and refugees. Development processes promoted by national and international economic development organizations are often predicated on changes in land use, urban renewal, and the construction of infrastructural projects such as dams, highways, and ports. These changes, in turn, entail the displacement of people from areas affected by these changes. Such displacement is stressful and brings about major changes in the modes of subsistence, political and social organization, and cultural identity of those populations. It can cause impoverishment, increased morbidity and mortality, and anomie (Cernea 1989:2).

Anthropologists have over many years engaged in longitudinal indepth research on these processes and are at a stage in which they can illuminate the basic commonalities in people's responses to exogenously imposed displacement (Cernea 1989:3; Scudder and Colson, 1982; Hansen and Oliver-Smith 1982). It has also sprouted activist groups that not only study the processes responsible for these flows but that lobby with international organizations such as the World Bank to ameliorate the lives of dislocated populations (Cernea 1988; Colson 1989).

Carol Smith, in this volume, reminds us that institutional and cultural analysis of the modern state is what anthropologists *must* do. It is no longer viable to try to understand local communities without understanding the institutional constraints posed by the presence of the state—that is, the national and international political context of local communities. Such study need not be purely negative but should, rather, focus on studying the conditions under which positive change occurs. Smith argues that we can learn more from successful cases than from failures, especially in documenting how social and political institutions were strengthened by given interventions. Other important questions for anthropology are to study the role of culture in shaping the power of the Third World state, the study of nationalistic forms that do not lead to terror, to examine the political impact of projects (rather than only its economics), and to elucidate what processes empower local people and strengthen civil society. Disentangling who invested in what, when, where, and why—and the impact of that investment on the state—is no less important than attention to whether local actors responded to development or not. The iconoclastic Cassandra reputation of anthropologists needs to transform itself into more positive words and action to change the very conditions we are in the habit of decrying.

Development and its Transformations

Broader and more appropriate measures of success in transforming societies are needed. For years Gross National Product (GNP) per capita was *the* measure of economic development. Moran, in chapter 7, evaluates the inadequacy of this measure and proposes a number of other measures. These alternative measures focus on the need to use per capita improvement in well-being, through important indicators such as declining infant mortality and educational attainment that measure a well-distributed GNP—in contrast to GNP per capita, which merely divides an aggregate measure by the total number of people, thereby hiding the distribution of economic benefits. In this regard anthropology has steadily spoken up and has been listened to at the highest levels, at least in some cases. An engaged anthropology has contributed to transforming the evaluation of success in development projects (see Horowitz, chap. 11).

The complex interrelations between ecology, productivity, and political economy require that, to understand the global transformations of traditional societies, anthropologists move away from the study of single communities at one point in time, away from relativism and away from moral neutrality (see Horowitz, chap. 11). Instead, an anthropology concerned with understanding the contemporary world needs to be multilevel, multisite, comparative and longitudinal in scope (see Colson and Kottak, chapter 4). It must set aside moral neutrality and assume a posture of engagement and a commitment to just social change. This is no easy task. It requires reassessing the conceptual foundations of the discipline and the methods that are brought to bear upon the subjects studied. Colson and Kottak provide an agenda for a transformed anthropology—one concerned with linking levels of analysis across time and space. In addition, the final chapter by Horowitz reviews the transformation of anthropology toward practical concern for the dire problems facing human beings.

In this view the local community is no longer a typical representative of other communities but has a distinct history of social and cultural relations that must be teased out. In turn, to overcome the theoretical sterility of this brand of historical particularism it becomes necessary to sample a number of communities within a region in order to determine the range of variation that is present within those societies over time. Thus, local communities are studied as nested sites within a regional system whose relations to more inclusive systems must be investigated. To achieve this, Finan, in chapter 10, proposes a stepwise research design and the participation of local communities in the research process.

The danger of excessive particularism is overcome through comparisons of the situations endemic in the contemporary world and the shared experiences of peoples throughout the world. Many peoples throughout the Third World have been incorporated in the past three hundred years into colonial systems, have experienced dislocation to distant labor markets, have been subjected to alien political rule, have seen their institutions ignored, have seen their reproductive behavior and their religious beliefs changed through missionization, and, more recently, have been incorporated into commercial production for international markets. Their land, water, and air has grown increasingly polluted, and they are experiencing, simultaneously, the old epidemic diseases as well as some of the chronic diseases associated with developed economies.

Out of attention to these shared experiences of our species comes an anthropology with a view of human society that shows how some local communities' leaders were able to resist the efforts of external forces to destroy local social formations, while others failed, and the reasons for this failure (see Smith, chap. 2); how respect for political leaders was preserved in one case and the conditions under which it may have been lost; and how a population achieved excellent health and access to food, while another declined in well-being (see Messer, chap. 8; and Shimkin and Frate, chap. 9).

The fact is that local populations studied at a single point in time are ephemeral in nature, human behavior is contingent, and their transformations are often dramatic in nature. These dynamic transformations cannot be understood in a local community at one point in time. Instead, understanding the changing nature of human sociality requires comparison of variable communities through time as they are nested at different levels of analysis. This is a very different kind of anthropology. It is an anthropology concerned less with the exotic than with the richly varied lives of people everywhere, with their biological makeup, their transformations through time, and increasingly with the human rights to life, food, and health.

Anthropology has passed from an era of cultural relativism, in which it avoided making universal claims about the rights of people, to a situation at present in which some anthropologists are engaged in protecting those rights throughout the globe. Some have renewed their ancient dedication to the preservation of cultural diversity, which in turn is but one dimension of the struggle of our species for survival on an increasingly endangered planet. This concern with cultural diversity must also seek ways to nest that diversity in a global culture that respects that diversity and makes space for diverse groups to construct their lives through information exchange and social order. As they engage these crises, anthropologists join other scientists and local people in search of ways to strengthen elements of civil society through making them participants in data collection not just for academic discourse but for local needs and political mobilization. Doing so is not a denial of science but, rather, the most sound basis for the ultimate value of anthropology as a science of humanity. This would be, indeed, a transformed anthropology.

REFERENCES

Balée, W.
    1988   Indigenous Adaptation to Amazonian Palm Forests. *Principes* 32 (2): 47–54.

Barlett, P., ed.
    1981   *Agricultural Decision-Making*. New York: Academic Press.

Barnes, J.
    1954   Class and Communities in a Norwegian Island Parish. *Human Relations* 7:39–58.

Barros, F. C., C. G. Victora, J. P. Vaughan, A. M. B. Teixeira, and A. Ashworth
    1987   Infant Mortality in Southern Brazil: A Population-based Study of Causes of Death. *Archives of Disease of Childhood* 62:487–90.

Brondizio, E., E. Moran, P. Mausel, and Y. Wu
    1994   Land Use Change in the Amazon Estuary: Patterns of Caboclo Settlement and Landscape Management. *Human Ecology* 22 (3): 249–78.

Butzer, K.
  1990 A Human Ecosystem Framework for Archaeology. In *The Ecosystem Approach in Anthropology,* ed. E. F. Moran. Ann Arbor: University of Michigan Press.
Cancian, F.
  1972 *Change and Uncertainty in a Peasant Economy.* Stanford: Stanford University Press.
Cashdan, E., ed.
  1989 *Risk and Uncertainty in Tribal and Peasant Economies.* Boulder: Westview Press.
Cernea, M.
  1988 Involuntary Resettlement in Development Projects. Washington, D.C: World Bank.
  1989 Anthropology, Policy, and Involuntary Resettlement. Paper presented at annual meeting, American Anthropological Association, Washington, D.C.
Cohen, A.
  1969 *Custom and Politics in Urban Africa.* London: Routledge and Kegan Paul.
Cohen, N.
  1989a Paleopathology and the Interpretation of Economic Change in Prehistory. In *Archeological Thought in America,* ed. C. C. Lamberg-Karlovsky Cambridge: Cambridge University Press.
  1989b *Health and the Rise of Civilization.* New Haven: Yale University Press.
Colson, E.
  1971 *The Social Consequences of Resettlement.* Manchester, Eng.: Manchester University Press.
  1989 Overview. *Annual Review of Anthropology* 18:1–16.
Dalton, George
  1967 *Tribal and Peasant Economies.* Austin: University of Texas Press.
Denevan, W.
  1970 Aboriginal Drained-Field Cultivation in the Americas. *Science* 169:647–54.
Evenari, M., et al.
  1971 *The Negev.* Cambridge, Mass.: Harvard University Press.
Frank, Andre Gunder
  1966 *The Development of Underdevelopment.* Boston: New England Free Press.
Gluckman, M.
  1958 *Custom and Conflict in Africa.* Oxford: Basil Blackwell.
Goodman, A. H., et al.
  1988 Biocultural Perspectives on Stress in Prehistoric, Historical, and Contemporary Population Research. *Yearbook of Physical Anthropology* 31:169–202.

Hansen, A., and A. Oliver-Smith, eds.
  1982 *Involuntary Migration and Resettlement.* Boulder: Westview Press.
Hansluwka, Harald
  1985 Measuring the Health of Populations, Indicators and Interpretations. *Social Science and Medicine* 20 (12): 1207–24.
Harrison, P. D., and B. L. Turner, eds.
  1978 *Prehistoric Maya Agriculture.* Albuquerque: University of New Mexico Press.
Hill, J.
  1989 Ritual Production of Environmental History among the Arawakan Wakuenai of Venezuela. *Human Ecology* 17 (1): 1–25.
Hoben, A.
  1982 Anthropologists and Development. *Annual Review of Anthropology* 11:349–75.
James, J. W.
  1972 Longitudinal Study of the Morbidity of Diarrhoeal and Respiratory Infections in Malnourished Children. *American Journal of Clinical Nutrition* 25:690–94.
Kielman, A. A., I. S. Uberoi, R. K. Chandra, and V. L. Mehra
  1976 The Effect of Nutritional Status on Immune Capacity and Immune Responses in Preschool Children in a Rural Community in India. *Bulletin of the World Health Organization* 54:477–83.
Klein, R. E., H. E. Freeman, J. Kagan, C. Yarborough, and J. Habicht
  1972 Is Big Smart? The Relation of Growth to Cognition. *Journal of Health and Social Behavior* 13:219–25.
Martorell, R.
  1989 Body Size, Adaptation and Function. *Human Organization* 48 (1): 15–20.
Martorell, R., H. L. Delgado, V. Valverde, and R. E. Klein
  1981 Maternal Stature, Fertility and Infant Mortality. *Human Biology* 53 (3): 303–12.
Mata, L. J.
  1978 *The Children of Santa Maria Cauque: A Prospective Field Study of Health and Growth.* Cambridge, Mass.: MIT Press.
Mead, M.
  1973 Changing Styles of Anthropological Work. *Annual Review of Anthropology* 2:1–26.
Messer, E.
  1984 Anthropological Perspectives on Diet. *Annual Review of Anthropology* 13:205–49.
Millman, Sara, and R. W. Kates
  1989 Toward Understanding Hunger. In *History of Hunger,* vol. 1, ed. L. Newman et al. London: Basil Blackwell.
Mitchell, J.
  1969 *Social Networks in Urban Situations.* Manchester, Eng.: Manchester University Press.

Moran, E., ed.
  1994 *The Comparative Analysis of Human Societies: Toward Common Standards for Data Collection and Reporting.* Boulder, Colo.: L. Rienner Publishers.
Moran, E., E. Brondizio, P. Mausel, and Y. Wu
  1994 Integrating Amazonian Vegetation, Land-use, and Satellite Data. *BioScience* 44 (5): 329–38.
Pollitt, E., and C. Thomson
  1977 Protein-Calorie Malnutrition and Behavior: A Review from Psychology. In *Nutrition and the Brain,* ed. R. J. Wurtman and J. J. Wurtman. New York: Raven Press.
Schneider, Harold
  1974 *Economic Man.* New York: Free Press.
Scudder, T., and E. Colson
  1982 From Welfare to Development: A Conceptual Framework for the Analysis of Dislocated People. In *Involuntary Migration in Resettlement: Problems and Responses of Dislocated People,* ed. A. Hansen and A. Oliver-Smith. Boulder, Colo.: Westview Press.
Seckler, D.
  1980 Malnutrition: An Intellectual Odyssey. *Western Journal of Agricultural Economics* 5 (2): 219–27.
Sen, Amartya
  1989 Food and Freedom. *World Development* 17 (6): 769–81.
Slater, R., B. Schutz, and S. Dorr, eds.
  1993 *Global Transformation and the Third World.* Boulder, Colo.: L. Rienner Publishers.
Smith, C.
  1984 Local History in Global Context: Social and Economic Transitions in Western Guatemala. *Comparative Studies in Society and History* 26 (2): 193–228.
Spurr, G. B.
  1983 Nutritional Status and Physical Work Capacity. *Yearbook of Physical Anthropology* 26:1–35.
Turner, B. L. and P. D. Harrison
  1981 Prehistoric Raised-Field Agriculture in the Maya Lowlands: Pulltrouser Swamp, N. Belize. *Science* 213:399–405.
Turner, V.
  1957 *Schism and Continuity in an African Society.* Manchester, Eng.: Manchester University Press.
Victora, C. G., F. C. Barros, J. P. Vaughan, and A. M. B. Teixeira
  1987 Birthweight and Infant Mortality: A Longitudinal Study of 5,914 Brazilian Children. *International Journal of Epidemiology* 16 (2): 239–45.
Wallace, Helen, and T. El Tahir Taha
  1988 Indicators for Monitoring Progress in Maternal and Child Health Care in Africa. *Journal of Tropical Pediatrics.* 34:158ff.

Wallerstein, Immanuel
    1976 *Modern World-System.* New York: Academic Press.
Wolf, E.
    1982 *Europe and the People without a History.* Berkeley: University of California Press.
Wright, R.
    1981 The History and Religion of the Baniwa Peoples of the Upper Rio Negro Valley. Ph.D. diss., Stanford University, Department of Anthropology.
    1988 Anthropological Presuppositions of Indigenous Advocacy. *Annual Review of Anthropology* 17:365.

Chapter 2

Development and the State: Issues for Anthropologists

Carol A. Smith

Anthropologists who do applied work probably know that the most significant factor influencing the success of their projects is the nature of the existing state in which they work. This is true whether they work in the First or Third World, whether they work for a governmental or nongovernmental institution (NGO). Yet little theoretical work has been done on the nature of the modern state by anthropologists, applied or theoretical. Nor do many anthropologists pay attention to the now extensive literature on the modern state developed by nonanthropologists (e.g., Skocpol 1979; Carnoy 1984; Corrigan and Sayer 1985; Evans, Rueschemeyer, and Skocpol 1985; Mann 1986; Migdal 1988). One senses that most anthropologists have conceded the large-scale institutional terrain to history, sociology, or political science, concentrating instead on what they know best, national culture or local communities.[1] Yet, as I will elaborate, institutional *and* cultural analysis of the modern state is what anthropologists who treat the problem of development in the Third World must do.

Anthropology does have a venerable tradition of theoretical work on state evolution and on premodern state institutions, but the knowledge produced by this tradition does not take us into the capitalist era. Apparently, most anthropological theorists of the state thought that institutional evolution stopped with early secondary state formation some three thousand years ago (e.g., Fried 1959). Those few anthropologists who have treated the rise of capitalism as a new social form (e.g., Wolf 1982; Mintz 1985) do little to analyze the particular nature of the capitalist state. Those anthropologists who treat the state in the modern world as an extension of traditional evolutionary theory in anthropology (e.g., Adams 1975) tend to produce highly abstract "energy" analyses, which are of little help to the practicing anthropologist.[2]

A different anthropological tradition briefly treated the rise and nature of "newly developing nations" (see, e.g., Geertz 1963), but this tradition died with modernization theory. Challenged first by dependency theorists in Latin America (Kay 1989) then by Marxists and world system theorists (Clammer 1978), most anthropologists who worked in this tradition drew back into studies of small communities or of cultural systems. Recent anthropological treatments of modern states (e.g., Fox 1990) discuss them as if they were only bearers or creators of new cultural or ideological traditions, rather than institutional forms worthy of analysis in and of themselves.

One cannot study the modern state without seeing it within the general context of supranational forces and organizations as well as the global interstate system. Indeed, there are many contexts, practical and theoretical, in which it is appropriate to concentrate on supranational entities. Yet we must go beyond world system theorists in our analysis of the variable characteristics of "peripheral," or Third World, states. For the development anthropologist it is especially important to deal with the particular characteristics of the Third World state within which he or she is likely to work, because state policies constrain the operation of the development agency with which the practicing anthropologist is associated—whether that agency be local, national, or a supranational organization—and ultimately determine local development priorities and practices. Michael Cernea notes that the "*two fundamental actors* in local development processes are local governments and local communities" (1988:11; emph. added). In my view neither local government nor community can be understood without an appreciation for how they are mutually constituted, ideologically inscribed, and institutionally constrained by the Third World state. Operating as individual activists, we may be able to do little to change the goals and efforts of such powerful actors as Third World states. But we will be much better prepared to assess the appropriateness and likelihood of success of a development project if we understand the general political context in which it is situated, which constrains not only development projects but also community relations and social action of all sorts.

My essay on this topic is divided into four main parts. First, I discuss general issues concerning states, parastatals, and the multistate environment, especially as they bear upon the activist or development anthropologist who works in the Third World. Here I basically ask the questions that we should ask ourselves whenever we take on the task of advising a "development project." Second, I discuss a variety of nonanthropological models of the modern state and discuss what we can borrow from them and what we must attempt to reformulate for ourselves. Third, I suggest what anthropologists can bring to the analysis of modern state institutions, using those few studies by anthropologists of state and nation in the Third World, together with several recent anthropological treatments of development projects in relation to states. I conclude with an outline for future theoretical work on the state and some suggestions that can hopefully serve as a practical guide for the development anthropologist—that is, a way to deal with the fact that states exist as crucial features of the development environment and heavily constrain the kind of development practice possible.

The Current "Development" Environment:
States, Multinationals, Parastatals, and NGOs

Anthony Smith (1986) suggests that development or modernization is the main legitimating ideology in Third World states and, as such, is its major concern. Hence, rulers in Third World states, whether despots or social democrats, believe that one of the state's primary functions is to create the conditions and infrastructure for rapid development. Given this fact, one might assume that there would be little conflict of interest between agents of the Third World state and the international development organizations through which anthropologists work. Obviously, however, there *are* conflicts of interest. But these conflicts center on the definition of development, rather than on the value of pursuing development goals.

Until approximately 1973 the development goals of most international agencies and Third World states were much the same. Apart from a few small groups such as the U.S. Peace Corps (whose mission was more diplomatic than economic), the emphasis was on "large-scale, capital-intensive interventions, such as ranches, major roads, irrigated perimeters, and big dams—projects that were expensive, required long-term expatriate technical expertise, involved elaborate top-down administration, were often resisted by local peoples—and more often than not did not work in the Third World context" (Horowitz 1988). The general development model was the Marshall Plan, which helped reestablish capitalist production in Western Europe. This model of development had little need or use for anthropologists, nor would Third World development programs have found a need for anthropologists had the capital-intensive model of development remained hegemonic.

One of the main effects of the capital-intensive development model, however, was the enormous Third World debt crisis we now live in. John Walton notes that between 1970 and 1983 the total debt of developing countries grew from $64 to $810 billion. Today most of these countries owe medium- and long-term debts that average one-third of their annual export earnings for export service alone, and the figure increases to 95 percent if short-term debt is considered. According to Walton, developing countries took out loans in the 1970s because they had palpable needs, not because they were greedy or forced to borrow. And the money was not necessarily squandered in corruption and high living. The borrowed money was used to create the *appearance of development,* thus bolstering local state legitimacy. The borrowed money also built some heavy industry and its elaborate infrastructure, elevated the social wage, provided openings for social mobility into rapidly expanding bureaucracies, and bought the modern weaponry that would protect the new states from aggressively growing neighbors—as well as from internal social unrest that often accompanies "modernization." Third World states pursued, in short, "a strategy of statecraft that united regimes of sundry political description that boasted the effects of development as a legitimizing principle" (Walton 1989:305). We must also recognize that at least Latin American countries experienced a very strong period of real capital growth during the 1960s and early 1970s.

By the early 1970s some of the negative effects of capital-intensive development models for the donor countries (and their bankers) were being noted. This, according to Elizabeth Colson, brought about a dramatic shift in the strategies that were to be pursued by First World development agencies:

> By then it was apparent that programs being urged upon Third World countries were not working as expected. Massive debts were being incurred. The poor were becoming more noticeable. [The U.S.] Congress then directed USAID to shift from capital-intensive projects to projects tailored to benefit the poorest of the poor, especially those in rural areas. McNamara's famous pronouncement

made about the same time called for a shift in World Bank programs to assist in the building up of the countryside. Other UN agencies and various bilateral agencies echoed the same concerns and redirected efforts in much the same fashion. (Colson 1982:3)

With the "revolution" in development goals, brought on by the debt crisis, came an enormous increase in nongovernmental, voluntary forms of development assistance, accompanied by a strong demand for anthropological expertise.

In the period between World War II and the early 1970s the efforts of small NGOs in the Third World were relatively small, and anthropologists rarely considered the kind of development agents needed. But between 1970 and 1985 NGO yearly disbursements for development in the Third World increased from an estimated $0.9 billion to 4 billion (Cernea 1988). According to Cernea, the essence of the NGO approach is "to mobilize people into organized structures of voluntary group action for self-reliance and self-development" (7). According to Cernea, the basic NGO strengths are that they can reach the rural poor in remote areas, promote local participation, operate at low cost, and adapt to local circumstances (17–18).

It is well to keep in mind, however, that the real advantage of NGOs is that they place few financial demands on either First or Third World states: they are self-help organizations, relying upon voluntary sources of both capital and labor. It should not be surprising, then, that political leaders in Third World states are much less enthusiastic about NGO development programs than First World development agents are.

Most people in the development world today accept the proposition that the development record of NGOs in the Third World is better (certainly less destructive) than the record compiled by the large multilateral lending institutions such as the International Monetary Fund (IMF). Yet the record is not fully established. And it is important to note some fundamental contradictions between the new "grassroots," or bottom-up, development strategies being touted today and the still development-ambitious Third World states. There are also potential contradictions between NGO development goals and the rural poor themselves. Colson (1982) notes that, while the new agents of development look to local communities to provide themselves with services that are normally government responsibilities (i.e., the construction of schools or health clinics), local communities typically use self-help schemes as a means to stake a claim on government services (i.e., they build the schools or clinics but with the expectation that the government will then staff them).

The real contradiction in current development schemes and Third World states, then, has to do with constituencies. Local Third World communities do not provide financial support to or form the constituency of international development organizations and thus have little control over the kind of assistance offered. At the same time the international community of development agents plan for people they do not know, living and working under conditions about which they have little comprehension. Equally important, they do not stay on to live with their results.

Perhaps most important, however, are the local political implications of international development work. Throughout the Third World today, most notably in countries in which a major donor state has important political interests, First World development projects do much of the work of meeting the basic needs (e.g., economic, health, educational, credit) that are typically provided by government in the First World—on the basis of which First World governments are made or kept accountable by their people or constituencies. By stepping into the public arena wherein civil society relates to the state, development agencies thus have powerful unintended effects. They can either stifle the development of local civil institutions or create civil institutions inappropriate to the local political context because the outside agencies have no means of creating the context by which these institutions can effectively deal with local government. In this manner they either threaten or prop up weak, corrupt, or otherwise unacceptable Third World governments. Development agencies rarely jeopardize the real sovereignty of the Third World state; more often they allow particular state regimes to remain sovereign that have no ties or serious responsibilities to their own popular constituencies.

The current development emphasis is on the creation and support of "micro-business enterprises" (noncapitalized businesses that are highly labor intensive), peasant credit and marketing cooperatives (which almost never become self-sufficient), and agrarian reform (of the sort that rarely threatens the political power of the national oligarchy but retains archaic economic structures). This emphasis helps maintain economic forms that are nonviable in the modern capitalist world—without continuous development assistance. Most social analysts, from Barrington

Moore (1966) through Alain de Janvry (1981), agree that development, or modernization, requires the eradication or transformation of the peasantry. Arturo Warman (1980) documents how the political imperatives of Mexico's "revolutionary" government maintained a marginalized peasantry long past the period in which rural people should have been brought into the national economy as "modern" producers. Currently, Mexico's people, including its peasants, are paying the price for agrarian conservatism (Sanderson 1986). Moore observes that the demise of the peasantry with modernization is indeed a social tragedy of immense proportions. But he also notes that the continued maintenance of marginalized groups in the capitalist world can simply prolong the agony.

My point here is not to suggest that development anthropologists desist from working with peasants, "marginals," or other "poorest-of-the-poor." It is only to point out that there are political consequences for following particular development strategies within the environment of a Third World state that is desperately trying to "modernize." Anthropologists are especially likely to see and attempt to redress the plight of the peasant or marginal, but, without any knowledge or concern about present political realities, their work in development can lead to disaster. In many parts of the Third World we now see certain grassroots groups created in all innocence by development agencies being violently mowed down by impatient Third World states. Guatemala, whose cooperative leaders and grassroots organizers were almost all murdered between 1978 and 1982 (Davis and Hodson 1982), provides a particularly harrowing, but not unique, example of this sort.

A final practical point about the relationship between international development agents and modern Third World states has to do with the role of development as culture and ideology within that political context (Dahl and Hjort 1984; Robertson 1984). Whatever agency in which the development agent works, whether a local or international NGO, the World Bank, or USAID, the development agent represents a particular development ideology. Development ideologies vary widely: some development agencies have a vision of cooperative communalism (which may or may not be appropriate to a particular political context); they may have a vision of grassroots empowerment; or they may simply have a vision of capital accumulation and growth. Only the latter ideology is likely to correspond to that held by the Third World state. And none of them may correspond to the desires and wishes of those people being developed, who may want nothing more than to be left alone—or nothing less than a total sociocultural transformation that the development agent is unprepared to assist or deal with.

In order for development agents to function effectively and honestly in a Third World context, they must be clear about their own goals in development work, their own biases about a "good and just society," and the like. This point has often been made. But it is equally important that the development agent analyze the ideology of the development agency with which he or she is associated and if and how that ideology corresponds to that of the Third World state in which the work is taking place. The incredible failures of development agencies working in the Third World over the last thirty years (see Colson 1985) cannot just be chalked up to ignorance or overenthusiasm. It is clearly relevant that development agents work in political environments in which the development goals of their funding source (such as the U.S.) and their working environment (a Third World state) are very likely to be at odds.

My point here is that we threaten the sovereignty of a people by ignoring their existing political institutions and hopes, whether realistic or not, as much as by ignoring their existing cultural preferences. So let us briefly examine some of what is known about the nature of modern Third World states and their political constituencies.

Theories of the State: Current Institutional Models

It is widely observed that the current world is more heavily influenced by institutional forms larger than the state—that is, the world market, world banking institutions, and various forms of multinational organizations, whether business or private. The implication is that currently proliferating world institutions (from Mobile Oil and the World Bank to Greenpeace and Amnesty International) now overshadow the administrative capacities of the state and thus deserve our attention in the present era more than the state does. Following Giddens (1987), I take the position that the existence of tightly knit international connections do not overshadow the administrative sovereignty of the state: "The influence of particular states within world politics may wax and wane, but we should not imagine that the centralizing of global connections on the one hand, and the sovereignty of states on the other, are mutually exclusive (291). If anything, the strength and significance of transnational connections have made the nation state *the* global form of world ordering.

A first important point, then, is that the modern state is quite different from early states or traditional empires, whose administrative capacities were always very weak. In order to understand the power and significance of the modern state in the modern international arena in which parastatal institutions are also prominent, we must draw a distinction between two entirely different social forms of power. One form, following the paths of the world market, penetrates everywhere, like water or missionaries, and wields influence through both money and world opinion, not insignificant forms of influence. But this form of power lacks localized apparatuses of control, which in the current era always fall under the domain of a state. The state form, in contrast, is inherently bounded, territorial, and organized for the administration of a particular social space. Mobile Oil or United Fruit (or even Amnesty International) may topple a particular state regime, but they cannot replace the state form; another regime, perhaps more to its liking, will take the place of the prior state regime, using the same basic functions of territorial administration as did the prior state.

The next thing we need to know about Third World states are the sources, nature of, and limits upon them as relatively autonomous social actors. Neither of the two classic ways of treating the state in the social science literature, liberal or Marxist, helps us understand the autonomous role of the state. Both standard approaches reduce the state (and state interests) to other elements in society—either to society as a whole (liberal theory) or to the dominant classes (Marxist theory)—calling upon the concept of the state mainly to describe a certain functional arena for action. Recently both liberals and Marxists have criticized the standard formulations, pointing out times and places in which the state has been an autonomous actor and suggesting how one might better understand it as such (e.g., Skocpol 1979; Carnoy 1984; Evans, Rueschemeyer, and Skocpol 1985; Mann 1986; Migdal 1988).[3] Unfortunately, few of these new theories of the state are especially illuminating about Third World states. Thus, I outline some of their arguments mainly to provide a framework for some of my own notions about the relationship between development and the Third World state.

Let us begin by assuming that the state is a set of institutions and personnel who administer a territorially demarcated area over which they attempt to monopolize the use of force (the Weberian definition). Where in this definition can we locate the source of state autonomy? According to Michael Mann (1986), the locus of state autonomy resides in the distinctive way in which state power is organized. Power relations exist everywhere and take many forms—ideological, economic, and coercive. The state can never fully monopolize power, nor are the means of state power unique. In other words, the state wields ideological, economic, and coercive power, just like the various institutions of civil society with which it often competes for power (e.g., religious and military groups, the dominant classes, local communities). What is peculiar to the state, as opposed to these other social institutions, is the way it organizes power through territorial administration. Because state power (in multiple forms) is channeled through a spatially centralized, concentrated, hierarchical organization over specified areas, it provides the context (social and political) for the exercise of all other forms of power; this provides the state with the potential to delimit and diffuse other forms of power and to use other forms of power for its own purposes.

This peculiarity of state power gives the state a particular interest vis-à-vis other institutions in society: an interest in controlling a bounded territory through its territorial forms of administration. This interest is two-sided: on the one hand, the state must maintain itself domestically, by controlling and incorporating the population it seeks to govern by means of its administrative system; and, on the other hand, the state must maintain itself with respect to competing territorial entities—that is, other states or forms of territorial organization. As long as a state exists in an arena of competing states, it must necessarily defend and maintain its administrative structures or else lose them to a stronger power (cf. Skocpol 1979).

Thus, a state formed through conquest or colonialism, the usual case in the Third World, only exists to the extent that it creates a territorial administration, with its own centers of power, and incorporates the populace it claims for itself into them—expelling or incorporating other contenders for power over the area, such as the preconquest native communities and kingdoms or the agents of political imperialism. While Third World states are rarely able to lessen their economic dependence on First World states, they have in the period following World War II invariably developed means of controlling the local peoples they claim to govern independent of externally imposed relations of production. Michel-Rolph Trouillot (1990) describes the nationalistic means developed by the Duvaliers to control the Haitian "nation" during a period of increased international aid; at the same time he demonstrates the lack of fit between economic and political control in Haiti over two centuries of Haitian history.

To maintain its administrative structures a state must also have some capacity to compete with or co-opt other groups in civil society in order to regulate social relationships, to extract resources, and to use those resources in determined ways (Migdal 1988:4). Because peasant communities have always attempted to regulate themselves and have usually resisted state extraction of their resources, the relationship between peasant communities and the Third World state in the twentieth century has typically been antagonistic. Other traditional groups in the Third World—for example, religious groups, traditional oligarchies, colonial settlers—have also resisted modern state power. But, because these groups are usually more useful in helping the state meet its own basic organizational goals, their relationship to the state has been more symbiotic than oppositional. The modern Third World state in turn often assists these other groups in achieving their ends, as long as these ends complement rather than conflict with the organizational goals of the state. Because peasant communities have retained relative autonomy vis-à-vis the state up to the modern period, they tend to be the most developed *independent* element in Third World civil society (for an elaboration of this point, see C. A. Smith 1990a).

Depending on the kinds of relationships established with various groups in civil society, states may be more or less powerful along several dimensions. Michael Mann (1986) identifies two dimensions of state power: one is despotic power, or the degree to which the state may undertake a range of actions without routine, institutionalized negotiations with various groups in civil society. The other dimension is infrastructural power, the state's ability to actually penetrate civil society and centrally coordinate the activities of civil society through its own infrastructure. According to Mann, state infrastructural power has grown exponentially through history, as societies have become more complex and as the burden of social regulation is increasingly turned over to a state. The exercise of despotic power has varied widely over space and time, existing in states that are infrastructurally strong as well as weak. But modern First World states typically exercise little despotic power, not only because of their consolidated infrastructural power but also because they have penetrated the institutions of civil society ideologically—largely through the development benefits they have produced and continue to produce. Third World states are likely to remain despotic until they can legitimate themselves through development. To do this, they must struggle to eradicate the strongest institutions of civil society in them, peasant communities. According to Joel Migdal (1988), these "archaic" institutions are the greatest impediment to "strong" Third World states.

In consequence Third World states are typically both weak and despotic, their infrastructural powers limited by their economic poverty and by their need to develop those powers exacerbating their despotic nature. In order to govern at all they must either rely on preexisting institutions (local community forms, local elites, or local middlemen), which are potential competitors to state power, or they must increasingly build up apparatuses of force (police and military) that are more likely to remain loyal to the state but that take resources away from development efforts. Since World War II, however, the Third World state has had a new option: it can rely on loans and direct assistance provided by development institutions that can meet some popular as well as state needs without directly threatening state power (Fitzgerald 1985). The only cost to the borrowing state is that it may lose some autonomy with respect to exercising despotic control; that is, the borrowing state must often engage in a limited form of "routine, institutionalized negotiations" with the donor state over the range of actions it may otherwise take arbitrarily.

Negotiations undertaken with donor states or institutions as opposed to civil institutions within the state itself are limited by the fact that the main threat the donor institution can make is to withhold assistance. Unlike civil institutions in local society, it can less easily threaten to topple the regime or transform the existing status quo.[4] Hence, modern Third World states need be less concerned about the exercise of despotic power, and they need have very little concern with local legitimacy. In this sense, then, the whole process of development aid between First and Third World institutions stifles the potential power of civil institutions in the Third World state. (A classic modern case is that of El Salvador, where U.S. assistance was virtually guaranteed to the Salvadoran state in the 1980s, regardless of the repressive acts taken by the state against the Salvadoran people (see Donner 1993).

The current conjuncture, in which First World states and other First World donor institutions have largely given up the policy of large-scale capital intensive development strategies to concentrate on "the poorest of the poor," has created new contradictions within Third World states.

Almost any student of development will concede that this new development strategy is quite unlikely to lead to self-sustaining growth for the Third World state. It is, at best, ameliorative, an exercise in "relief aid" that might lower the level of Third World indebtedness as well as dampen popular protest; at worst, it is an imposition of Western values about pulling oneself up by one's bootstraps through the powers of an untrammeled market and liberal ideology. In short, it is not a real development strategy at all.

One might expect the autonomy of the Third World state to be directly threatened by this new turn of events. Yet current studies of Third World states, especially in Latin America, while pointing to various kinds and sources of state weakness, mostly show its growing autonomy—with respect to both local oligarchs and foreign powers. Thus, while Walter LaFeber (1984) argued that Central American states were basically U.S. puppets until the recent period, James Dunkeley's (1988) study of Central American politics over the past thirty years shows that the U.S. has been less able to impose its will on the region even as it has increased its economic aid to the region twenty-fold (see also Trouillot's study of Haiti [1990]). Recent studies of Mexico, by Sanderson (1986) and Grindle (1986), describe a similar pattern—that is, declining international control, in this case combined with growing resistance to the state by invigorated elements in Mexican civil society.

E. V. K. Fitzgerald (1985), who also treats Mexico, argues that the peripheral state grows both increasingly strong and increasingly vulnerable in the course of capitalist development. Its strength arises from the development of a state apparatus capable of stimulating economic growth and controlling popular movements. Its vulnerability lies in its constant inability to collect the taxes necessary to finance increasing expenditures. Notably, despite their own long-term interests in the growth of an autonomous state (vis-à-vis international capital), domestic capitalists in much of the Third World continue to resist higher rates of taxation. In Guatemala, for example, a major battle raged in the 1980s between the military state and the traditional oligarchy over the issue of taxation (C. A. Smith 1990b). The main recourse of the state under these circumstances is to continue foreign borrowing. While strengthening the hand of the state against local interest groups, including local capital, this puts the state in a weak position in regards to international capital. Yet, again, the current world battle over the Third World debt shows that in some respects international capital (i.e., banks) are in the most vulnerable position of all. At this point in time many experts expect some sort of general repudiation of the Third World debt, which the citizens of First World states, who once enjoyed the terms of trade created by the debt, may ultimately have to pay (MacEwan 1989).

The overall picture of Third World states given to us by the experts, then, is that of an extended crisis, reminding one of Gramsci's bleak observations: "The crisis consists precisely in the fact that the old is dying and the new cannot be born; in this interregnum a great variety of morbid symptoms appear" (1971:276). On the one hand, the infrastructural powers of Third World states have grown in the recent period, even as their economic dependency has deepened. Growth in these powers threatens the growth of competing power sources in civil society. Yet the main competing groups in civil society are economically retrograde elements (i.e., peasants on the one hand, traditional oligarchs on the other hand). For economic transformation to take place in the Third World, these elements of civil society will have to lose power. Yet much development aid goes toward propping up both kinds of retrograde elements. The growing economic dependency of the Third World state (as opposed to economy) creates a continued structural crisis of the state deprived of the means to transform the economy. Meanwhile, we see the growth of state institutions that rival classic empires in their untrammeled use of despotic force and their high levels of bureaucratic corruption.

One might well ask at this point how an anthropologist might produce an analysis that could uncover the significant elements that produce such crises—especially given that my references so far have been to a nonanthropological literature and my discussion has remained at an extremely general level. To answer this question I will briefly describe several recent efforts by anthropologists to analyze Third World state crises, some of which emphasize culture, others of which emphasize development issues.

Current Anthropological Treatment of Third World States

What those few anthropologists who have dealt with modern Third World states have added to the theoretical analyses is a concern to theorize the relationship between state and "nation." Unlike theorists of the First World, who posit a relatively unproblematic relationship between state and nation (see, e.g., Gellner 1983), anthropologists have shown three problematic features of state- and nation-building characteristic of the Third World: (1) the modernity yet historical variability of the pattern; (2) the novel yet contradictory forms of power that nation building can give to an otherwise relatively "weak" state; and (3) the vast potential for novel and extreme forms of violence unleashed by the development of "nationalistic" forms of state power (see especially Anderson 1983; Tambiah 1986; Kapferer 1988; Fox 1990; Trouillot 1990; C. A. Smith 1990a).

As a result of Benedict Anderson's (1983) influence, many current anthropological studies of political culture, whether of states or of other "imagined communities" such as ethnic groups, emphasize the interaction between state institutions and ideology in the construction of a "deep, horizontal comradeship" basic to a nationalist sentiment. Nationalism, according to Anderson, is a modern sentiment of cultural solidarity or fraternity generated by modern colonialism, new forms of state power, and "print capitalism." While this new form of cultural solidarity may ultimately be responsible for much modern state and ethnic violence, it does so not so much by generating an urge to kill for the community but, rather, to die for it willingly (1983:16). Others have painted a much less benign picture of the phenomenon. Tambiah (1986) and Kapferer (1988), for example, emphasize the generation of both new and more totalitarian forms of state power alongside the propensity for generating unprecedented levels of popular violence in their analyses of militant Buddhist Sinhalese nationalism in Sri Lanka. In this regard they take a position closer to that of sociologists (e.g., Giddens 1987; Gellner 1983).

Trouillot is one of the few anthropologists to link forms of nationalism clearly to forms of state power. He argues that "the nation is a construct that operates *against the background of political power*. . . . Nation-building can operate within the state, against the state, or in the name of the state. The nation is not necessarily a cultural construct *backed* by political power. Rather, it is a cultural construct that offers some claim to homogeneity *in relation* to political power (1990:25). In his study of modern Haiti Trouillot shows that the Duvalier state was not different from previous Haitian states in its authoritarianism or use of violence but that it developed qualitatively new powers through a centralization in the executive, the eradication of civil forms of resistance, and a new kind of state violence that "broke down traditional solidarities within civil society" (168). In so doing, the Duvalier state used nationalism to turn *against* the nation. It is worth noting that the Duvalier state was able to accomplish this in the face of declining government revenues.

These few cultural studies of states and nations in the modern Third World provide, in their comparative and historical details, a basis for further understanding the elements used to construct modern state power, which have taken new and terrifying forms in the twentieth century. Not only do they convincingly show modern states to be major actors that take on lives of their own in relation to global forces, but they also show that "culture is not a mere adjunct of other forms of analysis and interpretation, such as economics, politics, and the like" (Kapferer 1988:18). New forms of state power are in fact based in fetishized forms of culture, symbolically disarticulated or decontextualized, such that they function in a new way, "constituting relations rather than constituted within relationships" (97). (See also the essays in Fox 1990.)

The more theoretical anthropological works on the state, which I have previously described, do not directly address development issues that could be of help to practicing anthropologists. (Trouillot 1990 is the main exception, though he does not describe the operation of the development projects that helped prop up the Duvalier regime in any detail.) The works that do treat development projects and agencies in relation to the state (three of which will be discussed here) do little to expand our theoretical understanding of the state, tending to treat the state (and nation) as unchanging parts of the development environment, related to development agents or efforts in an adversarial relationship rather than a mutually constituting one. (A. V. Robertson is the main exception here, though he touches only lightly on the manipulation of national identity involved in development projects.) In my conclusion I suggest how the two kinds of studies could be more fruitfully combined.

Orlove and LeVieil's (1989) study of fisheries development projects in Lake Titicaca provides perhaps the most typical case. There were three development projects: fish canneries (mostly private), trout farms (state and private), and trout cage culture (assisted mainly by international NGOs). Over a twenty-year period all failed. The fish canneries were successful at first: they had small capital requirements, experienced businessmen as owners, and a relatively strong local market. All failed within less than a decade because of overfishing by the local fishermen, who provided the canneries with fish. The various trout farms, which existed over a longer period of time, also failed because of a variety of production and marketing difficulties. About half of the trout farms were set up by a state agency (the Peruvian Ministry of Fisheries); the other half were run by either local cooperatives or private individuals. Notably, the state farms were the most efficient, but the NGO-funded projects were the last to collapse because their continued existence was not predicated on real profitability.

Orlove and LeVieil argue that state inability to control overfishing or to provide regular, professional, technical assistance was the major factor in the decline of all these experiments. They note the lack of coordination between various state ministries and their poverty of resources; they also charge the state ministries with waste, irresponsibility, and petty corruption. But their main conclusion is that state bureaucrats in both Peru and Bolivia are inefficient because they are unaccountable to the people they are meant to serve:

> We attribute the general governmental inefficiency to the general lack of accountability of the state to the peasant populations in the Lake Titicaca region; this lack stems from the great inequalities of wealth and power, compounded by a residual racism which discriminates against the peasants as Indians. The repeated failures of the agencies do not lead to changes in operation or in organization, because the purported beneficiaries of the projects cannot make their discontent heard. (1989:212)

It should be noted that Orlove and LeVieil could have made the same charge against the nongovernmental development organizations in the region (which also failed), but they did not. One senses the usual anthropological antipathy toward Third World state bureaucrats, whose particular patterns of failure (based on lack of commitment) seem more culturally obnoxious than do the patterns of failure of NGOs, whose personnel are usually highly committed, if disinterested in the prospects of independent success or self-sustainability.

Nonetheless, the fisheries case study does point to the main difficulty development agents have in working in Third World state environments: the lack of popular responsibility held by development agents in much of the Third World. The analysis, however, does not suggest any solution. Nor does it provide a careful assessment of the actual viability of the fisheries projects with respect to self-sustainability or development. Hence, my next case study is selected to show a different set of processes, the forms of development possible in a "revolutionary" state (Nicaragua, as described by Field 1987), where popular protest was mobilized to change the responsiveness of state agents.

Field describes the changing fortunes of an artisanal cooperative in the pre- and postrevolutionary periods of Nicaragua. The co-op, located in a small village near Masaya (San Juan Oriente), had long specialized in the production of ceramics. The co-op had been set up before the revolution by the Nicaraguan Central Bank. Like most cooperative organizations in the Third World, this particular coop had a very uneven record of success. At various points it nearly died because of a series of problems in production, credit, marketing, and personnel as well as the usual problem of corruption. After the revolution, however, the Ministry of Culture, interested in promoting artisanal production that might symbolize Nicaragua's preconquest past, decided to support the ceramics cooperative, without concern for the economic viability of the project.

The record of the postrevolutionary state ministry in actually supporting the cooperative project was no better than that of the prerevolutionary state agency. For example, the new kilns provided by the ministry for firing the ceramics did not reach the range needed to make a good product. Various parts needed for the new equipment were not available in Nicaragua. The ministry's marketing study completely misjudged local demand. Perhaps most debilitating (and typical), ministry officials, many of whom were holdovers from the prerevolutionary period, were both ignorant and patronizing about local development needs.

Eventually, relations between the local co-op and the ministry were strained to the breaking point. But within the open political environment of Nicaragua in the early 1980s it was possible for artisans, such as the potters in this co-op, to create an artisanal union through which their economic and social demands could be channeled directly to the state. By joining the artisanal union in 1985—with the support of the Sandinista Party, against the wishes of its own ministry—the potters in the San Juan cooperative were able design a more viable economic strategy than that they had been saddled with by the state ministry. More important, the artisanal union was able to call the state ministry to account, forcing major changes in the state's economic strategies affecting artisans.

The political empowerment of the local groups receiving state assistance in Nicaragua was not sufficient to create economic development on its own. But in this case political empowerment made the particular development project as viable as possible under existing economic (and political) constraints. More important, it forced state representatives of the development projects to take into account the economic demands of the people they are supposed to assist. The "real" economic development that may come out of these projects may be minimal. But, if projects of these sorts are broadened and strengthened, they could have a major impact on state development policy. The point made by this case is that it will be state development policy that determines what is to be and who is to benefit from economic development in the long run, as the following case study also illustrates.

The final case to be described is that of Malaysia between the 1950s and the early 1980s (Robertson 1984). What Robertson portrays is the growing importance of a state development agency, the Federal Land Development Authority, or FDLA, as both an agent of state policy and a major component of state bureaucratic growth and centralization. As Robertson describes it, Malaysia's development trajectory has two relatively unusual features: first, the postcolonial state has always taken planning for development seriously; and, second, it has done so more successfully than most Third World states. Robertson's third major point, I believe, is not so unusual: that, while the state's major development agency (the FDLA) was conceived by external development agents (mainly by the World Bank) as well as by the state, it has increasingly become an organic part of the Malay state rather than an expression of foreign, multinational interests.

Set up in 1956 with World Bank funding and direction, the FDLA was set up as a smallholder settlement scheme that was involved in the production, processing, and marketing of world exports (primarily palm oil and rubber). Relatively successful in promoting population redistribution in a very unevenly settled country and economic growth from its inception to the present, the FDLA, together with other forms of government planning, increasingly became a means of controlling rather than developing civil society, especially after the major ethnic turmoil in 1969. From that time to the present development planning involved centralizing and consolidating the powers of the state through the state's major and numerous development agencies. The effect was that "civil society was now clearly dependent on the state not simply to secure its welfare and progress but to save it from those malignant forces (in the particular form of either ethnic disunity or revolutionary threat) which threatened to destroy it from within" (ibid., 255).

In pursuing its development policy, the government assumed an expanded role in the economy such that Malaysia now has "one of the largest public sectors of all developing countries. Its ratio of public expenditure to GNP in 1972 was 39 percent, putting it close to the level of welfare states in Western Europe (ibid., 260). A principal justification for the state enterprises is that they establish and consolidate capital resources "in trust" for the ethnic Malays vis-à-vis the more prosperous and "enterprising" Malay Chinese (261). The FDLA became such a "trust" agency during the 1970s, such that by the late 1970s virtually all of its settlers were ethnic Malays. Thus, the development agency became a means for redistributing both economic and political power in civil society and the state.

At the same time, the FDLA became "perhaps the largest single agency landholding in the world" (ibid., 262). As the FDLA grew in size and power, pressure to sustain output targets changed it from a smallholder development agency into a form of estate system, in which settlers were paid wages and obtained no rights in land. Robertson describes this as a shift from the state attempting to meet the economic needs of the people to a situation in which the people must meet the economic needs of the state (269). The state, empowered by its economic as well as coercive power over settlers, currently intrudes into every aspect of settler life through numerous forms of state-organized committees. New development planning by the state also emphasizes "strengthening national security" against internal threats (275 ff.), not only by controlling the location of settler communities (in contested or potentially contested areas) but also by spending on security forces. Perhaps the most sinister intrusion of the state into community affairs has been the establishment of committees "formed to assist the security forces in facing any subversive and undesirable elements threatening the security and stability of (FDLA) villages" (287).

Despite twenty years of efforts to change the ethnic balance of economic power (mainly by favoring ethnic Malays over other ethnic groups in Malaysia), the development plans of the Malaysian state "has not done much to dissolve the racial categories which remain the most overt expression of disunity" (ibid., 289). At the same time the development plans of the state have exacerbated class tensions brought on by growing wealth disparities, which "are generally seen as an inevitable consequence of development and as an antidote to ethnicity" (283). Robertson notes that violent reactions against increasing income and property disparities as well as growing state control over civil life have been staved off by Malaysia's relatively high rate of economic growth in the 1970s (8 percent per year), which he is not sure is due to good planning or good fortune (the relative price stability for Malaysian exports and "the good luck to strike oil and reserves of natural gas—the dream of every poor country." But in any event the current situation is one in which "the dependency of the state on planned development is now as evident as the dependence of Malaysian society on the mediating capacities of the state" (290).

The three cases used to illustrate the anthropological treatment of the relationship between the Third World state and development projects and agencies were not chosen from an ample literature. But they illuminate a variety of relationships in widely diverse settings in which some of the development projects have been assessed as successful and others as failures. The authors of the Peruvian/Bolivian case study attribute failure in all kinds of development projects (state, private, and NGO) to the nature of the Peruvian/Bolivian state; the author of the Nicaraguan case study attributes the (relative) development success of a village cooperative to competition between elements in the state (a state ministry, an artisanal union, and the (state) revolutionary party); and the Malaysian case describes the growing interdependence of the state and a parastatal agency in both state and civil development processes, illustrating the importance of economic growth to state growth and the ability of the state to maintain civil order. Not surprisingly, there are no sympathetic portrayals of Third World states or their development agendas. But, also important, the state in every case plays a critical role and tends to be more successful in situations in which its competitors are local civil organizations (of one sort or another) rather than multinational donor organizations.

These studies suggest two points worthy of consideration by development anthropologists: first, development projects play a major role in determining the constraints under which a Third World state operates (its ability to penetrate civil society as well as to maintain relative social stability); and, second, the most effective development organizations are those that are in some ways directly responsible to their constituency. To further develop these contradictory points, let me briefly describe yet another case in which the Third World state, Guatemala, one of the world's greatest violators of human rights, has managed to develop a relatively "effective" development program.

Though I shall not use it as such, Guatemala can be used as a case to show the worst kind of development horror stories. USAID programs in Central America (which now take up some 20 percent of AID's budget) have not only been mostly failures, but they have been implicated in creating import dependency, supporting military control of rural areas, pinpointing community leadership that was subsequently eliminated, and having purely "political" aims with respect to propping up state regimes whose people are anxious, indeed desperate, to change them (Barry and Preusch 1988). Current programs in the Indian highlands by both NGOs and USAID have also played a major role in restructuring land tenure and local social relations in ways that seem mostly deleterious to the Indian communities (C. A. Smith 1990b). I note these development failures to put the relatively successful development project in proper context.

In 1985, before the democratic elections that put a civilian in charge of Guatemala's state for only the second time in over thirty years, Guatemala's military convened a multisectoral group to write a new constitution. One of the provisions of the new constitution, whose political implications are quite radical within the context of the highly centralized state typical in Latin America, is that 8 percent of general government revenues would be turned over to local (municipal) governments to be used for local development projects. A formula was developed, based on municipal population and current municipal revenues, to distribute the 8 percent in such a way that it would favor the "neediest" municipalities. Between 1986 and 1988 the program actually functioned that way—providing more funds per capita to the least developed areas of the country—though it appeared that the formula changed (to favor larger, richer municipalities) in 1989. The amount of money involved was quite substantial. Municipalities (townships) with populations of only some five thousand or so extremely poor peasants received as much as 240,000 quetzales (90,000 in U.S. dollars) per year for development projects. In most cases this was more than ten times the amount of development funding the community had ever gotten—certainly by the state.

Within certain constraints (general type of project, organization of development committees, donation of a certain percentage of community labor, need to spend the funds in a limited period of time) municipalities were free to allocate the funds to the projects they most needed (see Annis 1988). In the eleven municipalities in which I conducted interviews the favored projects were: roads, schools, clean water, market buildings, and *salones de uses multiples* (meetinghouses). One could certainly argue that such infrastructural projects, while basic to general development, had few processual features of the sort needed to implement anything like sustained growth. Municipalities could not hire technicians (though they did pay local workers to do most of the construction). They could not establish, for example, an agricultural extension service, something most places desperately need. Nor could they staff the schools, public health buildings, or other structures that they built. Thus, it would be easy to write off this program as development irrelevancy; the more cynical among us noted that most projects required the purchase of tons of cement, a resource controlled by one of the biggest monopolies in Guatemala.

Yet the political impact of the program has been dramatic. In at least three highland townships (of the eleven on which I collected information) corrupt or arbitrary mayors have been replaced by an irate citizenry. In many more townships they have been called to town meetings to account for the funds at their disposal. Corrupt political officials are rife in Guatemala, and Guatemalans (especially Guatemalan Indians) tend to be somewhat apathetic about them. But in a situation in which the stakes are high and in which the "development agent" can be held accountable to his or her constituency, people take political action—even in Guatemala, where political action of any sort is fraught with enormous risk. In consequence the political as well as economic development taking place within Guatemalan municipalities today is virtually unprecedented.

Municipal political activity has recently spilled over into education, on the heels of a poorly organized teachers' strike that had no popular support. (Teachers, who actually work about half-time as teachers, earn ten times more than local campesinos; they are also typical petty bureaucrats, usually non-Indian in Indian areas, and notably irresponsible.) On the assumption that they now had some political power over local institutions, irate parents, especially in Indian areas whose teachers tend to be especially irresponsible and arrogant, "locked out" the offending teachers and petitioned the Ministry of Education for new ones. Needless to remark, the ministry was not about to let parents make decisions about teacher placements, given that ministry officials make much of their income by selling teacher positions. Yet, in a number of cases, the ministry has agreed to teacher replacements—an enormous concession in Guatemala's political environment.

In the context of Guatemala, where a civilian is now president but all local observers agree that the Army High Command rules (see C. A. Smith 1990b), the development program described here cannot be seen as a model for others. It seems quite clear that the army mandated the 8 percent package to local political units in the hope of drawing the populace into national political life, legitimating the rule of the military and at the same time building up the infrastructure that was so heavily damaged during the army rampage through the highlands in the early 1980s. On the other hand, it is also clear that the municipal projects, despite numerous irregularities, have been the best managed and most "efficient" projects ever promulgated in Guatemala. The key to the success of the projects is simple: local political control over the development agents (in this case the municipal officers). While it is too early to reach any conclusions on this case, it does seem that the particular development project described here, promoted by even the most unsavory of Third World states, shows greater promise of reforming or strengthening elements of civil society than unlinked development successes in this same context would do.

These "successful" and "unsuccessful" development projects, when assessed in terms of the political agendas of the particular Third World state regimes in which they are taking place, show that the evaluation of development achievement is not a simple or unproblematic issue. In Robertson's words, "an interest in development . . . implies, inescapably, judgements of moral value." There are two basic points to consider here: one is what a particular Third World state achieves through development success in terms of its political goals (e.g., Malaysia) and one is what would happen to civil society, through state action, without development success (e.g., Guatemala). On the one hand, it seems fairly clear that development success is better than development failure in terms of meeting basic social needs for political stability as well as economic power; in certain circumstances, moreover, it can assist the development of civil organizations that can resist state excess in the target social system. But, on the other hand, the Malaysian case amply illustrates that development success can also promote extreme forms of authoritarianism, ultimately deleterious to the target population. This is the basic reason why development agents need to consider the general political environment in which they work and the forms of political organization their projects will promote.

Given the constituencies that they tend to champion, anthropologists have an inherent bias against states in general and the corrupt, inefficient, and despotic Third World state in particular. Yet, if we are really interested in Third World development, it seems that we must look for and carefully examine those few examples in which a state development scheme works or in which a working international development scheme is successfully transferred into the hands of a Third World state. All other forms of development success merely strengthen Third World dependency and weaken the Third World state (though not necessarily its despotic powers), which works against long-term development prospects. Weak Third World states not only remain underdeveloped, but they exact an enormous price for their weakness on their even weaker human subjects. And, much as we might want to, we cannot simply wish weak Third World states away.

Even Robertson, who seems horrified at the way in which the Malaysian state has used its development agencies to penetrate into civil society, seems to agree with this point:

> If the state were to end its reformist endeavors, the initiative would certainly pass to interests in Malaysia's segmented population. Such an eventuality would probably be very costly in human lives, and it is difficult to see how such turmoil could yield political and social structures which are clearly preferable to those which prevail today. (1984:292)

And later:

> It would be a grave delusion to imagine that the state itself will disappear, or even that its power over our daily lives will be significantly diminished in any future which we might currently imagine. A speculative social science cannot be so divorced from reality that its designs ignore or seek to disinvest this potent political force. Until we have a better understanding of the state, we have no coherent basis for recommending its transformation. (304)

An Agenda for Future Research and Experimentation

The anthropological studies described earlier, suggestive as they may be, are all relatively incomplete with respect to answering the basic questions of a development anthropologist. As noted, the best anthropological studies of Third World state culture and form (e.g., Anderson 1983; Kapferer 1988; Trouillot 1990) treat the global forces affecting Third World state development schematically, their strength lying in the sophisticated ways in which they have treated national culture and nationalism. Anthropologists who treat the issues of development and development agencies, in contrast, often overplay the role of global forces in creating the Third World state, allowing little role for autonomous state development and the role of culture in shaping the power of Third World states. New work on the state is needed to fill in the gaps.

An extremely worthwhile project, for example, would be for some student to examine the nature of development projects, state and international, that were established in Haiti during the Duvalier regime and to assess these projects in relation to their impact on state development during that period. Trouillot observes that the main development strategy during the Duvalier years was one of supporting "light industry" and tourism in Haiti's capital city, which "intensified economic and spatial polarization by increasing the gap between Port-au-Prince and the rest of the country" (1990:210), exacerbated Haiti's trade deficit, and, according to the World Bank, made almost no fiscal contribution to the national economy (213). Untangling who invested in what, when, where, and why—with particular emphasis on state effects and the cultural elements uncovered by Trouillot—would do a great deal to unmask the relationship between international lending/aid, of all sorts (multilateral loan institutions, NGOs, and state) and the development of particular state forms.

In similar fashion a restudy of Malaysian development planning that paid greater attention to the "nation-building" efforts of the state would also be useful. Robertson notes that after 1969 Malaysia's planners came up with a new Department of National Unity out of which a nationalist ideology was formulated. Throughout his study Robertson notes the importance of nationalist ideology in affecting government planning. A careful study of the cultural content of nationalist ideology, together with further attention to the way in which the state manipulated it, along the lines of Kapferer's study of Sri Lanka, might illuminate why the explosive ethnic tensions in Malaysia were kept in check while they erupted in Sri Lanka. In a sense, studies of nationalistic forms that do not lead to terror, which the case studies on nationalism suggest is inevitable—possibly because of the way in which the cases were selected—would be of considerable practical interest to any development specialists who typically works in nations in which the potential for ethnic turmoil is extremely high.

This brings me to a final point, one that has been made by others (Colson 1985) but bears repeating. In a sense we learn less from case studies of development failure than we do from those showing (even limited) success. The list of failures is too long, the details too repetitive, and the information they provide merely feed our already powerful cultural biases. For this reason studies that can show how local-level political as well as social institutions were strengthened by development projects may be more helpful to the socially concerned development agent than any other. Obviously, the development agent delves into Third World state and local politics at great risk. I do not advocate that we do so. But I do advocate that we look for examples in which a development project was not only successful in economic terms but also in local political terms and present them to the scholarly and development community so that we may begin to think about (and argue about) how development work can further these kinds of processes.

We must also consider ways in which we can assist development projects in a practical way by designing them in ways that can help empower local people politically vis-à-vis the invariably intrusive Third World state. Let me provide an example of how we might do this by describing a development project with which I am presently associated.[5] The project involves training local people in a culturally and linguistically diverse region (western Guatemala) to do their own (anthropological) research on economic infrastructure, processes, and needs in their own cultural-linguistic areas. In phase 1 of the project potential researchers (most with only secondary education) were selected by a local indigenous project director by means of various criteria, the most important of which were that they belonged to, lived in, and spoke the language of the area of investigation; that they had the potential to advise development projects in their areas; and that they respected the local culture, including local definitions of *development*. (My role was to train these people and help them devise a survey instrument to assess need and potential in 135 particular communities of the region.) Currently, the researchers are preparing a summary of their findings, with proposals for particular kinds of development projects in different parts of the region, which will be supplied to the various development agencies working in Guatemala. Phase 2 of the project (currently under way) involves carrying out studies in selected communities of the local political or quasipolitical organizations who could best manage these projects—that is, the groups who most clearly represent their local constituency. Phase 3 of the project (no doubt the most difficult part) will involve convincing potential donors to turn over the management of the projects suggested by this study to these local political groups, giving them the right to direct the projects in particular ways and to hire and fire the technical assistants who are involved in the project.

To date this project has no direct involvement with the Guatemalan state, nor does it plan to have any in the future—though it does plan to propose and/or to direct projects to the municipal governments that control the "8 percent" of government revenues previously described. At the same time there is nothing directly threatening to the state about the project, for it will work through existing state infrastructure. The aim is to provide a model of development to the state in which the beneficiaries of projects have power over the kind of project and the people directing it in their communities, a model that will be convincing because it is relatively effective. At this point I should once again emphasize that it would be completely utopian to assume that this project, even if successful, would bring about economic development in Guatemala. There are too many other factors at play. But it would, if successful, help strengthen elements in civil society with which the Guatemalan state would eventually have to negotiate in order to formulate and effectively carry out its own development policies. In so doing, it would help transform the state into one that is more likely to have successful development policies.

NOTES

1. The best treatments done so far have either considered the state as it exists in relation to national culture, or "the nation" (see, e.g., Anderson 1983; Tambiah 1986; Kapferer 1988; Trouillot 1990), or as it exists in relation to multinationals or international development agencies (see, e.g., Wolfe 1986; Field 1987; Robertson 1984). No major work attempts to deal with both aspects of modern state formation.

2. The only anthropologist I know who continues to work in the evolutionary style of the early students of the state whose work is of considerable relevance to development agents is Alvin Wolfe (see, e.g., 1986).

3. According to most of the cited authorities, liberal social scientists mean

by *the state* the institutions of territorial governance and control; they assume that various interest groups compete for control over those institutions, that the state itself has no particular interest, and that one can treat only particular state regimes when talking about state interests. Marxists, in contrast, assume that the interests of the state are those of the dominant classes, be they capitalist or noncapitalist; they too assume that the state has no interest independent of the classes directing it.

4. Obviously, such cases exist, namely, the recent U.S. invasion of Panama. But, while cases of direct foreign intervention are dramatic, they are nonetheless relatively rare.

5. Further descriptions of this project can be found in an unpublished report for the Interamerican Foundation, "An Analysis of Economic Variation, Development Projects, and Development Prospects in the Highlands of Western Guatemala" (March 1990).

REFERENCES

Adams, Richard N.
    1975   *Energy and Structure: A Theory of Social Power.* Austin: University of Texas Press.
Anderson, Benedict
    1983   *Imagined Communities: Reflections on the Origin and Spread of Nationalism.* London: Verso.
Annis, Sheldon
    1988   Can the World Bank Be a Grassroots Funder in Rural Guatemala? MS.
Barry, Tom, and Deb Preusch
    1988   *The Soft War: The Uses and Abuses of U.S. Economic Aid in Central America.* New York: Grove Press.
Blömstrom, Magnus, and Björn Hettne
    1984   *Development Theory in Transition.* London: Zed Books.
Carnoy, Martin
    1984   *The State and Political Theory.* Princeton: Princeton University Press.
Cernea, Michael M.
    1988   Nongovernmental Organizations and Local Development. World Bank Discussion Paper no. 40. Washington, D.C.: World Bank.
Clammer, John, ed.
    1978   *The New Economic Anthropology.* London: Macmillan.
Colson, Elizabeth
    1982   Planned Change: The Creation of a New Community. Berkeley: Institute of International Studies, University of California.
    1985   Using Anthropology in a World on the Move. *Human Organization* 44:191–96.

Corrigan, Philip, and Derek Sayer
  1985 *The Great Arch: English State Formation as Cultural Revolution.* London: Basil Blackwell.
Davis, Shelton, and Julie Hodson
  1982 *Witness to Political Violence in Guatemala: The Suppression of a Rural Development Movement.* Boston: Oxfam America, Impact Audit no. 2.
Dahl, Gudrun, and Anders Hjört
  1984 Development as Message and Meaning. *Ethnos* 49:165–85.
de Janvry, Alain
  1981 *The Agrarian Question and Reformism in Latin America.* Baltimore: Johns Hopkins University Press.
Donner, Mark
  1993 The Truth of El Mozote. *New Yorker,* 6 December, 50–129.
Dunkerley, James
  1988 *Power in the Isthmus: A Political History of Modern Central America.* London: Verso.
Evans, Peter, Dietrich Rueschemeyer, and Theda Skocpol, eds.
  1985 *Bringing the State Back In.* London: Cambridge University Press.
Field, Les
  1987 *"I Am Content with My Art": Two Groups of Artisans in Revolutionary Nicaragua.* Ph.D. diss., Department of Anthropology, Duke University.
Fitzgerald, E. V. K.
  1985 The Financial Constrain on Relative Autonomy: The State and Capital Accumulation in Mexico, 1940–82. In *The State and Capital Accumulation in Latin America, vol. 1,* ed. Christian Anglade and Carlos Fortin, 210–40. London: Macmillan.
Fox, Richard, ed.
  1990 *Nationalist Ideologies and the Production of National Cultures.* Washington, D.C.: American Anthropological Association, AES Monograph Series 2.
Fried, Morton
  1959 *The Evolution of Political Society.* Boston: Viking.
Gramsci, Antonio
  1971 *Selections from the Prison Notebooks.* Ed. Quinton Hoare and Geoffrey Nowell-Smith. New York: International Publishers.
Geertz, Clifford, ed.
  1963 *Old Societies and New States.* Glencoe, Ill.: Free Press.
Gellner, Ernest
  1983 *Nations and Nationalism.* Oxford: Basil Blackwell.
Grindle, Marilee S.
  1986 *State and Countryside: Development Policy and Agrarian Politics in Latin America.* Baltimore: Johns Hopkins University Press.
Giddens, Anthony
  1987 *The Nation-State and Violence.* Berkeley: University of California Press.

Horowitz, Michael M.
    1988 For a More Cost Effective Foreign-Aid Program. *Development Anthropology Network* 6:1–3.
Kapferer, Bruce
    1988 *Legends of People: Myths of State.* Washington, D.C.: Smithsonian Institution Press.
Interamerican Foundation
    1990 An Analysis of Economic Variation, Development Projects and Development Prospects in the Highlands of Western Guatemala. Unpublished text. p57a.
Kay, Cristobal
    1989 *Latin American Theories of Development and Underdevelopment.* London: Routledge.
LaFeber, Walter
    1984 *Inevitable Revolutions: The United States in Central America.* New York: Norton.
MacEwan, Arthur
    1989 *Debt and Disorder: International Economic Instability and U.S. Imperial Decline.* New York: Monthly Review Press.
Mann, Michael
    1986 *The Sources of Social Power,* vol. 1. Cambridge: Cambridge University Press.
Migdal, Joel
    1988 *Strong Societies and Weak States.* Princeton: Princeton University Press.
Mintz, Sidney
    1985 *Sweetness and Power: The Place of Sugar in Modern History.* New York: Viking.
Moore, Barrington, Jr.
    1966 *The Social Origins of Dictatorship and Democracy: Lord and Peasant in the Making of the Modern World.* Boston: Beacon Press.
Orlove, Benjamin, and Dominique LeVieil
    1989 Some Doubts about Trout: Fisheries Development Projects in Lake Titicaca. In *State, Capital, and Rural Society,* ed. B. S. Orlove, M. W. Foley, and T. F. Love, 211–46. Boulder, Colo.: Westview Press.
Robertson, A. V.
    1984 *People and the State: An Anthropology of Planned Development.* Cambridge: Cambridge University Press.
Sanderson, Steve E.
    1986 *The Transformation of Mexican Agriculture: International Structure and the Politics of Rural Change.* Princeton: Princeton University Press.
Skocpol, Theda
    1979 *States and Social Revolutions.* Cambridge: Cambridge University Press.
Smith, Anthony D.
    1986 State-Making and Nation-Building. In *States in History,* ed. John A. Hall, 228–63. Oxford: Basil Blackwell.

Smith, Carol A.
> 1990a *Guatemalan Indians and the State: 1540–1988.* Ed. C. A. Smith. Austin: University of Texas Press.
> 1990b The Militarization of Civil Society in Guatemala: Economic Reorganization as a Continuation of War. *Latin American Perspectives* 17:8–41.

Tambiah, S. J.
> 1986 *Sri Lanka: Ethnic Fratricide and the Dismantling of Democracy.* Chicago: University of Chicago Press.

Trouillot, Michel-Rolph
> 1990 *Haiti: State against Nation.* New York: Monthly Review Press.

Walton, John
> 1989 Debt, Protest, and the State in Latin America. In *Power and Popular Protest,* ed. Susan Eckstein, 299–328. Berkeley: University of California Press.

Warman, Arturo
> 1980 *We Come to Object: The Peasants of Morelos and the National State.* Baltimore: Johns Hopkins University Press.

Wasserstrom, Robert
> 1989 Rural Labor and Income Distribution in Central Chiapas. In *State, Capital, and Rural Society,* ed. B. S. Orlove, M. W. Foley, and T. F. Love, 101–17. Boulder, Colo.: Westview Press.

Wolf, Eric R.
> 1982 *Europe and the People without History.* Berkeley: University of California Press.

Wolfe, Alvin
> 1986 The Multinational Corporation as a Form of Sociocultural Integration above the Level of the State. In *Anthropology and International Business,* ed. Hendrick Serrie. Williamsburg, Va.: College of William and Mary.

Chapter 3

Grassroots Organizations and Grassroots Support Organizations: Patterns of Interaction

Julie Fisher

> We are optimists because we have known hunger. You in Europe can afford the luxury of pessimism because you do not know what it is.
> —Mustapha Cissokho, Senegalese peasant leader

> No one knows enough to be a pessimist.
> —Norman Cousins

The Third World today is characterized by an extraordinary mix of catastrophe and human ingenuity. The disastrous dimensions of the ills confronting the Third World are all too obvious. They include grinding poverty, deforestation, the continuing population explosion, the debt crisis, and, now, AIDS. Not so obvious are the vast dimensions of the growth of voluntary organizations trying to deal with these problems.

The rapid growth of the voluntary or independent sector in much of the Third World grows out of what have been called the "twin challenges of empowerment and development" (Berg 1987:38). In Asia, Latin America, and, more recently, Africa this organizational explosion is creating a coalition between some of the most and least educated people in each society. Young intellectuals and technically trained professionals are creating nonprofit development organizations that seek out and assist grassroots village and neighborhood groups. Village and neighborhood groups are networking with one another and in many cases seeking out or even hiring their own technical assistance.

This process is an anthropologist's dream come true, yet it has been largely overlooked as an anthropological subject. As a political scientist interested in development, I hope to bring this explosive phenomenon to the attention of anthropologists and to introduce a research agenda for anthropologists.

Most indigenous development organizations can be roughly divided into grassroots organizations (GROs) and grassroots support organizations (GRSOs). Grassroots organizations (GROs) have members and assist their own communities. Grassroots support organizations (GRSOs) are composed of paid professionals that assist communities other than their own by working with GROs. Today it is estimated that there are over 200,000 GROs and roughly 35,000 to 50,000 GRSOs in Asia, Africa, and Latin America, most of them organized since the early 1970s (Durning 1989; Fisher 1993).

Beginning in the 1970s, the availability of foreign assistance provided idealistic young Third World professionals with an alternative to the choice between dead end government jobs or migration to the developed countries. They were able, instead, to create thousands of GRSOs concerned with development, environment, the role of women, and primary health care. They also formed networks with one another and with GROs. By working through GROs, these professionals further stimulated organizational processes at the grassroots.

GROs, however, have also become far more active on their own. Faced with the deterioration of their environment and the increasing impoverishment of the 1980s, both traditional and newly created GROs are organizing horizontal networks among themselves. In some cases they have created GRSOs from below by hiring their own experts. An African chief explained that the drought "has become a weapon for us. With abundance, each one worked for himself. We have discovered plants that grow more rapidly. Hunger has become a teacher that has forced us to think" (Pradervand 1988:12).

This organizational explosion has gained further momentum from increasing numbers of international conferences and exchanges about development and from the spread of personal computers. Never before in history have local organizations been so able to communicate what they have learned with one another, and spread their ideas within and between nations.

The proliferation of NGOs (nongovernmental organizations) has left academics and development practitioners struggling to catch up with a new political and social reality. I have elsewhere (Fisher 1993) discussed the broad dimensions of this general phenomenon. This chapter, however, deals with GROs and their relationship to GRSOs. More specifically, it focuses on initial indicators in those relationships likely to enhance success in meeting the challenge of sustainable development.

Central to this initial assessment is the conviction that, in the words of Atherton Martin, an agronomist from Dominica, "Nothing grows from the top down." Although anthropological attention has been more focused on culture than institutions, anthropologists, because of their long-standing immersion in indigenous ways of life, are uniquely suited to contributing to an understanding of NGOs. Despite the quantum jump in the rhetorical commitment to grassroots participation among development practitioners and many successful attempts to involve local communities, the subtle assumption that "capacity building" is a one-way street is still widespread. *The need to understand existing capacity before doing anything else can be promoted more effectively by anthropologists than by any other academic discipline,* particularly if they become actively involved in the process of writing about, and working in, development.

Until now those anthropologists who have written about GROs have been more likely to focus on their origins or current activities, not their capacity for transformation or what Scott Gugenheim, an anthropologist at the World Bank, calls an *"antropologia de la acción."*[1] As this narrative proceeds, therefore, important issues or questions that lend themselves to an anthropological approach will be raised.

The next section focuses on GROs—their numbers, classification by origin and function, as well as the forces behind their recent proliferation. Then a discussion of the horizontal GRO networks and movements is followed by a brief description of GRSOs. This is followed by a discussion of empowerment and development—two interrelated goals that depend on institutional, environmental, and economic sustainability. Finally, the balance of the chapter deals with the types of relationships between GROs and GRSOs that are most likely to lead to sustainable empowerment and development. More intensive anthropological research on these patterns could highlight indigenous solutions to interrelated global poverty, environment, and population crises. It would also help provide development activists with the knowledge they need to spread what works and to learn from what fails.

GROs: Facts and Figures

In 1940 the First International Conference on Indian Life resolved to recommend support of the continued existence of the *ayllu,* the unit that holds land in common in several Latin American countries, both for the advantages it affords for mechanization and because of the social function it fulfills (Mead 1955).

Although GROs are also called "base groups," "people's organizations," or "local organizations," there is general agreement that they are membership organizations working to improve and develop their own communities. The broader term *local organizations* can be used to include other kinds of community groups such as burial societies or kinship networks as well as GROs working on development. This section will give a general statistical and geographic overview of GROs.

Numerical evidence on GROs is difficult to collect, but the thousands of officially registered organizations that exist only on paper are probably balanced by thousands of remote groups, known only to few, if any, outsiders. A 1977 study of the Dominican Republic carried out by the secretariat of agriculture identified 1,116 informal but registered associations of small farmers that had formed to share labor or joint marketing. As of 1986 the number of *unregistered* GROs, including women's groups and groups for unemployed youths, was estimated at double that figure (Vetter 1986: 3).

During the past twenty to thirty years tens of thousands of GROs have been created, and existing organizations have assumed new functions all over Asia, Latin America, and much of Africa.[2] A majority of the estimated twenty to thirty thousand Latin American squatter settlements have created their own community organizations. Pradervand (1990) estimates that there are at least twelve thousand to fifteen thousand grassroots groups in the Sahel countries and perhaps an equal number of women's groups in Kenya. Village organizations are particularly widespread in Asia, and new kinds of organizations such as women's groups have proliferated rapidly.

Precisely because of the considerable evidence of GRO proliferation, there is an enormous need for anthropological community-based studies of GROs. Such studies could focus on their evolution from more traditional local organizations and their relationships with one another and with outsiders.

GROs are less common in the Middle East, perhaps because Koranic culture emphasizes the duty of the individual, not the importance of organizing for social change (Esman and Uphoff 1984:97; Schneider 1985:34). Yet the hundreds of GROs active on the West Bank were not all connected with the Intifada. Some 650 GROs in Lebanon are filling the political vacuum caused by the civil war.³ Suggestive of the kind of study that anthropologists with Middle Eastern expertise might undertake is Van Nieuwenhuijze and his colleagues' (1985) assessment of traditional local organizations in Egypt as "nuclei of potential development."

To understand the diversity of GROs I will first discuss variations in their origins—important in understanding their character, internal culture, and relationships with GRSOs. The second classification, by function, focuses on the potential impact of GROs on empowerment and development.

Classification by Origin
GROs are not an entirely new phenomenon, and many have evolved from traditional organizations. Yet they are also founded as new organizations within a community, either by community residents or by outsiders. One way to categorize their origins as a kind of continuum would be as follows:

Traditional: historical origins in the community
    Examples: village councils, rotating credit societies
New organizations founded by community members
    Examples: women's groups
New organizations founded by villagers who have returned from the city
New organizations, founded by outsiders such as GRSOs, INGOs (international nongovernmental organizations), governments, or official donors (both bilateral and multilateral)
    Examples: borrowers groups, credit unions

Clear categorization of GROs by origin is difficult, since written accounts often exclude their history. Nor is it easy, in the absence of historical-anthropological analysis, to determine whether a recently established organization evolved from a more traditional local organization that may or may not have been involved in development. Thus, the continuum presented here can categorize the general evolutionary process as well as the origins of particular organizations. The tendency for local organizations to shift to larger concerns seems to have accelerated in recent years (Annis 1989; Painter 1986). Most of this discussion concerns "new" GROs. But first a few words about the history and evolution of traditional local organizations as well as the role of early outsiders.

Many village and community councils are descendents of much earlier forms of organization or ways of cooperating to achieve limited purposes. In Trinidad and Tobago in 1947 there were 317 local "friendly societies" that offered sickness, maternity, and death benefits to their members (Wells and Wells 1953). Other organizations, however, resembled GROs more closely. John Useem, in his study of the Palau Islands in the Pacific in the 1940s, found fifty active societies, organized by sex, age, and status, that were "primary instruments by which districts and villages engage in organized projects" (Mead 1955:144).

African tribes are often considered antithetical to change. By the 1750s in Tanzania, however, it was difficult to find a group that could be described as a consanguineous tribe under a traditional leader. New groupings of people began to share languages such as Kiswahili, and the tribe became a geographical entity that organized informal work groups. Among the Kuria of north-central Tanzania, village work groups dug irrigation canals, chased missing cattle, and extinguished fires (Anacleti 1986). Hyden (1983:15) describes African religious and kinship networks as an "economy of affection" that contributes to building schools and bridges.

In the Andean countries, cooperative labor arrangements dating back thousands of years provide an important cultural basis for the development of GROs. Local organizations traditionally focused on community improvements as well as shared agricultural labor. Some of the thirty-seven community improvement projects carried out in Mancos, Peru, between 1895 and 1967 required hard physical labor. This was "performed by the people under the traditional *faena*—a labor tax which dates back to the Incaic mita and lasts days, weeks, and even years" (Fishel 1979:54).

Even such apparently static organizations as Indian castes may be historically relevant to the development of GROs. The Nadar caste has built schools, colleges, libraries, and a cooperative bank over decades that are now used by other castes (Ralston, Anderson, and Colson 1983:80). By the late 1970s many caste associations, while still associated with maintaining power and status, had begun to work on economic and social problems. (Somjee 1979:39).

Because of governmental inability to provide basic services, traditional local organizations have been engaged in development far longer in other Asian countries.[4] In Nepal a chronically weak central government forced local organizations to maintain irrigation systems, construct roads, plant trees, and build schools (Dhungel 1986). Local organizations in Thailand construct and maintain irrigation systems, flood control facilities, temples, wells, ponds, roads, and bridges (Calavan 1986). Anthropologists could obviously contribute to a deeper understanding of the antecedent, or parent, organizations of GROs. Field studies of particular communities or regions could also draw on knowledge of earlier ethnographic studies in the same areas.

Traditional GROs were never wholly isolated from outside influences. Religious groups have had a complex, sometimes positive impact on local organizations for hundreds of years. During the sixteenth century, for example, a Spanish missionary bishop, Don Vasco de Quiroga, actually strengthened self-help traditions among the Puerepas tribe in Michoacan, Mexico. In Kenya, by the late nineteenth century, missionaries were training teachers already supported by local communities, and were providing materials to build schools. The postindependence Harambee movement grew out of this tradition and strengthened it by encouraging competition between different areas and school committees.

Curiously, some of the earliest development interventions by outsiders were more sensitive to grassroots participation than later international interventions emphasizing ready-made projects. Among the first development projects were those initiated in China in the 1920s by the Rural Reconstruction Movement, a pioneer in integrated rural development through community organization.[5] Equally innovative was the work of the YMCA in India under Spencer Hatch, initiated in 1921 in Martandam, Travancore. Based on the maximum use of local resources and technologies, it led to the development of cooperative marketing societies, village libraries, and a village leadership training school (Alliband 1983:29).[6] Historiographic studies of earlier anthropologists might further illuminate the complex social change issues surrounding the role of outsiders in traditional villages.

Among the most significant and potentially powerful "outsiders" are those born in a community who return to found a new local organization. Although this has become increasingly common in the Third World in recent years, it is based on ample historical precedent. Town improvement unions were founded in Nigeria in the late 1930s by the sons and daughters of villagers who had studied abroad (Okoli 1982:71).

The Growth of GROs since 1970

Many new GROs evolved from more traditional tribal groups. The *naams* of Burkina Faso originally acculturated young men into the tribe but now elect leaders, attract new members, and encourage crop diversification. They have constructed twenty-five maternity hospitals and are replacing the government in constructing pharmacies, schools, and village clinics. Among the other traditional African groups now involved in development are the *m'botai* of the Oulofs, the *walde* of the *peulhs,* the *Kafo* of the Mandinka, and the *tons* of the Bambara (Pradervand 1988:8).

Since the early 1970s these gradually evolving traditional organizations have been joined by greater numbers of new GROs. There are two major reasons for this. The first is the interrelated impact of population growth, environmental degradation, and poverty, compounded by skyrocketing debt and the macroeconomic decline of the 1980s. The second is the increasing availability of outside support for both GROs and GRSOs. This combination of bottom-up and top-down resources is crucial to the future of sustainable development in the Third World and to the environmental future of the planet. The quality of this process of interaction is enormously complicated, however, and may help determine its eventual dimensions and impact.

Among the dramatic kinds of events propelling the creation of GROs are wars, political repression, and natural disasters. In Afghanistan tens of thousands of GROs not only constituted the base of resistance to Soviet intervention but also provided social services. Under the Pinochet dictatorship in Chile hundreds of urban grassroots cooperatives, employment agencies, and educational groups emerged. In Asia grassroots activists are self-consicously tying human rights to environmental rights (Gain 1991). The 1975 floods in Bangladesh and the Mexican earthquake ten years later led to a proliferation of GROs.

Deepening poverty is an even more powerful organizer of GROs. As population and land pressures have worsened, the poor of the Third World have begun to organize themselves. Women became the majority in thousands of African GROs when so many men migrated to the city because of drought and famine. Having to walk farther to find food and water motivates women to do more than survive. In Kangoussema, Senegal, women walk seventy kilometers round-trip to sell their vegetables for a net profit of five to ten French francs. The male president of a mixed group in Senegal was quoted as saying that "women organize themselves better, because they have more determination" (Pradervand 1988:7).

Trading rural poverty for the challenges of urban survival has for many years led squatters in Latin America and some parts of Asia to organize neighborhood associations. Latin American neighborhood improvement associations are founded during invasions of unoccupied land (Fisher 1984). Moreira Alves (1984) counted over eleven hundred in São Paulo. In Hyderabad and Bombay women's community improvement organizations are particularly active.

Outside assistance promoting the creation of GROs is increasingly available from developing country governments, international NGOs (INGOs), and official bilateral and multilateral donors. Governments are generally more likely than other outsiders to exert top-down control over GROs or to ignore existing organizations while creating new organizations that favor local elites (Fisher 1993:32–33). GROs created by governments, however, can have some impact on the tendency to organize later. The urban neighborhood organizations set up by the Colombian government in the late 1950s were rather paternalistic. Yet, when the Rural Reconstruction Movement began working in Colombia in the 1960s, it found that cooperatives succeeded in 60 percent of the communities previously organized by the government and other outsiders, whereas success in communities with no prior projects was only 29 percent (Edel 1969:49; Fisher 1984).

Similarly, Esman and Uphoff's (1984:166) broad literature search revealed that no locally established organization had become totally dominated, or "spoiled," by government connections and that organizations with no government ties did not perform any better. GROs may have a stronger sense of identity than many well-meaning outsiders assume. Further anthropological analysis might uncover some of the reasons for this.

Although international voluntary assistance is increasingly channeled through GRSOs, it has sometimes fueled the growth of GROs more directly. In Sierra Leone, for example, increased international assistance led to a dramatic proliferation of GROs. INGOs also create GROs directly through their community organizers. Save the Children organized a network of fifty-seven women's clubs in Colombia to promote small enterprise development and health education (Fisher 1986).[7] Official multilateral organizations also provide financial support to GROs. UNICEF, for example, has worked through neighborhood improvement associations in Lima and Rio and provides cereal mills to villages that organize themselves in Burkina Faso (Lecomte 1986:21). Although only about 5 percent of World Bank loans included GRSOs or GROs as of 1990, the bank encourages governments to cooperate with these organizations and is increasingly working with GROs in its agricultural projects.[8]

Because of the generally positive image of international voluntary assistance, official bilateral donors increasingly work through INGOs. In some countries the long-term impact of such cooperation is already visible. The Pan American Development Foundation established the *Fundacion Dominicana de Desarrollo* in the Dominican Republic almost thirty years ago to provide credit and technical assistance for GROs. The foundation's program was then expanded with help from the Inter-American Foundation and AID. "The end result of all these factors has been the creation of a special climate where a highly successful program of one group can ripple out and be replicated by many others, where private and public agencies can enter into formal agreements to implement new development methodologies together" (Vetter 1986:3).

The most sustainable and potentially positive result of outside assistance probably stems from training or nonformal education. One observer has attributed the density of GROs in Burkina Faso to the large number of INGO training programs first initiated in the 1960s and 1970s. GROs are less pervasive in Mali, where there were few international training programs during those years (Lecomte 1986:115).

Despite the increasing tendency to work through GRSOs that may themselves empower GROs and the widely acknowledged need to promote participation of the "beneficiaries" of development projects, neither INGOs nor official donors devote adequate attention to the real potential of development from below. Donors continue to select project areas for reasons not related to the existence of indigenous GROs or the activities of GRSOs.[9] Their next step is then to "create" GROs and attempt the difficult task of "empowering" people from above.

There is, therefore, an urgent need for anthropological input. This was highlighted by a study of northern donor assistance to Bolivia, sponsored by the Workshop for Andean Oral History and partially written by Aymara Indians trained in anthropology. It concluded that, although almost a dozen development agencies had projects in northern Potosi, "none understood how the *allyus* were organized or how it functioned." Nor had donors worked with Bolivian GRSOs that understood the importance of the *allyu* as the traditional precooperative. The report concluded, "At this moment, the *allyus* are being dismembered!" Fortunately, Oxfam, the international donor, responded by withdrawing funding from existing projects and supporting the nascent efforts of *allyus* to establish broader networks (R. C. Smith 1987:6).

Classifying GROs
GROs can be roughly divided into local development associations (LDAs), interest associations, and cooperatives (including precooperatives) (Uphoff 1986). Local development associations are area-based inclusive membership organizations engaged in a wide range of local development activities. Although they often lack outside technical or training support, they are widespread in the Third World. Seventy-one of ninety-two specific squatter settlements studied in eleven Latin American countries had *juntas de vecino,* or neighborhood improvement associations, and they have been increasing in numbers since the early 1970s (Fisher 1984:63).

As multifunctional organizations, LDAs are likely to flourish where tasks are predictable, resources are available, and there is an assured supply of water (Esman and Uphoff 1984). A serious crisis, however, such as a flood or landslide can also create or reactivate LDAs. Both the focus and the scope of local activity may also be significantly affected by outside assistance. The traditional *cabildos* of the Sikuani tribe in Colombia were central to a health and water project developed with assistance from the Inter-American Foundation, several Colombian GRSOs, and the regional health service (Herrera and Lobo-Guerrero 1988:32).

Some LDAs reflect the social hierarchy of the community and may be allied with local government or national government administrators against alternative organizations. The officers of the LDAs in Yemen are from prominent local families, although prior involvement in self-help activity has become a necessary qualification for leadership. In other cases LDAs grow out of "alternative" interest associations (IAs) such as landless groups. In Mali the *kabala* (village associations) are run by women, and in Kenya the local women's groups are beginning to function more like LDAs.

LDAs are often capable of substantial accomplishment. A group in San Francisco, Bolivia, with some help from a French NGO, built a fourteen-kilometer road by hand across a mountain to improve village marketing of fruit and vegetables (Schneider 1985:33). *Juntas de vecinos* often build schools before petitioning the authorities for a teacher (Fisher 1984:64). Whether such accomplishments tend to emerge from traditional community councils that did not get involved in development in the past is another issue worthy of further anthropological study. A comparative study of community achievement in a wide area could use the age or indigenous origins of LDAs as a key variable.

Interest associations are defined either by a single development function (functional IAs) or by the type of person joining the group (categorical IAs). They tend to be more exclusive in membership than LDAs but may have more members than cooperatives. Among traditional groups defined by function are water users' associations, work groups, and pastoral organizations. More recently established types include village health committees and parent groups. Groups defined by personal characteristics (women's groups, landless groups, religious groups, and hometown associations) may be multifunctional.

Obviously, such distinctions begin to blur with increased mobilization. Peasant association and rural unions, for example, can have characteristics of both functional and categorical IAs. The Honduran Women's Peasant Federation (FEMUC) unites 294 GROs in thirteen of eighteen departments of the country and both cooperates with and maintains its autonomy from the male-dominated National Union of Peasants (Yudelman 1987). Nonetheless, the general categories, described in more detail in the following pages, are a useful way of beginning to understand the variety of IAs.

GROs with a single functional interest tend to be common in countries where soil and water are poor and work tasks are complex. In Botswana, for example, where such organizations are "legion" they manage catchment dams, dig and operate wells, and rent or purchase tractors as a group (Uphoff 1986:126). The link between construction and operation of irrigation or other shared systems "can be particularly striking when the construction task is unusually difficult" (F. Korten 1986:285). Farmers in Bali built a two-kilometer tunnel through a mountain to bring water to their fields.

Water users' associations are common in Indonesia, Pakistan, the Philippines, Sri Lanka, Thailand, Mexico, Peru, and Ecuador. Most operate under a traditional "water master," who has the trust of the group and can adjudicate disputes. Studies of strong associations in the Philippines and Indonesia show that they have high ratios of leaders to members, with responsibility for maintenance based on the layouts of the irrigation canals (Bagadion and Korten 1985:73).[10] *Galeria* organizations in Mexico use traditional methods for tapping and conveying underground water (Enge and Whiteford 1989).[11]

Pastoral organizations in East Africa construct water storage areas, burn old grass to promote the growth of new shoots, search for natural resources during droughts, and utilize herd structuring (Dyson-Hudson 1985:170). Pastoralist societies based on communal pasture ownership are generally nonhierarchical. In the Peruvian highlands individual peasants own cropland, but pasture land is owned and managed in common.

Functional interest associations also form around educational and health objectives. Parent associations are common in squatter settlements in Santiago de Chile, Lima, and Panama City (Fisher 1977:214). The "bench schools" of the Atlantic coast of Colombia have been in existence since the beginning of the nineteenth century. In Calcutta there were one hundred informally organized, unregistered schools with over seven thousand students in 1977 (Sivaramakrishnan 1977:106). Village health committees are generally promoted by governments, GRSOs, and INGOs. Particularly noteworthy were the village preventive health and family planning groups promoted by several GRSOs in Thailand in the 1970s based on the efforts of village health workers (Coombs 1980). Although continued outside support is probably more essential for these groups than almost any other type of GRO, the strongest Panamanian local health groups continued to function effectively even as government support declined (Uphoff 1986:300).

Environmental (particularly forestry) associations, are among the fastest-growing functional interest associations. Forest protection groups organized by Proshika, a Bangladesh GRSO, increased from 260 in 1986 to 1,944 by 1991 (Khan 1991). The Village Forest Councils in India were an outgrowth of Chipko, an environmental movement started by peasant women who lie down in front of bulldozers and hug trees to save them from being bulldozed.

The most common type of categorical interest association, women's groups, are also the most rapidly proliferating type of GRO in the Third World. The International Women's Tribune Center in New York is the contact and referral office for thirteen thousand groups in one hundred sixty countries. In rural Brazil the growth of the women's movement has been "explosive" (Durning 1989:28). The Kenyan organizations alone have over six hundred thousand members (Wanyande 1987:96).

Women's organizations often grow out of traditional rotating credit societies. In Ghana and Nigeria, where women's enterprises have a long history, women have developed their own savings and credit organizations. "Mother's clubs," common in Latin America, have a kind of instant cultural acceptability that a more obvious "women's movement " might lack, even though they can change the way women think about themselves and the way they act in their communities.[12] South Asian women, on the other hand, are organizing GROs around more feminist issues. Strengthened by GRSOs such as Bangladesh Rural Advancement Committee (BRAC) and the Grameen Bank in Bangladesh and the Working Women's Forum in India, low-income women have demonstrated against a number of notorious rape cases, dowry deaths, and bride burnings.

Religious groups are a second type of categorical interest association. In Central America and Brazil, Catholic theologians and activists were impressed with the way the poor survived by helping one another and began organizing GROs in the 1960s. Like those in Central America, the estimated eighty thousand Brazilian base communities are religious organizations grouping forty to one thousand people each, empowered to perform the sacraments in remote areas lacking priests. But they also promote land tenure groups and squatter neighborhood organizations, and members join other organizations such as labor unions (Moreira Alves 1984:83). Basic Christian communities are also active in the Philippines, and GRO and GRSO activists in many other countries got their start in church programs.

Islamic GROs are more active in Indonesia than in the Middle East.[13] It is estimated that there are more than twenty-six hundred *pesantren,* or Islamic boarding schools, involved in community development on the island of Java alone. With roots in the anticolonial struggle dating back to the nineteenth century, *pesantren* began as antidotes to Western cultural values but in recent years have developed social and economic programs, supported by informal links to government officials and a network of intellectuals (Eldridge 1984–85). *Pesantren* have also promoted Islamic and non-Islamic cooperatives.

Hometown or provincial associations are a third type of categorical interest organization. In Cairo, Caracas, and parts of Buenos Aires there are "provincial neighborhoods," whereas in other cities people from the same hometown or province may be dispersed but still keep in contact. Hometown associations not only provide employment and housing help for new migrants; they also organize to provide assistance to their rural hometowns. Some of them evolve into active GRSOs (Fisher 1993:42).

Since there have been a number of anthropological studies of functional interest groups, literature searches could contribute to understanding their relationships to the generally newer categorical interest associations and to the current challenges of sustainable development. Studies of "new" interest associations of all types could be based on the life histories of activists (see Smith, chap. 2) in relation to what Hirschman (1984) calls the "conservation and mutation of social energy."

Precooperatives and cooperatives are membership organizations that pool their private resources, rather than managing a public resource such as water or pasture land. Although they produce private goods and services, they have a larger ownership base than other kinds of businesses. The two most common types of traditional precooperatives in the Third World are informal work groups and rotating credit associations. Borrowers' groups, usually set up with GRSO or INGO assistance, are a more recently established type of precooperative. Cooperatives can be classified as credit unions (also called savings and credit societies), consumer cooperatives, service cooperatives (providing inputs and marketing services to members), and production cooperatives (in which land or other means of production are owned in common as well).

Informal work groups generally work on one farmer's field one day and rotate to another member's property the next, usually on a seasonal basis. They may also hire their services out to other farmers as a group, sharing the proceeds. In Liberia there are at least nineteen different traditional patterns of shared labor, differing in size, permanent character, and reciprocal obligation (Cernea 1982:126).[14]

Rotating credit societies have been identified in more than forty developing countries (ibid., 128). The *tandas* of Mexico, *tontines* of Zimbabwe and Cameroon, *chaer* of Thailand, and *bisi* of Pakistan are based on a monthly membership contribution, with the entire amount is distributed to a different member at the end of the month. Although contributions earn no interest, rotating credit societies regularize savings, involve no expense, and minimize the problem of collection. Some African associations have over four hundred members (Ralston, Anderson and Colson 1983:108–11). In Egypt, where *jam'iyyat* are widespread, they avoid the Islamic prohibition on usury. Rotating credit societies are evolving into credit unions in Cameroon and into processing and marketing cooperatives in South Asia. In Kenya they are investing in corn mills for their members (Cernea 1982:129).

More studies focusing on rotating credit societies would be particularly relevant to development, even though anthropologists have already focused on their cross-cultural similarity (Ralston, Anderson, and Colson 1983) and their infinite variety. Seibel and Massing (1974), for example, identified sixteen different types in Liberia alone.

Although borrowers' groups sometimes replace or evolve out of rotating credit societies, they are generally organized in response to the availability of outside credit (or onetime grants) provided by INGOs or GRSOs. Among the best-known examples are the thousands of groups organized by the Grameen Bank of Bangladesh. Although Grameen group members establish some individual enterprises with the proceeds of their grants and loans, precooperative group businesses are more common. Women seem to be particularly active in starting group-owned businesses in the Third World. The Trickle Up Program estimates that of the 10,334 small group businesses they have promoted with onetime grants of one hundred dollars, 56 percent are led by women (Leet and Leet 1989).

Credit unions that link precooperatives to the formal banking system are developing in a number of countries. In 1987 there were over twelve thousand savings and credit societies in Africa, with almost three million members (Dichter and Zesch 1989:2). In many countries, however, they are not sufficiently connected with one another or with the market. One indigenous credit union in Cameroon became the country's sixth bank in 1975. Four years later the government appointed a new director, the bank failed, and the members reverted to their original informal mechanisms (Hyden 1983:126).

Formal cooperatives (including credit unions) are widespread in the Third World, with an estimated twenty million members in Latin America alone.[15] Although cooperatives are more likely than other GROs to be registered officially, they usually lack technical assistance and knowledge of accounting and marketing. They often try to achieve so many objectives that conflicts of interest emerge (Tendler 1983). Cooperatives are particularly ill suited to seasonal economic activities if loan payments have to be made monthly.

Another reason for their frequent failure is that they are more likely than other GROs to have been promoted by governments or foreign donors.[16] As products of the special historical circumstances of nineteenth-century Europe, they were "imported" into the Third

World during the 1950s and 1960s, at a time when there was confidence that Western know-how could somehow solve the problems of Third World poverty. Uphoff (1986:130) traces corruption in the Kenyan cooperatives to the way foreign structures were imposed.

On the other hand, Technoserve's experience with multifunctional agrarian reform cooperatives in Peru and El Salvador demonstrates that they can become successful enterprises and can also provide basic social services for their members (Fisher, forthcoming a). When typically excluded groups such as women or the landless are able to join or organize cooperatives, motivation and commitment can rise. The women's dairy cooperatives in Andhra Pradesh and Bihar are so profitable and honest that men are bringing milk to them rather than to the male-dominated cooperatives.[17] The legitimacy and viability of cooperatives can also be enhanced by the broader institutional context surrounding them and their linkages with other GROs. A participatory evaluation of the effectiveness of rural cooperatives in Honduras concluded that cooperatives worked better in communities with many GROs than in communities with few such organizations (Merschrod 1980:21). There has been remarkably little research, however, by anthropologists or others, addressing the conditions under which more equitable organizations emerge and can be scaled out.[18]

GRO Federations and Horizontal Networking

> We had the good fortune to obtain some aid; let us pass it on to people poorer than ourselves. The mill that UNICEF has given us is a father-mill: he must make a son to take his place when he is old and weary, and a daughter to give to the neighboring village. Set the price of milling so that these children can be raised. (Lecomte 1986:21)

There are three basic kinds of horizontal networks at the grassroots level in the Third World today—regional networks of individual GROs, more amorphous grassroots movements that extend beyond one locality, and informal economic networks. Although networking among GROs has increased dramatically in recent years, some traditional local organizations were tied to one another in extensive lineage systems. The historical antecedents for amorphous protest movements include the Spartacus rebellion in ancient Rome, the Russian peasant movements coalescing around pretenders to the throne, and the American slave revolt led by Nat Turner. Traditional barter arrangements between villages preceded informal economic networks.

GRO networks may be purely indigenous or promoted by outsiders. LDA networks such as the citizens' council movement in India and squatter neighborhood federations in Latin America are often founded by GRO activists from a number of neighboring communities (Alliband 1983; Fisher 1984). Networks of religious IAs, cooperative federations, and some networks of women's organizations are more likely to have been organized by outsiders.

Typical of networks organized by outsiders are the Maison Familles Ruraux centers organized by French agricultural schools in seventeen countries. Each *maison* unites a small group of villages and undertakes such projects as building clinics and technology centers or providing agricultural credit. In Senegal there are hundreds of regionally federated groups linked to both French NGOs and Senegalese GRSOs (Rouille D'Orfeuille 1984).

LDA networks, because they are multifunctional, are more likely to assume quasigovernmental roles on a regional level than other types of GRO networks. Squatter neighborhood federations in Latin America frequently provide water taps, organize transportation, and build schools (Fisher 1984). In Yemen the Coordinating Council for Local Development Associations, with government support, receives complaints, contributes one-third of the cost of building local schools, pays a portion of teacher salaries, and has managed to remain relatively autonomous (Tutwiler 1984).

Yet interest associations are also creating horizontal linkages. An example of a women's network is Madres Educadores, a network of community daycare centers in poor urban neighborhoods throughout Colombia. Community kitchens in Lima and Santiago cooperate with one another in obtaining outside assistance.[19]

GROs defined by ethnicity are increasingly united by environmental goals. In the Philippines, Manobo tribal activist Edtami Mansayagan organized seventeen different ethnolinguistic groups in a joint protest of two thousand people against outside exploitation of Mount Apo, sacred to different Luad peoples.[20]

There is also evidence that GRO networks enhance the success of their individual members. The El Ceibo federation of thirty-five cocoa cooperatives in Bolivia sells $1.5 million worth of cacao per year, controls more than half of the national harvest, and has a small chocolate factory (Carroll 1992). An evaluation of the Panamanian health committees concluded that the main reason they remained effective after government support declined was that they themselves created an active federation of health committees (La Forgia 1985).

Although some formal networks utilize protest techniques, protest is more common among amorphous grassroots movements. During the 1970s regional movements in India were organized by landless tribal people. In Colombia, during the same period, peasants, small farmers, and students tried to redress the grievances of the poor through protest demonstrations and civic strikes (B. H. Smith 1990). A regional protest movement in Juchitán, Mexico, won a special municipal election in 1980 after fraud was officially acknowledged (Rubin 1987:4).

The defining characteristic of more recent protest movements is the access of the poor to natural resources, as the line between economic and environmental protest disappears. Indeed, the poor of the Third World were expressing their need for "sustainable development" years before the Brundtland Commission brought the term to international attention. In Brazil rural peasant movements sprang up all over the Amazon region in the late 1970s to protest deforestation and peasant expulsion by landowners. Tribal groups in the Caribbean and the forests of Brazil, Chile, Colombia, Bolivia, and Peru are also forming protest networks, supported by Cultural Survival and other outside donors. Thousands of peasant women in India's Chipko movement have successfully halted the planting of eucalyptus and teak as a replacement for indigenous mixed forests.[21]

Protest networks in Latin America have begun to evolve into a more formal federated pattern, with the need for increased coordination and representation to the larger society. CIDOB (Center of Indigenous Peoples and Communities in Eastern Bolivia), a representative body with delegates, grew out of attempts by several tribes to defend their land against the economic explosion based on oil, sugar, and cocaine. Yet the grassroots political culture of such movements can also reinforce egalitarianism. Although CIDOB had help from a GRSO formed by Bolivian anthropologists, the decision to hire them was made by the group itself. In addition, its federated structure grew out of the strong intercommunity traditions of the Chiriguano tribe. AIDESEP (Inter-Ethnic Association for the Development of the Peruvian Jungle), organized as a protest movement in 1980, now groups two-thirds of the 300,000 Indians in the Peruvian Amazon, represents hundreds of GROs, and lobbies for land titles, while refusing capital for development that could create a potential source of power over local communities. Contributions are channeled directly to local groups (Reed 1987; Cabarle 1991).

There are also horizontal economic networks at the grassroots level with characteristics of both GRO networks and grassroots movements. When first organized, they may resemble movements because they are not necessarily based on local GROs. Unlike movements, however, they focus directly on development rather than on political protest. In Togo the Association of Village Enterprises requires that its members produce both enough for themselves and a surplus to share with other villages. Jatun Pukara in Potosi, Bolivia, unites seventeen communities producing grains and wool and uses the profits from excess village crops to reinforce and consolidate new organizations (IRED 1988:12). Although alternative economic movements are often initially constructed on barter, they tend to enter the money economy when they have acquired enough economic knowledge and muscle to avoid exploitation.[22] Anthropological studies of the relationship of alternative economic networks to traditional patterns of exchange would be a valuable contribution to the growing interest in "scaling out" local development efforts.

Networks and movements, by providing a mechanism for scaling out, can communicate what works internationally as well as nationally.[23] In addition, participatory evaluation in conjunction with neighboring groups can be a vast improvement over a single GRO evaluating itself, even if it has support from a GRSO. GRO networks also offer the promise of wider economic markets and exchange mechanisms that can bypass exploitative middlemen.

Networking also has its costs, however. Unforeseen side effects can occur, such as a large increase in the number of vegetable gardens that accentuates water problems. Because of insufficient knowledge of the national market, action in one village may undermine what happens in another, despite communication between villages. Networking can take up valuable time and resources, and rapid growth can lead to feuding and mistrust.

Grassroots Support Organizations

Although some GRSOs are membership organizations, they are generally staffed by paid professionals and are less likely to use volunteers than nonprofit organizations in developed countries (Fisher 1993:178–79). GRSOs usually work with existing GROs or help create new ones where none exist. Unlike GROs, which may make profits, GRSOs are nonprofit organizations, although some are developing for-profit subsidiary activities. The evolution of GRO networks into GRSOs demonstrates, however, that there is sometimes a fine line between GRSOs and GROs. In addition, some GRSOs are small and locally based. The organizational mutations, combinations, and inventions occurring in the developing countries are difficult to track yet help sustain the burst of organizational activity that began in the 1970s.

GRSOs are less likely than GROs to have evolved from traditional antecedents.[24] One observer, describing their creation after 1970 by unemployed intellectuals in numerous countries who could count on plentiful foreign assistance, went so far as to call them a "baby boomer" phenomenon (McCarthy 1989).

Whatever the individual motivations of activists, a kind of nonideological GRSO commitment to becoming "deprofessionalized" has emerged in Asia, Latin America, and, to some degree, Africa, as caste, class, and gender hierarchies are being challenged. Interactions with poor communities simultaneously enhance this new professionalism and ensure its continuing differentiation from the conventional roles of the educated elite. The founders of GRSOs include professionals who break away from government programs, nationals who work for INGO field offices becoming more autonomous, and combinations of people from both the developing and developed countries. A Burkinabe sociologist and a Frenchman founded the Six S Association, with a branch fundraising office in Geneva. Founders have included priests, hydraulic engineers, African emigrés to Europe, organizers of GRO federations, and, more commonly, social scientists (Rouille d'Orfeuille 1984; Schneider 1985:183).

The founders of women's GRSOs are less likely to be upper middle class in origin. In Tamil Nadu, India, six young *harijan* (formerly untouchable) women college graduates returned to their village and trained fifteen organizers, each in charge of a landless laborers' association of several thousand in five districts. The movement has built clinics and trained widows as paraprofessional health workers (Fatima 1984).

Women professionals, however, are also heavily involved in GRSOs, especially through professional membership organizations. Women lawyers in India and Bangladesh probably have the broadest and most capable volunteer base of any GRSOs in the Third World. The Bangladesh association has a traveling volunteer project that has taught basic legal rights to women in sixty-eight thousand villages.

I have elsewhere (Fisher 1993) estimated, very conservatively, that there are approximately twenty thousand functioning GRSOs in Asia, at least six thousand in Latin America and three thousand five hundred to four thousand in Africa. Although a plurality work on integrated rural development, they are active in a wide range of development sectors, including alternative tourism, development theater, and consumer advocacy. The Brazilian Association of Canoeing and Ecology (ABRACE) dramatizes deforestation through Amazonian tours and provides preventive and curative medical care at the same time (Brundtland 1990). Sometimes an interest in development grows out of and combines with other issues, such as human rights. Even more important in recent years has been the sometimes overlapping interest in environmental deterioration, microenterprise development, and women.

The linkage between environmental deterioration and poverty has led to a vast increase in the number of environmental organizations preaching sustainable development through grassroots support activities, political lobbying, and networking. Three hundred GRSOs from twenty-two Indian states attended a national conference on the World Bank and the environment in December 1988 and launched a National Alliance of Environmental Groups. The Environmental Liaison Center in Kenya is in "regular contact" with some ten thousand research organizations, technical institutes, universities, and other organizations, including one thousand seven hundred in Africa and three thousand three hundred in Asia and Latin America (Muchiru 1987:113).[25]

GRSOs concentrating primarily on poverty alleviation are increasingly aware of the need to focus on sustaining natural resources. In Senegal, with help from the Six S Association, the local *naams* organizations build caged rock dams to trap water and slow soil erosion.[26] The National Council of Kenyan Women organized the Greenbelt Movement to teach women to distinguish between problems like desertification and symptoms like famine. It has established 670 local tree nurseries involving 15,000 farmers who have planted more than 2 million trees (Postel and Heise 1988:39).

Microenterprise development reaching vast numbers of people has become a primary strategy for alleviating poverty. Asian GRSOs pioneered the minimalist credit methods of reaching thousands of people through borrowers' groups. And, although men are included in many borrowers' groups, microenterprise development depends in many countries on the dramatic increase in women's groups.

GRSOs have also developed other creative methods of reaching vast numbers of poor people through their linkages with GROs. The Association of Development Agencies in Bangladesh (ADAB) surveyed a small sample of thirty of their largest members (out of an estimated one thousand two hundred GRSOs) and found that they employed over seven thousand workers, mostly in rural areas, and served over 10 percent of the rural population (Khan and Bhasin 1986:15). The Iringa Rural Nutrition Program in Tanzania with a multilevel organizational structure was able to reduce malnutrition from 56 percent to 38 percent in four years (Pelletier 1991). Six S had organized three thousand GROs with four hundred thousand members in nine West African countries by 1987 (IRED 1987:4).

GRSOs focusing on family planning have proliferated less rapidly than those focusing on poverty or environmental deterioration, however, and GRSOs with an interest in population are often affiliates of the International Planned Parenthood Federation. The whole complex of cultural issues surrounding reproduction is a crucial topic for further anthropological research on GRSOs, so long as it encompasses cultural assumptions about population within the developed countries (Fisher 1993).

One of the most remarkable and widespread characteristics of GRSOs is their commitment to participatory research. Many evolved from independent or university research institutes that gradually became more activist through their experience with GROs (ibid., 1993: 107). In the settlement of Ajusco near Mexico City residents have enlisted the help of university professionals in fighting relocation, growing vegetables, planting thousands of trees, and writing a proposal to the local authorities for a productive ecological settlement including mushroom cultivation, pest control, fish farming, rabbit rearing, and recycling. UNIJUI, a Brazilian organization, operates within the state-sponsored University of Rio Grande do Sul and involves five thousand students and two hundred professors from twenty disciplines. Local GROs have, in turn, helped redesign the university curriculum (Frantz 1987).

Although GRSOs as a subject may lie outside the terrain of ethnology, they are themselves interacting with it and are creating a kind of common global culture of development, closer to the terrain of anthropology than of governance. Applied anthropologists should consider joint research projects with GRSOs that build on participatory techniques.

GRSOs can be classified as those that only work to enhance living standards (charitable, developmental), those concentrating on organizing and empowering the poor, and those that do both (Landim 1987). A GRSO in Zaire called Jopaje is self-financing, owns a mill, and sells agricultural products in its own store. But it is also battling price speculation by the customary chiefs.

Another way of classifying GRSOs is to divide them into those created from below and those created from above. GRSOs created from below by GRO federations or by graduates of top-down aid are strongly egalitarian and committed to empowerment; however, those created by former villagers sometimes use a more charitable/developmental approach. GRSOs created from above also vary widely, but a commitment to empowerment seems to be more pronounced in organizations founded since the early 1980s. Some of the older Asian GRSOs depend heavily on the charisma of key leaders.

There are, of course, some GRSOs led by outright charlatans, exploiting the availability of foreign funding. Others are honest but sell their technical services to foreign donors in the absence of strong grassroots linkages. As Brown and Korten (1989:21) have pointed out, however, "To focus on the performance and scale of individual VOs [GRSOs] is to risk losing sight of the aggregate phenomena that they represent."

In fact, a commitment to empowering the poor is remarkably widespread among GRSOs. Despite the many differences among GRSOs, the author of a major OECD study of nineteen countries concluded that he found attention to the poorest people everywhere (Schneider 1985:188). A sample survey of Thai GRSOs found that 62 percent gave priority to the least-developed areas of the province or district in which they were working (Tongsawate and Tipps 1985:54). Latin American GRSOs were characterized by one observer as being "extremely effective" in reaching the poor and in helping communities to rediscover ancient collective work practices (Twose 1988:24).

GRSOs are also pushed toward alternative, collegial management styles through their contacts with one another. An Argentine study concluded that the most effective GRSOs were those actively engaged in networking with one another (Martinez Nogueira 1987). Yet their autonomy, as well as accountability, ultimately depends on their vertical linkages with people at the grassroots level.

Empowerment and Development

Before looking at relationships between GROs and GRSOs, let us look briefly at their major interrelated goals—empowerment and development. Participation is an instrumental means for achieving empowerment, just as enterprise development and nonformal education are among the means of achieving socioeconomic development.

Socioeconomic progress, however, also depends on participation, whether it emerges spontaneously from below through GROs or is promoted by GRSOs, INGOs, or official donors (Lance and McKenna 1975; Cheema 1986). Thirteen of twenty-five World Bank projects failed a long-term sustainability test, defined as an acceptable net flow of benefits from the project's investments after completion. First among the main causes of failure was not involving GROs to enhance beneficiary participation. Successful projects, on the other hand, had in common a "clear attempt by design, to enhance the institutional capacity in some form," and were based on partnerships with existing GROs (Cernea 1987:5). Other factors related to success such as technical improvements, socioeconomic compatibility, favorable policy environment, and recurrent cost financing/recovery were all strongly related to institutional development as well.

The most obvious gains from participation are the quality of information and a lowering of project costs. Bridges built in the Philippines, Nepal, and Mexico were washed out after farmers had told engineers not to build them in those locations because of high seasonal crests. Construction committees in Nepal organized by the local *panchayats* (LDAs) built sixty-two dams at one-fourth the cost of construction by the government (Uphoff 1986:63, 284).

On the other hand, if participation is promoted or encouraged in isolation from economic development, then the potential for mutual reinforcement is as neglected as if participation were ignored, because economic achievement can spark participation.[27] This need not imply an abandonment of social goals, however, since literacy, for example, has been tied to agricultural productivity, and investing in women liberates enormous economic energy. Social development objectives can also enhance participation. A study of Latin American GRSOs found a strong correlation between poverty reach and participation, either because the poorest people were easier to organize or because those GRSOs targeting the poorest of the poor were more participatory in their approach (Carroll 1992:34, 67).

It is not enough, therefore, to argue that "growth and equity are more complementary than competitive." (Lewis 1986:26). It is also that the particular social, economic, or participatory focus chosen should have the maximum number of spin-off effects. If there was a problem with the much needed emphasis on "basic needs" in the 1970s, it was the assumption that integrated rural development at the community level (health care, functional literacy, etc.) could somehow lead to overall economic advances. A targeted but massive (nongovernmental or governmental) social initiative with potential economic spin-off effects (providing health and family planning services to women of childbearing age or making it illegal for banks to deny credit to women) can have a more substantial impact on income than social development, thinly spread.

Even the sequential and partial achievement of the processes of empowerment and development is becoming increasingly dependent on the ability of both GROs and GRSOs to promote environmentally sustainable development and to sustain themselves as institutions as well. Although I have dealt with the internal capabilities of GROs and GRSOs elsewhere (Fisher 1993), and anthropological research on this topic would be valuable, the remainder of this chapter will focus on GRO-GRSO relationships, the key most likely to unlock their potential for long-term accomplishment.

GRO-GRSO Linkages

Although linkages and networking can positively impact many types of governmental and nongovernmental organizations, GROs and GRSOs have particular comparative advantages that complement each other. An Inter-American Foundation study of funded organizations concludes that GRSOs have the capacity for "organizational, economic or technological innovation, as well as for rapid response to unforeseen opportunities. Yet membership organizations [GROs] have the potential . . . to have a much deeper, and potentially more far-reaching social impact." GRSOs may have the greatest grassroots development impact by providing services that strengthen GROs as membership organizations (Fox and Butler 1987:4). GROs and GRSOs have, in other words, a better chance than other top-down/bottom-up relationships for overcoming "the central paradox of social development," originally described by David McClelland (1970) as "influencing people to build capacity to act on their own behalf " (D. C. Korten 1983:220).

What factors increase the likelihood that GRO-GRSO combinations will be able to promote sustainable development and overcome the unequal power relationship upon which any top-down/bottom-up connection is based? The functional differences among GRO-GRSO linkages in terms of grassroots empowerment and development have not been reviewed statistically, so we can only hypothesize based on available evidence. In other words, "We know participation is good, but do we know the key factors which interact to broaden and deepen it?" (Fox and Butler 1987:6).

Outlining the patterns of GRO-GRSO relationships that appear to be more closely linked to successful participatory development will help indicate directions for in-depth anthropological research. It will also provide potential donors with initial selection indicators as well as potential strategies for enhancing institutional sustainability. These indicators include the use of existing GROs, the use of GRO networks, specialized help to many GROs, the evolution of a GRO network into a GRSO, villagers who return to their communities ready to help, informal GRSO networks, and ties to universities.

The first and most obvious indicator of effectiveness is the use of existing GROs. Because GRSOs can skip the difficult first stage of trying to empower people from above, planning and evaluation techniques to provide a community with additional tools for determining its own future can be initiated sooner. GRO members can learn to write down their observations of organizational performance. Such "process documentation" is more difficult to achieve when new organizations are created (Esman and Uphoff 1984). Where peasants or squatters have already founded GROs, the process of participatory planning also has a greater potential impact on outsiders, through deepening their awareness of what they can learn as well as teach.

Sometimes the role of a traditional GRO may be apparently unrelated to development. The relationship of the Six S Association in Burkina Faso to the traditional *naams,* however, shows that the role of traditional GROs can change and that there are enormous advantages to be gained by building on what is already in the village. Six S chose the *naams* because, as youth organizations, they were the only traditional groups among the Mossi in which there was no social inequality. As the "first African creation of a society that is neither a copy of Western ideas nor a return to ancestral custom," Six S works through the *naams* to safeguard positive traditional values like mutual help (Ouedrago 1986:89).

The potentially important role of anthropologists in identifying and supporting many more such indigenous institutions is illustrated by the work of two Chilean GRSOs. Both the Sociedad de Profesionales para el Desarrollo Rural (SOPRODER), a GRSO that works with the Mapuche, and Taller de Estudios Rurales (TER), which works with the Aymara, include anthropologists. SOPRODER's approach is based on an understanding of the reciprocal exchanges of resources and labor that helped the Mapuche redistribute resources and protect fragile lands before forced deed registration by the government in 1979 led to migration and began to unravel the complex web of mutual obligation. SOPRODER encourages local Mapuche groups to become experts on wheat production, animal husbandry, and health, to meet with groups from other villages, and to organize a horizontal federation (Wali 1990:16). TER has found that preserving the *allyu* is essential to preserving the fragile ecology of the altiplano and compatible with both horizontal networking and intelligent modification of traditional technologies.[28]

Where local organizations do not exist, GRSOs can nonetheless provide some creative substitute techniques. For example, the Kottar Social Service Agency in India only enters a community if asked. It then is in a far better position to help local people create new organizations (Uphoff 1986:190). BRAC in Bangladesh began by promoting and creating local organizations, but the movement of landless groups that it helped to launch is now self-sustaining enough that BRAC is able to begin working with many new groups that it has not created.

The advantages of working with a horizontal network of existing GROs are a second indicator of successful linkages between GROs and GRSOs. GRSO investments in training and devolution of planning and evaluation to a horizontal network are obviously more productive than equal time spent organizing a single community organization, and numbers of beneficiaries is in itself a rough measure of effectiveness. It may also be that creative organizations are more likely to link up with others, both horizontally and vertically.

Linkages between GRSOs and GRO networks do, however, have

some other inherent advantages. GRSOs can assist GRO networks to empower themselves even where GRSOs themselves are reluctant or unable to confront local or national power structures (B. H. Smith 1990). Because networks spread leadership skills and reduce dependence on a few dynamic local community leaders, they can enhance institutional and even economic sustainability, linked in one World Bank study to local organizational density (Cernea 1987:12). Esman and Uphoff (1984) found that there was a strong correlation between the overall performance ratings of GROs and their horizontal and vertical nongovernmental linkages, with horizontal networking the more powerful of the two explanatory variables.

The Six S Association has made horizontal networking among neighboring village *naams* a condition of assistance. Networks must work solely with their own resources for two years to qualify for assistance. Support is provided for regional cohesion but only indirectly for particular activities. By avoiding dispersion and inexperienced beginners, Six S had reached three thousand *naams* in three countries with a membership of four hundred thousand by 1987 (Lecomte 1986; IRED 1987:4).

To be sure, technical assistance from Six S is spread thin, but this is accepted philosophically by local groups, since dry season activities such as catchment dams do not threaten productive activities taking place during the rainy season. Area committees produce their own educational tools on soap making, solar drying, agroforestry, and cereal banks (Lecomte 1986; IRED 1987:24). This educational process may actually be strengthened because peasants are allowed to learn from failure and seek out technical assistance from one another as well as from outsiders. Nine years after Six S was founded, levels of funding to the *naams* had declined, providing evidence of sustainability (OECD 1988).

Although investments in GRO networks are potentially productive in the long run, they are not a quick fix for GRSOs, particularly where there are no existing GROs. The Palawan Center for Appropriate Rural Technology in the Philippines has formed eight village-level peasant associations that work on agriculture, education, and health among swidden slash-and-burn farmers. Appropriate technology is used as the "entry point," followed by consciousness-raising, and the associations have organized a regional association affiliated with the National Peasant Association. The farmers did not view the associations as their own, however, because too much emphasis had been placed on leadership training and not enough on mass education (Belamide 1986).

A third pattern to look for in identifying effective assistance is a GRSO that provides specialized or sectoral assistance to large numbers of GROs, which may or may not be affiliated with one another. CENPRODES, sponsored by the Episcopal Conference of Colombia, has helped hundreds of GROs prepare funding proposals for European NGOs. The number of assisted projects designed and operated by recipients themselves increased from 8 percent in the first three years to 29 percent between 1981 and 1983 (B. H. Smith 1990).

Better known are large GRSOs, such as the Grameen Bank, that work with thousands of borrowers' groups not usually tied to one another. Only 4.2 percent of Grameen loans have been granted to borrowers with more than a half-acre of land, yet incomes are 43 percent higher than non–bank members in the same villages (Hulme 1990). The Grameen model has spread to many other countries, including Malaysia, where AIM (Amanah Ikhtiar Malaysia), in deference to Islamic values, charges a fixed management fee rather than interest.

A number of GRSOs also embody a fifth indicator of effectiveness, which is creating GRSOs from below, thus bypassing the unequal power relationship between insiders and outsiders. A farmers' association among the Tiv in Nigeria is built on traditional rotating credit arrangements, with two hundred base centers, eight regional centers, and one national council (OECD 1988). A Sri Lankan GRO network called Vinivida has a clearinghouse for exchange of information and access to development services and outside assistance. And LDAs organized in Zimbabwe during the struggle for independence have district associations, regional markets, and workshops for making tools.

Entrepreneurs who hire the right experts are usually assumed to be from the middle or upper class. But as GROs organize networks they become the entrepreneurs, and the conventional notion of hierarchy is stood on its head when they locate and hire their own professionals. Since a functional definition of hierarchy is determined by who works for whom, a bottom-up hierarchy, while challenging existing class structures, is not a contradiction in terms.[29] Also challenged by these patterns is the assumption that outside linkages necessarily increase GRO dependency.

A sixth powerful indicator of effective GRO-GRSO combinations occurs when people leave their village, obtain an education, and then found a GRSO to assist their home village. Lecomte (1986:84) notes that grassroots development activists in Africa have typically traveled outside their communities and have then returned. As innovators, these activists are a "driving force" in their own communities and "yet in a way outside it." One of the more dramatic examples of this began in the village of Wuro-Sogi in Senegal, where over one-fourth of the labor force had migrated either to France or to Dakar. In the 1960s these migrants set up a mutual assistance fund for their village that provided a motor pump during a drought, trained villagers to maintain it, and helped the local LDA to obtain additional outside assistance (OECD 1988).

"Support movements" that include both grassroots activists and intellectuals are a sixth important indicator. Although GRSOs have organized formal networks among themselves in most countries, they sometimes belong to less-formal networks that include individual professionals and GROs as well. Support movements, like other GRO-GRSO combinations, include people helping their own communities and people helping other communities. Yet they are continually evolving and developing more complex forms of interaction. Lokoyan in India, for example, has over two thousand members, including individual intellectuals, GRSOs, and GROs. In Mexico a number of intellectuals are linked to over four hundred GROs in what Gustavo Esteva (1987) describes as a "hammock" conforming to the shape of the user. This network's half-million dollar donation fund has revolved at least four times, with 95 percent returned. By providing GROs with more varied and diffuse forms of assistance, informal networks probably enhance GRO autonomy and make it more difficult for a particular GRSO to become corrupt or beholden to elites.[30]

There are also international networks built on this informal pattern of interaction, including the Asian Cultural Forum on Development (ACFOD), founded in 1976, with the stated purpose of "bringing the grassroots to the international level." One of ACFOD's first projects was to encourage international exchanges among rural theatres. ACFOD trains GRO as well as GRSO leaders and promotes international exchanges between GROs (Sabur 1986). Some international-local connections bubble up from below. A remarkable woman in Papua New Guinea named Matarina founded a women's group in her village as an illiterate teenager. At age twenty-eight she was coordinating four GROs, training leaders at the local government center, producing educational cassettes on development, traveling to other provinces, and was recognized at the national level. She has created an informal international network on women in development that includes a Fiji network, feminist academics from the University of the South Pacific, the Women and Development Network of Australia, the Australian Council of Churches, aboriginal communities in Australia, and women's development leaders in Fiji, Tonga, Samoa, and Vanuatu (Cox 1987:22–23).

Finally, it seems to me that, if one were to look at the development institutions in a given country, it would be worthwhile to pay special attention to GRSOs that are tied to universities, not only because of the intellectual resources they command but also because they have tended to utilize several other effective linkage patterns, especially participatory research. FUNDAEC, for example, was founded in Cali, Colombia, in 1974 by a group of professors who saw that the Green Revolution was only helping plantation owners. According to Dr. Farzam Arbad, one of the founders, "what is usually taken to the peasants is information, not knowledge. . . . A rural population needs a university, not just primary or technical schools, to act as its learning institution" (*AIRD News* 1987:11).

This list of indicators is meant to be suggestive, and reflects the institutional perspective of a political scientist in this collection of essays. Anthropologists could further explore these indicators by focusing on such cultural explanations as the complex and varying impact of underlying tribal or lineage systems on networking. One anthropological study of the LDAs in Yemen, for example, concludes that they were more successful in Anis, where there is a strong tribal system, than in Jibad Rayma, where tribal ties are weak (Swagman 1988). Segmentary lineage systems such as that of the Tiv in Nigeria may account for the ease with which the farmers' network has spread, yet kinship patterns in other areas may inhibit freedom of action (Ralston, Anderson, and Colson 1983:69–70; Horowitz 1986).

Perhaps even more interesting to anthropologists, who continually confront the modernization or even extinction of traditional culture, is the emergence of a new global culture of change, based on an appreciation for and a commitment to preserving and building on indigenous organizational knowledge.

Conclusions

Although the long-term results of the linkage patterns described in this chapter are not predictable, they can help achieve at least four important preconditions for long-term and widespread impact. First, they promote networking and enhance the possibilities for continual feedback and learning. Second, they help support and sustain effective innovations. Third, they dilute inequities inherent in the "central paradox of development." And, fourth, they provide the organizational mechanisms, if not necessarily the substance, of being able to scale out. If we are to understand the substance of what works, then anthropologists need to contribute their understanding of underlying historical and cultural patterns.

Nothing is inevitable in this process. Trained "leaders" may leave their communities because they are able to obtain jobs elsewhere. University professors may have their own private agendas despite their rhetorical commitment to the poor. Yet there is evidence that networking and mutual learning processes reinforce each other and enhance the possibilities for institutionally sustainable development.

Will self-help activity sustain itself over the long run? Much of the grassroots activity is so fueled by the dimensions of the intertwined poverty, environment, and population crises that people will probably not give up once modest gains are achieved. Although earlier studies of Latin American squatter settlements demonstrated that activism declined and was only reactivated when needed, the survival crisis has become so permanent that the process of decline and reactivation may be a luxury that GROs can no longer afford.[31] Uphoff's long-term participation in the Gal Oya irrigation project in Sri Lanka has led him to question whether the selfish behavior of "free riders" or those who degrade the commons for their own benefit inevitably replace collective rationality. Although conflict over water in Gal Oya was inevitably tied to an inadequate supply, there were also "incentives to increase that supply . . . thereby reducing conflict and enhancing productivity, converting a zero-sum situation to a positive sum one by collective action."[32]

A second major component of sustainability is outsiders who want to work themselves out of a job and know when to do it. If a GRSO (or INGO) pulls out too soon, it may leave little behind. If they stay too long, they may establish a pattern of dependency. Some GRSOs carefully plan their own departure. DESEC in Bolivia begins working intensively in a rural community but then sets up community centers and specialized committees that eventually become linked to a regional federation of community centers and a national federation that is gradually assuming a stronger assistance role (Uphoff 1986:335). The *Fundación del Centavo* in Guatemala limits loans and technical assistance for GROs to four years and does not try to ensure that all groups survive. By stressing its own limited financial resources and setting limits on credit, it discourages dependency (336). By being willing to accept some failures, it may actually increase the percentage of organizations that survive and prosper. It also preserves an option for the poor—that of allowing them to desert an organization that is not serving their needs.

Finally, sustainability depends on encouraging people to buy into their own development through contributions in labor or money to the common task. One study concluded that the most successful GRSOs in India were those that require token payment and/or a work requirement from even the poorest people (Panini 1987).

The probability of sustainable economic development is another story. If economic development is a precondition for GRSOs being able to move on to new communities, then there is a strong argument for paying attention to GRSOs that focus on income generation, community-based enterprise development, and promoting alternative economic ties that begin to have a macroeconomic impact through bypassing exploitative middlemen. Economic networks that create their own GRSO or obtain outside technical assistance can further enhance the probability of achieving economic sustainability. The Potato Producers' Association of Cochabamba, a network of GROs from three hundred sixty Bolivian communities, is administering a revolving loan fund with assistance from CEDEAGRO and capital from a consortia of European and U.S. donors (R. C. Smith 1987).

The combined impact of linkages and an economic approach to development is also flagged in a summary of evaluations on small enterprise development (Hunt 1984:183). Key institutional factors promoting success included support for GROs, cooperation between public and private organizations, new managerial skills emerging from participation, and networking where institutions maintained a high level of autonomy and coherence in goals and strategy. Autonomy and the lack of elite dominance were in turn related to a democratic context and linkages to other indigenous and external agencies.

Robert Michels's (1915) iron law of oligarchy has understandably conditioned the thinking of generations of societal observers. The evidence presented, however, indicates that the link between individual "human nature" and oligarchic behavior may not be inevitable. Since it has become nearly impossible in many countries for individuals to advance themselves, they have begun to organize collectively in ways that both pre- and postdate industrial bureaucracy (Fisher 1994). Although individual GROs and GRSOs can become sources of privilege and patronage for the few, the linkages between GROs, GRSOs, governments, and INGOs, coupled with the computer revolution, provide enhanced capabilities for organizational learning. This may improve not only the quality and sustainability of local development projects but also the ability to have a broader impact, particularly if "top down" economic policies begin to focus on sustainable, equitable development as well. The recent cholera epidemic in Andean America underlined the critical need for state infrastructural investment.[33]

Because their survival is at stake, people at the grassroots level may learn more quickly from the failure of development projects than those from outside who do not suffer the direct consequences of their own mistakes. Hirschman's (1984) concept of the conservation and mutation of social energy seems particularly applicable to GROs. In Bufat Village, Cameroon, the Taiwanese promoted agricultural cooperatives in the early 1960s that failed soon after they left. With help from their traditional chief, however, the villagers themselves decided to create "communities" of eight hundred inhabitants organized into a general assembly and executive committee. The communities have built six schools, five health posts, two water supply projects, and a cultural center. Rice yields have increased, and a rice husking plant has been built along with coffee, cocoa, and livestock plantations. The communities are planting trees, growing new forage crops, and have joined an agricultural credit program sponsored by the national rural development fund (Pavard 1986).

The effectiveness of GRSOs, horizontal networks of GROs and GRSOs, and their impact on governments and other outsiders ultimately depends on the groups at the bottom of the organizational pyramid. This chapter has dealt with some of the failures and frustrations of GROs. But there is an immense amount of evidence that GROs are not only the strongest and broadest part of the pyramid; they are also, in themselves, the *sine qua non* of effective development.[34]

Anthropologists not only have specialized knowledge of grassroots organizations and their antecedents; they also understand that "organic forms of local social organization are prerequisites to successful development" (Wali 1990:12). Their skills and commitment can contribute to the organizational revolution occurring in the Third World. Perhaps most important of all is their potential contribution to protecting and enhancing indigenous organizational and technical knowledge, without which there can be no empowerment or development. The loss of this resource in a world that is becoming increasingly dependent on sustainable development strategies would be a disaster.

NOTES

1. Letter to the author, 11 July 1991.
2. There are fewer GROs in northeastern India, Burma, and the Asian Marxist countries. I have seen few reports of GROs or GRSOs in some African countries such as Chad, Mauritania, the Central African Republic, and Niger.
3. Discussion with the Middle East division of Save the Children, September 1989.
4. For a discussion of the Third World state and its inability to provide needed services, see Carol Smith's article in this volume. She points out that, because peasant communities have retained relative autonomy up to the modern period, they tend to be "the most independent element in Third World civil society."
5. What is now the International Institute for Rural Reconstruction remains active today, with autonomous affiliates in many countries.
6. Other early interventions in India were less successful. A project in Sriniketan was initiated in 1922 by a group of intellectuals and activist artists who lacked technical skills. Its budget was nine times that of Martandam, but longitudinal data developed in 1958 revealed little long-term improvement (Alliband 1983:33).
7. In some cases dormant GROs are reactivated with outside help. The 1980 agrarian reform in El Salvador turned two hundred sixty expropriated haciendas into cooperatives. Many of these were failing and in danger of dissolution when Technoserve, a U.S. PVO (private voluntary organization) began providing them with technical assistance in agronomy, accounting, and marketing. TNS has provided assistance to over one-fourth of the Salvadoran agrarian reform cooperatives, and one of them, Las Lajas, grossed over a million dollars in 1986 (Fisher, forthcoming a).
8. Interview with David Beckmann of the World Bank, May 1990.
9. GRSOs are sometimes chosen because of their superior international public relations capability, rather than because of their ability to work with GROs.
10. Water user's networks are sometimes promoted by outsiders. The water council movement in a drought-prone area of Maharashtra, founded by Gram Fourav Pratishthan, a GRSO, is a particularly innovative example. Assistance depends on group irrigation plans and must include the landless. Because the landless receive the same water share as members who own land, the landless acquire a bargaining chip within the organization. Sugarcane cultivation, which requires a great deal of irrigation, is prohibited (Deshpande et al. 1986).

11. According to Enge and Whiteford, these methods date back to the *ganat* organizations in ancient Persia.

12. In the Sibundoy Valley in Colombia women who had hung their heads in shyness during the first meetings of women's clubs organized by Save the Children eventually became valued contributors to family income, and some participate in community council meetings (Fisher 1986).

13. Local Islamic organizations not involved in development are more common, however. See Ralston, Anderson, and Colson 1983:90–91.

14. According to Painter (1986) work groups in Niger are related to lineage systems.

15. Annis's (1987) estimate is in accordance with national estimates by Thompson 1990:394; Ritchey Vance 1991:33; and Carroll 1992:211.

16. The coastal cooperatives created by the Peruvian agrarian reform of 1969 were given excellent land, but when they began to earn profits the government taxed them so heavily that their prospects were damaged.

17. Discussion with Karen McGuinness of the Ford Foundation.

18. Letter to the author from Scott Gugenheim, 11 July 1991.

19. Goff 1990:21; Friedmann 1989:12.

20. Discussion with Mansayagan at the Asia Society, spring 1991. Even cooperatives that are creatures of the state find that networking enhances autonomy and bottom-up political impact. In Mali the autonomous Federation of Rural Groups, made up of twenty cooperatives, meets regularly with the regional political cadre and has had some impact on government policies (Rouille D'Orfeuille 1984).

21. Environmental movements are also strong in other mountainous areas of India. In the Doon Valley, at the base of the Himalayas, the Dehradun movement opposes limestone quarrying, since limestone in fractured form provides the best and largest aquifer for sustaining water resources (Shiva 1986).

22. GRO networks, movements, and hybrids of both types of horizontal organization are forming national federations in some countries. In Senegal the Federation of Farmers' Associations (FONGS) buys grain from peasant groups and sells it to other groups in the federation in order to build a revolving loan fund for development. In Peru regional water users' associations have organized a national federation.

23. Networks such as IRED (Development Innovations and Networks) and IFDA (International Foundation for Development Alternatives) in Switzerland document grassroots activism and promote international exchanges between GROs as well as GRSOs. There are also a rapidly growing number of regional and interregional South-South networks such as APPEN (Asian People's Environmental Network).

24. Some traditional charities have evolved into development assistance organizations, however (see Eldridge 1984–85). Hospitals in a number of countries have created primary health care outreach programs that function like GRSOs.

25. These figures obviously include government, international, and pure research organizations as well as GRSOs.

26. Six S stands for Se Servir au Sahel au Saison Seche (making use of the dry season in the Sahel).

27. The increasing interest in microenterprise development has only partially met this need. GRSOs such as PRADAN in India, which promotes larger community-based enterprises and work consciously to alter markets, are still the exception to the rule.

28. With the return to democracy in Chile, the government has created decentralized corporations called Condicion Especial de Pueblos Indigenas (CEPI) to funnel loans and resources. This is being organized by Jose Bengoa, an anthropologist who has worked with SOPRODER (Wali 1990).

29. I am indebted to my husband, Richard Peck, for this idea.

30. There are also more formal GRSO networks or consortia that now include GROs. A group of Bangladesh GRSOs including BRAC, Proshika, and Friends in Village Development have formed an interorganization resource building group. This phenomenon is also occurring among subnational GRSOs, "a most promising trend, given the lopsided dominance of Dhaka-based agencies" (PACT 1989:31).

31. For earlier citations, see Fisher 1984:67–76.

32. Uphoff 1992:327–33.

33. I am indebted to Scott Guggenheim for this example. A more complete discussion of the relationships between GROs, GRSOs, and governments will be found in Fisher, forthcoming b.

34. Maize farmers in Zimbabwe who belonged to groups outproduced individual maize farmers, and the effect of group membership became more powerful as rainfall and soil conditions worsened (Bratton 1983:315). The yields for rain-fed farmers in Kenya who belonged to GROs were significantly higher than for those who did not belong, even though group members had lower ratios of extension agents per farmer than nongroup members (Oxby 1983:54).

REFERENCES

AIRD News
    1987   6(3).

Alliband, Terry
    1983   *Catalysts of Development: Voluntary Agencies in India.* W. Hartford, Conn.: Kumarian Press.

Anacleti, A. Odhiambo
    1986   Rural Groupings and Organizations—with special reference to Tanzania. *The Courier* 99 (September–October).

Annis, Sheldon
    1987   The Next World Bank? Financing Development from the Bottom Up. *Grassroots Development* 11(1): 24–29.

1989 Can Small-Scale Development Be Large-Scale Policy? In *Direct to the Poor: Grassroots Development in Latin America,* ed. Sheldon Annis and Peter Hakim, 209–18. Boulder, Colo.: Westview Press.

Attir, M. O., Burkhart Holzner, and Zdenek Suda, eds.
1982 *Directions of Change: Modernization Theory, Research and Realities.* Boulder, Colo.: Westview Press.

Bagadion, Benjamin U., and Frances F. Korten
1985 Developing Irrigators' Organizations: A Learning Process Approach. In *Putting People First: Sociological Variables in Rural Development,* ed. Michael Cernea, 52–90. New York: Oxford University Press.

Belamide, Eileen
1986 Building Self-Help Groups: The Philippine Experience. *Ideas and Action* 171:13–18.

Berg, Robert
1987 Non-Governmental Organizations: New Force in Third World Development and Politics. MS, Michigan State University, Center for Advanced Study of International Development. Distinguished Speakers Series no. 2.

Bratton, Michael
1983 Farmer Organizations in the Communal Areas of Zimbabwe: Preliminary Findings. MS, Departments of Land Management and Political and Administrative Studies, University of Zimbabwe, Harare. Cited in Uphoff 1986:147.

Brown, L. David, and David Korten
1989 The Role of Voluntary Organizations in Development. Boston: Institute for Development Research.

Brundtland Bulletin
1990 Geneva: Centre for Our Common Future. Vol. 7 (March).

Cabarle, Bruce
1991 Community Forestry and the Social Ecology of Development. *Grassroots Development* 15(3): 3–9.

Calavan, Michael
1986 Community Management in Rural Northeastern Thailand. In *Community Management: Asian Experience and Perspectives,* ed. D. C. Korten, 93–104. W. Hartford, Conn.: Kumarian Press.

Carroll, Thomas F.
1992 *Intermediary NGOs: The Supporting Link in Development.* Hartford, Conn.: Kumarian Press.

Cernea, Michael
1982 Modernization and Development Potential of Traditional Grass-Roots Organizations. In *Directions of Change: Modernization Theory, Research and Realities,* ed. M. O. Attir et al., 121–39. Boulder, Colo.: Westview Press.
1985 (ed.) *Putting People First: Sociological Variables in Rural Development.* New York: Oxford University Press.

1987 Farmer Organizations and Institution Building for Sustainable Development. *Regional Development Dialogue* 8(2):1–24.

Cheema, G. Shabbir, ed.
1986 *Reaching the Urban Poor: Project Implementation in Developing Countries.* Boulder, Colo.: Westview Press.

Coombs, Philip H.
1980 *Meeting the Basic Needs of the Rural Poor.* New York: Pergamon Press.

Cox, Elizabeth
1987 Networking among the Rural Women in the South Pacific. *Ideas and Action.* 175:18–23.

Deshpande, V. D., S. P. Salunke, and David Korten
1986 Water for People. In *Community Management: Asian Experience and Perspectives,* ed. D. C. Korten, 183–200. Hartford, Conn.: Kumarian Press.

Dhungel, Dipak P.
1986 The People's Movement and Experiment in Nepal. *Community Development Journal* 21(3): 317–25.

Dichter, Thomas W., and Scott Zesch
1989 *Savings and Credit Societies in an African Context: Insights and Lessons on Internal Management from the Kenyan Experience.* Case Histories in Enterprise Development, Sector Study Series. Norwalk, Conn.: Technoserve.

Durning, Alan B.
1989 *Action at the Grassroots: Fighting Poverty and Environmental Decline.* Worldwatch Paper 88, Washington, D.C.: Worldwatch Institute.

Dyson-Hudson, Neville
1985 Pastoral Production Systems and Livestock Development Projects: An East African Perspective. In *Putting People First: Sociological Variables in Rural Development,* ed. Michael Cernea, 157–86. New York: Oxford University Press.

Edel, Matthew D.
1969 The Colombian Community Action Program: Costs and Benefits. *Yale Economic Essays* 9(2).

Eldridge, Philip
1984– The Political Role of Community Action Groups in India and Indonesia: In Search of a General Theory. *Alternatives: A Journal of World Policy 10* (Winter).

Enge, Kjell, and Scott Whiteford
1989 *The Keepers of Water and Earth: Mexican Rural Social Organization and Irrigation.* Austin: University of Texas Press.

Esman, Milton J., and Norman T. Uphoff
1984 *Local Organizations: Intermediaries in Local Development.* Ithaca, N.Y.: Cornell University Press.

Esteva, Gustavo
1987 Regenerating People's Space. *Alternatives* 12(1): 125–52.

Fatima, Burnad
    1984   Rural Development and Women's Liberation: Caste, Class and Gender in a Grass-Roots Organization in Tamil Nadu, South India. *Bulletin* (Institute for Development Studies, Sussex) 15:45–56.
Fishel, John T.
    1979   Political Participation in a Peruvian Highland District. In *Political Participation in Latin America,* ed. J. Booth and M. A. Seligson, 2:51–61. New York: Holmes and Meier.
Fisher, Julie
    1977   *Political Learning in the Latin American Barriadas: The Role of the Junta de Vecinos.* Ph.D. diss., School of Advanced International Studies, Johns Hopkins University.
    1984   Development from Below: Neighborhood Improvement Associations in the Latin American Squatter Settlements. *Studies in Comparative International Development* 19(1): 61–85.
    1986   Colombia: When Women Are United. In *Already I Feel the Change: Lessons from the Field 1,* 263 pp. Save the Children.
    1993   *The Road from Rio: Sustainable Development and the Nongovernmental Movement in the Third World.* Westport, Conn.: Praeger Publishers.
    1994   Is the Iron Law of Oligarchy Rusting Away in the Third World? *World Development* (February). Vol. 22, No. 2, pp. 129–143.
    Forthcoming a. *Turning Workers into Owners: Technoserve's Experience with Agrarian Reform Cooperatives in Peru and El Salvador.* Norwalk, Conn.: Technoserve.
    Forthcoming b. *Cultivating Civil Societies: NGOs, Governments and International Donors.* Westport, Conn.: Praeger Publishers.
Fox, Jonathan, and John Butler
    1987   Research Project Preview: Membership Organization Dynamics: Lessons from the Inter-American Foundation Experience. IAF memorandum, 18 May.
Frantz, Telmo Rudi
    1987   The Role of NGOs in the Strengthening of Civil Society. *World Development* 15 (supp., Autumn): 121–27.
Friedmann, John
    1989   Collective Self-Empowerment and Social Change. *IFDA Dossier* no. 69 (January–February): 3–14.
Gain, Philip
    1991   Case study done for Beyond Boundaries: Issues in Asian and American Environmental Activism. Asia Society, New York, 24–26 April.
Goff, Brent
    1990   Mastering the Craft of Scaling Up in Colombia. *Grassroots Development* 14(1): 13–22.
Herrera, Xochitl, and Miguel Lobo-Guerrero
    1988   From Failure to Success: Tapping the Creative Energy of Sikuani Culture in Colombia. *Grassroots Development* 12(3): 28–37.

Hirschman, Albert O.
- 1984 *Getting ahead Collectively: Grassroots Experiences in Latin America.* New York: Pergamon Press.

Horowitz, Michael
- 1986 Ideology, Policy and Praxis in Pastoral Livestock Development. In *Anthropology and Rural Development in West Africa,* ed. Horowitz and Painter, 251–72. Boulder, Colo.: Westview Press.

Horowitz, Michael, and Thomas M. Painter, eds.
- 1986 *Anthropology and Rural Development in West Africa.* Boulder, Colo.: Westview Press.

Hulme, David
- 1990 Can the Grameen Bank Be Replicated? Recent Experiments in Malaysia, Malawi, and Sri Lanka. *Development Policy Review* 8(3): 287–300.

Hunt, Robert W.
- 1984 Voluntary Agencies and the Promotion of Enterprise. In *Private Voluntary Organizations as Agents of Development,* ed. R. F. Gorman, 165–200. Boulder, Colo.: Westview Press.

Hyden, Goran
- 1983 *No Shortcuts to Progress: African Development Management in Perspective.* Berkeley: University of California Press.

Innovations et Reseaux pour le Developpement (IRED)
- 1987 Geneva: Innovations et Reseaux pour le Developpement. *IRED Forum,* no. 25.
- 1988 Geneva: Innovations et Reseaux pour le Developpement. *IRED Forum,* no. 27.

Khan, Mafruzah
- 1991 Participatory Management of Local Resources: Proshika's Initiatives in Forest Management. Dhaka, Proshika.

Khan, Nighat Said, and Kamla Bhasin
- 1986 Role of People's Organizations. *IFDA Dossier* 53:3–15.

Korten, David C.
- 1983 *Bureaucracy and the Poor.* Hartford, Conn.: Kumarian Press.
- 1986 *Community Management: Asian Experience and Perspectives.* Hartford, Conn.: Kumarian Press.

Korten, Frances
- 1986 The Policy Framework for Community Management." In *Community Management: Asian Experience and Perspectives,* ed. D. C. Korten, 275–91. Hartford, Conn.: Kumarian Press.

La Forgia, Gerard
- 1985 *Local Organizations for Rural Health in Panama: Community Participation, Bureaucratic Reorientation and Political Will.* Ithaca, N.Y.: Rural Development Committee, Cornell University. Cited in Uphoff 1986:208.

Lance, L. M., and E. E. McKenna
- 1975 Analysis of Cases Pertaining to the Impact of Western Technology in the Non-Western World. *Human Organization,* 34(1): 87–94.

Landim, Leilah
- 1987 Non-Governmental Organizations in Latin America. *World Development* 15 (supp., Autumn): 29–38.

Lecomte, Bernard J.
- 1986 *Project Aid: Limitations and Alternatives.* Paris: OECD Development Center Studies.

Leet, Glen, and Mildred Robbins Leet
- 1989 Trickle Up Program: 1988 Global Report. New York: Trickle Up Program.

Lewis, John P.
- 1986 Development Promotion: A Time for Regrouping. In *Development Strategies Reconsidered,* ed. J. P. Lewis and V. Kallab, U.S. Third World Policy Perspectives no. 5, pp. 3–35 Overseas Development Council. New Brunswick, N.J., and Oxford: Transaction Books.

McCarthy, Kathleen D.
- 1989 The Voluntary Sector Overseas: Notes from the Field. Working Papers: Center for the Study of Philanthropy, City University of New York.

McClelland, David C.
- 1970 The Two Faces of Power. *Journal of International Affairs* 24(1): 29–47.

Martinez Nogueira, Roberto
- 1987 Life Cycle and Learning in Grass Roots Organisations. *World Development* 15 (Suppl. on Development Alternatives: The Challenges for NGO's): 169–78.

Mead, Margaret
- 1955 *Cultural Patterns and Technical Change.* New York: Mentor Books.

Merschrod, Kris
- 1980 Participation in Program Evaluation at the Regional Level in Honduras. *Rural Development Participation Review* (Rural Development Committee, Cornell University, Ithaca, N.Y.) 2(1): 18–22.

Michels, Robert
- 1959 (orig. 1915) *Political Parties.* New York: Dover Publications.

Moreira Alves, Maria Elena
- 1984 Grassroots Organizations, Trade Unions, and the Church: A Challenge to the Controlled Abertura in Brazil. *Latin American Perspectives* 11(1): 73–102.

Muchiru, Simon
- 1986 NGOs and African Development: Contributions, Capabilities and Needs. MS. Nairobi: African NGOs Environmental Network, April. Cited in Berg 1987:21.

Okoli, F. C.
- 1982 Organizing for Community Development in Anambra State of Nigeria: Toward a Strategy of Development Humanism. *African Review* 9(2): 62–77.

Organization for Economic Cooperation and Development
   1988   *Voluntary Aid for Development: The Role of Non-Governmental Organisations.* Paris: Development Cooperation Directorate.
Ouedraogo, Bernard
   1986   "Development without Damage"—The *Naam* Groups Tackle Drought. *Courier* 99 (September–October): 89–90.
Oxby, Clare
   1983   Farmer Groups in Rural Areas of the Third World. *Community Development Journal* 18(1): 50–59.
Private Agencies Collaborating Together (PACT)
   1989   *Asian Linkages. NGO Collaboration in the 1990s: A Five Country Study.* New York: PACT.
Painter, Thomas
   1986   In Search of Peasant Connection: Spontaneous Cooperation, Introduced Cooperatives, and Agricultural Development in Southwestern Niger. In *Anthropology and Rural Development in West Africa,* ed. Horowitz and Painter, 197–219. Boulder, Colo.: Westview Press.
Panini, M. N.
   1987   India. *Ideas and Action* 3:20–21.
Pavard, Claude
   1986   Rural Structures as Agents of Development—the Bafut Experimental Project. *Courier* (September–October): 99.
Pelletier, David
   1991   *The Uses and Limitations of Information in the Iringa Nutrition Program, Tanzania.* Ithaca, N.Y.: Cornell Food and Nutrition Policy Program.
Postel, Sandra, and Lori Heise
   1988   Reforestation with a Human Touch. *Grassroots Development* 12(3): 38–40.
Pradervand, Pierre
   1988   Afrique Noire: La Victoire du Courage. *IFDA Dossier* 64:3–12.
   1990   *Listening to Africa: Developing Africa from the Grassroots.* Westport, Conn.: Praeger Publishers.
Ralston, Lenore, James Anderson, and Elizabeth Colson
   1983   *Voluntary Efforts in Decentralized Management.* Berkeley: University of California Press.
Reed, Richard
   1987   Federations of Indian Communities: Strategies for Grassroots Development. *Cultural Survival Quarterly* 11(1): 16–20.
Ritchey Vance, Marion
   1991   *The Art of Association: NGOs and Civil Society in Colombia.* Country Focus Series no. 2. Washington, D.C.: Inter-American Foundation.
Rouille D'Orfeuille, Henri
   1984   *Cooperer Autrement: L'engagement des organisations nongouvernementales aujourd'hui.* Paris: L'Harmatton.

Rubin, Jeffrey.
    1987   Election, Repression, and Limited Reform: Update on Southern Mexico. *LASA Forum* (Latin American Studies Association) 18(2): 1–5.
Sabur, M. Abdus
    1986   The ACFOD Experience. *IFDA Dossier* 55 (September–October).
Schneider, Bertrand
    1985   *La Revolution des Pieds Nus-Rapport au Club de Rome.* Paris: Fayard.
Seibel, Hans Dieter, and Andreas Massing
    1974   *Traditional Organizations and Economic Development: Studies of Indigenous Cooperatives in Liberia.* New York: Praeger. Cited in Uphoff 1986:117.
Shiva, Vandana
    1986   Ecology Movements in India. *Development* 3:64–65.
Sivaramakrishnan, K. C.
    1977   Slum Improvement in Calcutta. *Assignment Children* 40:87–115.
Smith, Brian H.
    1990   *More than Altruism: The Politics of Private Foreign Aid.* Princeton: Princeton University Press.
Smith, Richard C.
    1987   Bolivia: Aid Reconsidered. *Oxfam America News* (Spring).
Somjee, A. H.
    1979   *The Democratic Process in a Developing Society.* New York: St. Martin's Press.
Swagman, Charles F.
    1988   *Development and Change in Yemen.* Salt Lake City: University of Utah Press.
Tendler, Judith
    1983   *What to Think about Cooperatives: A Guide from Bolivia.* Washington, D.C.: Inter-American Foundation.
Thompson, Andres
    1990   Democracy and Development: The Role of NGOs in the Southern Cone (Argentina, Chile and Uruguay). In *The Nonprofit Sector in the Global Community,* ed. Kathleen D. Carthy, San Francisco: Jossey-Bass.
Tongsawate, Maniemai, and Walter E. J. Tips
    1985   *Coordination between Governmental and Non-Governmental Organizations in Thailand's Rural Development.* Monograph no. 5. Bangkok: Division of Human Settlements Development, Asian Institute of Technology.
Tutwiler, Richard
    1984   Ta awun Mahwit: A Case Study of a Local Development Association in Highland Yemen. In *Local Politics and Development in the Middle East,* ed. Louis J.Cantori and Iliya Harik, 166–92. Boulder, Colo.: Westview Press.

Twose, Nigel
- 1988 The Role of Indigenous NGOs in Africa. *Panoscope* 5 (March): 23–24.

Uphoff, Norman
- 1986 *Local Institutional Development: An Analytical Sourcebook with Cases.* W. Hartford, Conn.: Kumarian Press.
- 1992 *Learning from Gal Oya: Possibilities for Participatory Development and Post-Newtonian Social Science.* Ithaca, NY.: Cornell University Press.

Van Nieuwenhuijze, C.A.O., M. Fathalla Al-Khatib, and Adel Azer
- 1985 *The Poor Man's Model of Development.* Leiden: E. J. Brill.

Vetter, Stephen
- 1986 Building the Infrastructure for Progress: Private Development Organizations in the Dominican Republic. *Grassroots Development* 10(1): 2–9.

Wali, Alaka
- 1990 Living with the Land: Ethnicity and Development in Chile. *Grassroots Development* 14(9): 12–20.

Wanyande, Peter
- 1987 Women's Groups in Participatory Development: Kenya's Development Experience through the Use of Harambee. *Development* 2–3.

Wells, A. F., and D. Wells
- 1953 *Friendly Societies in the West Indies.* London: Colonial Research Publications, HMSO. Cited in S. Craig, Political Patronage and Community Resistance: Community Councils in Trinidad and Tobago. In *Rural Development in the Caribbean,* P. I. Gomes. New York: St. Martin's Press, 1985.

Yudelman, Sally
- 1987 *Hopeful Openings.* Hartford, Conn.: Kumarian Press.

Chapter 4

Linkages Methodology for the Study of Sociocultural Transformations

Elizabeth Colson and Conrad Phillip Kottak

Increasingly, anthropology is developing models of its subject matter that are isomorphic with the structure of the modern world. Various recent multilevel, multisite, and multitime research projects exemplify this development. Such projects are one indication of the shift toward the study of process, of an engagement with history, and of an anthropology that takes care to consider the role of political and economic power in forming what Meyer Fortes called "the field of social relations," by which he meant "the range of social relations, in time and space" (Fortes 1945:xi).

That range is now international. Probably no one alive today has not met someone from another country. Even in remote areas local people now take their cues not just from immediate others but from a multitude of strangers who impinge on them, directly or via the mass media.

> The . . . isolation of small communities . . . is in sharp decline because of the advance of urbanization, industrialization, and bureaucratization. Significantly, all these processes modify not only the objective relationships, but also the quality of the subjective relationships of those who live in little communities. These quantitative and qualitative dimensions of sociocultural change, and the rate at which they occur, have led to increased interest everywhere in social planning and in centralizing the allocation and distribution of resources. (Gallagher and Padfield 1980:4)

Linkages

Linkages is a convenient term to encompass the multistranded involvement in the world system that ethnographers must now consider in conceptualizing the influences affecting values, categories, institutional arrangements, and other symbolic systems. The linkages perspective is the antithesis of traditional anthropological "holism," which looked inward, assuming the existence of some entity, either a culture or a society, complete and autonomous. Linkages, crucial to social transformations, work to destabilize, rather than maintain, local systems over time.

A definition of linkages in relation to research methodology and content was the goal of a working group of anthropologists who first met in 1986.[1] All of us were concerned with the impact of international and national forces, including development projects, on our research locales. This concern inevitably raised questions about feedback between local-, regional-, and national-level institutions and responses. Most members of the linkages group had worked more than once in the same region. They knew the advantages of observing how people respond to different opportunities and perturbations at various stages of their lives. Our awareness that geographical mobility and modern communication systems make community boundaries very permeable led us to question old definitions of social units.

Seeking ways of dealing with mobility and tracking people across space and time, we affirmed the value of research samples (both communities and mobile individuals) that could be followed through time. What kinds of links did they have with others, including external agencies? This line of inquiry entailed a census approach (to provide information on demographic, occupational, and other changes), a network approach (to trace the far-flung sets of relationships associated with geographical mobility and external interventions), plus survey and ethnographic techniques. Monitoring change also required dated inventories: of governmental and nongovernmental agencies, of transportation and other infrastructure, of the mass media, of the range of goods available, household items, prices, and crucial events such as epidemics. Such inventories provide variables allowing us to differentiate communities and individuals.

One focus of linkages research is longitudinal study. Another is systematic intercommunity comparison, which requires several sample populations chosen because they vary with respect to key criteria. These samples can be from the same region, and the data collected part of the same study. They can also be from different regions (even different countries), if anthropologists can provide minimum core data (Epstein 1978:220) to make comparison possible. Linkages research extends to the levels at which policies are worked out, examining archives and official records and interviewing planners, administrators, and others who impinge on the study population. The aim of such approaches is to link changes at the local level to those in regional, national, and world systems.

Our varied databases provide answers to specific questions about the results of interventions. We recognize that effects are not always immediate; time is necessary to register long-term consequences. People may respond one way in an emergency, but their responses change as they live with and assess alterations in their environments. Linkages research is planned as an ongoing process requiring teamwork. Time and personnel are needed to follow a dispersing population, to study different sites, to interview at many organizational levels, to explore archives and records, and to do follow-up studies. Involvement of host country colleagues, including local assistants and other community residents, is a key to continuity. Research is wasted if it can't be communicated; teamwork helps make data usable for others. Thus, *linkages* also refers to cooperation by people with common research interests in creating a community of data.

The studies being done by members of the linkages group are explicitly comparative. Focusing on transformation and development, they blend ethnography and survey, synchrony and diachrony. Ideally, several anthropologists work together as an international team. Some linkages projects are restudies that build on earlier ethnographic work. One example is a research project on the cultural context, meaning, and impact of Brazilian television, developed and directed by Conrad Kottak between 1983 and 1987.[2] That project (some of the results of which are described in chap. 5 in this vol.) emerged from Kottak's earlier work in Arembepe, Brazil (begun in 1962),[3] but it also included three other communities previously studied by anthropologists. Kottak and his Brazilians and American colleagues continue to monitor some of those communities, building longitudinal core data. An example of research in which the monitoring of change was part of the original design is the longitudinal study of the interplay of social and economic processes in Gwembe District, Zambia. This study, planned in 1956 as a longitudinal project by Elizabeth Colson and Thayer Scudder, continues.[4]

Such studies, involving repeated visits, also create linkages in the form of commitment to those studied and the claims they continue to make on anthropologists. Modern communication systems make continued involvement inevitable. We can hardly escape knowledge of the continuing history of those among whom we have worked. Anthropology has become much more conscious of political and economic power, of hierarchy and inequity. As members of a world system, we can no longer take for granted the structuring of power relationships that advantage some and disadvantage others. Nor can we treat them in purely intellectual terms as symbolic structures or literary tropes. As Eric Wolf (1989) has pointed out, they have real consequences for real people. They are more than discourse.

From Isolate to World System

Linkages researchers are obviously not alone in their concern with social change and development, their view of culture as a process rather than an entity, and their realization that communities consist of people who have variant opportunities and make different choices. We also join the many anthropologists who have questioned the shibboleth of cultural relativism. Our world needs some agreement on basic human rights and ways of guaranteeing them. Anthropologists have seen local people fall victim to development projects, revolutionary violence, and warfare provoked by external interventions and the dictates of international markets. Not surprisingly in today's world, many anthropologists now focus on violence and violation (Carmack 1988; Kapferer 1988; Loizos 1981; Parnell 1988; Tambiah 1986).

Many agents of multinational organizations have as their raison d'être interference in the lives of others to promote "development." We are not cultural relativists when we judge their activities. It is no accident that *Cultural Survival* emerged in the 1970s to offer an anthropological critique of intervention. Studies of development organizations and their policies are now common (e.g., Colson 1983; Hoben 1982; Justice 1986; Kottak 1991; Robertson 1982).

Contemporary anthropologists can no longer even hope to do ethnography among people isolated from world markets or unaffected by centers of political and economic power. Archaeologists and historians familiar with records on Asia, Africa, and the Pacific have even questioned the historic existence of the ethnographic isolate. Eric Wolf (1982) has focused on the centuries-old interplay between state systems and "the people without history." More than 80 percent of the "cultures" in the World Ethnographic Sample are anything but pristine—having had a major encounter with a nation-state before any anthropologist ever reached them (Bradley et al. 1990). Most societies have been subject to colonialism or other political centralization. No matter what the subject or the research locale, we need to consider documents describing the interdependencies between local systems and larger economic and political networks (cf. Feirman 1985; Guyer 1988).

Anthropologists could believe in the static "ethnographic present" only when we were unaware of the extent to which local cultures are products of world history. In the 1930s, when little archaeology had been done, when dating techniques were rudimentary and imprecise, and when much archival information remained unexamined by historians, it was easier to think in terms of static societies, equilibria, and integrated systems. One recent example of the impact of archaeological and historical evidence on anthropological thinking is the challenge to the Kalahari San as representatives of early hunter-gatherers. We know now that for centuries the San have been intermittently pastoralists and agriculturalists and in touch with pastoralists and agriculturalists (Elphick 1977; Solway and Lee 1990).

Challenges also come from the accumulating ethnographic record. Few contemporary anthropologists enter regions where no one has ever worked. We have their publications, sometimes even their field notes. We must account for the differences between their findings and our own—not by adopting the stance of a dueling ethnographic individualist (Freeman 1983) but by paying full attention to the forces of history and intracultural variation. Modern anthropological research is incomplete if we fail to examine the documents that chart decades of local and regional interrelations and attempted interventions. Historical events and responses are now routinely built into the ethnographic record, much to its enrichment.

Modern ethnographic records should be thought of as referring to different stages in the encounter of local populations with the world system. Ethnography should focus on the adjustments that occur continuously as people meet different challenges. Whether studying mental healing (Mullings 1984) or agriculture (Pottier 1988), contemporary anthropologists can draw on data unavailable to their predecessors.

Geography also limits us less than in the past, when it could take months to reach a research site and return visits were rare. Once in the field the ethnographer's social universe used to be the distance he or she could cover comfortably on foot, bicycle, boat, or horse. New systems of transportation that allow local people to move about also enable anthropologists to widen the catchment area of their research and to return repeatedly. Ethnographic articles in the main journals routinely include data from two or more field stays. Continuity and change are now built into the anthropologist's experience and field notes (Bond 1990). The perception of what change means for villagers becomes more poignant as our old friends ponder with us what is happening to them and what the world will be like for our children.

Some of our richest ethnography comes from those who have gone back—sometimes just once, sometimes several times. Monica Wilson had known the Nyakyusa for more than thirty years when she wrote *For Men and Elders* (1977). Wendy James's study of "the flux and flow of indigenous and imported practices, and the waxing and waning of Christianity and Islam" among the Uduk of Sudan draws on her observations of the conflicting forces affecting those people over thirty years (1988:vii). Roger Keesing used his repeated visits to Guadalcanal to "situate Kwaio religion not on some abstract plane of formal structure, but in the minds and acts of individuals and in the social life of communities" (1982:3). Caroline Humphrey (1983) used government documents, accounts by other ethnographers, and her own revisit to document the interplay between ideology and economy that influenced how collective farmers in Siberia thought about the Soviet system and how this affected their productivity and relations with one another.

Restudies, whether by the original fieldworker or another, are now common. They encourage the development of methods to deal with flux—even though they may not have been planned with that goal.[5] The conditions that encourage restudies have also made it possible for anthropologists to plan and carry out longitudinal fieldwork, in which time is part of the research design. Each such study must deal with economic fluctuations, migration, changing political influence, and changes in national and local ideologies. Anthropologists planning such studies would accept the dictate of John Bennett (1982:298), who initiated a decade of research on Saskatchewan family farms in the 1960s, that "the cultural typological approach," with "its built-in assumptions of homeostasis and unchanging ethos," must be rejected because it fails to account for the rapidity of change.

The theoretical assumptions underlying long-term studies clash with some earlier formulations. We do not assume cultural integration, social equilibrium, harmony of values, or uniformity of response by individuals. Repeated visits show that people and communities respond differently to opportunities and hardships, depending on their resources, their social positions, their previous experiences, and the degree to which they have dealt with outsiders. There are multiple linkages between local residents and people and institutions throughout the world. The belief that community members share common values is a powerful myth, but experience can be shared only to a point. No matter how egalitarian or homogeneous communities may seem to a short-term visitor, their members have different values and interests. This is one source of change.

Local concerns—health, subsistence, self-respect, cognitive frameworks to make sense of experience—depend on engagement with wider systems. The inhabitants of distant cities provide reference groups on which local people base judgments. The speed with which styles spread confirms the interconnectedness that is now a part of the anthropologist's universe of study. The T-shirt flourishes everywhere. "Ethnic" clothing and jewelry inspire Western designers and are reexported to the world at large. People in South American barrios and African cities incur debt to finance Western-style weddings. Youngsters in small towns and rural areas dance "disco." Many communities maintain their local styles of dress, dance, and performance in order to entertain jet-set tourists (Crick 1989; Kottak 1990, 1992; Graburn 1983; Smith 1977, 1989; Volkman 1990).

Linkages between rural and urban areas are ancient, although they first excited anthropological attention in the 1930s—for example, in studies of African labor migration and settlement in the new towns of southern and central Africa (Hellman 1948; Richards 1940; Schapera 1947; Wilson 1941-42). These studies were the forerunners of recent work on migration and resettlement (Eades 1986; Hansen and Oliver-Smith 1982; Morgan and Colson 1987; Talai 1989), including involuntary resettlement (see *Practicing Anthropology* [1990]). In the 1940s and 1950s studies of adjustment to city life dominated the research on Africa. These studies led to "network" and "situational" analysis to confront the rapidity with which people changed their behavior in different settings (see Mitchell 1987). Since then the Third World has witnessed an explosive growth of cities, which now provide the standards by which most people measure their well-being and success (Lloyd 1979).

Our species, with astonishing steadfastness, has viewed cities as filled with action, glamour, variety, opportunity, and the promise of an easier life, as can be seen dramatically when flying over any Third World capital, where shantytown suburbs are crammed with emigrants from outlying areas. Each new arrival is hopeful of making his fortune within the "lights of the city" and confident he will escape the backbreaking labor that has traditionally been his way of life. (Schwartz 1980:vii)

Communication systems radiating from the cities tell rural people what they lack and teach them that they must change if they want to share the wealth and pleasures of town. Government policies place rural interests below those of city dwellers, especially the bureaucratic elites, whose own reference groups are the international elites of the industrial world.

Exposure to external institutions and alternative ways of life comes through many channels, including the media. Seasonal, temporary, and permanent migration maintain social networks between rural people and their urban kin. Improved transportation transforms cities into market centers and information pools for a wide area. National and international agents invade the hinterland as tourists, development agents, conservationists, officials, and representatives of competing religious sects. Radio, television, and the videocassette recorder reach distant areas. The spread of literacy is a stated goal of all governments. The media, providing common fare, work toward a certain homogenization of standards. Audio and video recorders, however, have another potential. Local people use them to communicate with distant relatives, to preserve their traditions, and to record their interests (see Michaels [1986] on the use of videocameras in homegrown television in Walbiri, central Australia).

Any methodology that tries to extract the purely local from the wider system will miss much of what is going on and much that concerns the people being studied. For much that is significant anthropologists can rely neither on participant observation nor intensive interviews with selected informants regarded as the repositories of tradition. Local informants may be as mystified as we are with the exercise of power from regional, national, and international centers. The chain of intermediaries has many links; the knowledge that this is so can itself create a sense of alienation and dependency.

It is this larger context that we need to find ways of examining. These multiple linkages must be part of our research focus. The cities and towns visited by members of the sample population become a further extension of the study. Participation in a larger social universe is a goal held out to people in the hinterland. The terms on which incorporation takes place are usually to their disadvantage, however, because their skills and resources prevent them from entering the system at what they regard as an honorable level. This was not true for a short period following the end of the colonial system in many parts of Africa, Asia, and Papua New Guinea, when rapid promotion was the order of the day and even primary education gave entry to the upper echelons of the civil service. Village children could aspire to become cabinet officers, United Nations employees, university professors, and high civil servants. Younger siblings could expect their help with education and jobs. Older kin benefited from the accomplishments of the young.

Three decades later class differences are hardening. It is more difficult to use education to enter even the lower echelons of secure employment. Nevertheless, we think that the desire of people in the hinterland to share in what they see as the advantages of the expanded world is fueling rapid transformations that are now taking place. A larger world appeals to human imagination and curiosity, the desire for information and experience, and the search for greater comfort and an easing of toil. People seize upon the contacts offered them, or create their own linkages, because they hope to exploit the larger system.

We assume that certain constants of human motivation and response underwrite the patterns of incorporation reported from many parts of the world. Nevertheless, the interplay between national and regional centers and those within their spheres of influence varies according to the degree to which communication is frequent, instantaneous, and pervasive; with the resources the centers can deploy to reward incorporation; and with the power exercised by the centers.

Multisite and Multitime Research in Brazil

Our own applications of linkages methodology will be used to illustrate these points. For Brazil, where television is now pervasive, Kottak's research project on its cultural context and effects examines how TV has changed local life. The rationale for the research was the realization that television is one of the most powerful information disseminators, socializing agents, and public opinion molders in the contemporary world. Yet few social scientists had examined in depth what happens when communities become exposed to TV. Previous studies had been done mainly in English-speaking countries and had focused on a limited target group (usually children) or range of effects (usually psychological—e.g., violence). Other than in a few studies of Canadian Indian response to television (Granzberg and Steinbring 1980; Molohon 1984), anthropologists had paid little attention to television—perhaps reflecting the discipline's characteristic resistance to cultural homogenization, which TV's spread is usually seen as aiding. Kottak and his (mostly Brazilian) colleagues had to devise a methodology appropriate to the linkages created in Brazil by the new information channels. They had to combine in-depth, on-the-ground ethnographic observation with survey research, the combing of media records, and content analysis of programs.

Brazil has the world's most-watched commercial network (Rede Globo). Kottak became intrigued with the effects of television in Brazil in 1980 when he revisited Arembepe, Bahia state, which he had first studied in 1962. Compared with the 1960s, when Arembepeiros had been starved for information about the outside world, by 1980 their familiarity with nation and world was well advanced, and television seemed to be the main reason.

Richard Pace, an anthropologist who participated in Kottak's television project, reached similar conclusions for the Amazonian town of Gurupá,[6] which he studied between 1984 and 1986:

> Before the spread of television, conversation often focussed on local events, local gossip, soccer, or an occasional diffuse comment on regional or national politics. A foreign anthropologist was often asked vague questions such as what kind of jungle grows in the United States, are all Americans rich, and what are cowboys like? With the spread of television, however, conversation took on a more cosmopolitan, more diverse nature. Events in North America, Europe, and the Middle East were discussed in detail. National politics were scrutinized. (It was the year [1985] that the military regime gave powers back to a civilian government.) I found myself discussing the goals of the American space program, the ideology of President Reagan, poverty in the United States, international terrorism, and the geophysical causes of earthquakes. (1987:20–21)

By 1980 Brazil had more TV sets than the rest of Latin America combined. The percentage of Brazilian households with television increased from 7 percent to 51 percent between 1964 and 1979, and the figure exceeds 80 percent today. Through communications satellites, reception dishes, and retransmitting ground stations, people in remote villages now receive national programming. Reflecting Brazil's huge population (150+ million) and its degree of economic development (the world's tenth largest economy), the middle class includes about fifty million people, a tantalizing market (second in the Western hemisphere) for television and the culture of consumption.

The Globo network, which blossomed under the aegis of an authoritarian centralized state and military dictatorship, moved quickly and efficiently to hook a product-and-information hungry population. Today Globo, which dominates Brazil's airwaves as no single network has ever done in North America, mainly shows its own productions and consistently attracts a nightly audience of sixty to eighty million people. All of Brazil's most popular TV programs are native productions. The most-watched are the national news and the *telenovelas* that Globo broadcasts nationally six nights per week. They consistently draw 60 percent to 95 percent audience shares.

The research project directed by Kottak from 1983 to 1987 was a multitiered study, investigating Brazilian television at national and local levels. It blended ethnography and survey to assess television's impact. The bulk of the national-level work was done between August 1983 and August 1984. Kottak interviewed television industry experts and personnel and did archival and statistical research in Brazil's established media research organizations.[7] Concurrently, the project also included an initial, mainly qualitative, program content study.

The next stage was a local-level impact study involving systematic fieldwork by Brazilian and American researchers. This began in January 1985 in four communities in different regions. The aim was to gather qualitative and quantitative data (using standard protocols) to permit systematic comparison of communities and people with different degrees of exposure to television. In-depth fieldwork was done in those four communities, located in the south (Ibirama), south central (Cunha), northeast (Arembepe), and Amazonian (Gurupá) regions.

Each site fitted another aspect of the research design, longitudinal study, building on prior research. Each community had been previously studied, providing information on what life had been like before television. One weakness with the original project design, however, was that all four communities were rural and poor. As the researchers tried to compare those sites with national-level information from urban sources, they realized that a link was missing. They needed to extend their field procedures, including ethnographic observation and structured interviewing, to the urban, socioeconomically contrasting settings in which most Brazilians now live. Thus, two wealthier and more urban settings in the states of Rio de Janeiro (Niterói) and São Paulo (Americana) were selected for study in 1986. These studies were necessarily briefer than the first four.

With fieldwork continuing through 1987, the project has examined the varied cultural, social, economic, and psychological effects associated with the introduction of television to the study populations.[8] (Kottak discusses some of the findings in chap. 5.) Besides television this research project has also considered many other sources of exposure to external situations and currents of change.[9] Systematic comparison incorporating a time dimension showed that television's most profound effects on people, society, and culture take place gradually. Effects may well be imperceptible (both to natives and researchers) at a given time. Yet the research design (studying a gamut of communities and people exposed to television for different lengths of time) did reveal many areas of influence.

The project confirmed that TV impact occurs in stages. There is an initial stage (stage 1, in progress in Gurupá) of strangeness and novelty. The medium (the set) rather than the message (content) is the mesmerizer. Stage 2 (Cunha, Arembepe) is a ten- to fifteen-year period of maximum receptivity. People accept, reject, interpret, and rework TV messages. Because TV saturation is still only partial, many statistical correlations between viewing and other factors are obvious. Televiewing produced the strongest correlations in the stage 2 communities of Arembepe and Cunha.

Ibirama is entering and Americana and Niterói are fully in stage 3. Once TV has reached most homes in a community, statistical measures of its impact there become less evident. This is because, as an innovation pervades a population, its presence differentiates less and less among people. This third stage, however, during which TV impact *appears* to be least, has a subtle, though powerful, legacy. Stage 4, exemplified by Americans of the baby-boom generation and younger, encompasses the cumulative effects of TV on full-grown natives who have spent their lives in a society pervaded by television and the behavior patterns and mass culture it spawns. During this fourth phase the more profound and long-term sociocultural effects of television become evident (Kottak 1990).

Kottak and his associates concluded that TV's role in promoting or hindering social interaction depends both on the culture it enters and the stage of community saturation. An initial effect (stages 1 and 2) is to promote social contact, by bringing people from different households together to watch. In stages 1 and 2 set ownership and hours of operation correlate very strongly with number of household visitors. In stage 3, however, with set ownership widespread, people stay home to watch their own sets.

The project also supported the researchers' prior assumption that cultural, political, and economic variation *within* towns, regions, and nations is vital in understanding the effects of technology on human behavior. TV impact is not a matter of simple, automatic, programmed responses to irresistible, omnipotent stimuli. Viewing, interpretation, and impact all take place in the context of the prior culture(s) and experiences of members of the audience. Viewers are not the passive "couch potatoes" who populate American commentary. Instead, they are human beings who make discriminations and choices about television in ways that make sense to them. They watch to validate beliefs, develop fantasies, and find answers to questions that the local setting discourages or condemns. People use TV to relieve frustrations, build or enhance images of self, chart social courses, and formulate daring life plans. Sometimes the interaction between viewer and set leads to unrealistic plans, false hopes, disappointment, and frustration. The process of TV impact is not, however, one in which an all-powerful Big Brother zaps a defenseless zombie.

We take prior culture(s) and subcultures into account when we consider why different programs attract different audiences. Program choices and preferences reflect preexisting social categories and contrasts, power differentials, and variant predispositions within the local culture. Audiences use television in varied ways. They go on watching because they find meaning in its images and content. In Ibirama, for instance, Alberto Costa (n.d.) concluded that women and young adults of both sexes were particularly attracted to *telenovelas*. These relatively powerless social groups used Globo's *telenovelas* to challenge conservative local norms.

Audience preferences vary not only between nations but also with local (and regional) cultural contrasts and categories. Preexisting cultural categories and views influence indigenous creations and audience behavior. But long-term exposure to messages feeds back on social reality and gradually modifies old beliefs, attitudes, and behavior—contributing to a changing (mass) culture. Unifying themes may emerge, but the result is not simply homogenization. New differences and divisions may also arise, and preexisting distinctions and conflicts may be reinforced, even intensified.

Building on experience with the television project, Kottak and his Brazilian associates designed new research on industrialization and commercial expansion, focusing on environmental hazards and risk perception in Brazil. Again the investigation is proceeding at two levels: (1) national, Brazil as a whole, into which the government introduced a policy of industrialization in the early 1950s; and (2) local, across a range of sites differently exposed to risks (Costa, Kottak, Prado, and Stiles 1995; Kottak and Costa 1993).

Once again the field research design is systematic intercommunity comparison (based on quantitative and qualitative data). This methodology adds an analytic level to traditional "risk analysts," which studies populations *directly exposed* to environmental hazards such as nuclear repositories. Given *that* research design, public reactions to a threat are inevitably interpreted within a stimulus-response framework (a threat causes certain responses).[10] By contrast, the design being used by the Kottak team assumes that variation in environmental awareness and risk perception can be most accurately understood by studying a range of sites differentially exposed to hazards. Comparison is essential. Any approach limited to endangered groups can't help but see risk perception mainly in response to an immediate stimulus. After an initial focus on nuclear energy, the Brazilian environmental problems being investigated expanded to include forest degradation, air and water pollution, and other hazards.

Illustrating the linkages methodology, this Brazilian ecological research recognizes that environmental risk perception is linked to larger processes of change. Contributing to these processes are external and internal economic, political, and social pressures related to a group's position in the world system. Change, however, also depends on and varies with traditional cultural values and beliefs. The research on risk perception has four rationales:

1. Technological innovation, risk perception, and environmental awareness are cultural phenomena.
2. These are generated through processes of social and cultural change at the national and the local level in response to the economic and political position that a group occupies in the world system.
3. These changes also depend on the internal dynamic of the cultural models existing in any society both at macroscopic (national) and microscopic (local) levels.
4. Historically, concerns about nuclear energy and radioactivity (combined with the mass media's reporting of worldwide ecological movements) first spurred development of ecological awareness at the national level in Brazil—a process later fueled by the media and by the United Nations Conference on the Environment and Development (UNCED), held in Rio de Janeiro in June 1992.

This new research has international significance and again unites a multinational team (a linkages goal). Such research foci as TV impact and environmental risk perception illustrate the kinds of issues that are likely to be explored when long-term association with a research community exposes researchers to the consequences of various technological interventions. The study of ecological awareness and risk perception in Brazil will complement existing studies of hazards in industrial societies. The results may enhance public understanding that technological innovations are differently understood, interpreted, evaluated, and justified according to the assumptions and values of those who develop or receive them. The empirical and theoretical aims of the project are complementary. The communities being studied have been chosen to represent a gamut of differential exposure to environmental threats, minor to extreme.

Two of the sites (Arembepe and Ibirama) were also included in the television study, so that longitudinal monitoring (another linkages goal) continues.[11] Arembepe is increasingly plagued by water pollution—a fact that has yet to penetrate local risk perception. The Kottak team originally chose Ibirama, a town without evident environmental problems in a forested area of Santa Catarina state, as a control site. Recently, however, Ibirama's traditional timber industry has been confronted with environmental legislation prompted by the national concern over deforestation. Near Ibirama are substantial patches of surviving Atlantic forest, and

118   Transforming Societies, Transforming Anthropology

since 1990 the area around Ibirama has become a deforestation hot spot. Alberto Costa, who began fieldwork in Ibirama in 1985, continues to study that town as it reacts to environmental legislation. One eventual aim of this linkages research on environmental issues is to use satellite images showing historical change in the Brazilian forests to elicit local perceptions of deforestation and its significance at our known sites.

Social Transformation in Gwembe District

Another multilevel, multitime, multisite, comparative study, at Gwembe District, Zambia, also illustrates linkages methodology. Gwembe District has multistranded links with overlapping larger systems—provincial, national, and international. Transportation and communication networks, labor markets, marketing boards for cash crops, international capitalism, and political mobilization interpenetrate the local systems of relationships and evaluation. The people of Gwembe are aware of this, from their experience on the ground and the mass media (to which, however, they are much less exposed than Brazilians are). External forces have transformed their geographical and social environments. One result has been the creation of four small townships in a district that in 1956 had no marketing centers and few shops.

In the 1950s most Gwembe men had worked as labor migrants in what is now Zimbabwe or South Africa, yet people still puzzled over scraps of information about the rest of the world. They asked: Is England a city as large as Bulawayo? Is it to the south or the north? Is America another city? What is Hungary?

The people of Gwembe no longer ask these questions. Although television and telephone reach only three townships, people travel to the cities to visit kin and seek work and thus have media exposure. In the 1980s fewer newspapers reached the villages than in the 1960s and 1970s. This is one sign of the decline of the national economy, which has resulted in a shortage of newsprint and deterioration of roads. Nevertheless, people rely on radios (one or two in most villages since the early 1960s) for world news, weather forecasts, and word of the death of kin settled elsewhere in Zambia. The postal service, largely nonexistent in the 1950s, is not always efficient, but mail does arrive. Jets fly overhead and link the capital of Zambia to other African capitals and to London, Paris, and New York. Everyone knows some Gwembe man or woman who has been to Europe, America, India, or Japan.

In the early 1950s strangers, even from nearby regions of Zambia, rarely visited Gwembe. Since then a multitude have arrived. Some stay a few hours, others months or years. Visitors to Gwembe include Japanese, Chinese, Indians, Sri Lankans, Italians, Yugoslavs, Germans, Dutch, Irish, Britons, Australians, Canadians, Americans, and Africans from many countries. Foreigners come as tourists, anthropologists, prospectors, missionaries, international consultants, employees of mining and agricultural corporations, and workers for the voluntary organizations active in the district since the 1970s.

Local people know something about international relations. They are keenly aware of how the decline in copper prices has affected the Zambian economy and of what it means to be subject to South African raids. Every village has an urban diaspora to remind it of fluctuations in the economy. Those who remain in the village use deteriorating buses and cars to move between village and town. They think of themselves as citizens of Zambia, a larger entity that has been created over the past thirty years.

The longitudinal study of Gwembe District, like other such studies—such as that of Tzintzuntzan, Mexico begun in 1945 (Foster 1978; Kemper 1978)—has had to develop a research methodology adapted to geographical and social mobility and changing degrees of international embeddedness. It has also had to find ways of dealing with the fact that communities have different resources, access to roads and other amenities, and levels of administrative overview.

Gwembe District covers 12,611 square kilometers. Its population grew from about 55,000 in 1956 to 96,879 in 1980 (Serpell and Munachona 1986:4, 8). For decades about 45 percent of the able-bodied men have been absent as labor migrants at any time. The 1980 census gave a sex ratio of 88.5; the district continues to lose many men. Most Gwembe people live in villages with 100 to 800 inhabitants. Of the small towns that emerged in the 1960s one has a coal mine, and three are administrative centers. The Gwembe population exploits a much larger pool of resources than the district offers. They have access to the towns and industries of Zambia. (Until 1965 they also had easy access to Zimbabwe.)

The Zambia-Zimbabwe border forms one boundary of the district; this offers both opportunity and danger. During the Zimbabwe War of Independence in the 1970s, Gwembe was a theater of guerrilla warfare, which damaged its infrastructure and killed some villagers. The border, however, also encourages a trade in smuggled goods, including gemstones illicitly mined in the Gwembe hills, and gives poachers access to the game reserves of Zimbabwe.

The Gwembe research project is multisite, because no single village or neighborhood could adequately represent Gwembe's diversity (Colson and Scudder 1975; Scudder and Colson 1978). Four villages and their surrounding neighborhoods, in different localities, form the research core. They and their inhabitants have been followed for four decades. Periodic village censuses (1956–57, 1962–63, 1965, 1972–73, 1981–82, and 1987–88) provide basic data on demography, economy, and other variables chosen to monitor changes in kinship and ritual behavior. Censused people who have moved are traced and interviewed (if possible) to see how their careers compare with those of people who have stayed in the village and to provide information about the social relationships that persist over time and their contribution to the local economy. Information on labor migration, visits between town and country, remittances, and other linkages illuminate the extent to which rural and urban belong to a single system. Besides the village samples, Colson, Scudder, and their associates have constructed other samples as needed to pursue particular questions. One example is a snowball sample of Gwembe men and women who attended secondary school before 1972. In that crucial year for understanding elite formation, the number of secondary school leavers surpassed the supply of jobs requiring secondary education.

Zambian assistants have kept records of local events and daily diaries of food bought and eaten. From field notes it is possible to reconstruct prices for different periods. Shifts in village preferences are documented by shopping lists provided by villagers wishing goods from urban shops. Field notes also contain observations based on attendance at moots, local courts, village and district meetings, church services, funerals, and rituals associated with households and neighborhoods.

Such information is supplemented by interviews with traders and officials, technical workers, political leaders, and expatriates employed by missions and international voluntary agencies. It has also been possible to obtain access to government and other records, both published and unpublished, including those of special missions. Zambian social scientists who have worked in the district also provide insights into the changes taking place.

Successively different questions have come to the fore, while basic data on communities and individuals continue to be collected. The first focus of study was the impact of a large hydroelectric dam, which flooded much of the Zambezi River plain and subjected the Gwembe people to forced resettlement. Yet the dam also spurred road building and other activities that brought the people of Gwembe more closely in touch with the rest of Zambia (Colson 1971; Scudder 1972; Scudder and Habarad 1991).

When the dam was built, primary education was poorly developed, and few men had attended secondary school. By the late 1960s education had become a major concern at Gwembe and was playing an important role in major transformations then taking place. Accordingly, Scudder and Colson (1980) designed research to examine the role of the system of national education in providing access to new opportunities and in increasing social differentiation within the district and nation. At the same time, it was evident that drinking alcohol was a growing problem. A third major study therefore examined the interplay of markets, transportation, and exposure to town values implicated in the transformation of domestic brewing and a radical change in drinking patterns (Colson and Scudder 1988).

Using the data recorded over years of revisits, it has also been possible to examine the role of markets, extension services, development agencies, and mining, all of which have transformed local agriculture. These linkages have made Gwembe (and the rest of Zambia) more vulnerable to international price structures, the directives of the World Bank and the International Monetary Fund, and the pressures of other international agencies. In the 1980s Gwembe villagers, like other Zambians, talked of the desirability of *forex* (foreign exchange). They were aware of the legal and black market rates of exchange. In the mid-1980s economic vulnerability led to the expropriation of village land to the advantage of transnational agribusinesses financed from Germany, the United States, Ireland, and Hong Kong (Scudder 1985; Scudder and Habarad 1991).

The wealth of data gathered through longitudinal study at Gwembe has made it possible to examine many other aspects of change. One example is the transformation of local courts, which have come under closer supervision from the center and are held to standardized procedures laid down by the Zambian lawyers (trained in Europe and America) in the Ministry of Justice (Colson 1976). Other studies have dealt with the changing position of the elderly. (Most of the rewards associated with the growth of the Zambian economy went to young educated men and women who could take advantage of the opportunities created by the policy of Zambianization of posts in civil service and business organizations after independence [Colson and Scudder 1981].)

Longitudinal data on political action and local governance underlie the recent study of villagers' innovative use of the lower echelons of the political party organization to supplement local institutions that no longer function effectively (Habarad n.d.). Data on religious beliefs and practice, again collected over decades, are being analyzed to explicate the ways in which religious concepts and ritual behavior are remodeled through the enlargement of social space, increased social differentiation and economic specialization, a shift from subsistence agriculture to market orientation, the perception of new kinds of threats from a much wider range of possible opponents, and the contrasting teachings on world history offered by Christian missions and other educators.

From the beginning the Gwembe study was planned to be more than an ethnographic account of a single time segment. It was designed to examine the impact of large-scale development projects and national development strategies. Along with other longitudinal studies it has shown the limitations of synchronic studies and the pitfalls of the once standard one-year study (a single year being assumed sufficient to familiarize the fieldworker with the basic patterns of the annual round, with any year standing as representative of all years).

The findings from Gwembe apply to experiences of incorporation and transformation in much of the Third World (see Bodley, 1988). During the last hundred years Gwembe has been incorporated into a colonial system, has had its men forced into distant labor markets, has been subject to alien political rule and then the politics of independence, and has been missionized by Christian churches. More recently Gwembe has been subject to foreign development missions, has had its environmental base profoundly altered by one of the world's largest man-made lakes, has suffered the forced resettlement of most of its population, and has shifted to a cash economy dominated by commercial agriculture. Gwembe is now increasingly losing land to highly capitalized foreign enterprises. Mining activities and pesticides used in commercial agriculture are endangering water supplies and lake fisheries.

Immunization of children and other health measures have lowered death rates, but diseases from the world pool periodically make life hazardous. Droughts and high food prices increase malnutrition. Since the early 1980s, like the rest of Zambia and much of central and eastern Africa, Gwembe has been menaced by the spread of AIDS, for which its population is trying to find an explanation. The frequency of recent droughts, often back to back, may be an indication that Gwembe is also now affected by the climatic shifts associated with the buildup of pollutants in the atmosphere (largely due to activities in the Northern Hemisphere) and the destruction of the tropical rain forests, again mainly a reflex of international markets.

Gwembe is no remote and exotic enclave, unique in its experience. Rather, it is an epitome of situations endemic to the contemporary world. This is what makes this longitudinal study a good barometer for examining the linkages between changes at the local level and the shifting policies and demands of the international system.

Methodological Questions

Neither the Kottak projects in Brazil nor the Gwembe study fit the category of community study. Nor do they rely on random samples of individuals chosen to represent some larger universe. Each study does seek to capitalize on the advantages associated with earlier methods of intensive ethnography. In each project the design calls for the creation of several sample populations in different locales, chosen because they contrast with one another in significant fashion. This variation forms the focus for research. The intention is to illuminate processes of change rather than to make statements about cultural cohesion.

Such large and complex research arenas yield overwhelming masses of data. It becomes difficult to keep a perspective and to use all the information effectively. This is one of the unsolved problems created when research integrates data collected over time, studies interactions at many levels, and compares sample populations and individual careers using many variables. To permit other researchers to use and build on our work, the data must be intelligible. Because our longitudinal and comparative studies are meant to provide known samples that can be used when new questions arise, appropriate data preparation and storage are essential. This poses a challenge to traditional anthropological funding agencies, which are accustomed to financing small-scale studies by lone fieldworkers, often providing no funds for analysis. Linkages projects produce masses of data, and grant budgets (like those in the other social sciences) must recognize the need for coding and analysis.

By the 1980s it was evident that the Gwembe data had to be systematized in some fashion. This was necessary to test intuitions and hypotheses against the detailed census and checklist information and to make that information available to successors in the research and others who could gain from comparing what was happening in Gwembe with what was happening at other research sites.

Comparison must go beyond simply saying "this is different and this is similar." We need to know how different and how similar, whether the comparison is of a single population through time or of different synchronic samples. Comparison must consider both rates (which sum up similarities) and variation (even members of a small community differ, and individuals are not consistent over time). Comparison must also recognize that populations may have superficially different but functionally equivalent responses and that they may deliberately modify their responses in order to define themselves against perceived others (Nader 1989).

We need time-dependent studies if we are to understand processes. Such studies, however, create problems of storage and recovery and require proper methods of analysis. Realization of the need to transform anthropological research design and methodology was one impetus for forming the linkages group. Those of us with experience in long-term research had previously realized that research questions were being transformed by the time spans now available to the anthropologist but that we were still groping for techniques appropriate to such research (Foster et al. 1978).

The increasing sophistication of computer technology provides the technology for the fine-grained comparisons based on the kinds of samples anthropologists now collect. Since field workers may lack the requisite analytic and computer skills, collaboration again emerges as an important component of this kind of research. The goals of systematic synchronic and diachronic comparison have encouraged collaboration in the field among several anthropologists. The complexities of analysis have also produced new kinds of linkages—between field anthropologists and those who can adapt computer technology to handle masses of data. The latter find the richness of the data intellectually challenging, while the field anthropologists gain from being forced to think more clearly about what kinds of questions need to be asked and with what degree of precision.

The linkages group has used the Gwembe database as a testing ground for creating the computer programs appropriate for longitudinal research in anthropology. Douglas White, of the University of California at Irvine; James Lee, of the California Institute of Technology; and their students have constructed time series rates on mortality, fertility, marital unions, labor migration, household and homestead size, and many other variables. These time series can be used to test various hypotheses about the effects of environmental factors, government policies, economic fluctuations, and other external interventions.

Success here will provide tools for others who do, or plan to do, similar research. Success will also mean that the Gwembe database can be used as a research tool by other anthropologists. Several such databases will help anthropologists make more effective arguments when they critique or participate in planning technological interventions.

Conclusion

The theoretical underpinnings and the methodologies associated with multitime, multisite, multilevel, studies, which we call the linkages approach, builds on earlier work in anthropology, as we stated earlier. Julian Steward's large-scale and comparative projects (1956, 1967) designed to examine cultural transformations have influenced our ideas about embeddedness and multistranded linkages. The pioneering work carried out on urbanization and the rural-urban continuum associated with Max Gluckman, Clyde Mitchell, and others at the Rhodes-Livingstone Institute provide other sources of influence. More recently the regional analyses of Carol Smith (1984, 1987) and the world systems approaches of Mintz (1985), Wallerstein (1974, 1980), and Wolf (1982) have reinforced our recognition that local societies are never isolates. Local cultures must be understood in much larger contexts. Tools for comparative analysis have been developed by survey researchers, by anthropologists working with the Human Relations Area File and the World Ethnographic Sample, and by others interested in systematic comparison.

Although what we are doing and advocating is increasingly common in anthropology, the linkages approach makes a contribution by combining the strengths of the long-term study and the possibilities for teamwork, systematic comparison, ordering, and analysis provided by computer technology. Our methodology permits fine-grained synchronic and diachronic comparisons to test intuitions and hypotheses about the meanings of the interconnections that link local responses to shifts in large-scale systems.

Anthropologists have provided basic ethnographic information for much of the world. Good ethnography now depends, however, on recognizing that the world system supplies much of what informs local action and that we must pay attention to the past and the future as well as to the present. Television, radio, newspapers, travel, education, proselytizing religions, multinational organizations, military machines, and international markets are institutions that affect us all. These modern linkages belong in the anthropological record.

NOTES

We thank Thayer Scudder for reading and commenting on an earlier draft of this chapter. We have also benefited from the comments of our fellow members of the AAA Presidential Panel on Social Transformations in Preindustrial and Industrializing Societies. We have previously published a similar paper entitled "Multilevel Linkages: Longitudinal and Comparative Studies," by Conrad Kottak and Elizabeth Colson, in *Assessing Cultural Anthropology,* ed. Robert Borofsky, 396–412 (New York: McGraw-Hill, 1994).

1. The original group included Lilyan Brudner-White, Michael Burton, Elizabeth Colson, Scarlet Epstein, Nancie Gonzalez, David Gregory, Conrad Kottak, Thayer Scudder, and Douglas White. Later it was joined by Robert Van Kemper and Chad McDaniel.

2. Kottak's television research has been supported by three agencies, in addition to the University of Michigan (through a sabbatical leave): (1) the Wenner-Gren Foundation for Anthropological Research, for a grant to study "The Electronic Mass Media and Social Change in Brazil" (1983–84); (2) the National Science Foundation for a research grant (NSF-G-BNS 8317856-Kottak) to study "The Social Impact of Television in Rural Brazil" in the states of Bahia, Para, Santa Catarina, and São Paulo (6/84–11/86); and (3) the National Institute of Mental Health for a research grant (DHHS-PHS-G-5-R01-MH38815-03-Kottak) to investigate "Television's Behavioral Effects in Brazil," supporting field team research and data analysis in six Brazilian rural communities (1/1/85–12/31/88).

3. Along with Isabel (Betty) Wagley Kottak, Conrad Kottak has been studying Arembepe, Bahia state, a coastal town whose population now numbers about two thousand people, since 1962 (Kottak 1992). Youngest of our TV project research sites, Arembepe was settled late in the nineteenth century by freed slaves from sugar plantations in Bahia's Recôncavo region. In 1985, for the TV project, two other researchers joined the Kottaks. Iraní Escolano, a Brazilian, was at that time a graduate student in survey methods at Hunter College of the City University of New York. Pennie Magee, an anthropology graduate student at the University of Florida, had previously spent many years in Brazil.

4. Elizabeth Colson first visited Gwembe District in 1949. In 1956 she and

Thayer Scudder began a long-term study initially tied to research on the impact of a large hydroelectric dam and the resettlement of the population of the area to be flooded. Scudder and Colson have revisited the district frequently, in 1956–57, 1960, 1961–62, 1965, 1967, 1968, 1972–73, 1975, 1978, 1981–82, 1983, 1987, and 1989. Jonathan Habarad joined the study in 1987 and spent eighteen months in Gwembe. Douglas White, James Lee, and their students have been involved in the analysis of the village census data since 1987. The research has been supported by the Rhodes-Livingstone Institute (now the Institute for African Studies in the University of Zambia), FAO, the Joint Committee on Africa of the Social Science Research Council and the American Council of Learned Societies, the John Guggenheim Foundation, and the National Science Foundation through grants in 1972–73, 1981–82, 1987, and 1987–88.

5. This became apparent at the first conference on long-term field studies in social anthropology held in 1975 (Foster et al. 1978).

6. Gurupá or Itá is another longitudinal site, originally studied by Charles Wagley in 1949 (Wagley 1953), subsequently by Darrell Miller and Richard Pace (1987, 1993).

7. Later, to round out the national-level component of the research, in the summer of 1986, Joseph Straubhaar of Michigan State University's Department of Telecommunication, whose previous research had also focused on Brazilian television, worked with Rio-based project consultant Lucia Ferreira Reis gathering additional information in Rio and São Paulo. They obtained data from the major Brazilian public opinion and media research organizations. These data were obtained for the cities transmitting the television signals received in each project community, for the period during which research was going on in the communities, to be compared with the community data to provide a regional- and national-level perspective on television diffusion and impact and to permit rural-urban contrast.

8. In addition to Kottak's book (1990), which provides an overview of the main research findings, articles are being prepared on such topics as TV and race, TV and family planning, and TV and economic development.

9. We also investigated various links with the external world, including telephone use, frequency, destination and purpose of travel outside, military service, and prior urban residence. Our questionnaires contained several queries concerning information sources other than television, including newspapers, magazines, books, radio, and movies.

10. For examples of, and commentary on, traditional risk analysis, see the following: Cooper 1985; Hansson 1983; Kasperson and Gray 1983; O'Riordan 1983; Paschen, Bechmann, and Frederichs 1983; Starr 1983; and Trunk and Trunk 1983.

11. Pilot work for this research began in 1989, with modest funding from three agencies: the Michigan Memorial Phoenix Project (Project no. 714—The Social Context and Impact of Nuclear Energy in Brazil) and two Brazilian agencies, ANPOCS and FAPERJ. Most of this research has been supported by the National Science Foundation and by the Office of Forestry, Environment, and

Natural Resources, Bureau of Science and Technology, of the U.S. Agency for International Development, under NSF Grant no. BNS-9112030 (8/15/91–7/31/94).

REFERENCES

Beckett, Jeremy
    1987   *Torres Strait Islanders: Custom and Colonialism*. New York: Cambridge University Press.

Bennett, John W.
    1982   *Of Time and the Enterprise: North American Family Farm Management in a Context of Resource Marginality*. Minneapolis: University of Minnesota Press.

Bodley, John H., ed.
    1988   *Tribal Peoples and Development Issues: A Global Overview*. Mountain View, Calif.: Mayfield.

Bond, George
    1990   Fieldnotes: Research in Past Occurrences. In *Fieldnotes: The Makings of Anthropology*, ed. Roger Sanjek, 273–89. Ithaca, N.Y.: Cornell University Press.

Bradley, Candace, Camella Moore, Michael Burton, and Douglas White
    1990   A Cross-Cultural Historical Analysis of Subsistence Change. *American Anthropologist* 92(2): 447–57.

Buckser, Andrew
    1989   Sacred Airtime: American Church Structures and the Rise of Televangelism. *Human Organization* 48(4): 370–76.

Carmack, Robert M., ed.
    1988   *Harvest of Violence: The Maya Indians and the Guatemalan Crisis*. Oklahoma: University of Oklahoma Press.

Colson, Elizabeth
    1971   *The Social Consequences of Resettlement: The Impact of the Kariba Resettlement upon the Gwembe Tonga*. Manchester: Manchester University Press.
    1976   From Chief's Court to Local Court. In *Freedom and Constraint*, ed. Myron J. Aronoff, 15–19. Assen and Amsterdam: Van Gorcum.
    1982   *Planned Change: The Creation of a New Community*. Berkeley: University of California, Institute of International Studies.

Colson, Elizabeth, and Thayer Scudder
    1975   New Economic Relationships between the Gwembe Valley and the Line of Rail. In *Town and Country in Central and Eastern Africa*, ed. David Parkin, 190–210. London: Oxford University Press.
    1988   *For Prayer and Profit: The Ritual, Economic, and Social Importance of Beer in Gwembe District, Zambia, 1950–1982*. Stanford, Calif.: Stanford University Press.

Cooper, M. G., ed.
    1985 *Risk: Man-Made Hazards to Man.* Oxford: Clarendon Press.
Costa, Alberto
    In press A Voice for the Silence: Television, Culture, and Change in Ibirama. In *Television's Social Impact in Brazil,* ed. Conrad Phillip Kottak, n.p. In press.
Costa, Alberto, Conrad Kottak, Rosane Prado, and John Stiles
    1995 Ecological Awareness and Risk Perception in Brazil. NAPA Bulletin 15. *Global Ecosystems Creating Options through Anthropological Perspectives,* ed. Pam Puntenney, 71–87. Washington, D.C.: American Anthropological Association.
Crick, Malcolm
    1989 Representations of International Tourism in the Social Sciences: Sun, Sex, Sights, Savings, and Servility. *Annual Review of Anthropology* 18:307–400.
Eades, Jeremy, ed.
    1986 *Migrants, Workers, and the Social Order.* London: Tavistock Publications.
Elphick, Richard
    1977 *Kraal and Castle: Khoikhoi and the Founding of White South Africa.* New Haven, Conn.: Yale University Press.
Epstein, T. Scarlett
    1978 Mysore Villages Revisited. In *Long-Term Field Research in Social Anthropology,* ed. George Foster et al., 209–26. New York: Academic Press.
Feirman, Steven
    1985 Struggle for Control: The Social Roots of Health and Healing in Modern Africa. *African Studies* 28(2–3): 73–147.
Fortes, Meyer
    1945 *The Dynamics of Clanship among the Tallensi.* Oxford: Oxford University Press.
Foster, George
    1978 Fieldwork in Tzintzuntzan: The First Thirty Years. In *Long-Term Field Research in Social Anthropology,* ed. George Foster et al., 165–84. New York: Academic Press.
Foster, George, Thayer Scudder, Elizabeth Colson, and R. V. Kemper
    1978 *Long-Term Field Research in Social Anthropology.* New York: Academic Press.
Freeman, Derek
    1983 *Margaret Mead and Samoa: The Making and Unmaking of an Anthropological Myth.* Cambridge, Mass.: Harvard University Press.
Gallagher, Art, Jr., and Harland Padfield
    1980 Theory of the Dying Community. In *The Dying Community,* ed. Art Gallagher Jr. and Harland Padfield, 1–22. Albuquerque: University of New Mexico Press.

Gallagher, Art, Jr., and Harland Padfield, eds.
  1980 *The Dying Community.* Albuquerque: University of New Mexico Press.
Graburn, Nelson, ed.
  1983 The Anthropology of Tourism. *Annals of Tourism Research* (special issue) 10(1). New York: Pergamon.
Granzberg, G., and T. Steinbring
  1980 *Television and the Canadian Indian.* Winnipeg: University of Winnipeg Press.
Guyer, Jane
  1987 Feeding African Cities. In *Feeding African Cities,* ed. Jane Guyer, 1–54. Bloomington: Indiana University Press.
Habarad, Jonathan
  N.d. Neighborhood and Nation in Gwembe District, Zambia. Unpublished manuscript.
Hansen, Art, and Anthony Oliver-Smith, eds.
  1982 *Involuntary Migration and Resettlement: The Problems and Responses of Dislocated People.* Boulder, Colo.: Westview Press.
Hansson, Bengt
  1983 The Assessment of Nuclear Risk: Some Experiences from the Swedish Energy Commission. In *The Analysis of Actual versus Perceived Risks,* ed. Vincent T. Covello, W. Gary Flamm, Joseph V. Rodricks, and Robert G. Tardiff, 69–80. New York: Plenum Press.
Hellman, Ellen
  1948 *Rooiyard: A Sociological Study of an Urban Slum.* Rhodes-Livingstone Paper no. 13. Manchester: Manchester University Press.
Hoben, Alan
  1982 Anthropologists and Development. *Annual Review of Anthropology* 11:349–75. Palo Alto: Annual Reviews.
Humphrey, Caroline
  1983 *Karl Marx Collective: Economy, Society and Religion in a Siberian Collective Farm.* Cambridge: Cambridge University Press.
James, Wendy
  1988 *The Listening Ebony: Moral Knowledge, Religion, and Power among the Uduk of Sudan.* Oxford: Clarendon Press.
Justice, Judith
  1986 *Policies, Plans, and People: Culture and Health Development in Nepal.* Berkeley: University of California Press.
Kapferer, Bruce
  1988 *Legends of People, Myths of State: Violence, Intolerance, and Political Culture in Sri Lanka and Australia.* Washington, D.C.: Smithsonian Institution.
Kasperson, Roger E., and Arnold L. Gray
  1983 Risk Assessment Following Crisis in the United States: The Kemeny Commission. In *The Analysis of Actual versus Perceived Risks,* ed.

　　　　　Vincent T. Covello, W. Gary Flamm, Joseph V. Rodricks, and
　　　　　Robert G. Tardiff, 129–56. New York: Plenum Press.
Keesing, Roger M.
　　1982　*Kwaio Religion: The Living and the Dead in a Solomon Island Society.* New York: Columbia University Press.
Kemper, Robert Van
　　1978　Fieldwork among Tzintzuntzan Migrants in Mexico City: Retrospect and Prospect. In *Long-Term Field Research in Social Anthropology,* ed. George Foster et al., 189–207. New York: Academic Press.
Kottak, Conrad
　　1990　*Prime-Time Society: An Anthropological Analysis of Television and Culture.* Belmont, Calif.: Wadsworth.
　　1991　When People Don't Come First: Some Lessons from Completed Projects. In *Putting People First: Sociological Variables in Rural Development,* 2d ed., ed. Michael Cernea, 429–64. New York: Oxford University Press.
　　1992　*Assault on Paradise: Social Change in a Brazilian Village,* 2d ed. New York: McGraw-Hill.
Kottak, Conrad, and Alberto Costa
　　1993　Ecological Awareness, Environmentalist Action, and International Conservation Strategy. *Human Organization* 52(4): 335–43.
Lloyd, Peter
　　1979　*Slums of Hope: Shanty Towns of the Third World.* London: Penguin Books.
Loizos, Peter
　　1981　*The Heart Grown Bitter: A Chronicle of Cypriot War Refugees.* Cambridge: Cambridge University Press.
Michaels, Eric
　　1986　*The Aboriginal Invention of Television in Central Australia, 1982–86.* Canberra: Australian Institute of Aboriginal Studies.
Mintz, S.
　　1985　*Sweetness and Power: The Place of Sugar in Modern History.* New York: Viking Penguin.
Mitchell, J. Clyde
　　1987　*Cities, Society, and Social Perception: A Central African Perspective.* Oxford: Clarendon Press.
Molohon, Kathryn
　　1984　Response to Television in Two Swampy Creek Cree Communities on the West Coast of James Bay. *Kroeber Anthropological Society Papers* 63–64:95–103.
Morgan, Scott, and Elizabeth Colson, eds.
　　1987　*People in Upheaval.* Staten Island, N.Y.: Center for Migration Studies.
Mullings, Leith
　　1984　*Therapy, Ideology, and Social Change: Mental Healing in Urban Ghana.* Berkeley: University of California Press.

Nader, Laura
    1989   Comparative Consciousness. Paper given at the 1989 annual meeting of the American Anthropological Association, Washington, D.C., November.
O'Riordan, Timothy
    1983   Coping with the Risks of Nuclear Power Plants in the United Kingdom. In *The Analysis of Actual versus Perceived Risks,* ed. Vincent T. Covello, W. Gary Flamm, Joseph V. Rodricks, and Robert G. Tardiff, 101–28. New York: Plenum Press.
Pace, Richard B.
    1987   *Economic and Political Change in the Amazonian Community of Itá, Brazil.* Ph.D. diss., Department of Anthropology, University of Florida. Ann Arbor: UMI Research Press.
    1993   First Time Televiewing in Amazônia: Television Acculturation in Gurupá, Brazil. *Ethnology* 32(2): 187–206.
Parnell, Philip C.
    1988   *Escalating Disputes: Social Participation and Change in the Oaxacan Highlands.* Tucson: University of Arizona Press.
Paschen, H., G. Bechmann, and G. Frederichs
    1983   Nuclear Power Plant: West German Management of Risk—A Problem Analysis. In *The Analysis of Actual versus Perceived Risks,* ed. Vincent T. Covello, W. Gary Flamm, Joseph V. Rodricks, and Robert G. Tardiff, 81–99. New York: Plenum Press.
Pottier, Johan
    1988   *Migrants No More: Settlement and Survival in Mambwe Villages, Zambia.* Bloomington: Indiana University Press.
Practicing Anthropology
    1990   Involuntary Resettlement and Development Anthropology. *Practicing Anthropology* 12(3).
Richards, Audrey
    1940   *Bemba Marriage and Present Economic Conditions.* Rhodes-Livingstone Paper no. 4. Livingstone: Rhodes-Livingstone Institute.
Robertson, A. L.
    1982   *The People and the State.* Cambridge: Cambridge University Press.
Sanjek, Roger, ed.
    1990   *Fieldnotes: The Makings of Anthropology.* Ithaca, N.Y.: Cornell University Press.
Schapera, I.
    1947   *Migrant Labour and Tribal Life: A Study of Conditions in the Bechuanaland Protectorate.* Oxford: Oxford University Press.
Schwartz, Douglas
    1980   Foreword. In *The Dying Community,* ed. Art Gallagher Jr. and Harland Padfield, vii–ix. Albuquerque: University of New Mexico Press.
Scudder, Thayer
    1982   The Impact of Big Dam–Building on the Zambezi River Basin. In

The Careless Technology: Ecology and International Development, ed. M. T. Farvar and J. P. Milton, 206–35. New York: Natural History Press.

1985 *A History of Development in the Twentieth Century: The Zambian Portion of the Middle Zambezi Valley and the Lake Kariba Basin.* Working Paper no. 22. Binghamton, N.Y.: Institute for Development Anthropology.

Scudder, Thayer, and Elizabeth Colson

1980 *Secondary Education and the Formation of an Elite: The Impact of Education on Gwembe District, Zambia.* London: Academic Press.

Scudder, Thayer, and Jonathan Habarad

1991 Local Responses to Involuntary Relocation and Development in the Zambian Portion of the Middle Zambezi Valley. In *Migrants in Agricultural Development,* ed. J. A. Mollet, 178–205. Oxford: Oxford University Press.

Serpell, Namposya, and Monica Munachonga

1986 *Needs Assessment Survey of Rural Women in the Gwembe and Namwala Districts of Southern Province, Zambia.* Report no. 1, Gwembe District. Prepared for the Department of Agriculture, Ministry of Agriculture and Water Development, Home Economics Section, Lusaka, Zambia.

Smith, Carol A.

1984 Local History in Global Context: Social and Economic Transitions in Western Guatemala. *Comparative Studies in Society and History* 26:109–33.

1987 Regional Analysis in World-System Perspective: A Critique of Three Structural Theories of Uneven Development. *Review* 10(4): 597–648.

Smith, Valene, ed.

1989 (orig. 1977) *Hosts and Guests: The Anthropology of Tourism,* 2d ed. Philadelphia: University of Pennsylvania Press.

Solway, Jacqueline, and Richard Lee

1990 Foragers, Genuine and Spurious: Situating the Kalahari San in History. *Current Anthropology* 31(2): 109–46.

Starr, Chauncey

1983 Coping with Nuclear Power Risks: A National Strategy. In *The Analysis of Actual versus Perceived Risks,* ed. Vincent T. Covello, W. Gary Flamm, Joseph V. Rodricks, and Robert G. Tardiff, 251–57. New York: Plenum Press.

Steward, Julian

1956 *The People of Puerto Rico: A Study in Social Anthropology.* Urbana: University of Illinois Press.

Steward, Julian, ed.

1967 *Contemporary Change in Traditional Societies,* 3 vols. Urbana: University of Illinois Press.

Talai, Vered Amit
    1989 *Armenians in London: The Management of Social Boundaries.* Manchester: Manchester University Press.
Tambiah, S. J.
    1986 *Sri Lanka: Ethnic Fratricide and the Dismantling of Democracy.* Chicago: University of Chicago Press.
Trunk, Anne, and Edward Trunk
    1983 Impact of the Three Mile Island Accident as Perceived by Those Living in the Surrounding Community. In *The Analysis of Actual versus Perceived Risks,* ed. Vincent T. Covello, W. Gary Flamm, Joseph V. Rodricks, and Robert G. Tardiff, 225–33. New York: Plenum Press.
Volkman, Toby Alice
    1990 Vision and Revisions: Toraja Culture and the Tourist Age. *American Ethnologist* 17(1): 91–110.
Wagley, Charles
    1953 *Amazon Town: A Study of Man in the Tropics.* New York: Macmillan.
Wallerstein, I.
    1974 *The Modern World-System: Capitalist Agriculture and the Origins of the European World-Economy in the Sixteenth Century.* New York: Academic Press.
    1980 *The Modern World System II: Mercantilism and the Consolidation of the European World-Economy, 1600–1750.* New York: Academic Press.
White, Douglas
    1989 Microcomputer Tools for Anthropological Research. *Development Anthropology Network* 7(1): 9–16.
Wilson, Monica
    1977 *For Men and Elders.* New York: Africana.
Wolf, Eric
    1982 *Europe and the People without History.* Berkeley: University of California Press.
    1989 Facing Power: Old Insights, New Questions. Distinguished Lecture, American Anthropological Association annual meeting, Washington, D.C.

Chapter 5

The Media, Development, and Social Change

Conrad Phillip Kottak

The mass media play an increasingly prominent role in national and international culture. They propel a globally spreading culture of consumption, stimulating participation in the cash economy (Hujanen 1976). The electronic mass media instantaneously transmit information and images within and across national boundaries. Particularly for nonliterate people, the most significant mass medium is television. Many researchers have commented on television's pervasive impact on society. Comstock et al. (1978) see it as a major socializing agent competing with family, school, peers, community, and church. Television executives have become "key gatekeepers" (Saldich 1979:22), regulating public access to information, a role played historically by political and religious leaders. Television directs public attention toward some things and away from others (Gerbner and Gross 1976; Hood 1987). Hirsch (1979) stresses television's role in focusing attention on national-level events.

The Media and National Identity

As print has done for centuries (Anderson 1991), the electronic mass media can also spread, and even create, national and ethnic identities. Like print, television and radio can diffuse the cultures of different countries within their own boundaries, thus enhancing national cultural identity. For example, millions of Brazilians who were formerly cut off (by geographic isolation or illiteracy) from urban and national information now join in a common communication system, thanks to national TV. Television gives contemporary Brazilians a sense of regular participation in national events.

Cross-cultural studies contradict a belief Americans ethnocentrically hold about televiewing in other countries. This misconception is that American programs inevitably triumph over local products. This doesn't usually happen when there is appealing local competition. In Brazil, for example, the most popular network (TV Globo) relies heavily on native productions. American imports like "Dallas" and "Dynasty" have drawn small audiences. TV Globo's most popular programs are *telenovelas,* locally made serials that are similar to American soap operas (Straubhaar 1982). Globo plays each night to the world's largest and most devoted audience (sixty million to eighty million viewers throughout the nation). The programs that attract this horde are made by Brazilians, for Brazilians. Thus, it is not North American culture but, rather, a new pan-Brazilian national culture that Brazilian TV is propagating. Brazilian productions also compete internationally. They are exported to over one hundred countries, spanning Latin America, Europe, Asia, and Africa.

We may generalize that programming that is culturally alien won't do very well anywhere if a quality local choice is available. Confirmation comes from many countries. National productions have proved their popularity in Japan, Mexico, India, Egypt, Nigeria, and China (see Abu-Lughod 1993; Ivy 1988; Lull 1988, 1991; A. P. Lyons 1990; H. D. Lyons 1990; Mankekar 1993; Spitulnik 1993). In a survey during the mid-1980's 75 percent of Nigerian viewers preferred local productions. Only 10 percent favored imports, and the remaining 15 percent liked the two options equally. Local productions are successful in Nigeria because "they are filled with everyday moments that audiences can identify with. These shows are locally produced by Nigerians." Thirty million people watched one of the most popular series, "The Village Headmaster," each week. That program brought rural values to the screens of urbanites who had lost touch with their rural roots (Gray 1986).

All cultures express imagination—in dreams, songs, fantasies, myths, and stories. Today, however, more people in many more places imagine "a wider set of 'possible' lives than they ever did before. One important source of this change is the mass media, which present a rich, ever-changing store of possible lives." (Appadurai 1991, 197). In Appadurai's view the United States has lost its role as principal "puppeteer of a world system of images" (a media-saturated world in which the imagination plays a growing role in social life) (1990, 4). The United States remains a media center, but one among many. It has been joined by Canada, Japan, Western Europe, Brazil, Mexico, Egypt, India, and Hong Kong.

Censors and Gatekeepers

The electronic mass media, especially television, bring information directly to the people—a likely factor in democratization in South Africa and the demise of the former Soviet Union (Manaev 1991). One wonders whether slavery would have endured so long had TV sets brought daily information about external options and events to shanty residents.

Commercial TV, supported mainly by advertising, tends to be freer of direct government controls than is broadcast television in countries with more government financial support and supervision, such as those in the former Soviet empire and many African nations (Hirsch 1979). Before glasnost Russian television, via eighty million sets reaching 90 percent of the citizenry, was a nationally pervasive propaganda tool. Four channels, all based in Moscow, carried the same programs—the official news, speeches of the Supreme Soviet, lessons in geometry, grammar and computers, and youth classes about obligations in society (Morrison 1986).

The overt propaganda role of television has also been evident in Africa. So concludes a report by the International Development Research Council, a Canadian research group, after a study of Cameroon, Congo, Gambia, Ivory Coast, Niger, Nigeria, Senegal, Zaire, Zambia, and Zimbabwe. The report found that (despite a few bright spots such as Nigeria) "television in Africa has generally become a government mouthpiece" (Gray 1986). Typical African TV content includes political speeches, reports on visits of foreign dignitaries, development experts speaking European languages, dubbed cartoons, and dramas featuring upper-class characters dealing with Western problems.

Much less competition and variety mark broadcasting in such countries than in nations where television is mainly commercial. Obviously, however, there can be censorship of commercial TV as well as of government-funded or government-run television. Even with commercial television governments typically allocate access to the airwaves and play some role in regulating scheduling and content of news, documentaries, ads, propaganda, information, and entertainment programs. Several forms of censorship affect commercial television:

1. external—government,
2. external—public opinion,
3. external—sponsors,

4. intermediate—network executives, and
5. internal—self-censorship by creators.

Although lacking the prestige of an elite art form, television, as the mass medium par excellance, can have tremendous power. As Hirsch has observed,

> political leaders and office-holders are generally far more alert and sensitive than social scientists and journalists to the structural characteristics which distinguish television from other news media and provide it with a different form of power. (Hirsch 1979, 255)

Brazil's former military government from 1964 to 1985, for example, never doubted the power of television and was vigilant in supervising its content. A 1962 law granted broadcast licenses for fifteen years, revokable at any time. Broadcasters had to be much more careful than their counterparts in the United States, where licensing is longer term. In a 1975 speech the Brazilian minister of culture cited television's huge potential influence as the reason for state control. Among the content features requiring government attention he mentioned violence, distorted presentations of reality, and foreign morality, values, and customs (Miranda and Pereira 1983). Responding to the threat of government interference or network controls, reporters, writers, directors, and commentators censor themselves, both consciously and unconsciously. This "internal censor" can be particularly stifling as a brake on creativity.

The Special Significance of Brazil

In 1982 I became interested in television in Brazil, which, as noted, has the world's most watched commercial network (Globo), which shows mainly its own productions, particularly *telenovelas*. A research project I planned and directed from 1983 to 1987 on the impact of television in Brazil included fieldwork at seven sites in different geographical areas of the country. The four main sites were in the southern state of Santa Catarina (Ibirama), the south-central state of São Paulo (Cunha), the northeastern state of Bahia (Arembepe), and the Amazonian state of Pará (Gurupá). Each of these sites had been studied at least twenty years earlier, before television's arrival. This research project investigated television's role in molding knowledge, attitudes, perceptions, emotions, images of the world, and economic development.[1]

Some aspects of this study are discussed further in my chapter with Colson in this volume (chap. 4). Here I draw heavily on this Brazilian research, because of its unusually rich data base, which makes it possible to examine several relationships involving the mass media, social change, and development. Whenever possible I consider the extent to which certain findings may apply cross-nationally.

To assess the influence of television in Brazil, it was vital to our research design to compare people with varying degrees of exposure. We were able to locate and interview, particularly in Gurupá and the rural zone of Arembepe, many people with almost no exposure to television. Indeed, one of our reasons for choosing Gurupá, an Amazon town, was that, when fieldwork began, it lacked a satellite dish and had only a dozen sets. These relied on expensive antennas to receive very poor signals from the state capital (Pace 1993).

Despite many similarities, which permitted controlled comparison, our four main sites contrasted in two important respects: time of television's introduction and ethnic background (Cunha is Luso-Brazilian; Ibirama, German-Polish-and-Italian-Brazilian; Arembepe, Afro-Brazilian; and Gurupá, Indian-Brazilian). Most important for a TV impact study, television had reached the sites at different times. We could therefore assess relationships between length of TV exposure (as a predictor variable) and many other (dependent) variables (while controlling for the effects of such intervening variables as income and class). Our project used a set of uniform quantitative and qualitative procedures to collect data at each site.[2]

Information

> While basic attitudes and behaviors are quite seldom affected by single programs or informational campaigns, the mass media may be far more effective in conveying generalized information to the mass audience than studies following traditional research designs have so far suggested. (Hirsch 1979)

My interest in the role of the media in social change grew out of my previous research in Brazil, which began in 1962 in Arembepe, then a fairly isolated fishing village (Kottak 1992). Before TV Arembepeiros, like other rural Brazilians, had been cut off from national and international information through limitations on transportation and mobility, educational deficiencies, poverty, and widespread illiteracy.

The advent of television gave villagers the chance to embark on an adventure of instantaneous national and international participation. Our informants again and again made the point that TV brings knowledge of the outside world. As one young man put it, "You sit here in this little place and learn about the whole world because you have TV." Awareness of national and global events is much greater among viewers than among unexposed people. Regular viewers have more general knowledge and can recognize and interpret more information from outside—both images and ideas.

I first noticed television's effects in Arembepe in 1980, when I returned following a seven-year absence. After the arrival of electricity in 1978 villagers, with reliable access to TV, became much more informed about international events. I could contrast this information explosion with the mid-1960s, when villagers had eagerly used me as a source of information about the outside world. In 1980, as one fisherman remarked, "The whole world is open to Arembepe." Instead of being asked "Are there elephants in America?" or "What happens to the water when the tide goes out?" I was told about a fishermen's strike in France and labor unions in Poland. I was asked about the chances and merits of President Carter and Senator Edward Kennedy, who were competing for the 1980 Democratic presidential nomination. People also wanted to talk about politics, during the first free elections since the 1964 military takeover. Television seemed to be the main reason for Arembepe's new familiarity with the nation and the world.

Social Navigation and Migration

By training villagers in national norms, television makes it easier for them to deal with the outsiders they meet. It is difficult for Americans to appreciate this role of television as facilitator of social interaction because we so rarely encounter anyone who was not raised in the daily presence of the mass media. Because of its mainly urban content, Brazilian television brings the city to the country and the metropolis to smaller cities and towns. It also introduces Brazilian urban lifestyles to other Latin American countries, where Globo's well-produced *telenovelas* are very popular. Life in such overpopulated, polluted, crime-ridden megacities as Rio and

São Paulo is dramatically different from daily existence in Brazil's villages, towns, and small cities. But Globo's *telenovelas* characteristically present images of urban glamour and sophistication. Videocameras caress the natural and architectural attractions of Rio and São Paulo, ignoring their more sordid aspects, which, however, news broadcasts regularly report.

News programs, which are also popular, convey more negative images of the city, particularly about crime. Because TV transmits contradictory images, with *telenovelas* positive and news negative, it is not surprising that we found no clear directional effects of televiewing on images of city life. Rural Brazilians did view Rio (the setting of most *novelas*) more positively than São Paulo. But we found no discernible effects of television on answers to "Would you like your children to live in a big city?"

Literacy

Compared with Brazil, a much longer and greater exposure to print media and radio has mediated television's impact in North America and Western Europe. Brazil, which outlawed printing presses until the nineteenth century, has never been particularly reading oriented. By stimulating rural appetites for information, television has actually spurred greater use of print media by Brazilians. To understand this effect we need to consider some underlying contrasts in cultural attitudes about reading.[3] Many Brazilians view reading as antisocial. Books belong to the public world of school, formal education, work, and the rules and records of the bureaucratic state. Print is part of the outside, impersonal world of street and work rather than the inside, intimate world of home and family (cf. DaMatta 1987, 1991).

Given Brazil's print media history and attitudes about reading, most Brazilians were media deprived when television reached them. In the United States, Canada, and Western Europe television may be the mass medium par excellance, but it is nevertheless one among many familiar media that have been available for decades. Television's infiltration of the home has been much more exclusive in Brazil. For most Brazilians— and for people throughout the nonliterate world—television has become the primary, often exclusive, conduit to regional, national, and international information. Especially for nonelites TV is the main gate to the global village.

Brazilians do not perceive either television or radio, both of which may be used socially, as being as antisocial as print. Although radio was widely available in Brazilian cities and county seats by the 1950s, its penetration of rural areas has been more recent. Small transistor radios became a rural fad in the early 1960s, and by the mid-1960s the portable radio had become a status symbol among rural men with disposable cash. Showing their radios off, and so that others might listen (i.e., using radio socially), these men carried their sets around their villages. They tuned in soccer games, music, and news—including international reports from the Voice of America, broadcast in Portuguese.

In the 1960s the people of Arembepe, like those in most other rural areas, had little exposure to print. The most educated local schoolteacher had only a fourth-grade education. Almost no one read for pleasure. Arembepeiros did enjoy picture magazines brought back from the city, and a few occasionally read pamphlet versions of regional ballads.

Our research findings challenge the "commonsense" assumption that televiewing has a negative effect on reading. Instead, we found that televiewing correlates with greater use of print media. This was especially evident in the three communities in our study that had received television most recently. Only education was a stronger predictor than televiewing of scores on a reading index we devised.[4]

The number of current TV hours watched correlates strongly with reading, supporting our hypothesis that heavy televiewing is associated with general information hunger. Televiewing hooks villagers on information and stimulates curiosity, which motivates many people to read more. Given literacy and the availability of print media, heavy viewers are precisely the people who are also most apt to devour books, magazines, and newspapers. There was a strong statistical correlation between number of books in the home and daily TV hours.

Participation in the Cash Economy

Commercial television—whether in the United States, Brazil, or elsewhere—tends to dote on people who can afford to live, or aspire to, glamorous lives. Rich TV families encourage the culture of consumption by illustrating it. Characters must be able to afford the products that sponsor the show. Advertising can be direct (as commercials) or indirect (with consumer goods introduced as part of entertainment program content). *Telenovelas,* watched in more than one hundred countries, including most of Latin America, spur consumption by having characters chat about their wishes for products. For example, two young men discuss their hopes of purchasing a house or car or having meat on the table ("like rich people"). Two women extol a new corn popper or toaster oven. Outdoor locales show a sponsor bank, in front of which characters stop to talk, with the bank logo easily visible.

Through television information about products (their existence, appearance, function, availability, and current price) directly and regularly reaches people in remote areas. Effects are evident to the ethnographers who originally worked at the research sites a generation ago. New consumer patterns show up in hairstyles, diet, and clothing (e.g., sneakers vs. sandals).

One of our questions designed to elicit information about the culture of consumption was "If you won the lottery, what would you do with the money?" Most people said they would put it in a savings account. We also asked our respondents (many of them rural folk who used to be bank wary) if and when they had opened a savings account, because TV constantly advertised this investment option. No one in Arembepe had a savings account in the mid-1960s, but many did by the mid-1980s. Current televiewing level (average daily hours watched) was an excellent predictor of having a savings account.[5] Better roads and bus service also provide villagers with easier access to banks and make participation in a consumer economy much easier.

The decision to open a savings account was not just TV-conditioned behavior but also a rational response to an attractive use of surplus money. A savings account offered both interest and "monetary correction" (additional guaranteed monthly interest equaling the inflation rate). Savings accounts have been popular in Brazil because they have offered a risk free investment in an international economy that is not risk-free. The existence of millions of savings accounts with monetary correction (and, therefore, TV's impact on economic behavior) has helped fuel the inflation for which Brazil is famous.

Another example of TV's impact on consumers' behavior is a widespread correlation and probable negative public health effect. With its fashionable society women and powdered milk ads, Brazilian television promotes early weaning and bottle feeding. We found that heavy viewers tended to breastfeed less (and to wean earlier) than did other Brazilian women.[6] The public health effect is likely to be negative because (1) babies who are nursed acquire antibodies and immunities from mother's milk, (2) mother's milk is often richer in nutrients than is a combination of powdered milk and locally available supplements, and (3) powdered milk is sometimes mixed with polluted water, which causes infantile diarrhea and other illnesses.

TV hones the wish to be prosperous and upwardly mobile. *Subir na vida,* to rise in life, is one of the most common *telenovela* expressions. Most *novelas* are modern-day Cinderella stories. A young woman or man from a lower-status family falls in love with and eventually marries someone from a richer family. The interclass friendships and romances shown on Brazilian television link members of classes A (upper), B (middle), and sometimes C (upper working). Only occasionally is there a romance between a working-class character and someone from the upper or upper-middle class. Even rarer in entertainment programming are members of class D (lower working, unemployed poor), with their impoverished, untelegenic lifestyles. Even the fantasy world of the *telenovela* recognizes that such people have virtually no chance to "rise in life" by marrying someone from the elite group.

Measuring the Cultivation Effect

There is a reciprocal relationship between the mass media and culture. The preexisting culture influences indigenous creations and program choice. Long-term exposure to messages then feeds back on social reality, changing old beliefs, attitudes, and behavior. This process contributes to the development of a new mass culture. One important aim of our Brazil TV project was cross-cultural comparison: Did research results from North America also hold true for Brazil? George Gerbner and his colleagues in the "Cultural Indicators Project" at the University of Pennsylvania's Annenberg School of Communications have found that American heavy viewers perceive the "real world" as being similar to the world represented on television (Gerbner and Gross 1976; Gerbner, Gross, Jackson-Beeck, Jeffries-Fox, and Signorielli 1978; Gerbner, Gross, Morgan, and Signorielli 1980; Signorielli, Gross, and Morgan 1982). Gerbner and Gross conclude that American "television viewing . . . makes a separate and independent contribution to the 'biasing' of conceptions of social reality within most age, sex, educational, and other groupings" (1976:191). Labeling this biasing process the "cultivation effect," Gerbner and his associates examined relationships between heavy television watching and distorted perceptions of social reality.

The demographic and socioeconomic characteristics of heavy viewers in Brazil set them off from heavy viewers in the United States, among whom children, the elderly, lower-income people, blacks, and females are statistically overrepresented. Our Brazilian heavy viewers, by contrast, scored higher on most socioeconomic measures than did the lighter viewers. In our total sample, at most sites, and, most notably, in both our high- and low-income samples,[7] daily televiewing hours tended to increase with class, household income, and urban residence. As in the United States, however, females were significantly heavier viewers than males, particularly in our upper-income sample. We would therefore expect the Brazilian version of Gerbner's cultivation effect to be particularly marked among women.

How did we measure cultivation effects? Uniquely, our research design permitted us to distinguish between two key TV exposure variables. First was current viewing level (average daily hours [ATVHOURS]), which is routinely used in American research. Second and far more significant was length of home TV exposure (HOMEEXPO). American research must rely solely on current viewing level to assess TV's influence, because there is little variation in length of home exposure, except for variation based on age. Americans aged forty-five and younger have never known a world without TV. Some American researchers have tried to use age as an indirect measure of TV's long-term effects. Their assumption is that viewing has a cumulative effect, its influence increasing (up to a point) with age. Yet, that approach has difficulty distinguishing between the effects of years of TV exposure and other changes associated with aging. By contrast, our Brazilian sample included people in the same age groups but exposed to TV for different times. Years of age and years of home exposure were two separate variables.

For many of our statistical analyses we used stepwise multiple regression. This measures the separate effects (as well as the combined effects) of several "potential predictors" on a dependent variable. For example, to predict "risk of heart attack" (the dependent variable), potential predictors would include sex, age, family history, weight, blood pressure, level of serum cholesterol, exercise, and cigarette smoking. Each one would make a separate contribution, and some would have more impact than others. Someone with many "risk factors," however, would have a greater risk of heart attack than someone with few predictors.

We used a standard set of nine to eleven potential predictor variables. Through stepwise multiple regression we examined their effects on hundreds of dependent variables (Kottak 1990). Our potential predictors included: gender, age, skin color, social class, education, income, religiosity, years of home TV exposure (HOMEEXPO), and current televiewing level (ATVHOURS). Multiple regression analysis measures the separate and independent influence of each predictor on the dependent variable (holding the others constant).

Our research design provided three different ways of measuring exposure to television: length of site exposure, length of individual exposure, and current individual (and household) viewing habits. (1) The first wave of TV sets with good reception reached our field sites in different years (from 1955 to 1984), providing a continuum of exposure among the communities. (2) Our respondents started watching television at different times (outside or inside the research site or their homes). (3) Our informants had different current viewing habits; in some households the set remained on almost all day; in others sets were absent, broken, or rarely turned on. Some people were heavy viewers; some watched rarely, others not at all. What kinds of effects of watching television were we able to document statistically?

The Media and the Demographic Transition

The first effect to be discussed was discovered by chance. I first considered the possibility that TV might be affecting Brazilian family size when I read an intriguing article in the *New York Times*. Based on interviews with Brazilians, that report used their impressions and speculations to assert that TV was influencing Brazilians to limit family size. Fortunately, I had the quantitative data to test this hypothesis—which my statistical results suggest has merit.

Our findings echo many other studies conducted throughout the world in showing that the strongest predictor of smaller family size is a woman's educational level. Our two television variables (ATVHOURS and especially HOMEEXPO), however, were better predictors of smaller family size than were many other social indicators, including income, class, and religiosity. This was true despite the fact that there has been little conscious use of television to get Brazilians to limit their progeny. The contraceptive effects of TV exposure have been totally unplanned. The mechanisms by which TV content and exposure influence family planning may be suggested, but further research is needed on the mechanisms behind the correlations.

In the four communities with the longest exposure to television the average woman had had a TV set in her home for fifteen years, and she had had 2.3 pregnancies. In the three communities in which TV had arrived most recently, the average woman had had a home set for four years, and she had had 5 pregnancies. Thus, length of site exposure is a useful predictor of reproductive histories. Of course, television exposure at a site is an aspect of that site's increasing overall access to external systems and resources, which usually include improved methods of contraception. But the predictive power of HOMEEXPO showed up not only when we compared sites but also within age cohorts, within sites, and among individual women in the total sample.[8]

What social mechanisms underlie these correlations? As the *New York Times* article mentioned, family planning opportunities (including contraception) are greater in Brazil now than they used to be. But, as Manoff (1994) notes, based on experience in Africa, Asia, and Latin America, family planning is not ensured by the availability of contraceptives. Popular demand for contraception has to be created, often through "social marketing"—planned multimedia campaigns (Manoff 1994).[9] In Brazil, however, there has been little direct use of TV to get people to limit their progeny. Because the contraceptive effects of television have nothing to do with policy, educational campaigns, or public service announcements, we may wonder how television may be encouraging Brazilians to plan smaller families.

First, we can note that Brazilian TV families have fewer children than traditional small-town Brazilians do. Narrative form and production costs limit the number of players in each *telenovela* to about fifty characters. *Telenovelas* are usually gender balanced and include three-generation extended families of different social classes (so that some of the main characters can "rise in life" by marrying up). These narrative conventions limit the number of young children per TV family. I think that a cultivation effect may operate as people get used to seeing, day after day, nuclear families smaller than the traditional ones in their towns. Furthermore, the aim of commercial television is to sell products and lifestyles. Brazilian TV families are routinely shown enjoying consumers' goods and leisured urban lives—to which viewers learn to aspire. *Telenovelas* may convey the idea that people can have lives like their characters' if they emulate their characters' apparent family planning.

I think that the effect of Brazilian television on family planning is a corollary of a more general teleprompted shift from traditional toward more liberal social attitudes. Further fieldwork is needed to determine how television actually works to influence reproductive choice and family planning.

Sex-Gender Attitudes

I suspect that television's cultivation effects are particularly strong when national productions are more popular than imports—as in the United States, Brazil, Japan, Mexico, India, Egypt, and Nigeria. It is not simply television as technology (as a medium) but also specific, recurrent, and culturally appropriate TV content (messages) that does the cultivating. Different themes and values dominate content in different nations, producing different effects.

Brazilian televiewing correlates consistently and strikingly with liberal views on sex-gender issues, as assessed in an index derived from ten questions. This was one of our firmest statistical confirmations of television's impact on attitudes. Television strongly influenced sex-gender views, independently of other intercorrelated predictor variables, such as gender, education, and income. The heavier and longer-exposed viewers were strikingly more liberal—less traditional in their opinions on such matters as whether women "belong at home," should work when their husbands earn well, should work when pregnant, should go to bars, should leave a husband they no longer love, should pursue men they like, and about whether men should cook and wash clothes and whether parents should talk to their children about sex. All these questions elicit TV-biased answers, in that Brazilian television (particularly *telenovelas*) depicts an urban-modern society in which sex-gender roles are less traditional than in small communities.

Are these effects or just correlations? That is, does Brazilian TV make people more liberal, or do already liberal people, seeking reinforcement for their views, simply watch more television? Do they look to TV and its urban-elite world for moral options that are missing, suppressed, or disapproved in their own, more traditional, towns? I have concluded that liberalization is both a correlation and an effect. There is a strong correlation between liberal social views and current viewing hours. Liberal small-town Brazilians may well watch more TV to validate personal views that the local setting suppresses. Confirming that long-term TV exposure also has an effect on Brazilians' attitudes, however, there is an even stronger correlation between years of home viewing by individuals and their liberal social views.

It is difficult to separate effects of televiewing from mere correlations when we use current viewing level as a predictor variable. Questions like the following always arise: Does television create fears about the outside world, or is it that already fearful people are more likely to stay home and watch more TV? Effects are clearer when length of home exposure can be measured. Logically, we can compare this predictor and its influence over time to education and its effects. If the cumulative effects of formal education increase with years of schooling, then it seems reasonable to assume some similar influence as a result of years of home exposure to television.

Heavy *telenovela* viewers are probably predisposed to liberal views. Over time, however, content, entering homes each day, reinforces those views. TV-biased and TV-reinforced attitudes spread as viewers take courage from the daily validation of their unorthodox (local) views in (national) programming. More and more townsfolk encounter nontraditional views and come to see them as normal.

Environmental Awareness and Risk Perception

In a more recent research project that I direct,[10] an international team is investigating the causes and extent of environmental awareness and environmentalist action, in relation to the media and through field studies at a series of Brazilian sites differently exposed to environmental hazards. Our main hypothesis is that: although an actual threat is necessary for risk perception, such perception does not arise inevitably through rational analysis of risk. Instead, environmental risk perception emerges from encounters involving local ethnoecologies,[11] imported ethnoecologies (often propagated by the media), and changing circumstances (including population growth, migration, and industrial expansion).

This research arose from our recognition that Brazilian economic development has proceeded in a society that has lacked generalized environmental awareness and effective ecological controls. Only in the 1980s did Brazilian political forces start emphasizing environmentalism, which remains a secondary (but growing) political force, with mainly urban support. Environmental awareness has been undeveloped outside the main cities.

In recent years nationally publicized ecological issues have included radioactive accidents, the burning of the Amazonian rain forest, the murder of labor leader Chico Mendes, and the effects of gold extraction, highway construction, and other intrusions of the world system on indigenous peoples and their territories. The media have also reported about the hazards posed by riverine mercury, industrial pollution, and inadequate waste disposal.

Our initial work—in two towns—focused on nuclear energy in relation to risk perception and environmentalism. The towns studied were Angra dos Reis and Ibirama. Angra dos Reis, in Rio de Janeiro state, is a seaside resort and has Brazil's only nuclear reactor. The people of Angra dos Reis have endured a series of rumors about various dangers from the reactor. They have protested at various stages of its construction, inauguration, and operation. Despite rumors and scares, Angra has never experienced anything approaching a nuclear accident, although the town has had its share of oil spills, water pollution, and other sanitation problems.

According to Rosane Prado (1990), our project researcher in Angra, the dominant local image of what has happened to the town is "beauty betrayed." With its picturesque seaside setting, Angra dos Reis has been a favorite resort for the elites of Rio. Along with the colonial port town of Paratí further south, Angra has kept much of its tourist appeal despite its ecological problems. Continued tourism in Angra illustrates how Brazilians, even elites, minimize environmental hazards, including a nuclear plant that has been widely publicized as hazardous.

We originally chose Ibirama, a town without evident environmental problems in a forested area of Santa Catarina state, as a control site, for comparison with Angra dos Reis and its hazards. (Alberto Costa has been doing anthropological research in Ibirama since 1985.) Recently, however, Ibirama's traditional timber industry has been confronted with environmental legislation prompted by the national concern over deforestation (Kottak and Costa 1993).[12]

For analysis of our quantitative data we used a standard set of eleven (potential) predictor variables to assess aspects of ecological awareness and risk perception. As in the TV study, we have used stepwise multiple regression, this time to examine the effects of these predictors on thirty-one measures of risk perception. Our eleven predictors are: site (living at a "high-risk" vs. a "low-risk" site), gender, age, skin color, social class, education, household income, religiosity, print media exposure, length of home TV exposure, and current televiewing level.

In our statistical results so far, the people of high-risk Angra dos Reis scored significantly higher on measures of risk perception than did the people in the control community (Ibirama). The people of Angra dos Reis from all social backgrounds had an in-depth knowledge of local, national, and international cases of environmental hazards and disasters. By contrast, only upper-class Ibiramenses with higher levels of education and more exposure to the media had comparable knowledge. These findings support the contention of traditional risk analysis that exposure to an environmental hazard increases risk perception.

Still, the people of at-risk Angra did not regard nuclear energy, on which their town's economy is partially dependent, as all bad. They were no more likely than the people of Ibirama to oppose economic development—for example, by calling industry disadvantageous. Nor were the people of Angra more likely to say "natural is better," "local life is worse now than it used to be," or "change here has been for the worse." Nor even did the questions "Is nuclear energy dangerous?" and "Does nuclear energy cause environmental pollution?" produce significant differences between our high-risk site and our control community.

Next we examined the role of the media. We wondered which was the better predictor of environmental awareness: television exposure or print media exposure.[13] Our statistical analysis has confirmed the prominent role of the media, particularly television, in fostering risk perception. In our combined sample (Angra and Ibirama) HOMEEXPO (years of exposure to television in one's home) was the best predictor of the opinion that the community is dangerous.[14] HOMEEXPO was also the strongest predictor of knowledge about extralocal environmental threats. Overall, tested against thirty-one measures of risk perception (nine indices and twenty-two individual variables), HOMEEXPO made eleven predictions, versus just three for our PRINT index.

TV stimulates risk perception, but a local threat has an additive effect. People who feel at risk enlarge their use of the media for information about all risks. We found in high-risk Angra that heightened local risk perception has stimulated greater use of all the media to obtain information about hazards.

Our Brazilian research so far also confirms that risk perception doesn't necessarily correlate with action or with participation in environmental groups. In Angra dos Reis most people are acutely aware of environmental dangers. But only those from the higher social classes join environmental organizations. In Ibirama membership in groups concerned with environmental protection is restricted to a few upper-class members of the local branch of the Green Party. This group's influence on local environmental awareness has been minor compared with that of television. Overall, people in Angra were no more likely than people in Ibirama to say they would like to participate in an ecological movement. But residents of Angra dos Reis were more likely to say that something should be done to prevent pollution as well as to know an ecology movement member.

Our study so far suggests that risk perception may be more developed in groups and cultures that are less endangered objectively. (Compare a fitness-obsessed member of the North American upper-middle class with an impoverished fisher from the highly polluted Brazilian town of Arembepe.) Brazil appears to have many more unregulated ecological hazards than the United States does, but Brazilians worry much less about them. Brazilian environmental awareness is most developed in places and groups that are most directly influenced by the media and by international environmental concerns and ecological mobilization, rather than among those who are most endangered.

Of course, the mass media also hone risk perception in the United States. Seeking audience-grabbing stories, news agencies focus on every conceivable "risk"—from Alar-tainted apples and Chilean grapes to poisoned Tylenol. Also, the rise of cable TV, talk radio, and twenty-four-hour newscasting has blurred the distinction between the national and the local, bringing all reported threats closer to home. Constant rebroadcasting magnifies risk perception. Geographical distance is obscured by the national media and their barrage of information; a threat in Milwaukee or Buffalo is perceived as one nearby. This is yet another example of television's role in focusing attention on national-level events (Hirsch 1979).

Cultural Imperialism
Cultural imperialism refers to the spread or advance of one culture at the expense of others, or its imposition on other cultures, which it modifies, replaces, or destroys—usually because of differential economic or political influence. One illustration would be the advance of a national culture at the expense of regional and local ones (Bourdieu 1982). Another would be a colonial situation, such as when children in the French colonial empire were taught French history, language, and culture from

standard textbooks also used in France. Tahitians, Malagasy, Vietnamese, and Senegalese learned the French language and culture by reciting from books about "our ancestors the Gauls."

Ironically, many contemporary French intellectuals, seemingly forgetting France's colonialist past, are quick to complain about U.S. cultural imperialism. In 1992 French intellectuals protested the opening of Euro Disney as a threat to French and European culture, and the former French minister of culture Jack Lang has lamented the extent to which U.S. films and TV programs dominate popular culture in many countries.

Studies of the media in many cultures show that the matter isn't as simple as the French intellectuals imagine. People aren't passive victims of cultural imperialism. Contemporary people—often with considerable creativity—constantly revise, rework, resist, and reject the messages they get from external systems. To understand the role of the media in culture change, it is important to recognize that meaning is not inherent or imposed but, rather, locally manufactured. People assign their own meanings and value to the texts, messages, and products they receive. Those meanings reflect their cultural backgrounds and experiences. When forces from world centers enter new societies they are indigenized—modified to fit the local culture (see Ginsburg 1991; Weatherford 1990). This is true of cultural forces as different as fast food, music, housing styles, science, terrorism, celebrations, and political ideas and institutions (Appadurai 1990).

The notion of cultural imperialism is flawed because it views people as victims rather than as creative agents in their own transformation. For example, Michaels (1986) found *Rambo* to be a popular movie among aborigines in the deserts of central Australia, who had manufactured their own meanings from the film. Their "reading" was very different from the one imagined by the movie's creators and by most Americans. The native Australians saw Rambo as a representative of the Third World battling the white officer class. This reading expressed their negative feelings about white paternalism and existing race relations. The native Australians also created tribal ties and kin links between Rambo and the prisoners he was rescuing. All this made sense, based on their experience. Native Australians are disproportionately represented in Australian jails, and their most likely liberator would be someone with a personal link to them. These readings of *Rambo* were relevant meanings produced from the text, not by it (Fiske 1989).

Cultural Resistance

Many critics worry that modern technology, including the mass media, is killing off traditional cultures by homogenizing products to reach more people. But others see an important countervailing role for modern technology in allowing social groups (local cultures) to express themselves, and thus in disseminating particular subcultures (Marcus and Fisher 1986:122). Modern radio and TV, for example, constantly bring local happenings (e.g., a "chicken festival" in Iowa) to the attention of a larger public. The North American media play a role in stimulating local activities of many sorts. Similarly in Brazil, as in many nations, local practices, celebrations, and performances are changing in the context of outside forces, including the mass media and tourism.

In the Brazilian town of Arembepe TV coverage has stimulated participation in a traditional annual performance, the Chegança. This is a fishers' dance-play that reenacts the Portuguese discovery of Brazil. Arembepeiros have traveled to the state capital to perform the Chegança before television cameras, for a TV program featuring traditional performances from many rural communities. Here one sees television's role in allowing social groups to express themselves and in publicizing local cultures.

One national Brazilian Sunday night variety program (Fantástico) is especially popular in rural areas because it shows such local events. In several towns along the Amazon River annual folk ceremonies are now staged more lavishly for TV cameras. In the Amazon town of Parantíns, for example, boatloads of tourists arriving any time of year are shown a videotape of the town's annual Bumba Meu Boi festival. This is a costumed performance mimicking bullfighting, parts of which have been shown on Fantástico. This pattern, in which communities preserve, revive, and intensify the scale of traditional ceremonies to perform for TV and tourists, is expanding.

Brazilian television has also played a top-down role, however, by spreading the popularity of national (and international) holidays, like Carnival and Christmas (Kottak 1990). TV has aided the national spread of Carnival beyond its traditional urban centers, especially Rio de Janeiro. Still, local reactions to the nationwide broadcasting of Carnival and its trappings (elaborate parades, costumes, and frenzied dancing) are not simple or uniform responses to external stimuli. Like other syncretisms, these new forms of popular expression are cultural creations that develop from the interplay of local, regional, national, and international forces.

Rather than direct adoption of Carnival, or rote imitation of it, local Brazilians respond in various ways. These reactions include "stimulus diffusion" and "creative opposition." Stimulus diffusion describes the process by which a group modifies a custom by adopting images and behavior associated with an external practice, without borrowing the practice itself. We see stimulus diffusion when Brazilians don't take up Carnival itself but, instead, modify their local festivities to fit Carnival images. Creative opposition occurs when people change their behavior as they consciously and actively avoid or spurn an external image or practice. We see creative opposition when local Brazilians deliberately reject Carnival, sometimes by celebrating traditional local festivals on a previously unimagined scale, sometimes by rejecting certain local practices perceived as similar to the disdained external practice.

In Brazilian towns national Carnival coverage seems more often to inspire stimulus diffusion than direct borrowing through simple imitation. Local groups work hard not on Carnival per se but on incorporating its elements and themes in their own ceremonies. Some of these have grown in scale, in imitation of Carnival celebrations shown on national TV. But local reactions can also be negative, even hostile. One example is Arembepe, where Carnival has never been important, probably because of its calendrical closeness to the main local festival, which is held in February to honor Saint Francis of Assisi. In the past villagers couldn't afford to celebrate both occasions. Now, not only do the people of Arembepe reject Carnival; they are also increasingly hostile to their own main festival. Arembepeiros resent the fact that Saint Francis has become "an outsiders' event," because it draws thousands of tourists to Arembepe each February. The villagers think that commercial interests and outsiders have appropriated Saint Francis.

In creative opposition many Arembepeiros now say they like and participate more in the traditional June festivals honoring Saint John, Saint Peter, and Saint Anthony. In the past these were observed on a much smaller scale than was Saint Francis. Arembepeiros celebrate them now with a new vigor and enthusiasm, as they react to outsiders and their celebrations, real and televised.

The Media in a Translocal World

Globalization describes the accelerating links between nations and people in a world system connected economically, politically, and by modern media and transportation. Arjun Appadurai (1990:1) characterizes today's world as a "translocal" "interactive system" that is "strikingly new." Whether as refugees, migrants, tourists, pilgrims, proselytizers, laborers, business people, development workers, employees of nongovernmental organizations (NGOs), politicians, soldiers, sports figures, or media-borne images, people travel more than ever.

The electronic mass media have come to play a key role in preserving ethnic and national identities among people who lead transnational lives. As groups move, they stay linked to one another and to their homeland through the media. Diasporas have enlarged the markets for media and travel services targeted at specific ethnic, national, or religious audiences. In 1992, for a fee, a Public Broadcasting System (PBS) station in Fairfax, Virginia, offered more than thirty hours a week to immigrant groups in the Washington, D.C., area, to make programs in their own languages. "Somali Television," for instance, is a half-hour program with about five thousand Somali viewers, who can see their flag and hear their language on TV each week. Starting the program is a reading from the Koran, with clips of mosques from around the world (thus contributing, too, to a transnational Islamic identity). Formerly, an entertainment segment featured folk dances and Somali music. As Somalia's civil war dragged on, the entertainment segment was replaced in 1992 by images of bony children and parched countryside. "Somali Television" also features obituaries, rallies, and a segment called "Somalia Today," which has interviews with diplomats, immigration lawyers, and travel agents discussing airfares. Guests represent various tribes and subclans. "Somali Television" became a vital link between emigrant Somalis and their homeland. This was particularly true before images of Somalia became widespread on network news in late 1992 and early 1993 (*New York Times*, 18 December 1992).

Contemporary global culture is driven by flows of people, technology, finance, images, information, and ideology (Appadurai 1990). Business, technology, and the media have increased the craving for commodities and images throughout the world. This has forced nation-states, including "Iron Curtains," to open to a global culture of consumption.

Almost everyone today participates in this culture. Few people have never seen a T-shirt advertising a Western product. Michael Jackson's "Beat It" blasts through the streets of Rio de Janeiro, while taxi drivers from Toronto to Madagascar play Brazilian lambada tapes. Peasants and tribal people participate in the modern world system not only because they (willingly or unwillingly) work for cash but also because their products and images are appropriated by world capitalism. They are commercialized by others (like the San in the movie *The Gods Must Be Crazy*). And, seizing their own destinies, often helped by outsiders, indigenous peoples also market their own images and products through outlets like the Body Shop and Cultural Survival. Some social commentators see contemporary flows of people, technology, finance, information, and ideology as a cultural imperialist steamroller. This view ignores the selective, synthesizing activity of human beings as they deal with external forces, images, and messages. Anthropological studies show that domination is usually met by resistance and that cultural diffusion is a creative process.

Anthropology and the Media: Prospects, Issues, and Questions

Although several studies have been done, media anthropology remains an emerging field. This paper has described relations between the media and the cultural forces at the local, regional, national, and international levels. Certain findings of American TV researchers have been assessed using the Brazilian case—an especially relevant one given that nation's size, the national extent of commercial TV, the dominance of local productions, and the mass impact on popular culture of the world's most watched commercial television network (Globo).

General and specific questions remain, however, about the relation between media and other cultural forces and the role of the media in processes of social transformation. Some key general questions are these:

1. In what ways can perspectives from traditional and contemporary cultural anthropology (including the linkages methodology discussed in the last chapter) shed further light on the content and impact of television and other mass media?

2. What lessons can be learned from a range of studies of the sociocultural context of media (a) creation, (b) distribution, (c) reception, and (d) impact?
3. What cross-cultural generalizations may be made about the media in relation to society and social change?

To provide a foundation for such generalizations, and to promote better understanding of the universal, general, and specific relationships between culture and the media, some concrete questions and lines of investigation may be suggested. What unifying and divisive roles do the media play in promoting social identities? We have seen that the media play a role in promoting national identity, but print, radio, and television may also be used to foster various kinds of "identity politics" and to encourage ethnic conflict within nations. We may also ask what role the media may play in creating or strengthening identities beyond the national level, for example, among members of the same religion, occupation, or gender? How do the media challenge traditional institutions and authorities, including governments, churches, schools, and kin groups?

What determines the kinds of programs and messages that are produced, received, accepted, reworked, and/or rejected in particular countries and cultures? What makes foreign messages acceptable and popular in some places, while local productions dominate in others? How do cultural, social, economic, and political factors interplay in determining such preferences?

To what extent are the findings discussed in this paper replicable and recurrent in countries other than the United States or Brazil. For example, how often and how widely does television heighten risk perception, cultivate distrust of traditional authorities, stimulate political protest and action, spur consumption, transform celebrations, and affect public health and family planning.

Despite the emergence of media anthropology as a subfield, most generalizations about the media reported by the media continue to be based on unsupported, ethnocentric judgments, or on a narrow range of research in North America—usually psychologically oriented. This ethnocentrism in the evaluation of the media and their influence on society and social change can be remedied through continued cross-cultural research.

NOTES

1. The Department of Social Anthropology of the National Museum, a division of the Federal University of Rio de Janeiro, cooperated in this project by offering Conrad Kottak an institutional affiliation and by providing field researchers Rosane Prado and Alberto Costa and Brazilian liaison Roberto DaMatta. Our four primary research sites, studied mainly in 1985, were representative communities in the states of Santa Catarina (Ibirama), São Paulo (Cunha), Bahia (Arembepe), and Pará (Gurupá). Alberto Costa worked in Ibirama, Rosane Prado in Cunha, Richard Pace in Gurupá, and four fieldworkers in Arembepe (Iraní Escolano, Pennie Magee, Isabel Kottak, and Conrad Kottak).

2. We used two printed interview schedules, for more than one thousand eight hundred structured interviews, ranging over hundreds of variables. We used one schedule for households (n = 847) and another for individuals (n = 1032).

3. The only communities in our study with significant traditions of reading were Ibirama, settled initially by Germans, including many Protestants, and Americana-Santa Barbara, whose American settlers were mainly Protestants.

4. In the overall sample current viewing hours was the second of only two predictor variables entered (after education, which had a much greater effect) in our standard multiple regression equation, with the reading index (based on whether the respondent regularly reads books plus magazines plus newspapers) as the dependent variable. Current viewing hours produced a final beta of .11, with a final multiple R of .64. The predictive value of current daily televiewing was even more dramatic in Cunha, where there is higher literacy and greater print availability. There current viewing hours had a final beta of .25 and produced an R^2 change of 4 percent. (The final multiple R was .66.)

5. Current viewing hours was the second of seven predictor variables entered in our standard multiple regression equation, with a yes response to "Do you have a savings account?" as the dependent variable. In order of predictive value of the variables, people with savings accounts tended to be: of higher local class, heavier viewers, well educated, male, religious, light-skinned, and to have (controlling for associated variables just listed) *lower* household income. Current viewing hours had a final beta of .14. (The final multiple R was .35).

6. In Cunha, for example, the average female heavy viewer had nursed her last infant just eight months, versus thirteen months for medium viewers and eighteen months for light viewers.

7. Because there were radical differences in average income from site to site, we could not simply divide our total sample by income, since the more cash-oriented sites (Ibirama, Niterói, and Americana) would have been drastically overrepresented in the richer half. Rather, our first procedure was to divide the sample for each site into higher- and lower-income groups. The six higher segments were then added together, as were the lower ones, to form two income-differentiated samples of 400+ and 500+ individuals, respectively.

8. HOMEEXPO is the best predictor of fewer pregnancies in Niterói, Angra, and among wealthier women. HOMEEXPO is the next best predictor (after education) of fewer progeny in the total sample.

9. Family planning succeeded in Bangladesh only after a social marketing campaign stressing contraception but was aimed mainly at husbands (Manoff 1994).

10. Pilot work for this research began in 1989, with modest funding from three agencies: the Michigan Memorial Phoenix Project (project no. 714—The Social Context and Impact of Nuclear Energy in Brazil) and two Brazilian agencies, ANPOCS and Faperj. Most of this research has been supported by the National Science Foundation and by the Office of Forestry, Environment, and Natural Resources, Bureau of Science and Technology, of the U.S. Agency for International Development, under NSF Grant no. BNS-9112030 (8/15/91–7/31/94).

11. Every society has an ethnoecology—a traditional set of environmental perceptions and a cultural model of the environment and its relation to people and society.

12. When Americans (and even Brazilians) think of deforestation in Brazil, they almost always have the Amazon in mind. More than 90 percent of the original Amazon forest remains, however, compared with less than 10 percent of the Atlantic forest, which once fringed the Brazilian coast. Much of the surviving Atlantic forest is in the state of Santa Catarina. That small state has half of 1 percent of all the forest in the world.

13. We used the number of years the respondent has watched TV at home (HOMEEXPO) and average daily televiewing hours (ATVHOURS) to assess the impact of television. We devised an index called PRINT to measure the respondent's use of books, magazines, and newspapers.

14. Ibirama and Angra does Reis have had electricity and thus local access to television for about the same length of time, but in each town some people have had TVs in their homes longer than others.

REFERENCES

Abu-Lughod, L.
    1993   Finding a Place for Islam: Egyptian Television Serials and the National Interest. *Public Culture* 5(3): 493–513.

Anderson, B.
    1991   *Imagined Communities: Reflections on the Origin and Spread of Nationalism,* rev. ed. London: Verso.

Appadurai, A.
    1990   Disjuncture and Difference in the Global Cultural Economy. *Public Culture* 2(2): 1–24.
    1991   Global Ethnoscapes: Notes and Queries for a Transnational Anthropology. In *Recapturing Anthropology: Working in the Present,* ed.

R. G. Fox, 191–210. Santa Fe: School of American Research Advanced Seminar Series.

Bourdieu, P.
   1982 *Ce Que Parler Veut Dire.* Paris: Fayard.

Comstock, George, Steven Chaffee, Natan Katzman, Maxwell McCombs, and Donald Roberts
   1978 *Television and Human Behavior.* New York: Columbia University Press.

DaMatta, R.
   1987 *A Casa e a Rua.* Rio de Janeiro: Guanabara.
   1991 *Carnivals, Rogues, and Heroes: An Interpretation of the Brazilian Dilemma.* Translated from the Portuguese by John Drury. Notre Dame, Ind.: University of Notre Dame Press.

Fiske, John
   1989 *Understanding Popular Culture.* Boston: Unwin-Hyman.

Gerbner, George, and Larry Gross
   1976 Living with Television: The Violence Profile. *Journal of Communication* 26(2): 173–99.

Gerbner, G., L. Gross, M. Jackson-Beeck, S. Jeffries-Fox, and N. Signorielli
   1978 Cultural Indicators: Violence Profile no. 9. *Journal of Communication* 28(3): 176–207.

Gerbner, G., L. Gross, M. Morgan, and N. Signorielli
   1980 The "Mainstreaming" of America: Violence Profile no. 11. *Journal of Communication* 30(3): 10–29.

Ginsburg, F.
   1991 Indigenous Media: Faustian Contract or Global Village? *Cultural Anthropology* 6(1): 92–112.

Granzberg, G., and J. Steinbring, eds.
   1980 *Television and the Canadian Indian.* Winnipeg: University of Winnipeg.

Gray, Jerry
   1986 With a Few Exceptions, Television in Africa Fails to Educate and Enlighten. *Ann Arbor News,* 8 December, C2.

Gutis, P. S.
   1987 American TV Isn't Traveling So Well. *New York Times.*

Hirsch, Paul M.
   1979 The Role of Television and Popular Culture in Contemporary Society. In *Television: The Critical View,* ed. Horace Newcomb, 249–79. New York: Oxford University Press.

Hood, Stuart
   1987 *On Television,* 3d ed. London: Pluto.

Hujanen, T.
   1976 *Immigrant Broadcasting and Migration Control in Western Europe.* Tampere, Fin.: Institute of Journalism and Mass Communication, University of Tampere.

Ivy, M.
    1988   Tradition and Difference in the Japanese Mass Media. *Public Culture* 1(1): 21–29.

Kottak, Conrad P.
    1990   *Prime-Time Society: An Anthropological Analysis of Television and Culture.* Belmont, Calif.: Wadsworth.
    1992   *Assault on Paradise: Social Change in a Brazilian Village,* 2d ed. New York: McGraw-Hill.

Kottak, Conrad P., ed.
    1982   *Researching American Culture: A Guide for Student Anthropologists.* Ann Arbor: University of Michigan Press.

Kottak, Conrad, and Alberto Costa
    1993   Ecological Awareness, Environmentalist Action, and International Conservation Strategy. *Human Organization* 52(4): 335–43.

Lull, James
    1991   *China Turned On: Television, Reform, and Resistance.* New York: Routledge.

Lull, James, ed.
    1988   *World Families Watch Television.* Newbury Park, Calif.: Sage.

Lyons, A. P.
    1990   The Television and the Shrine: Towards a Theoretical Model for the Study of Mass Communication in Nigeria. *Visual Anthropology* 3(4): 429–56.

Lyons, H. D.
    1990   Television in Contemporary Urban Life: Benin City, Nigeria. *Visual Anthropology* 3(4): 411–28.

Manaev, O.
    1991   The Influence of Western Radio on the Democratization of Soviet Youth. *Journal of Communication* 41(2): 72–91.

Mankekar, P.
    1993   National Texts and Gendered Lives: An Ethnography of Television Viewers in India. *American Ethnologist* 20(3): 543–63.

Manoff, Richard K.
    1994   How Family Planning Came to Bangladesh. Letter to the editor. *New York Times,* 16 January, 4–16.

Marcus, G. E., and M. M. J. Fischer
    1986   *Anthropology as Cultural Critique: An Experimental Moment in the Human Sciences.* Chicago: University of Chicago Press.

Michaels, E.
    1986   *The Aboriginal Invention of Television in Central Australia, 1982–1986.* Canberra: Australian Institute of Aboriginal Studies.

Miranda, Ricardo, and Carlos Alberto M. Pereira
    1983   *Televisão: O Nacional e o Popular na Cultura Brasileira.* São Paulo: Brasiliense.

Morrison, Patt
    1986   MTV with a Twist. *Ann Arbor News,* 14 December, B3.

New York Times
    1992   Alexandria Journal: TV Program for Somalis Is a Rare Unifying Force. 18 December.

Pace, Richard
    1993   First Time Televiewing in Amazônia: Television Acculturation in Gurupá, Brazil. *Ethnology* 32(2): 187–206.

Prado, Rosane M.
    1990   Beauty Betrayed: Risk Perception at a Nuclear Reactor Site in Brazil. Paper presented at the eighty-ninth annual meeting, American Anthropological Association, New Orleans.

Saldich, Anne Rawley
    1979   *Electronic Democracy: Television's Impact on the American Political Process.* New York: Praeger.

Signorielli, N., L. Gross, and M. Morgan
    1982   Violence in Television Programs: Ten Years Later. In *Television and Behavior: Ten Years of Scientific Progress and Implications for the Eighties,* vol. 2. *Technical Reports,* ed. David Pearl et al., 158–73. Washington, D.C.: National Institute of Mental Health, U.S. Government Printing Office.

Spitulnik, D.
    1993   Anthropology and Mass Media. *Annual Review of Anthropology* 22:293–315.

Straubhaar, Joseph D.
    1982   The Development of the Telenovela as the Pre-eminent Form of Popular Culture in Brazil. *Studies in Latin American Popular Culture* 1:138–50.

Weatherford, E.
    1990   Native Visions: The Growth of Indigenous Media. *Aperture* 119:58–61.

Chapter 6

Anthropology, Human Rights, and Social Transformation

Ellen Messer

The twentieth century has witnessed the creation of more states in more places than ever before. In the process of state formation, the rights of individuals and groups have been severely curtailed. . . . During the next century, basic human rights probably will be generally agreed upon by the states, in many cases the very states that violate human rights. If anthropologists are to have any influence over the standards that are adopted, they must begin to raise the issues increasingly and in more visible arenas.
—Jason Clay (1988a)

Anthropology has had no impact on human rights.
—Ana-Magdalena Hurtado (1990)

Since the close of World War II the United Nations (UN) has been assembling declarations, legislation, and enforcement mechanisms to promote human rights. Both the ongoing efforts to establish a global community and to base membership on a universal but evolving standard of values constitute perhaps the greatest social transformation of this century and a process in which the leaders and societies of emerging industrializing nations have played no small part. Representatives of many different national and religious traditions have met together to promulgate human rights by consensus. They have affirmed that there must be some basic standard of human rights, although they have disagreed on what specific rights, or protections against violations, entail. Cultural values diverge around even the central question of who is counted as a human being. In view of such fundamental misunderstandings many question how universal standards can be promoted (see, e.g., Adegbite 1968, for an example of Third World views; Clay 1988a,b, for a critical anthropological appraisal).

Both human rights activists and legal experts (e.g., Tomasevski 1989; Alston 1990a) and UN agencies charged with implementing human rights policies, such as the UN Economic, Social, and Cultural Organization (UNESCO), demand more information on pluralistic conceptualizations of "universal" human rights, in order to improve formulations, instruments, and reporting. As the UN expands to include Third World and newly independent states, the urgency grows to learn more about moral norms and civil standards of behavior in different cultural contexts, so that national, regional, community, and religious leaders can be brought into discussions of evolving human rights standards. Further investigation is needed of the contexts in which rules and standards are applied, especially which individuals are counted as full human beings or persons and who are outcasts and why. A principal limitation of the UN human rights documents and machinery has been their failure to penetrate below, or to look outside, the level of the state to identify human rights notions as well as sources of violation. The role for anthropologists in clarifying human rights would seem to be obvious.

Anthropologists and Human Rights

Why Anthropologists Seem to Have Been Uninvolved in Human Rights
In view of anthropologists' contributions to formulating these human rights questions and answers, anthropologists should have been integrally involved and interested in human rights. Two reasons are often cited for their apparent uninvolvement: (1) the burden of cultural relativism (see, e.g., Downing and Kushner 1988); and (2) their greater interest in indigenous rights and the rights of collectivities over and against the rights of the individual specified in the original human rights concept and documents. Both are evident in the official statement of the American Anthropological Association (AAA) in 1947, which rejected the notion of (universal) human rights. This statement, with these sentiments, then contributed to the impression both inside and outside of anthropology that anthropologists have been uninterested in human rights (e.g., Downing and Kushner 1988a,b; Renteln 1988a,b). Another reason, cited by the editors of *Human Rights and Anthropology,* for anthropologists' disinterest in human rights (a view contradicted at least in part by the extensive bibliography of the volume) is the political sensitivity of doing fieldwork. Anthropologists reporting human rights abuses implicitly or explicitly question the politi-

cal legitimacy of sovereign states and national notions of progress. In so doing, they imperil the continued fieldwork of anthropologists in particular political contexts and locations and their behind-the-scenes advocacy on behalf of the peoples they study.

Even with such constraints anthropologists still must explain why we have published so few comparative studies of human rights formulations or the ways different societies establish guidelines for conduct. How do concepts of "rights" and "obligations" translate into codes of behavior? Or how do notions of "personhood" and "human being" create categories of privileged or underprivileged, respectively protected or denied protection under law at multiple levels in plural societies? Anthropologists could be contributing to better international legislation and monitoring instruments (Downing and Kushner 1988) in a world that human rights legal experts recognize to be increasingly pluralistic and marked by the need to protect collective as well as individual rights (e.g., Crawford 1988; Alston 1990a).

Reciprocally, constraints of cultural relativism and national politics do not explain why anthropologists do not refer more to the human rights framework in theoretical or policy-oriented analyses of social transformation. And anthropologists are only beginning to draw on human rights rhetoric and instruments in their advocacy for particular economic, social, and cultural rights to land, to food, to health, and to self-determination. Anthropologists could be contributing to international formulations and reporting mechanisms that might help make such rights enforceable (see Zalaquett 1984). In this case constraints lie not only with anthropologists but also with the existing reporting mechanisms of the UN and nongovernment organizations (NGOs) that up until the present have preferred to deal mainly or exclusively with civil and political rights of individuals and not to incorporate socioeconomic, development, or indigenous rights into their reporting framework.

Where Anthropologists Have Contributed or Might Contribute to Human Rights

Alternatively, the viewpoint that anthropologists have been uninterested in human rights may mask the considerable involvement of anthropologists, and adoption of anthropological principles, in the evolving human rights debate. Boas and Durkheim, along with the students they educated, demonstrated utmost concern over definitions of human beings, how sociocultural units defined individual and group identities, and the behaviors that followed from such classifications. Margaret Mead was centrally involved in the construction and signing of the 1948 Universal Declaration of Human Rights (Newman 1989). Individual anthropologists, both prior to and following the declaration, have been active in promoting the rights of indigenous peoples, the rights of workers, the rights of women, and the rights of other oppressed groups (e.g., Kuper 1982, 1986; Stavenhagen 1990).

As a discipline, anthropology continually has pressed for better cognizance and appreciation of the multiple human rights standards existing in different cultures and the utilization of these understandings to improve global conceptualizations and implementation (e.g., Schirmer, Renteln, and Weisberg 1988; UNESCO 1987). Promoting awareness of the value of cultural diversity as a prerequisite for the survival of the global community and the human species has been a separate but related human rights task (Lévi-Strauss 1952; Barnett 1988).

Anthropologists also have shaped human rights rhetoric and instruments as, drawing on cross-cultural studies, they question whether particular moral concepts or rights and obligations are universal or culturally relative and further explicate the dimensions of inequality by which states or groups exclude individuals or collectivities from human rights protections on the basis of race, language, or other cultural grouping. They also help formulate the special human rights protections needed by those groups that are especially vulnerable to abuses, such as indigenous peoples, migrants, refugees, women, children, and the elderly. They assist also in clarifying the rights to health, land, water, food, and freedom from all types of violence, including genocide, ethnocide, torture, and slavery (Schirmer, Renteln, and Weisberg 1988). In sum, the alternative viewpoint accepted here is: anthropologists have been very active in human rights but could be even more active.

In view of past activities this chapter considers additional areas in which anthropologists might contribute to human rights policy, planning, and implementation. A first challenge is to formulate more precisely the concepts of "human" and "person," in order to raise awareness of the dynamics by which exclusion and violence prevail in situations of ethnic polarization. These anthropological understandings of human classification might well be used to predict and redress the political, economic, and sociocultural dimensions of human rights abuses.

A second concern is to promote the implementation of economic, social, and cultural rights, along with the so-called solidarity, people's, or third generation *collective* rights to development, clean environment, and peaceful existence, which emerged in discussions by Third World nations in the 1980s (see Crawford 1988).

A third issue is to explicate the linkages among institutions and values that tie together ideas and instruments of human rights at various social and institutional levels. Political philosophers (e.g., Falk 1980, 1988) tend to see human rights as growing out of either "statist" or "indigenous" frameworks, but these often prove mutually contradictory or at best incongruous. States legislate certain rights, such as the right to food through food security legislation, only to be contradicted at the local level, where regional officials may not implement policies fully or equitably or where indigenous norms may lead to neglect of certain social outcasts. Anthropologists offer frameworks and data to systematize discussions of how rights are conceptualized and obligations assumed or abrogated at different social levels or by different social institutions.

A fourth and overarching issue is to analyze the evolution of human rights rhetoric and institutions. Human rights constitutes the world's first universal ideology (see Weissbrodt 1988:1), but the words and concepts keep changing over time. How has the existence of a body of human rights literature contributed to formulations of human rights concepts and expressions at local, regional, religious, and national levels? How can human rights rhetoric be formulated so as to enable local people to voice common concerns? In sum, how can rhetoric be transformed into action? What is the process by which values, rights, and obligations are translated into action across social levels?

To place such transformations in context, I begin the discussion by tracing the development of human rights legislation historically, against a 1940s background of cultural relativism. I then proceed to consider notions of human being and personhood, as these are expressed in collective and individual rights and obligations. The final sections suggest the various ways in which anthropologists continue to be involved in human rights policy; in the formulation of plural cultural understandings relating to definitions of rights and definitions of human beings; and in the international efforts to secure certain rights, such as a universal right to freedom from hunger.

The United Nations and Human Rights

By human rights we refer here to the Universal Declaration of Human Rights (1948), the International Covenants on Civil and Political Rights, and on Economic Social, and Cultural Rights (1966), additional UN Conventions against all forms of discrimination (racist and cultural); protocols for protection of rights of the especially vulnerable migrant, refugee, and besieged populations; stated protections for the rights of indigenous, minority, or other culturally threatened groups; and attempts to formulate universal protections for women and children. We include the standards of human rights promoted through various UN agencies: the right to work and freedom of association (the International Labor Organization [ILO]), the right to culture (UNESCO), the right to health (World Health Organization [WHO]), and the right to freedom from hunger (Food and Agriculture Organization [FAO]; World Food Programme [WFP]), etc. Also included are a set of solidarity rights related to peace, socioeconomic security, and environment, which are implemented by additional legal instruments and agencies (Zalaquett 1984), and rights of indigenous peoples.

Drafting of a common set of human rights standards began in 1946, in the aftermath of World War II and the Holocaust. The Nuremberg trials in particular intensified a desire by Western philosophical and legal scholars to reaffirm concepts of natural rights and the rights of man and citizen, which had been legal beacons in the history of emancipation in Western parliamentary democracies (Zalaquett 1981).[1] Representatives from the many non-Western or nondemocratic nations that were to become the United Nations accepted the initiative on human rights as an outgrowth of a universal tradition[2] or an international set of standards to which they might contribute.

Three Generations of Rights

Professionals working in the human rights fields, principally scholars and activists in international law and political philosophy, have always seen themselves as creating a universal moral standard, a system of values, on which all can agree (Zalaquett 1981; U.N. 1988). As a result of plural contributions into international rights constructions, human rights notions and covenants generally are viewed as having evolved in three stages: (1) civil and political rights; (2) economic, social, and cultural rights; and (3) special human development issues relating to human rights. A fourth stage of indigenous rights is currently evolving.

The first set of rights sought to guarantee all human beings political freedom of expression, movement, and person. Civil and political rights drew on the liberal tradition of Western parliamentary democracies and the universal traditions of rights expressed in some fashion in all societies and governments. The second set of rights formulated guarantees to employment and fair working conditions, a standard of living that would ensure health, well-being, and social security, education, participation in the cultural life of the community, and the special rights of motherhood and childhood. These economic, social, and cultural rights drew on the distinct Marxist-socialist and welfare state conception of rights—namely, that citizens have rights in a state, rather than against it. Strictly speaking, socialist governments never accepted the notion of natural rights, although they signed the documents. They instead promoted the notion of economic, social, and cultural rights, the legal instruments for which the United States, among other nations, signed but never ratified (Alston 1990b).

The third generation of emerging rights addressed: (1) peace and disarmament; (2) protection of the environment and natural resources; (3) the search for a just economic order; and (4) freedom from extreme want. African national leaders who rejected the so-called universalism of civil-political rights as ethnocentrically Western (e.g., Zvogbo 1979; Legesse 1980)[3] interpreted these alternative rights (to development) as a logical corollary to political rights of self-determination, while international lawyers, promoting the human rights framework, pragmatically interpreted the formulation of such a third generation of rights to be a logical corollary of the diversity and dynamics of international law and society that is part of the UN human rights system (e.g., Alston 1990a). Notwithstanding some initial protest that such derivative rights compromise and gut the human rights concept (e.g., Donnelly 1984), this third generation of so-called solidarity rights has gradually received formalization in regional and finally international UN treaties. Moreover, the rhetoric of human rights has changed in recent years from clarifying how the three "generations" are conceptually distinct to orchestrating their harmonics (Mayor 1990). Indigenous rights constitute yet a fourth generation, which certifies people's and community rights alongside those of the individual. All these discussions of "what are rights?" and which rights take precedence in any society also raise serious discussion of who is included in the category "human" modifying the rights concept.

Human Rights and Human Classification

Discussions over the derivation, legitimacy, or universality of human rights argue over whether there exists a universal concept of individual and natural man, or human beings as human beings apart from their social context. A twenty-year perspective on human rights in 1966 mentions that, ultimately, notions of human rights can be compared cross-culturally by evaluating what are the duties of the more fortunate to improve conditions of the underprivileged (Glean 1966; Raphael 1966). Of particular concern is how value systems affect who is counted as a person and, therefore, a beneficiary of legal rights and privileges. But there has been curiously little discussion specifically on issues of human classification within the societies (global, national, community) that must accept and implement those rights. Few discussants mention that the enlightened civil and political tradition of Western parliamentary democracies excluded initially at least women, slaves, and non-property-owning males as full members of the dominant society and that some of the most vocal proponents of human rights declarations were from South African nations, which excluded blacks, and Near Eastern nations, which excluded members of minority religious or ethnic groups from citizenship (Adegbite 1968). Throughout the history of human rights implementation national governments flagrantly abused human rights, although they had signed the treaties and covenants, and the institutions and nations that had agreed to protect human rights failed to intervene (e.g., Adegbite 1968; Kuper 1977, 1982; Jacobs 1984).

Beyond political expediency the reasons for such omissions can be found also in the international legal framework. International legal scholars did not deal with the thorny issue of how personhood and citizenry might be defined within nations. Instead, they formulated possible abuses against various classes of persons in the international arena and left internal human classification issues (at least initially) to national governments. Human rights formulations drew on three traditions in international law: the abolition of slavery;[4] humanitarian law, specifically, how to protect the human rights of prisoners and noncombatants held captive in war zones;[5] and statutes on the Protection of Minorities.[6] Provisions against genocide and the violation of cultural rights and for protection of migrants and refugees that dealt with the rights of those who might be abused as nonpersons within the statist framework constituted additional innovative legislation by separate commissions. Codes singled out Gypsies, ethnic Slavs, females, and minors for protection and suggest how, by international mandate, the UN was trying to create the terms for social inclusion. Demands for minority rights eventually coalesced into demands for solidarity rights, cultural rights, and indigenous rights. Separate legislation has also promoted the rights of women, children, and the elderly. But these international compromises have been worked out in contexts of considerable debate, disagreement, and strife—and there are few mechanisms for enforcement beyond moral persuasion, sanctions, or embarrassment.

In sum, questions of personhood have been dealt with as conventions or statements of specialized commissions or agencies—i.e., as additions—to what might be termed the nature and content of the universal human rights framework. Debates centered on the character and legitimacy of these rights in relation to the first-generation political and civil rights but they eschewed discussions of personhood that might have suggested that certain individuals or collectivities were denied rights because they were not classified as full human beings. In the aftermath of the Holocaust the victorious states desired to enshrine human rights in a legal framework. Legal experts found the anthropological discourse about social exclusion from rights based on particular cultural frameworks of human classification counterproductive. In their view, if a right is human, then it must be universally applicable; if only the privileged enjoy the right, then one is talking more about elite entitlements than human rights, and the concept is destroyed.

The American Anthropological Association was invited to contribute a professional perspective on universal rights. Philosophers were sponsored to deliberate on the same topic. Both concluded that notions of human rights might not be universal and certainly were not to be entrusted exclusively to state government authority (Maritain 1943) if universal adherence to human rights was the goal. But the international human rights commissions rejected both the anthropological and the philosophical framework (on jurisdictional grounds) as inimical to their desired goal: of lawyers drafting a universalistic framework and diplomats debating it. As a result, the relevance of the anthropological discourse on cultural relativism for human rights formulation, implementation, and monitoring was never carefully explored.

Anthropologists, Human Rights, and the United Nations

The 1940s Context of Cultural Relativism
Early in its deliberations the Human Rights Commission(s) formulating the Universal Declaration solicited inputs by anthropologists. They perhaps were looking for answers to questions such as: (1) whether or not other cultures have a concept of human rights and if these might resemble that of the proposed Universal Declaration (and proposed covenants), or (2) whether the values of elites who were to ratify the human rights declarations and covenants correspond to the traditional value systems in the countries they represent and what implications these might have for global comprehension and compliance.[7] American cultural anthropologists, still heavily immersed in cultural relativism, consistently recognized that all societies have some basis for evaluating and enforcing what may be deemed correct or permissible behavior. Moreover, both individuals and societies refer to some superhuman or legal authority (national constitution or international treaty) as the basis for behavioral norms. But, rather than respond to these questions, and thus contribute from the perspective of cultural relativism to the activities of formulating rights, the AAA officially opposed the enterprise.

The official AAA statement insisted that rights are culturally relative and issued a statement of advocacy for the rights and autonomy of indigenous peoples, in opposition to any universal formulations. Foreseeing the violation of tribal peoples, the AAA Executive Board, in its Report of the AAA for the year ending 1944, expressed "the hope that in the settlement of this present world war the rights of so-called primitive peoples to their way of life and the possession of property be respected." Specifically, the AAA Executive Board, in a "Statement on Human Rights" drafted by Melville Herskovits in 1947, went on record against formulations of universals in human rights. The statement made three major points: (1) it demanded respect for cultural differences along with individual differences; (2) it validated this position by insisting that there had not yet been discovered a technique for *qualitatively* evaluating cultural differences; and (3) it emphasized that "standards and values are relative to the culture from which they derive" (AAA 1947:539–43). This position effectively ruled out any accord of the AAA with the commission drafting a Universal Declaration. Thus, the UN Universal Declaration was constructed against a background of official, although controversial, AAA opposition.

As its critics were quick to point out, however, this position is indefensible both emotionally and intellectually. Anthropologists who advocated tolerance for all cultural values tend to be intolerant of cultural norms of intolerance, and if they are intolerant of intolerance, then the position is a sham. This paradox had already appeared in Boas and was replicated in Herskovits. Additionally, it can be (and was) argued that there are social, technical, and biological measures of culture and human well-being, even if one rejects moral valuations.

Curiously, the defensible elements of the document that had implications for human rights formulation and implementation were neither debated nor elaborated. The statement notes that all human beings biologically are *human* beings and deserve basic human rights. This same message had already been delivered in a more elaborate and eloquent form by American physical anthropologists as their contribution to the UN position papers on race. But there appears to have been no communication between physical and cultural anthropologists about their respective documents nor emphasis that this is a central lesson and principle that anthropology has to offer the public. The document also stresses a hard core of *similarities* among cultures that consistently has been overlooked (ibid., 541). Anthropologists might have pursued the question of how a particular "universal" right is developed in other cultures and how a particular cultural formulation of a right relates to any universal. But it was many years before anthropologists pursued these questions systematically (see, e.g., Renteln 1988a; Na'im 1992).

As a corollary, the statement asserts "the aims that guide the life of every people are self-evident in their significance to that people." But the statement and subsequent discussions never looked beyond the status quo into the historical contexts in which distinctive cultural notions of human rights were developed—or the contexts in which they might change. In their debates over universals vs. cultural relativism, anthropologists never questioned what happens to those goals, the corresponding norms, and behaviors as the human ecology or human relations to the political environment change. Customs such as infanticide, underfeeding of children and women, and abandonment of the elderly, which cultural relativists sought to rationalize and nonrelativists sought to condemn, might cease to be of self-evident utility under conditions of improved health and food resources. The goals the Universal Declaration and the accompanying human rights treaties assumed, or aimed to bring about, were conditions of plenty, or at least adequacy, in which hard choices of who should eat and who must die would be unnecessary. Even in Herskovits' terms, one could argue that, if conditions could be changed to increase access to resources, some of the "less benevolent" practices of particular cultures might be abandoned. But Herskovits and other anthropologists *who were asked*[8] forewent such possible discussion. Herskovits remained firm in his support of cultural difference, insisting that all cultures are "selective" and rely on internal forces of cultural change in changed cultural contexts to bring about a more benevolent way of life (1951:30).[9]

Finally, while the anthropologists' Statement on Human Rights deplored the attempt to provide a qualitative moral or legal standard for evaluating cultures, it did not rule out a quantitative standard for evaluating the consequences of culture—i.e., the consequences of living a culture pattern can be measured (evaluated) by nutrition, health, homicide or violence rates or profiles, or other objective criteria. Such evaluations are different from statements of preference, application, or advocacy of any particular standard as good or adequate for judging culture (see Barnett 1948). Subsequent contributions by anthropologists (e.g., Mead 1950; see Messer 1993) explored these directions.

Subsequent Contributions to Human Rights Commissions
After experiencing rejection, anthropologists (and philosophers) largely abandoned the philosophical and legal discussion within the Human Rights Commission, even as they continued to advocate political, economic, and cultural rights for indigenous groups, for minorities, and for other oppressed groups, whose needs for protection evolved along with the emergence of states. Under the sponsorship of UNESCO they contributed to cross-cultural discussions of rights (see *Human Rights Teaching*). They also participated in human rights debates as part of their crusade (sometimes shared with philosophers) against the common "enemy" of modernization and their defense of "the victims of progress" (e.g., Bodley 1975). Additionally, anthropologists worked within UN commissions on special aspects of human rights, such as genocide and apartheid. They spearheaded efforts to understand the etiology of intergroup hostilities that result in such atrocities for the purpose of preventing them (e.g., Kuper 1977, 1982, 1986). Additionally, they have continued to be involved in efforts to achieve human rights for indigenous peoples and for traditional communities more generally (Stavenhagen 1990; Messer 1993).

Anthropologists have also contributed to UN efforts to conceptualize the conditions under which women, children, the elderly, and "involuntary migrants" might enjoy human rights. These as well as all of the human rights issues mentioned previously are related to the issue of human classification and cultural classification and to fundamental sociocultural questions of notions of persons, rights, and obligations.

Human Classification

Both social and cultural anthropology provide conceptual frameworks to structure human rights understandings, especially cultural privileges of inclusion and exclusion. Inequality, definitions of ingroup (or outgroup), ethnic conflict, and genocide are all topical areas explored by anthropologists that have implications for predicting and modifying human rights behaviors. They also provide arenas for exploring the relevance of anthropological concepts and methods to human rights policies and protections.

Human beings or persons have rights to demand and expect certain behaviors from others who share their common moral community. Each constitutes a biological or sociocultural category, which can be analyzed from both native and observers' points of view. Human rights activists assume a universal definition of *human being* deserving universal rights on the basis of a shared "humanity." But in most cultures, including those informing Western human rights doctrine, not all individuals are considered to be complete members of humankind or full social persons. Those considered by some criteria to be defective, or not to have the full set of characteristics, include in certain cultural contexts: (1) women; (2) children; (3) the disabled, the ill, and the elderly; and (4) those with "other" physical, linguistic, cultural, or behavioral characteristics.[10] In addition, strangers of different genealogical, geographic, linguistic, or cultural background may be denied full social personhood and civil rights.

Such classifications of groups or individuals as not fully human remains a chief excuse for human rights abuses. American, British, and French anthropological studies offer insights on customs and behaviors of inclusion versus exclusion that follow from such classifications; principles extend as well to relationships of communities to states and of states within the world order. In examining "the dilemma of cultural diversity and equivalency in universal human rights standards," Schirmer (1988), for example, evokes the truism that classification of individuals as "other" or nonhuman allows violence and killing of otherwise fellow humans at any sociopolitical level. The other, to cite some particular contexts, may be an unnamed Eskimo child, not yet human according to their classification, who is allowed to die from neglect; a victim caught by Borneo headhunters, who consider those outside their boundaries to be nonhuman and fair game for attack; or indigenous peoples and poor *ladinos,* denied personhood by Guatemalan military leaders, landowners, or industrialists, who thereby justify denying them basic rights. Wartime provides another special context in which it has proven easy to slip into dehumanizing the other—and into human rights abuses—as did Americans during the Vietnam War (Polgar 1968).

Beyond describing dehumanization and its consequences, anthropologists offer at least three conceptual frameworks for describing the dynamics and, in certain cases, preventing or remedying the resulting human rights abuses: the ingroup-outgroup distinction, pluralism and ethnicity, and genocide.

Ingroup-Outgroup
Boas provides our first (dual) legacy on human classification and its consequences through a comparative study of peoples, classified on the basis of race, language, and culture, and a cross-cultural study of what he found to be universal tendencies to classify humans as of one's own group or others and human tendencies to include or exclude in one's own cultural terms.

> Among many primitive people, the only individuals dignified by the term human beings are the members of the tribe. It even happens in some cases that the language will designate only tribal members as "he" or "she," while all foreigners are "it" like animals. (1943:161)

Although all groups have certain standards—such as prohibitions against lying, theft, and murder—Boas noted that these standards seemed not to be applied to those outside of one's own social unit:

> The one outstanding fact is that every human society has two distinct ethical standards, the one for the in-group, the other for the out-group. Everybody has close associations with some group, however constituted, and as such has certain duties to other members of the group. . . . We do not observe any progress in the standards of

human society. We only recognize a softening of the hostility between the conflicting groups, at least in times of peace. (1939:22)

Simply put, moral law was obligatory when acting toward members of one's own community; the same obligation did not extend to those of other communities. Moreover, Boas encountered among technologically and historically diverse groups what seemed to be a universal human tendency to classify ingroup versus outgroup, from which followed the practice not to make human rights of the ingroup extend to the outgroup.

While seeking to describe the diversity in human races, languages, and cultures, Boas tried to learn also how people acquire negative stereotypes of other groups. He attempted to discern how people acquire the notion that only the members of one's own tribe are fully human and that others are not automatic recipients of the same rights accorded to fellow kin, community, or nation. All of this work carries with it a critique of "progress," as such human tendencies to discriminate appeared in technologically advanced as well as in primitive societies. Another dimension that he might have probed, but did not, was the role competition over political or economic resources played in generating intergroup hostilities and dehumanization. Instead, he focused on cultural criteria and, on the basis of American data, demonstrated that the tendency to preserve the purity of the group through discrimination against outsiders was not biological in origin and was therefore preventable, if not reversible. In the new socioeconomic environment of America immigrant national "types" tended to assimilate.

Boas therefore was also sure that discrimination could be eliminated and focused on education and assimilation as possible remedies. Youth, early on in life, would have to be indoctrinated by outstanding individuals in their own culture to be citizens of the world rather than of their more insular and particular cultures. But on the basis of recent historical observations, and his recognition that everyone must first be taught to be a member of some particular culture, he despaired of this ever occurring (Messer 1986). He also proposed assimilation by intermarriage as a way to eliminate physical and behavioral indicators of difference.

Many fellow anthropologists even at that time disagreed with his assimilationist position. Voices for cultural relativism recognized that "every society has values and imposes restraints" but remained silent on Boas's observation that ingroups treat members of outgroups by different rules. Cultural relativism stressed universal values such as "right . . . justice . . . and beauty" variously interpreted. Proponents agreed that objective indices of cultural inferiority or superiority cannot be established (Herskovits 1951:22), but did not rule out quantitative or qualitative measures of violence (Williams 1947). They hoped "by starting from relativism and its toleration . . . to work out a new set of absolute values and standards, if such are attainable at all or prove to be desirable" (Kroeber 1949:320). And even Boas argued that indigenous populations and cultures should be preserved. What the Boasian legacy provides for the human rights discourse, then, is a direction for investigating where abuses are likely to occur through an analysis of ingroup-outgroup distinctions in particular cultures and a positive directive to use human rights teaching as an approach to minimizing outgroup stigmatization.

Ethnicity and Pluralism

Alternatively, anthropologists study human classification, personhood, rights, and obligations within a framework of ethnicity and cultural pluralism. This framework examines interethnic dynamics, the circumstances under which states emerge, and persistent ethnic hostilities within states (see, e.g., Guideri, Pellizzi, and Tambiah 1988). Key issues within this vast literature are the dynamism, flexibility, and resilience of ethnic identity in pluralistic state contexts that may also involve regional organizations, intergovernmental organizations, and NGOs (see chap. 2 by C. A. Smith). Ethnic dimensions of human rights and Third World state policies can be studied by region, religion, and also gender (see Messer 1993).

The circumstances under which an ethnic group or state assimilates rather than distances or violates strangers constitute a special case for understanding human rights and social obligations. Colson (1970), monitoring the absorption of immigrants into Zambian Tongan society over several decades, raises the general question of "what factors encourage people to deal with aliens as potential recruits to their own order rather than as representatives of opposing interests or bearers of a unique and different heritage who must receive special status." She concludes that absorption rather than marginalization or rejection of aliens seems to depend on the political structure, especially the presence of state authority. States tend to define different status groups based on different modes of livelihood; accordingly, component groups tend to maintain and emphasize differences. Nonstate societies, "those lacking differentiated authority systems," by contrast, "show a homogeneity which belies the actual history of their recruitment"; they tend to assimilate strangers and to de-emphasize differences. Prior to the penetration of the Zambian state Tongans usually tried to recruit aliens into their social organization via patron-client relations, quasi-kinship modes, and personal relations that did not treat others as foreigners. In the face of state authority, by contrast, Tongans more and more tend to view themselves as one ethnic identity in opposition to others. They also tend to see foreigners as agents of alien communities who do not come to merge and contribute but, rather, maintain their distinctiveness and deprive locals of resources.

Such social transformations constitute part of the larger process by which states or their surrogates (multinational corporations, intergovernmental organizations, or nongovernmental organizations) engender interethnic conflict and violence and interfere with the absorption or tolerance of involuntary migrants by host groups. Understanding these intergroup-state dynamics provides a framework for anticipating abridgments of human rights norms (and legislation) by *ethnic* communities and peoples within states.

Violence and Genocide
Combining Boas's concerns with their investigations of interethnic violence, anthropologists have focused also on human classification and genocide, or on who can be attacked with impunity because they are not of one's group and therefore not worthy of full moral consideration. Kapferer (1988), in a carefully documented account of ethnic violence in Sri Lanka, demonstrated how violence by the state, Buddhist monks, and ordinary citizens against those they identified as ethnically different was rationalized and built on a nationalist Sinhalese myth. Ethnic Tamils, perceived as threatening to the Sinhalese Buddhist state order, were classified as evil, outside of that order, and expungeable. State, monk, and citizen condoned their violence against Tamils with reference to a founding myth. In this myth Dutugenmunu, "a righteous Buddhist king" suffering over the knowledge that he has sent millions to slaughter in the process of founding and defending the Buddhist Sinhalese state, is comforted by Buddhist monks, who declare, " 'only one and a half human beings had been slain. . . . One had come into the [three] refuges, and the other had taken on himself the five precepts.' . . . All the others are stated to be 'not more esteemed than beasts' as they are not

Buddhists" (1988:69–70). Kapferer captures the sense of violence, domination, and exclusion that characterizes Buddhist epic traditions relating to state culture and does not necessarily offer a very hopeful outlook.[11]

Genocide more generally falls within this pattern of excluding the other from human status by mythic or other rationalization and then killing, massacring, enslaving, raping, annihilating by scorched earth, arbitrary imprisonment, or any other treatment prohibited against citizens (Fein 1984:5; cited in Doughty 1988). These behaviors create a self-fulfilling proposition; they literally dehumanize their victims and leave them without the protections of a common humanity. By conforming to forced inhuman conditions, the others, such as black Africans in South Africa, materialize white notions and actions of inhumanity; analogously, Jews, bestialized in Nazi concentration camps, became living testimony to German brutality that systematically aimed to destroy their human spirits as well as bodies. Analysts of genocide, as well as lesser forms of discrimination, argue that dehumanization is commonly part of the dominant group's strategy to separate, segregate, socially isolate, and deny others membership in the wider community.

As in less severe forms of interethnic violence, the anthropological approach has been to spotlight ethnic rivalries and try to negotiate peaceful solutions before full-fledged conflict erupts. Unfortunately, since rivalries tend to be predicated not only on some mythic or symbolic past but also on competition for resources, prevention of human rights abuses usually entails well-reasoned cultural analyses as well as some transformation in political-economic structure and underlying conditions.

Policy Implications of Anthropological Studies of Human Classification

Inequality, ingroup-outgroup discrimination, and ethnic conflict all restrict definitions of who is counted human, but definitions of rights and persons are not static. They expand or contract under different circumstances. A developing role for anthropologists is to analyze the structural determinants of discrimination and human rights violations and also to identify and encourage the contexts that favor the expansion of human rights protections or a widening notion of human community. The foregoing sections suggest at least four approaches to research and related policy action.

The first is that of Boas, who studied the plasticity of human "types" and favored public policies that would remove differences via biological and cultural assimilation. He relied on education to create national "citizens of the world" and teach antidiscrimination. He also advanced research to demonstrate the physical and behavioral plasticity of human types. Put together, they were aimed to reduce prejudice and discrimination, at least among educated persons.

Evolutionary studies in anthropology suggest a second approach, which is to characterize the circumstances under which independent sociocultural groups are merged (assimilated, co-opted, coerced, or contracted) into a more integral social order, based on religious, political, or economic criteria (e.g., Johnson and Earle 1986). Such studies tend to emphasize as prime movers population growth and technoeconomic factors over political or cultural ones. They use these factors to account for the emergence of states and new national or international social orders, but they hardly describe the dynamics and resilience of ethnic identity or interethnic hostilities that continually threaten the stability of states. Nor do they offer plans of action for prevention or alleviation of ethnic tensions.

A third, and complementary, evolutionary approach is to study processes of interethnic and political-economic relations in relation to the emergence of states (see, e.g., Watts 1983; Guideri, Pellizzi, and Tambiah 1988). Such works again offer theoretical and practical insights but no plan of action to resolve abuses. In his overview of a collection of essays on interethnic relations and states, for example, Tambiah suggests that major transformations in political, economic, religious, and communications relations are all involved in the social transformations from kinship, caste, and local group loyalties to national and transnational (panhuman) identities. All contributed to the opening up of parochial to more inclusive social identities in particular historical periods. A case in point is the Western European nation-state, which involved subjugation by the emergent state government of more petty component identities, the expansion of capitalism and international trade, the rise of mass communication via the printing press, and the decline of power in the Catholic Church. Tambiah (1988) cautions that we probably should not anticipate that Third World nations will follow the same paths to democracy and secular humanism as did medieval to modern European states and their derivatives. These Third World societies, particularly those that are Islamic or Buddhist, are based on very different traditions that link people to land. Nevertheless, he suggests that any widening of rights and greater inclusiveness in the human community likely awaits similarly great social transformations.

A fourth approach is to learn from and apply previous experience through careful historical analysis of ethnic violence. Kuper (1977, 1982, 1986) provides probably our best example of how an anthropologist who studies human classification can translate analytical and academic research into policy. Drawing on studies of ethnic violence in Rwanda, Burundi, Zanzibar, and Algeria, Kuper analyzes how the process of ethnic polarization occurs and what opportunities potentially exist to transform oppressive social systems without violence. In points that correspond inversely to Tambiah's prerequisites for a more inclusive social order, Kuper notes in each instance how denials of economic structural transformations, political participation, and more open educational opportunities, plus the destruction of a "middle ground" of less polarized leadership, prevented advancement by deprived groups, which then pressed political-economic and sociocultural cleavages toward rupture. He suggests three measures of prevention, albeit none of them cures. One is for outside interventionists to manipulate political-economic ties to create or maintain a middle ground and a social fabric of greater complexity. This middle ground would render it less likely that the social simplification that accompanies the exaggeration of ethnic cleavages could occur. A second is for outside aid to be tied to improving the lots of deprived groups. A third and final dimension is to rely on interventions from outside the society (in political terms, the UN; in indigenous terms, God or religious authority) to end certain cycles of violence and human rights abuses. He exhorts UN agencies to ensure more equitable participation in plural societies and not to miss opportunities to prevent violence. In his view the UN Convention against genocide has proved obviously insufficient and unenforceable; the only solution is therefore prevention (Kuper 1977).

Anthropologists might contribute also their insights on how certain multiethnic Third World states have managed to minimize conflict, further human rights, and achieve a sense of national identity and community. Universal education, mass communication, and opportunities for all groups to participate in national economic improvement programs are undoubtedly elements—as demonstrated in the case of Tanzania (Shimkin 1990). Yet even such seeming success stories are qualified by their persistent failures to extend universal (national) rights and privileges to women. The very young and the very old also may find themselves deprived of official succor, especially under circumstances of dearth. We turn next to analyses of their classifications and deprivations.

Deprivation by Gender

Women, either all of the time or in specific contexts, may be viewed as different from men—a separate category of person or nonperson that never totally belongs to the social unit's category of person—or some fraction of full adult human status. Undergoing their own separate rites of passage, eating separately, and in some cases even consuming different foods, women may never be counted or treated as full persons within social groups dominated by males (Strathern 1972).

The political, economic, and sociocultural structures that deny women full personhood may also deny them human rights, such as rights to representation or rights to food, either all of the time or in certain contexts (e.g., McLaughlin 1974). Although most of the anthropological literature analyzing women's rights and personhood derives from nonindustrialized societies, women are also excluded from full social participation in modern states as well as international organizations. Economic development and modernization programs usually directed by and toward males often bypass female farmers, merchants, and entrepreneurs at all social scales. Even "women-in-development" programs that seek to improve the lot of women by singling them out for assistance tend to reinforce social structures that count women as partial persons. The process of trying to redress some of the material abuses that stem from the structure may fulfill the content while leaving women's social marginality intact. Programs such as the Bangladesh Rural Advancement Committee that manage to entitle and empower women at the same time are rare exceptions (see Chen 1986). National and international organizations also perpetuate patterns of gender discrimination by establishing "normal" standards that count women as some fraction of a male consumption unit.

In these national and international structures and organizations, as in local communities, definitions of personhood are embedded in cultural values that set women apart. The rights of women as human beings then come into conflict with cultural norms and attitudes that deny women full rights. Indian cultures provide a case in point, and anthropologists, such as Papanek (1989), have suggested a comparative regional approach for measuring the extent of human rights abuses stemming from local categories of gender difference affecting, for example, access to food. She advises the researcher to describe first the actual behaviors by which females get less of available (food) resources than males; second, the material consequences of differential resource allocations (e.g., skewed survivorship ratios); and, third, what ideas underlie such inequalities.

Especially relevant to the valuation of, and behaviors toward, categories of persons labeled "female" are their ascribed biological or cultural characteristics. In local cultural terms women may be categorized as needing less or less high-quality food. Foods may, in turn, be classified in local parlance as "hot" versus "cold," so that high-quality foods are interpreted as actually damaging to females. Alternatively, food self-deprivation may be construed to be of spiritual value especially for females. Women's self-restraint additionally may be understood to be tied to a biological ability to accept pain without cost. Women and men may have differences of opinion on such matters, and so a further issue in monitoring the damage resulting from gender-based (or other) allocation rules is whether the victims themselves feel violated or deprived. More "objective" accounts often leave out this critical subjective judgment of deprivation. A case in point is when economists insist that Third World populations are not hungry or malnourished but, rather, "small but healthy," without asking their sample members to report how they feel or, for that matter, checking with medical colleagues to see whether those who are small in fact are healthy (see Messer 1989a). Anthropologists thus potentially play a dual role: (1) establishing the objective terms by which "deprivation" is defined; and (2) offering subjects' judgments on analogous dimensions. Both offer policy makers additional information on who is hungry or deprived and at what levels actions need to be targeted to improve the situation.

Deprivation by Age

Age constitutes yet another criterion for denying full human status and access to resources. In many societies personhood, with its attendant rights and duties, is linked to full productive status; in situations in which resources are in short supply, those who cannot contribute to their own or the collective subsistence often find themselves deprived. In many cases the very young or old find themselves marginalized as customary socioeconomic patterns change. Anthropologists analyzing intergenerational work patterns report such social, structural, occupational, and resource changes and resulting human rights abuses. Pagezy (1988), in the course of ecological investigation in Zaire, discovered (to her obvious dismay) the formerly foraging Twa, now settled, abandoning their elderly to malnutrition or starvation as the young struggled for their own subsistence. The history of such neglect is not clear—that is, whether such disdain for the needs of the elderly was less the case under conditions of foraging or simply less obvious.

Hemmings-Gapihan (1985), in her study of changing social mores and labor organization by gender in Gourma, Upper Volta (Burkina Faso), argued that elderly women in that society traditionally controlled both land and labor; as they aged, they worked less without threat of loss to subsistence. But such customs of caring for elderly women appeared to be overturned by increasing emphasis on cash crops and male control of younger women's and men's labor. Although in each of these cases a simplifying analysis might interpret the erosion of rights entirely in political-economic terms (e.g., Watts 1983), the loss of respect for the old or infirm, who as a consequence lose land rights, food rights, and the right to subsistence and social security, is also a cultural judgment about which (partial) human beings are no longer included in the community or household that works together and shares provisions.

On the opposite pole marked age or gender categories can alternatively signal extra cultural protection or access to resources. Both women and children are favored in life and death situations in Western culture. The extra cultural value placed on children is especially evident within the ideologies and behaviors of the UN agencies, such as UNICEF, in which children are singled out for special allocations of food, health care, and protection from violence (e.g., Grant 1990). The rights of children, UNICEF insists, take precedence over national rights of sovereignty. To protect children's rights UNICEF advocates intervening in the internal affairs of states—the only circumstance under which this happens.

Additionally, much of famine relief aims explicitly at "saving the children," whether or not children are especially imperiled. Legesse (1990), for example, reports that eastern African pastoralists customarily protect their children's well-being in times of food shortage more so than neighboring farming populations. A happy scenario is where international relief agencies reinforce the benefits for children of pastoralists and add to the benefits for farmers' children. A not-so-happy scenario is where the need to intervene to feed hard-pressed East African adult pastoralists is judged to be unnecessary because the children, who have already been favored, appear to be well nourished. This can result in unrelieved hardship and suffering for adults.[12]

As is the case with gender-related access to food, anthropologists' community-based understandings of subjective and objective dimensions of preference can improve preventive and ameliorative food and health policies.

Summary

Better understandings of human classification and personhood make it possible to carry out predictive as well as after-the-fact analyses. Anticipating what categories of people defined by ethnic identity, gender, or age are likely to be denied access to critical resources such as food or health care, at all times or in times of dearth, by households, communities, states, or social agencies, can help identify groups and individuals vulnerable to rights abuses and help aid rapid response to their plight. Better understandings of human classification also can help pinpoint where political-economic structures do violence to human rights at community or national levels. Understanding the circumstances under which women, children, or the elderly lose basic subsistence entitlements assists those who might intervene to construct and use a human rights framework to identify vulnerable groups, both to constrain abuses and to create obligations.

Issues of human classification also enter into the understanding of who enjoys particular categories of social, economic, and cultural rights, another arena for anthropological contributions.

Economic, Social, and Cultural (ECOSOC) Rights

Political-economic as well as sociocultural structures deprive people of rights such as rights to adequate food and nutrition, health, a sustainable environment, and other essential prerequisites for livelihood. Although both theoretical and applied anthropologists study these issues, very little of their work has been tied explicitly to the human rights framework. As indicated earlier, one reason for this omission is that anthropologists have focused mainly on indigenous or collective rights. They have devoted less attention to documenting the socioeconomic and cultural rights of individuals, although the UN framework is based on individual rights. But, together with Third World critics of the UN international human rights framework, who share these critical views that it is ethnocentrically Western, anthropologists support the universal rights to be free from hunger, to enjoy health (or health care), and to earn a decent livelihood under humane conditions, even as they disagree on the numbers or procedures for defining acceptable levels or standards (e.g., Cohen 1993).

Anthropologists contribute to enlarging this ECOSOC framework of human rights through theory, practical reporting, and policy-related activities. Marxist interpretations offer one framework for examining the causes of ill health, hunger, and other abuses. The human rights framework offers anthropologists another global platform on which to voice concerns about political-economic institutions interpreted in particular contexts as interfering with human rights. To move from rhetoric to action, anthropologists also participate in practical programs and projects. Marchione (1984) offers several methodological approaches for examining the right to food; Clay, with colleagues at Cultural Survival, critiques the food relief work of governments and NGOs (1988b; Clay and Holcomb 1986; Clay et al. 1988); and Horowitz (1990) elaborates on structural causes of human rights abuses in the global food economy. Leading advocates of indigenous and other human rights are now employed at institutions such as the World Bank, where they draft guidelines to protect the rights of peoples affected by development projects (e.g., Cernea 1991). Carrying out predictive as well as post hoc analyses of how political-economic structures violate human rights at local to state levels, anthropologists can use a human rights framework not only to analyze the structural contexts but also to contribute to actions to constrain abuses and to create obligations. The anthropologists just cited are already drawing into the human rights arena cases of economic discrimination, which have their root causes in the inequities of the political economy. Additional examples can be found in Huss-Ashmore and Katz (1989, 1990) and Downs, Kerner, and Reyna (1991).

Institutions and Linkages

Explorations of sociocultural, political, and economic dimensions also raise the issue of linkages and levels in human rights reporting, compliance, and fulfillment. Until recently human rights research and advocacy had largely failed to conceptualize human rights formulation or implementation at any level between the state and the individual. More recently the human rights literature by anthropologists (e.g., Kuper 1977, 1981; Stavenhagen 1990) and scholars of religion (e.g., Rouner 1988) increasingly presents rights issues from the viewpoints of indigenous and minority groups and the different world religious traditions, especially as these other notions interfere with universal acceptance (Alston 1990a). Analysis of rights at local or intermediate social levels remains scarce, however, for both conceptual and methodological reasons. First, as already mentioned, some human rights scholars interpret what might be termed cross-cultural analysis of rights to obviate the principle of universality. Second, cross-cultural analysis leading to action entails new skills of conceptualization and negotiation (Na'im 1992).

Linking levels to connect theoretical notions of what rights are and who enjoys them to practical programs to fulfill rights or report abuses involves both sociocultural theory and also applied anthropology. Certainly, distinctive cultures hold distinctive notions of rights and duties. But in certain arenas rights conceived by distinctive cultures or religions might be rendered congruent if proponents focused on potential points of agreement rather than conflict with those of the international doctrines. With respect to the right to food, as a case in point, Islamic law and international UN human rights share the identical intent to protect people from hunger. How might the Muslim obligation to provide charity and to feed the hungry reinforce the international human rights principle? How might community organizations, local and regional food security mechanisms, including grain storage and hospitality customs, facilitate an implementation of the right to food through mediation among differing, but not necessarily antagonistic, cultural notions of rights to food and obligations to feed? How might anthropologists apply their sociocultural knowledge of the competing, but not always antagonistic, demands of multiple legal and human rights traditions to achieve a superior outcome for both the hungry and for those donating food? Analysis of human rights can emphasize mutually congruent and reinforcing traditions about food even where principles and other rights, such as freedom of religion, differ and where Islamic jurists insist Islamic law takes precedence over international doctrine (Farhang 1988).

Anthropology, Human Rights, and the State

Cultural understandings of rights principles and practices below the level of the state also offer new opportunities for human rights conceptualization, reporting, and achievement. The international legal codes presuppose state organization, political will, and values to create or bolster compliance. In clarifying the concept, Eide notes:

> the notion of human rights is intimately linked to the notions of "state." Only in the context of an organized society with public authorities does the notion of "human rights" make sense. "Human rights" refers to norms concerning the relationship between individuals (sometimes groups of individuals) and the state. (Eide 1984:152)

UN doctrine insists that human rights be monitored and addressed from the top down, but in practical terms rights are conceptualized and met at various levels. A challenge for anthropologists is to envision and then design strategies for meeting human rights that might better coordinate international, state, and local efforts.

Subsistence rights offer one illustration. Historical studies of land rights, water rights, community grain storage customs, and kinship and social organization all indicate how prestate communities protected subsistence rights and promoted social security. Ethnographic studies demonstrate, in addition, a range of coping strategies at the household level and also their demise under changing conditions. In particular, they report what role the state played in transforming local subsistence and risk-averse practices and the gaps between the breakdown of traditional modes of risk avoidance and the buildup of state capacity to assume responsibility for social security (e.g., Colson 1979; Moris 1989).

Such studies suggest both negative and positive implications: what states ought not to do, in order to preserve traditional local to regional mechanisms for securing subsistence rights, and what states ought to do to create new institutions to meet rights where the old have atrophied. They also suggest that states, in their current form, often are not able or choose not to meet the subsistence rights of all. Therefore, anthropologists (among others) might begin to investigate ways for local or crosscutting (e.g. religious) sociocultural groups to demand and secure rights. What might be ways to combine top-down (UN) with bottom-up "grassroots" strategies for rights?

For anthropologists linking elite or official with local levels involves paying more attention to the culture of bureaucrats and of those who protect and enforce human rights. One of the weaknesses of anthropologists' human rights reporting up to this point in time is that we tend to focus almost exclusively on the unempowered and the abusers. We do not give sufficient weight to the cultural characteristics of the empowered and the potential protectors or advocates. Nor has there been much attention directed toward cross-cultural analyses that illuminate how notions of rights and persons create categories of privileged and underprivileged at many levels in plural societies (e.g., Downing and Kushner 1988). Anthropologists might also contribute more to the ideas and instruments of international human rights in a world that anthropologists and human rights advocates increasingly recognize to be pluralistic and marked by the need to protect collective as well as individual rights (e.g., Crawford 1988; Alston 1990a). Human rights reporting instruments should include provisions for self-reporting by communities and individuals, not only the top-down monitoring of compliance by states according to human rights codes. Anthropologists are already contributing to the design and implementation of conceptual and reporting mechanisms (e.g., Stavenhagen 1990) but might contribute further.

An additional theoretical and practical concern is to analyze the meaning of human rights within the statist framework. How does the doctrine of universal human rights relate to national mores and rules of behavior? How have state governments behaved with respect to the universal framework? Whether or not states accept them in their entirety, nations sign onto the UN Charter and Universal Declaration of Human Rights because signing is a rite of passage for joining the UN and for recognition of sovereign status within the community of nations. Nations may later express divergence from the codes and refuse to ratify the legal instruments that are meant to implement them or to behave in accordance with the legal codes once ratified. Understanding the sociocultural as well as political-economic rationales, and responding to such discrepant behaviors, are also potential items for the anthropologists' agenda.

Asian nations, as a case in point (see Yamane 1982), show great diversity in legal and moral traditions at the local, state, and crosscutting religious levels. Only India, Japan, and Sri Lanka have ratified both international covenants on human rights; the Philippines has ratified the International Covenant on Economic, Social and Cultural Rights (as of 1980). Ratifications of the ILO resolutions on human rights are much lower in Asia than in other regions of the world. Notions of human rights therefore appear not to be widely shared among Asian cultural traditions.

There are several reasons for this seeming lack. The first is that rights and obligations in Asian traditions are viewed as more communal than individual, and, thus, demands for what the international framework construes to be individual rights may be made on the basis of family or community values, rather than individual rights in a state. Asian peoples additionally have found that collective rights may prove to be the most important route for gaining access to justice, since denials are often based on group membership. Reform of the justice system may also be a prerequisite for action on human rights. Second, many Asian individuals are so poor that any notion of human rights that does not refer to economic development and fulfillment of essential subsistence rights appears meaningless. Third, many violations are tied to the abusive conduct of transnational corporations, which control and constrain individuals' rights to work and earn a decent standard of living and furthermore often control access to land and to natural resources. Technically, they can be made to adhere to human rights codes via government regulations. But in practice governments often are either reluctant or too weak to do so.

All of these factors indicate that human rights, as defined in the international sphere, are widely abused in Asia, but formulaic human rights covenants do not offer a solution. Significant human rights abusers occur among nations that have and have not ratified the UN covenants. To advance human rights practice individuals must first be apprised of their rights, and gain the consciousness to protest repression and arbitrary disciplinary actions. NGO, government, and IGO actions must then establish the frameworks and channels for human rights reporting. A further possibility is for Asian nations to join together to form either NGO or intergovernmental organization (IGO) regional human rights associations between the level of the global international community and the state.

Nongovernmental Organizations
Dissatisfaction with human rights as the exclusive domain of governments potentially leads to new institutional forms of nongovernmental as well as intergovernmental organizations. Human rights–monitoring NGOs, such as the regional Human Rights Watch Committees and Amnesty International, evaluate standards, government compliance, and mechanisms for meeting obligations. These organizations, with

anthropologists in staff and leadership positions, report by region, country, and issue (e.g., women's rights) and rally public sentiment to embarrass and change the behaviors of abusers.

The Independent Commission on International Humanitarian Issues (ICIHI) is another investigative think tank. Its mandate is to address humanitarian issues that are dealt with inadequately by existing international mechanisms, to suggest possible new mechanisms, and to raise international public consciousness about the causes of human suffering (Aga Khan 1988:156). ICIHI evaluates state compliance with human rights standards, where and why behaviors do not conform to standards, and what the international community might do to improve universal human rights performance. Their human rights concerns include especially famine (the right to food) (ICIHI 1985; Messer 1989b) and indigenous rights (ICIHI 1988). ICIHI also suggests what concerned citizens and NGOs might do to circumvent the inadequacies or perfidies of governments to reach the people who are suffering deprivations.

Nongovernmental organizations set policies and practices at the local level, with activities that come under scrutiny by anthropologists, much the same as the activities of governments come under scrutiny. Their activities are complementary to the inadequacies or unwillingness of governments, and they constitute yet another aspect of the social-political-economic environment with which individuals, households, and local communities must contend in making a living, producing and reproducing their biological and sociocultural beings. Smith's essay in this volume (chap. 2) raises one possible limitation of this NGO bypass-government approach: it may interfere with the legitimate efforts of indigenous or other local communities to negotiate more lasting (or sometimes revolutionary) solutions to immediate problems of rights and longer-term obligations. The particular programs of NGOs (referring here to NGOs in general rather than human rights NGOs in particular) may be just as intrusive and destructive to the aspirations of local political leaders and cultures as those of a domineering national state. Sometimes the NGOs that enter communities have little understanding of the historical context of suffering that they are trying to end and have no long-term commitment to action. NGOs have also been known to interfere with the day-to-day functioning of national governments and the course of their negotiations with municipalities or local governments for programs and power sharing.

As is the case with other participants in the development process, the raison-d'être of NGOs is in part humanitarian but also self-interested. Their ideologies, motivations, and activities contribute to the overall process of economic development and human rights but in their own cultural terms. The culture and organizational structure of NGOs therefore constitute one other contrasting level and linkage in the definition and practice of human rights, especially in the struggle by indigenous communities for self-determination and protections of their collectivity against outside interference.

Transformations in Human Rights Rhetoric and Institutional Structure

The Rights of Collectivities

Overall reviews of the human rights literature of the past forty years, and especially the summaries appearing in 1988 on the fortieth anniversary of the Universal Declaration of Human Rights (e.g., Crawford 1988; Berting et al. 1990), emphasize how the world has changed. There are new international institutional actors in the guise of UN agencies, multilateral banks, and transnational corporations. The hegemony of the old superpowers is challenged by more than 150 newly independent nations, whose needs for economic development at times appear to overwhelm themselves and potential donors. NGOs, alongside governments, provide an extensive network of international, national, and local development and human rights agencies that since 1948 also have grown in numbers and activities.

Most human rights advocates[13] (e.g., Baehr 1990; Burger 1990; VanderWal 1990) recognize that human needs and demands, expressed through collective organization and action, have changed since 1948. Human rights, evolving along with these institutional changes, now include solidarity rights and the rights of collectivities, indigenous rights, and rights to a cultural identity (Berting et al. 1990). Expanding concepts and dimensions of rights do not negate earlier Western cultural inspiration; national constitutions of the new states almost without exception enshrine both civil-political and socioeconomic rights in their founding declarations. But cultural and collective rights emphasize that individuals achieve human dignity through cultural as well as biological survival and that cultural groups are entitled to a sustainable, peaceful, and enabling natural and socioeconomic environment. In other words, cultural groups must be protected, or individual rights to survival are at risk.

Advocates have slowly come to accept what have always been the anthropologists' understandings of indigenous rights: that threats to native lands and livelihoods, languages and societies, constitute abuses to human dignity and human rights.[14] Cultural identity may be as important as health for human dignity and self-confidence. Cultural pluralism, rather than threatening humankind, is in itself of value (Kamenka 1988:134). Translated into human rights parlance, efforts to eliminate cultural distinctiveness must be constrained, and conditions to further cultural survival must be obligated.

Other new categories of rights include "people's rights," which are interpreted by Third World leaders to be a logical outgrowth of the right to self-determination. Collectivities of Third World states demand their right to exist in a peaceful, prosperous, environmentally sustainable world (Marks 1980; Crawford 1988; Baehr 1990). Human rights rhetoric now also recognizes as legitimate the demands of indigenous groups to be protected within states (Falk 1988). Overcoming the threat to indigenous survival is interpreted as an "emergency," an imperative for the survival of the human species, even though indigenous groups and rights often challenge fundamental notions of economic "progress" and state sovereignty.

The need for protection of human rights is also evident where ethnic groups come into conflict in the process of state formation and disintegration. Government efforts at control and subordination generate demands for ethnic autonomy and rights, over and against government attempts to create an assimilative sociocultural order (Guideri, Pellizzi, and Tambiah 1988). As Stavenhagen summarized so succinctly, "The idea of a right usually arises when we have to face a situation in which violations of rights occur" (1990:256).

Cross-Cultural Formulations of Rights

The changing world order also encourages international human rights activists to explore more widely multiple cultural perspectives on human rights and their implications for standards and compliance. National governments, especially religious leaders, that are neither secular (humanist) nor Western continually must choose whether to comply with or disregard the 1948 Universal Declaration on Human Rights and subsequent instruments. To win their support for both legislation and adherence, evolving human rights standards need to resonate with these different traditions of religious and community law (e.g., Alston 1990a).

Although soliciting cultural and religious opinions on human rights is not new (see 1966 UNESCO conference reported in the *International Social Science Journal,* especially Glean 1966; Raphael 1966; and review in Robertson 1982), understanding their various points of view is much more urgent. Rallying Islamic and Buddhist principles on limits to violence and warfare, or obligations to feed the hungry or provide medical care to the sick are instances in which multicultural contributions might improve human rights performance. While rendering different value systems congruent is not easy, at least human rights lawyers and philosophers are taking the problem seriously. They accept the reality of differing concepts of rights held by different collectivities in a plural world. They also take note of the different concepts of persons who enjoy rights in different legal traditions or customary law.

The human rights commissions promulgating legal rights for a plural, international, global society then face the choice of whether to try to incorporate the distinctive viewpoints into a united but pluralistic whole or to homogenize the disparate viewpoints into a uniform whole (see, e.g., Kammerer 1988:279). The documents appear to follow the first model, incorporation of regional and indigenous human rights formulations into the expanding "whole" of international human rights. In consequence, the international (UN) human rights doctrine is "united" as a series of documents passed by the UN, but principles and practices continue to evolve in response to the "smoking mirrors" in the perennial struggle to create postimperial and new or postnational orders (Guideri, Pellizzi, and Tambiah 1988). The legal experts still wonder how to create and implement a universal human rights standard that will limit all forms of violence, including the quiet violence of hunger. Individuals, communities, NGOs, and religious and cultural groups suffering human rights abuses maintain a hope that the human rights framework can assist them in overcoming oppression.

The multiplying number of rights now recognized within the human rights framework testifies to the actions following on such hopes and the evolution of the human rights concept through debate. They also suggest an influential role for anthropologists.

Where Anthropology Prevailed

Although anthropologists, with a few exceptions (Stavenhagen 1990), maintain low profiles, anthropological concepts and concerns are well represented in this evolving human rights field. International human rights now incorporate notions of indigenous rights, cultural rights, and the rights of collectivities more generally. UNESCO and the ILO clarify and champion the rights of indigenous and minority peoples to enjoy their cultural heritage, including their natural resources. The Organization of African Unity has championed "Human and Peoples' Rights" (1981), the World Conference of Indigenous Peoples has issued its own "Declaration of Principles of Indigenous Rights" (1984), and the U.N. General Assembly has voted a "Declaration on the Right to Development" (1986) (see Crawford 1988, for commentaries on these documents). The ILO "Convention 107 concerning the Protection and Integration of Indigenous and other Tribal and Semi-Tribal Populations in Independent Countries" (1957) has been revised to strip it of assimilationist, integrationist, and paternalistic sentiments, to bring it more into line with the desires of indigenous groups to remain separate and sovereign (Burger 1988). Leaders of indigenous rights movements, moreover, have learned to frame their own human rights demands, outside of the dominance of Western academic culture (Varese 1988; Wright 1988, Wright and Ismaelillo 1982), thus changing the roles of anthropologists from torchbearers to consultants and advocates.

Ten years ago Legesse accurately described this process of change in the following terms: human rights are universal in intent but not in derivation (1980:123). UN delegates representing widely varying cultural traditions usually agree that there exists a universal concern for human rights, although they question the universality of any particular human rights notion. Over time representatives from different nations and cultures participate in a universalizing process in which all contribute to the expanding framework of human rights. Although some philosophers (e.g., Donnelly 1990) continue to define the logic of human rights in a strict sense as excluding collective rights or alternative non-Western notions of human rights (e.g., Howard 1992), others (e.g., Alston 1990a) accept the need to consider alternative formulations. While these latter also worry that alternative conceptions of human rights might water down their stature, they insist that pluralistic notions can be accommodated to retain and even strengthen the possibility of establishing universal standards with moral force, and practical enforcement mechanisms.

Indigenous rights are universally recognized to be imperative in today's world (see Stavenhagen 1990). Anthropologists, accordingly, have discarded the method of describing cultures by trait lists that proposed to measure cultural survivals versus assimilations (e.g., Tax 1952) as well as the tendency to analyze "other" cultures according to their degree of assimilation (see Guideri, Pellizzi, and Tambiah 1988:27). Instead, they are describing the processes by which rights and cultural identities are negotiated among states, peoples, and individuals and strengthening human rights advocacy in the areas of economic, social, and cultural rights with fact-finding that potentially contributes to human rights, development, and environmental policy. Cultural identity now is presented and demanded by indigenous representatives who are affirming their own biological and cultural superiority, rather than an identity "validated" (after being questioned) by the other, dominant culture (Varese 1988). In the process of indigenous peoples assuming their own voices, anthropologists also have moved from cultural analyses of "communities" to "regional" systems, including more in-depth analysis of ethnicities vis-à-vis states.

Conclusions

In a sense all of the essays envisioned in this volume on social transformation refer to basic human rights.[15] As anthropologists, we have questioned the units by which development and well-being are measured; the impact of development strategies on health; the intrusions of authoritarian state regimes (usually propped up by international aid); the well-being of indigenous populations; and the complex religious, political, philosophical, and economic factors that influence vulnerability to hunger and ill health. We have tried to analyze the new U.N. and NGO participants in development strategies and the linkages among them, communities, and governments and to connect these linkages to more conventional anthropological analyses of political economy, human and cultural ecology, and cultural and class identities. Along with other anthropologists we have debated the impacts of social transformations and tried to clarify the forces that limit human freedom and dignity and, where possible, tried to change them or mitigate their negative impact.

In total these efforts demonstrate a critical involvement in human rights concerns. Anthropologists also have been active in describing and comparing different cultural standards of behavior and how social mores and behaviors are transformed under changing material and ideological conditions. The definition of social person, or the relationship of the individual to the sociocultural group, has also been an anthropological concern (Harris 1989). Notwithstanding, anthropologists in the past have often been excluded from discussions of human rights because we are viewed as opposed to universalizing approaches and to the assimilationist, pro-development, or modernization, values that they seemed to entail. Anthropologists who argued for protection of collective, over and against individual rights, erected a barrier that kept this anthropological discourse from influencing the initial formulation of rights. This adversarial stance ostensibly was matched by the unwillingness of international legal scholars to take seriously different sociocultural definitions of human beings as these modify rights within a group, state, or human community. Such scholars have felt, rightly or wrongly, that entertaining possible exclusionary definitions of human beings does violence to the intellectual notion that certain basic rights *are* universal, which means that they are universally accepted and applied. Anthropologists in the human rights field also have asked different questions, about cultural survival and cultural diversity, and have scrutinized different units—particularly those below but also beyond the state level—in approaching human rights policies.

Despite these differences of opinion and approach, humans rights now incorporate anthropologists' notions of indigenous and collective rights (even if nonanthropologists have not been moved so far as to celebrate diversity as a virtue to the extent that anthropologists do). Moreover, the data suggest that anthropologists' alleged lack of participation in human rights activities lies more in the precision and narrowness of philosophical and disciplinary rhetoric and the connections between anthropologists and the human rights system. While marginalized in the conceptual debate, anthropologists never failed to address and try to expand the basic subject matter. Now others are beginning to address human rights from the bottom-up perspective. Some may even recognize that local definitions of personhood may be more important for realizing rights than the formula contained in some abstract legal document.

Since the 1940s anthropologists have largely moved away from the philosophical debate on whether universal rights are possible and have pressed for the rights of collective, oppressed, and vulnerable groups—all of which relate to various dimensions of human classification and discrimination. Our additional efforts try to clarify demands of the particular peoples pressing for rights and to monitor response. The most important arena for anthropologists remains a monitoring-reporting-advocacy role that also clarifies at what social levels rights are denied or fulfilled. As anthropologists, we continue to point out the discrepancies between human rights rhetoric and ratifications and human rights abuses. We provide evidence and approach the root causes of ongoing human rights abuses in political, economic, and sociocultural terms, as we champion the aspirations of indigenous peoples to maintain their cultures while protecting an adequate standard of living. All this means that the subject matter of anthropology extends beyond analyses of ethnic, class, and race relations, to notions of human rights in cross-cultural perspective. For conceptualization, strategic policy engagement, and action, this constitutes an expanded, although not a new, agenda for anthropologists.

NOTES

1. Both the Universal Declaration and instruments as a result have been alleged (positively or negatively, depending on point of view) to represent "the human rights concept of one culture, namely, the culture of parliamentary democracies," (Robertson 1982:8), which "have produced the best known formulations and institutionalized the most effective system of implementation both nationally and internationally" (9). Supporting this position, human rights experts cite precedents in the charters and declarations of the liberal democracies of Western Europe, which were based on Greek philosophy, Roman law, and Judeo-Christian tradition, Reformation humanism, and Enlightenment philosophy (see, e.g., Robertson 1982). Specific legal documents include the Magna Carta (1215), the United States Declaration of Rights (1774), and the French *Declaration of the Rights of Man and the Citizen* (1989). But these precedential philosophies and ages held radically different concepts of personhood that relegated whole categories of individuals to the status of noncitizen or slave. Moreover, the rights proclaimed in the supporting constitutional documents usually circumscribed who counted as a person (often property-owning males) and, therefore, who might enjoy such rights. These details were mentioned in many volumes on human rights that I perused in preparation for this essay. They cited laudably the U.S. and

French "mainstreams" that found expression in the Universal Declaration of Human Rights in 1948. Exceptions were Third World critics, who branded the so-called universal human rights framework ethnocentric (Adegbite 1968).

2. A twentieth-anniversary volume celebrating the Universal Declaration (Hersch 1969) drew on the varied traditions of nations to find unity rather than diversity in legal traditions. All societies and governments are built on some notions of rights and obligations that preserve the body politic and the public order. They also establish notions of membership and status; not everyone is counted as a human being and full member of society. Cross-cultural surveys always focus, however, on what notions constitute legal contractual rights and obligations. Notions of personhood are collapsed into two schematic dimensions: ruler and ruled. Thus, the shah of Iran saw a human rights precedent in the proclamations of Cyrus the Great, who conferred rights to liberty and security, freedom of religion, movement, property, and economic and social rights on his subjects. Middle and Near Eastern scholars pointed out the ancient Egyptian pharaohs and the Babylonian monarch Hammurabi encoded certain rights almost two thousand years before the Christian era.

3. Algerian (Fanon 1963) and Senegalese (Senghor n.d.) critiques of French "universalism" dramatize how tyrannical Western powers could be in their love of man.

4. An international legal position on the abolition of slavery evolved over the 150-year period 1807–1957 and included such milestones as British colonial law (1807), the antislavery act in Brussels (1890), the League of Nations International Convention on the Abolition of Slavery and the Slave Trade (1926), the proclamation against slavery in the United Nations Universal Declaration (1948), and the United Nations Covenants against the slave trade (1957–58). Antislavery declarations notwithstanding, some form of slavery had clearly persisted over this period, especially in the European colonies. British interests in Nigeria through the early twentieth century, for example, were willing to tolerate customs of indigenous slavery, although colonial documents clarify that this was not condoned to be respectable behavior, and British interests expected that modern state landholding and other practices would gradually cause slavery to disappear.

5. The Red Cross, other humanitarian organizations, and the League of Nations were involved in extending nutritional and health services to prisoners of war and bringing relief into zones of armed conflict or other disasters since the nineteenth century (Messer 1991). Subsequent UN treaties and associated protocols furthered such humanitarian efforts to protect the victims of violent conflict. UN agencies, including Food and Agriculture Organization (FAO), World Health Organization (WHO), United Nations' Children and Education Fund (UNICEF), and World Food Programme (WFP) designed special programs to deliver humanitarian supplies; a special UN High Commissioner on Refugees was created to deal with growing demands by refugees.

6. International organizations after World War I sought to protect minority individuals in multinational states. Official statements expressed the principle or

desire that all peoples should enjoy human rights but included no provisions for enforcement. Nowhere do the documents clarify how "peoples" are linked to "persons" and actions within international law.

7. Renteln (1988a:10) has formulated these questions with respect to measuring human rights, with a specific focus on principles of violence or retaliation.

8. This small controlling group, however, did not speak for all anthropologists, most of whom were never asked for their opinion (Dimitri Shimkin notes, pers. comm., July 1990).

9. This defense of cultural relativism, coming immediately after the atrocities of World War II, appears odd, even wrongheaded.

10. Harris's review (1989:602) distinguishes among the categories of individual (the human organism as a psychological experience) and person (standing in a social order as an agent-in-society). Persons, for example, have judgmental capacities, social entitlements, and mystical capacities (connections with superhumans) depending on their positions in the social order. Beings who lack such capacities lack full status. Which concerns dominate and define full human or personal status vary according to culture. The significance of such definitions for human rights formulation and fulfillment awaits further cross-cultural clarification.

11. For an alternative and more hopeful viewpoint, see Tambiah 1992.

12. UNICEF and NGO consultants, familiar with such allegations, insist they are false (Mary Anderson, pers. comm., January 1991).

13. Some political philosophers continue to argue the precise points of logic for individual rights in the face of changing concepts, attitudes, and interpretations (see, e.g., Donnelly 1990).

14. What culture means in the development context constitutes yet another debate. Legal experts entertain varying images of "development" and a more or less dynamic concept of culture. Certain international lawyers interpret the political momentum behind people's rights as due to the failure of Western lawyers to deal seriously with Third World needs and demands. "I suspect that much of the distaste of Western international formulations of international rights conceals a complacent commitment to the interests of Western States" (Prott 1988:106).

15. "Humanitarianism demands that whatever detracts from human wellbeing must be questioned, regardless of its effects on economic growth, political power, or the stability of a certain order. Abstractions such as growth, stability, and order are not ends in themselves, but have value only if they bring about the greater welfare of people" (qtd. from Aga Khan 1988:162).

REFERENCES

Adegbite, L. O.
    1968   African Attitudes to the International Protection of Human Rights. In *International Protection of Human Rights,* ed. A. Eide and H. Shue, 69–81. New York: Interscience.

Aga Khan, S.
   1988   Forty Years On: And So Much Left To Do. In *Human Rights*, ed. P. Davies, 155–63. New York: Routledge.
Alston, P.
   1990a Introduction. *Human Rights in a Pluralist World: Individuals and Collectivities*. Westport, Conn.: Meckler.
   1990b U.S. Ratification of the Covenant on Economic, Social, and Cultural Rights: The Need for an Entirely New Strategy. *American Journal of International Law* 84:865–93.
American Anthropological Association (AAA)
   1947   Statement on Human Rights. *American Anthropologist*, 49:539–43.
Baehr, P. R.
   1990   Human Rights as People's Rights. In *Human Rights in a Pluralist World: Individuals and Collectivities,* ed. J. Berting et al., Westport, Conn.: Meckler.
Barnett, C.
   1988   Is There a Scientific Basis in Anthropology for the Ethics of Human Rights? In *Human Rights and Anthropology,* ed. T. E. Downing and G. Kushner, 21–26. Cambridge, Mass.: Cultural Survival.
Barnett, H. G.
   1948   On Science and Human Rights. *American Anthropologist* 50:352–55.
Berting, J., P. R. Baehr, J. H. Burger, C. Flinterman, B. de Klerk, P. Kroes, C. A. van Minnen, and K, van der Wal, eds.
   1990   *Human Rights in a Pluralist World: Individuals and Collectivities.* Westport, Conn.: Meckler.
Boas, F.
   1939   Autobiography. In *I Believe: The Personal Philosophies of Certain Eminent Men and Women of Our Time*, ed. C. Fadiman, 19–29. New York: Simon and Schuster.
   1943   Individual, Family, Population, and Race. *Proceedings of the American Philosophical Society* 87(2): 161–64.
Bodley, J.
   1975   *Victims of Progress*. Mountain View, Calif.: Mayfield.
Burger, J.
   1988   Indigenous Peoples: New Rights for Old Wrongs. In *Human Rights,* ed. P. Davies, 99–110. New York: Routledge.
Cernea, M.
   1991   *Putting People First: Sociological Variables in Development,* 2d ed. New York: Oxford University Press.
Chen, M.
   1986   *The Quiet Revolution: Women in Transition in Rural Bangladesh.* Cambridge, Mass.: Schenkman.
Clay, J.
   1988a Anthropologists and Human Rights. Activists by Default? In *Human Rights and Anthropology,* ed. T. E. Downing and G. Kushner, 115–24. Cambridge, Mass.: Cultural Survival.

1988b Ethiopian Famine and the Relief Agencies. In *The Moral Nation: Humanitarianism and U.S. Foreign Policy Today*, ed. R. Nichols and G. Loescher, 232–77. Notre Dame, Ind.: University of Notre Dame Press.

Clay, J., and B. Holcomb
1986 *Politics and the Ethiopian Famine, 1984–85*. Cambridge, Mass.: Cultural Survival.

Clay, J., S. Steingraber, P. Niggli
1988 *The Spoils of Famine: Ethiopian Famine Policy and Peasant Agriculture*. Cambridge, Mass.: Cultural Survival.

Cohen, R.
1993 Endless Teardrops: Prolegomena to the Study of Human Rights in Africa. In *Human Rights and Governance in Africa*, ed. R. Cohen, G. Hyden, and W. Nagen, Gainesville: University of Florida Press.

Colson, E.
1970 The Assimilation of Aliens among Zambian Tonga. In *From Tribe to Nation in Africa: Studies in Incorporation Processes*, ed. R. Cohen and J. Middleton, 35–54. Scranton, Pa.: Chandler.
1979 In Good Years and Bad: Food Strategies in Self-Reliant Societies. *Journal of Anthropological Research* 35:18–29.

Crawford, J.
1988 *The Rights of Peoples*. Oxford: Clarendon Press.

Donnelly, J.
1984 The Right to Development: How Not to Link Human Rights and Development. In *Human Rights and Development in Africa*, ed. C. Welch and R. Meltzer, 261–84. Albany, N.Y.: SUNY Press.
1990 In *Human Rights in a Pluralist World: Individuals and Collectivities*, ed. J. Berting, et al. Westport, Conn.: Meckler.

Doughty, P.
1988 Crossroads for Anthropology: Human Rights in Latin America. In *Human Rights and Anthropology*, ed. T. E. Downing and G. Kushner, 43–72. Cambridge, Mass.: Cultural Survival.

Downing, T. E. and G. Kushner
1988a Human Rights Research: The Challenge for Anthropologists. In *Human Rights and Anthropology*, ed. T. E. Downing and G. Kushner, 9–20. Cambridge, Mass.: Cultural Survival.
1988b Introduction. In *Human Rights and Anthropology*, ed. T. E. Downing and G. Kushner, 1–8. Cambridge, Mass.: Cultural Survival.

Downs, R. E., D. Kerner, and S. P. Reyna, eds.
1991 *The Political Economy of African Famine*. Philadelphia: Gordon and Breach.

Eide, A.
1984 The International Human Rights System. In *Food as a Human Right*, 152–61. Tokyo: United Nations University Press.

Falk, R.
1980 Theoretical Foundations of Human Rights. In *The Politics of Human*

    Rights, ed. P. R. Newberg, 65–110. New York: New York University Press.
 1988 The Rights of Peoples (in Particular, Indigenous Peoples) In *The Rights of Peoples,* ed. J. Crawford, 17–37. Oxford: Clarendon Press.
Fanon, F.
 1963 *The Wretched of the Earth.* Trans. C. Farrington. New York: Grove.
Farhang, M.
 1988 Fundamentalism and Civil Rights in Contemporary Middle Eastern Politics. In *Human Rights and the World's Religions,* ed. L. S. Rouner, 63–75. Notre Dame, Ind.: Notre Dame University Press.
Fein, H.
 1984 Scenarios of Genocide: Models of Genocide and Critical Responses. In *Toward an Understanding and Prevention of Genocide,* ed. I. W. Charney, 1–23. Proceedings of the International Conference on the Holocaust. Boulder, Colo.: Westview Press.
Glean, M.
 1966 Introduction to Human Rights in Perspective. *International Social Science Journal* 18(1): 7–10.
Grant, J.
 1990 *The State of the World's Children: 1990.* New York: UNICEF.
Guidieri, R., F. Pellizi, and S. Tambiah, eds.
 1988 *Ethnicities and Nations: Processes of Interethnic Relations in Latin America, Southeast Asia, and the Pacific.* Houston: Rothco Chapel.
Harris, Grace
 1989 Concepts of Individual, Self, and Person in Description and Analysis. *American Anthropologist* 91:599–612.
Hemmings-Gapihan, G.
 1985 Women and Economy in Gourma, 1919–1978: A Study of Economic Change in Burkina Faso (Upper Volta). Ph.D. diss., Department of Anthropology, Yale University.
Hersch, J.
 1969 *Birthright of Man.* New York: UNESCO.
Herskovits, M.
 1951 Tender and Tough-Minded Anthropology and the Study of Values in Culture. *Southwestern Journal of Anthropology* 7:22–31.
Horowitz, M.
 1990 Victims of Development. *Development Anthropology Network* 7(2): 1–8.
Howard, R.
 1992 Dignity, Community, and Human Rights. *Human Rights in Cross-Cultural Perspective: A Quest for Consensus,* 81–102. Philadelphia: University of Pennsylvania Press.
Hurtado, A.-M.
 1990 Anthropology Has Had No Impact on Human Rights. *Anthropology Newsletter* 31(3): 3.

Huss-Ashmore, R., and S. Katz, eds.
   1989   *African Food Systems in Crisis,* Part 1: Microperspectives. New York: Gordon and Breach.
   1990   *African Food Systems in Crisis,* Part 2: Contending with Change. New York: Gordon and Breach.
Independent Commission on International Humanitarian Issues (ICIHI)
   1985   *Famine: A Man-Made Disaster?* New York: Vintage.
   1988   *Indigenous Peoples: A Global Quest for Justice.* London: Zed.
Jacobs, D.
   1984   *The Brutality of Nations.* New York: Alfred A. Knopf.
Johnson, A., and T. Earle
   1987   *The Evolution of Human Society: From Foraging Group to Agrarian State.* Stanford, Calif.: Stanford University Press.
Kamenka, E.
   1988   Human Rights: People's Rights. In *The Rights of Peoples,* ed. J. Crawford, 127–40. Oxford: Clarendon Press.
Kammerer, C.
   1988   Territorial Imperatives: Akha Ethnic Identity and Thailand's National Integration. In *Ethnicities and Nations: Processes of Interethnic Relations in Latin America, Southeast Asia, and the Pacific,* ed. R. Guideri, F. Pellizzi, and S. Tambiah, 259–92. Houston: Rothco Chapel.
Kapferer, Bruce
   1988   *Legends of People, Myths of State. Violence, Intolerance, and Political Culture.* Washington, D.C.: Smithsonian.
Kroeber, A. L.
   1949   An Authoritarian Panacea. *American Anthropologist* 51:320.
Kuper, L.
   1977   *The Pity of It All: Polarisation of Racial and Ethnic Relations.* London: Duckworth.
   1982   *Genocide: Its Political Use in the Twentieth Century.* New Haven, Conn.: Yale University Press.
   1986   *The Prevention of Genocide.* New Haven, Conn.: Yale University Press.
Legesse, A.
   1980   Human Rights in African Political Culture. In *The Moral Imperatives of Human Rights: A World Survey.* ed. E. Thompson, 123–38. Washington, D.C.: American University Press.
   1990   Personal communication.
Lévi-Strauss, C.
   1952   *Race and History.* Paris: UNESCO.
Marchione, T.
   1984   Approaches to the Hunger Problem: A Critical Overview. In *Food as a Human Right,* ed. A. Eide, W. B. Eide, S. Goonatilake, J. Gussow, and W. Omawale, 117–40. Tokyo: United Nations University Press.
Maritain, J.
   1943–71   *The Rights of Man and Natural Law.* New York: Gordon and Breach.

Marks, S.
    1980   Emerging Human Rights: A New Generation for the 1980s. *Rutgers Law Review* 33:435.

Mayor, F.
    1990   Preface. In *Human Rights in a Pluralist World: Individuals and Collectivities*, ed. J. Berting, et al., Westport, Conn.: Meckler.

McLaughlin, B.
    1974   Mediation of Contradiction: Why Mbum Women Do Not Eat Chicken. In *Women, Culture, and Society.* ed. L. Lamphere and M. Rosaldo, 301–19. Stanford, Calif.: Stanford University Press.

Mead, M.
    1950   *Food and the Family.* New York: UNESCO.

Messer, E.
    1986   Franz Boas and Kaufmann Kohler: Anthropology and Reform Judaism. *Jewish Social Studies* 48(2): 127–40.
    1989a Small But Healthy? Some Cross Cultural Perspectives. *Human Organization* 38(1): 39–52.
    1989b The Ecology and Politics of Food Availability. In *African Food Systems in Crisis, Part 1: Microperspectives,* ed. R. Huss-Ashmore and S. Katz, 189–202. New York: Gordon and Breach.
    1991   Food Wars: Hunger as a Weapon of War in 1990. Research Report RR-91-3, World Hunger Program, Brown University, Providence, R.I.
    1993   Anthropology and Human Rights. *Annual Review of Anthropology* 22:221–49.

Moris, J.
    1989   Indigenous versus Introduced Solutions to Food Stress in Africa. In *Seasonal Variability in Third World Agriculture,* ed. D. Sahn, 209–34. Baltimore: Johns Hopkins University Press.

Na'im, A. A. A.
    1992   Toward a Cross-Cultural Approach to Defining International Standards of Human Rights: The Meaning of Cruel, Inhuman, or Degrading Treatment or Punishment. *Human Rights in Cross-Cultural Perspective: A Quest for Consensus,* 19–43. Philadelphia: University of Pennsylvania Press.

Newman, L.
    1989   Personal communication.

Newman, L., ed.
    1990   *Hunger in History: Food Shortage, Poverty, and Deprivation.* London: Basil Blackwell.

Pagezy, H.
    1988   Coping with Uncertainty in Food Supply among the Oto and the Twa Living in the Equatorial Flooded Forest near Lake Tumba. In *Coping with Uncertainty in Food Supply,* ed. I. de Garine and G. A. Harrison, 176–209. New York: Oxford University Press.

Papanek. H.
    1989   Socialization for Inequality: Issues for Research and Action. *Samya Shakti.* New Delhi: Center for Women's Development Studies.

Polgar, S.
   1968   General Discussion. In *War: The Anthropology of Armed Conflict and Aggression,* ed. M. Fried, M. Harris, and R. Murphy, 81–82. New York: Natural History Press.

Prott, L. V.
   1988   Cultural Rights as Peoples' Rights in International Law. In *The Rights of Peoples,* ed. J. Crawford, 93–106. Oxford: Clarendon Press.

Raphael, D. D.
   1966   The Liberal Western Tradition of Human Rights. *International Social Science Journal* 18(1): 22–30.

Renteln, A. D.
   1988a A Cross-Cultural Approach of Validating International Human Rights: The Case of Retribution Tied to Proportionality. In *Human Rights: Theory and Measurement,* 7–40. New York: St. Martin's.
   1988b Relativism and the Search for Human Rights. *American Anthropologist* 90:56–72.

Robertson, A. H.
   1982   *Human Rights in the World: An Introduction to the International Protection of Humans Rights,* 2d ed. New York: St. Martin's.

Rouner, L. S.
   1988   *Human Rights and the World's Religions.* Notre Dame, Ind.: University of Notre Dame Press.

Schirmer, J.
   1988   The Dilemma of Cultural Diversity and Equivalency in Universal Human Rights Standards. In *Human Rights and Anthropology,* ed. T. Downing and G. Kushner, 121–97. Cambridge, Mass.: Cultural Survival.

Schirmer, J., A. Renteln, and L. Weisberg
   1988   Anthropology and Human Rights: A Selected Bibliography. *Human Rights and Anthropology,* 121–97. Cambridge, Mass.: Cultural Survival.

Sengor, L. S.
   N.d.   *Liberté 1: Negritude et Humanisme* 1:98. Paris: Edition du Seuil.

Stavenhagen, R.
   1990   Indigenous Rights. In *Human Rights in a Pluralist World: Individuals and Collectivities,* ed. J. Berting, et al., Westport, Conn.: Meckler.

Strathern, M.
   1972   *Women in Between.* New York: Seminar Press.

Tambiah, S.
   1988   Foreword. In *Ethnicities and Nations: Processes of Interethnic Relations in Latin America, Southeast Asia, and the Pacific,* ed. R. Guidieri, F. Pellizzi, and S. Tambiah, 1–6. Houston: Rothco Chapel.
   1992   *Buddhism Betrayed? Religion, Politics, and Violence in Sri Lanka.* Chicago: University of Chicago Press.

Tax, S., ed.
   1952   *Heritage of Conquest.* Glencoe, Ill.: Free Press.

Tomasevski, K.
　　1989　*Development Aid and Human Rights: A Case Study for the Danish Center.* New York: St. Martin's.
United Nations
　　1988　Human Rights. *UN Chronicle* 25(1) (March): 47–50.
UNESCO
　　1987　Anthropology and Human Rights. *Human Rights Teachings 6.*
VanderWal, K.
　　1990　Collective Human Rights: A Western View. In *Human Rights in a Pluralist World: Individuals and Collectivities,* ed. J. Berting, et al., Westport, Conn.: Meckler.
Varese, S.
　　1988　Multi-Ethnicity and Hegemonic Construction: Indian Plans and the Indian Future. In *Ethnicities and Nations: Processes of Interethnic Relations in Latin America, Southeast Asia, and the Pacific,* ed. R. Guidieri, F. Pellizzi, and S. Tambiah, 57–77. Houston: Rothco Chapel.
Watts, M.
　　1983　*Silent Violence: Food, Famine and Peasantry in Northern Nigeria.* Berkeley: University of California Press.
Weissbrodt, D.
　　1988　Human Rights: An Historical Perspective. In *Human Rights,* ed. P. Davies, 1–20. New York: Routledge.
Williams, E.
　　1947　Anthropology for the Common Man. *American Anthropologist* 49:84–90.
Wright, R. M.
　　1988　Anthropological Presuppositions of Indigenous Advocacy. In *Annual Review of Anthropology* 17:365–90.
Wright, R. M., and Ismaelillo
　　1982　*Native Peoples in Struggle: Cases from the Fourth Russell Tribunal.* Bombay: ERIN.
Yamane, H.
　　1982　Human Rights for the People of Asia. *Human Rights Teaching* 3:18–22
Zalaquett, José
　　1981　*The Human Rights Issue and the Human Rights Movement* [Background Information.] Geneva: Commission of the Churches on International Affairs of the World Council of Churches.
　　1984　The Relationship between Development and Human Rights. *The Human Right to Food,* ed. A. Eide et al., 141–51. Tokyo: United Nations University Press.
Zvogbo, E. J. M.
　　1979　A Third World View. In *Human Rights and American Foreign Policy,* ed. D. P. Kommers and G. D. Lescher, 90–107. Notre Dame, Ind.: Notre Dame University Press.

Chapter 7

Goals and Indices of Development: An Anthropological Perspective

Emilio F. Moran

The processes of global change, often referred to by the gloss "development," have accelerated in the twentieth century. Driven by economic planners who have adopted theories and analytic methods primarily from neoclassical and Keynesian economics, the process has produced numerous disorders in the distribution of resources within and between nations as well as some notable improvements in public health, nutrition, and wealth. The net result most would agree, however, has been an exacerbation of the differences between rich and poor nations and between the rich and the poor within nations.

The extrapolation of aggregate macroeconomic indices which measure so-called development from First World nations to other settings has been going on for the greater part of the twentieth century. Even though these indices were not specifically developed to measure improvements in individual or even aggregate welfare over the years, they have become obligatory indices in measuring how well development efforts have succeeded. Their current value in evaluating how successful development efforts have been in improving the welfare of individuals in a nation is brought into question in this chapter.

In the nineteenth century European economic historians began to develop theories that sought to explain how the process of transformation from predominantly agricultural to industrial production occurred—and how it might be promoted further. Western economic theories, some of them dating from the peak period of European colonialism in the late nineteenth century, have attempted to explain the experience of the West and to justify its economic actions (Robinson 1979). The promotion of growth by the West has resulted, on the positive side, in unprecedented amounts of wealth and, on the negative side, in unprecedented disparities in welfare and destruction of natural resources.

These disparities between nations have become, if anything, accentuated in the twentieth century. Just as these disparities between nations have grown larger, however, their interdependence has grown at a comparable rate. This interdependence has come about through the promotion and acceptance of Western economic concepts that purport to provide a value-free approach to understanding the wealth of nations and its change over time.

The best example of such a concept may be the use of gross national product (GNP) as the optimum measure of development. GNP—that is, the total flow of goods and services produced in a particular country measured at market prices—cannot and does not measure the distribution of that output among the people and thus is hardly an adequate measure of the improvement in welfare of the individuals of a nation.

To evade this dilemma it has been common to take a refuge in the calculation of per capita GNP as a more objective measure of economic success. The wealth and, by implication, the welfare of individuals is judged in terms of the growth of GNP per capita. As a prominent Cambridge economist has pointed out, "From the point of view of welfare, information about *average* income is meaningless unless we know how consuming power is distributed" (Robinson 1979:5).

The growing interconnectedness of the earth's national economies, together with the persistence of economic disparities and unequal terms of trade, represent a type of disorder that constitutes a major threat to global peace and stability—and to the ability of nations to provide adequate access to resources to a majority of the world's citizens. "Spokesmen for the Third World like to deploy comparisons of figures of national income per capita in order to demonstrate the difference between rich and poor countries, but there is nowadays great disillusionment with statistical GNP as the objective of development. Nevertheless, there have been few attempts to replace it in the simplifying operations that nations use to evaluate their progress" (ibid.).

This chapter provides one more critique of currently dominant aggregate economic indices of development, but it does so with the objective of encouraging anthropologists to join other social scientists in proposing alternative indices that provide a broader assessment of changes in social welfare than that which measures primarily output of goods and services. Such an effort should beware of existing efforts to invent other single indices of development status (e.g., Tata and Schultz 1988), a simplifying exercise likely to overlook the variability in physical, social, economic, and political systems.

Anthropology, as the social science with the longest history of attention to the local details of human life in broad context, is in a particularly good position to consider how it might engage the challenge posed by the need to measure and evaluate positive and negative changes in human welfare. The indices we might develop cannot be purely disaggregated ones, as this would make them of little value for certain kinds of aggregate analysis that nations must engage in. Rather, the indices must permit both aggregation and disaggregation, macro- and micro-analysis of the improvement in human welfare in nations. Nothing is likely to teach us more humility than to attempt to create an index such as this, as others who have tried have been quick to point out (Daly and Cobb Jr. 1989).

It would be naive to think that this chapter advocates the abandonment of neoclassical economics. The neoclassical paradigm is a body of theory of considerable robustness that has been highly productive in the study of economic behavior. Even indices like GNP, which I will criticize in this chapter, have their place. GNP is an effective reductionist way to compare the relative total wealth and power of nations. As a measure of productive capacity, it can hardly be improved on. When applied to the measurement of social welfare within nations, however, it overlooks the great disparities in distribution that can be produced in an expanding economy. One of the earliest critics of GNP was Simon Kuznets, who argued that the national accounts' focus on market transactions distorted the assessment of society's actual well-being. This is particularly the case when applied to Third World nations, where so much of the productive economic activity occurs *outside* the market (Waring 1989). This is a matter of considerable seriousness given that international assistance programs often target aid to those groups in most need, but they do not always identify persons entirely outside the market. This may have had negative results on the nutritional well-being of farmers, in particular. This is proving to be the case also in the more developed economies, in times of recession, when the informal sector expands to meet the needs of the population left out of the formal sector by policies aimed, say, at controlling inflation. Despite the large investments in development and the notable rise in GNP of most countries, there is growing evidence that there has been a decline in overall welfare in recent years even in the United States (Daly and Cobb Jr. 1989).

The GNP index is not wrong; it is misapplied in current practice. It hides unacceptable disparities in distribution created by development behind the apparent equity of per capita share of total GNP. It is easier to avoid the problems of distribution and to pretend that wealth will trickle more or less evenly to individuals. This is patently not the case. The GNP per capita has outlived its usefulness as an indicator of how well development efforts have succeeded in reducing the poverty of people in nations. It may still be useful in measuring the relative power and wealth of nations. It is difficult to comprehend why GNP continues to be such a broadly used gauge of economic performance when it excludes a large portion of women's productive but unpaid work within the home and when production that brings about environmental degradation is counted as value produced but an unspoiled environment is not (Waring 1989). This chapter is an invitation to anthropologists to join the economists and social scientists who find GNP and other current measures of development inadequate in working together toward producing them in ways that can be realistically implemented.

Economic Theory and the Disorders of Development

Economics lacks, to this day, a general theory of development (Gill 1967). "No clear-cut system of 'new development economics' has yet emerged to dominate the fields of economic development theory and policy as completely as the 'new economics' based on J. M. Keynes's work, dominated income and employment theory after 1936" (Hayami and Ruttan 1971:2).

Two approaches loom as most influential in the literature before the 1970s. One emphasizes the *growth stages* through which economies evolve (Rostow 1960); the other emphasizes the problems posed by the existence of *dual economies* (Jorgenson 1961; Ranis and Fei 1961). Efforts to arrive at a set of sequential stages that represent the process of economic growth go back to the nineteenth century and had their origin in Germany (Hoselitz 1960). Marx is considered the only one of a host of scholars that produced genuinely evolutionary economic theory (Schumpeter 1954). His scheme proposed five stages, each of which resulted from the struggle between those controlling the means of production (i.e., capitalists) and those who did not (i.e., labor). This struggle occurs around the opportunities for transformation in the relations of production created by a changing technology. Less comprehensive but no less influential in policy circles were the views of Friedrich List, who emphasized the importance of having a national industrial policy to transform economies from being agriculturally to industrially based. No major growth stage theory emerged until Rostow proposed his stages of growth (1960). Rostow's stages gave a preeminent role to the rapid growth of agricultural output during the early stages of economic development, and his views became commonplace among public policy practitioners, despite the rejection of his stages by most economists (Hayami and Ruttan 1971:15).

Dual economy approaches emerged in an attempt to understand the relationship (or lack thereof) between the traditional sector and the modern sector in countries feeling the influence of Western colonialism (ibid., 17). The early dualistic models were static and emphasized the limited interaction between the two sectors. They tended to reflect the frustration of colonial powers with their colonies' failure to respond quickly to the economic policies that they introduced. Their models found tropical/colonial conditions as too different from the West and found Western economics as inapplicable in dual economy situations (Boeke 1953). Boeke noted that Indonesians were guided primarily by "social needs," in contrast to Western societies, which are driven primarily by "economic needs." Despite the rejection of Boeke by his own Dutch colleagues, and others in the field of economics, Boeke's views made their way into decision-making circles, whose members found in his models a justification for not investing in agricultural development and giving sole attention to industrial policy.

More recent dualistic models have been characterized as "dynamic" because they proposed a solution to the apparent lack of interaction between the traditional and the modern sector. W. Arthur Lewis (1954) provided the intellectual takeoff for the models proposed later by Jorgenson, Fei, and Ranis. Their models sought ways to transfer labor and surplus from the traditional sector (subsistence agriculture) to the modern sector (mechanized agriculture and industry) through policy interventions. They neglected to take into account the additional costs of technological inputs to agriculture and the possibility that it may be "appropriate in some situations to have a net flow of savings into the agricultural sector" (Hayami and Ruttan 1971:23).

Development economics moved from the economic modernization phase of the 1950s and the 1960s to a phase of growth-with-equity in the 1970s. The former was defined largely in terms of growth in average per capita output, while the latter has attempted to include income distribution, employment, nutrition, and other variables (Eicher and Staatz 1984:3). In models before 1950 agriculture was given a rather passive role, while the interdependence of the agricultural and industrial sector became more recognized in the 1960s.

Considerable changes took place in the 1970s and into the 1980s through greater emphasis on microeconomic research, intersectoral linkages, rural factor markets, migration, and rural small-scale industries. These were, in part, responses to the growth of political economy and dependency models that criticized Western neoclassical economies. Dependency theorists argued that low-income countries were pauperized both through a process of unequal exchange with the industrialized nations and through the repatriation of profits from foreign-owned businesses (Frank 1966). They also attributed to the understanding that each country has a historical experience that affects how they respond to economic incentives and policies. They showed that economic development was more than just a matter of raising per capita GNP; it involved restructuring institutional and political relationships. In the words of de Janvry, "economic policy without political economy is a useless and utopian exercise" (1981:263).

These critiques, as well as the series of political disasters that struck a number of Third World countries from the 1960s on, led to a growing emphasis in economics on equity rather than on growth. It became increasingly apparent that rapid economic growth in some countries had deleterious and even disastrous effects (Eicher and Staatz 1984:13).

This resulted in greater attention to the agricultural sector, a greater effort at targeting projects to labor-absorbing projects, and welfare programs. An expansion of micro-level research on agricultural production and marketing, farmer decision making, the performance of rural factor markets, and rural nonfarm employment resulted. Anthropologists were called upon to participate in growing numbers during this phase and to contribute to the "social soundness" of development projects (Chenery et al. 1974; Chenery 1979; Streeten et al. 1981; Cernea 1987).

Important efforts at modeling the agricultural sector were produced in this period (Hayami and Ruttan 1971; Johnston and Kilby 1975; Mellor 1976; de Janvry 1981). Each of these emphasized different approaches to agricultural development. Hayami and Ruttan (1971) argued for the importance of identifying which mix of factors of production a country provided a comparative advantage in and through what changes in relative factor prices the process can be optimized. This implied that countries have different factor endowments and, thus, different growth paths—a notable improvement over previous models, which presumed that wholesale importation of agricultural technology from developed countries would lead to growth.

Mellor (1976) emphasized how the high-yielding varieties could become the cornerstone of policies leading to growth linkages in other sectors, with most of the employment actually occurring in the nonfarm sector. Johnston and Kilby (1975) proposed a view, with which anthropologists would generally tend to agree, that concentrating development efforts on the mass of small farmers would lead to faster growth rates of both aggregate economic output and employment—given the importance of the size distribution of farms on the demand for industrial products and through notable improvements in individual welfare that would result. Many other scholars (e.g., Dorner and Ranel 1971; Barraclough 1973; Berry and Cline 1979) supported the view of the importance of land reform to bring about equitable development, but political support for such reform waned in the 1970s; in some cases it was opposed by the rise of authoritarian regimes with development strategies concerned more with aggregate economic growth than with equity.

In the mid-1970s the "basic needs" approach was popularized by the ILO and subsequently by the World Bank (Seers 1970; Streeten et al. 1981). This approach argued that development projects should give priority to increasing the welfare of the poor (the poorest 40 percent) directly, through projects targeted at improving nutrition, education, housing, health, and so on. Anthropologists were called upon, once more, to help with these projects, and their contributions were important (Cernea 1987).

By the mid-1980s, however, a growing number of economists began to doubt the emphasis given to equity and to shift to a more growth-oriented strategy. Currently, both approaches coexist, and policy makers seem to fluctuate between growth- and equity-oriented projects. The recent rise of supply-side economics, another name for neoclassical growth-oriented economic theory, in major First World nations has led to a shift in practice that gives greater weight to the "invisible hand of the market" and to the benefits to be derived from GNP growth than to distributional issues.

The presumption of supply-side economists in international lending agencies and foreign aid organizations is that all countries ought to grow in economic activity and that, ideally, they should do so rapidly. Population growth has been a major driving force justifying the need to have a concurrent economic expansion to avert deterioration of standards of living. The fact that sustained economic growth has been a historical anomaly, and that where it has occurred it has been a product of unusual, unplanned circumstances, has not deterred development economists from trying to develop models and policies that can lead capital-poor nations to a path of sustained economic growth. A path of economic growth in contemporary societies, it is said, requires capital accumulation, in which current consumption is deferred and savings are invested in the further growth of capital. Presumably, the increased economic activity generated by capital investment leads to an expansion of employment and of markets for goods and services. As this process continues, further capital is accumulated and invested, leading to technological change to gain greater efficiency in the allocation of resources and to gain market share. This can be done through either favorable prices or product quality or both. Competition in technology leads, in turn, to educational improvements and greater specialization, which expands markets and demand for goods and services. In other words, the process becomes self-sustaining (Gill 1967:34).

This ideal model of development is rarely achieved. Under what conditions would a country dominated by an agrarian elite choose to part with its current privileges and conspicuous forms of allocating its wealth to, say, prestige give way to other forms of allocation favoring capital accumulation in technological innovation? In the absence of a large number of firms and competitors, such firms would opt for less risk, in the form of collusion through oligopolies. What would urge powerful elites to allocate significant proportions of GNP to education, science, and technology for all citizens? What would justify the technological modernization of agriculture when labor is abundant and cheap? What would move elites to change the tax structure so that they are more progressive and leave more of the income in the hands of the masses, who, as consumers, will buy the output of industrial growth, instead of having tax structures that favor leaving more of the income in their own hands, whose consumption will favor industrial growth of oligopolies under government incentives and protection? These *moral* choices are not addressed by most of neoclassical economics, even though such choices are made daily by those in powerful positions (Etzioni 1988). The moral dimensions of economic decision making have been lacking from the neoclassical economic models, with their apparent focus on the maximization of an individuals's utility and his lack of concern with the social order. In fact, most political systems have moral priorities that affect the ultimate economic decisions that are made. Economics has identified one important element in human behavior: the tendency toward selfishness of individuals—while overlooking that one of the tasks of any social and political system is to control and direct that selfishness in productive ways for the larger social good (Arrow 1983).

The Trouble with GNP as a Measure

Economics is most concerned with the efficiency of resource allocation over time (Bates 1983a:362). To deal with this concern it focuses on changes in per capita income and on changes in productive activities that make income changes possible (ibid.). The tool kit brought to bear on efficiency accounting of firms relies on econometric methods to determine whether, given their current resources, firms are using the technology that allows them to maximize output; whether they are selecting inputs and producing outputs in proportion to their relative prices thereby maximizing profits; and whether resources are being used to the point where the costs equal the benefits at the margin and whether the net benefits are greater than those generated by alternative uses of scarce resources (364).

The concern with *efficiency* is not surprising. Development economics is concerned with countries with scarce capital and scarce technology. The stress on capital is basic: capital can take resources out of consumption in one period of time so as to increase consumption at a later time, the productive possibilities of any group are determined by the capital at its command, and to increase per capita income one must increase the ratio of capital to labor (Bates 1983a:365). Harrod (1952) and Domar (1946) focused on the process of capital formation, while later theorists emphasized the stages of growth and the role of savings and investment in economic growth (e.g., Rostow 1961). Efforts to divert attention to people, or "human capital" as economists would have it, have appeared

(Schultz 1964) but they have failed to divert economic practice away from an emphasis on *real* capital.

Economists have been all too ready to give up on the search for better indices of social welfare. "As an indicator of welfare, national product is crude, but it is the best index we have. Some simple improvements can be made. Per capita product is doubtless a better gauge of welfare than total product. A factor can be added to count the part of growing product that the society takes in the form of additional leisure. *However the measure is improved, output cannot be equated with welfare* but it can serve as a rough register of changes in welfare" (Sirkin 1965:203; italics mine). This latter distinction is often forgotten by the practitioners of the art of economics. As the same author notes: "in an economy dedicated to the promotion of welfare of its members, growth should be defined as the increase of welfare. Since no direct measure of welfare nor any prospect of obtaining one exists, discussions of growth are conducted in terms of the increase of economic product" (ibid.).

The use of GNP and other measures of commoditization are a lot less crucial to measuring living standards than "freedom from drudgery, reduced exposure to risk of death, and an expanded range of choices open to individuals" (Hart, in Sen 1987:84). GNP might bear some marginal relation to living standards when a commoditized industrial economy is prospering, but it is less so when it is undergoing a recession or if an economy is only weakly monetized (ibid., 93). Yet it is in these latter circumstances that GNP tends to be used most often as an index and when it is most likely to mislead. It is perhaps more relevant to view human welfare in terms of "unaggregated characterizations of functionings and capabilities" and as "partial orderings of aggregated assessments" than as single number measures of opulence (Sen 1987:38). Thus, China, for example, has improved its overall per capita GNP considerably above India's, but it was unable to stave off devastating famine or offer freedom of the press and of expression to its citizens. Which one has a higher standard of living? Is a larger GNP merely an indicator of opulence? Or is it best seen as a constellation of freedoms— freedom from drudgery, freedom to live a long life, freedom to have rights to food guaranteed by society at large?

Despite the mounting evidence for the imperfection of the market, economists hold on to the presuppositions that prices are efficient allocators and that one can infer from aggregate decisions the rationality or irrationality of individuals. "Rational individual choices do not in general lead to socially rational outcomes. . . . [This] has been explored most actively by political science" (Bates 1983b:375). Popkin (1979) and Bates (1983a), among others, have explored the importance of aggregation procedures in the study of agrarian societies.

One of the confusions emerging out of economic theory lies in a subtle shift in level of analysis. When economists observe that *a society* uses its resources inefficiently, for example, it infers that individuals in it are making irrational or inappropriate allocation choices. This view is totally unwarranted, since individual choices, even when rational, do not necessarily lead to socially rational outcomes. What is rational or adaptive to the individual may be, and often is, irrational or maladaptive to the aggregate, or social group. This shift in analysis is a result of the lack of theoretical articulation between microeconomics and macroeconomics (Thurow 1983:4) and a lack of attention to moral ends and values in individual decisions (Etzioni 1988). Economic decision-making models in anthropology may indulge in some of the same fallacies, as a result of borrowing economic models without a sufficient assessment of their implications in terms of social welfare (Barlett 1980; Gladwin 1989).

The reliance of economic policy on per capita GNP as a measure of social welfare reflects these conceptual problems. This preference, as we have seen, held during the 1950s and 1960s, had a temporary decline in the 1970s, when basic needs and equity seemed to be promoted, and returned in the 1980s under the guise of supply-side economics. Policies that lead to greater per capita GNP are evaluated as "socially successful." Per capita GNP, consisting of the sum of the total value of the output of an economy divided by the number of persons in that society (Sirkin 1965:7), is used to evaluate the well-being of individuals in it. This practice is based on a number of incorrect assumptions: first, consumption is not an adequate measure of individual wealth, especially in societies in which not all goods and services are cleared through markets (e.g., reciprocal exchanges, subsistence production, gifts, barter) or in which the proportion of total consumption attributed to government consumption of goods and services makes up a disproportionate amount of total consumption (e.g., government expenditures in armaments). Second, GNP per capita is meaningful only if every additional unit of income generates the same satisfaction from each person. This is patently not the case, since a poor person is likely to value an additional unit of income more than a very rich person (Marshall 1920). Third, increases in total and per capita GNP do not take into account that these increases are not shared proportionally and that a 10 percent gain in income in the top 5 percent income group is likely to represent a larger proportion of total GNP than, say, a 10 percent gain in income for the bottom 5, 10, or even 20 percent of the population of a developing country.

GNP further distorts the welfare of individuals and nations through its inclusion of items such as military expenditures, which have grown in their proportion of total GNP faster than total GNP, averaging 7 to 9 percent, as compared to 2 to 5 percent for total GNP (Robinson 1979:124). When military expenditures are included, the meaning of GNP as a measure of welfare becomes very dubious.

To compound the problems introduced by the use of per capita GNP as a measure of social welfare, one can also point out the extremely poor quality of basic statistical figures issued by most countries (Hill 1986:32), based as they are on bad agricultural statistics to start with. Farmers, unlike professional economists, have a "disinclination to aggregate" the areas they operate and think of them individually in terms of the seed it takes to plant each field, the crops that each will support, or the history of its acquisition (ibid., 37). When forced to aggregate, farmers will respond with figures, but their accuracy is highly questionable. Moreover, most farmers lack any incentive to measure and aggregate the output from their various small plots. Some of the output may be sold, some consumed, other bartered, and other saved for seed. Some of the products have no harvest season but are harvested throughout the year in small quantities as needed, as is the case with cassava and plantains.

Anthropologists also know that official land records are seriously out-of-date, underestimate the value of properties, and neglect to include items most likely to increase tax assessments. When these landholdings are worked by different wives, as is true in polygynous societies, the difficulty increases, as the male household head may not even think of the land as his or it may not be recorded as such in land record offices. This is not to say that males are always head of households but, rather, that in many cases census takers make the mistake of going to the apparent male head of household to seek information. In other societies farm plots may be put in the name of different household members to circumvent legal limitations on the number of properties a household head may own. Anthropology, despite its attention to the interdependence of individuals and societies, has not tackled this problem of aggregation in economics and contributed its own insights to the consequences of such interdependence on policy. The basic factor that leads to the problem of analytical shift in levels is the very interdependence of individuals. The greater the interdependence and the lesser the autonomy, the more the decision of individuals are likely to lead to socially undesirable outcomes.

Another major presumption biasing many macroeconomists' approaches to development is their apparent ignorance of existing inequalities in local systems (Hill 1986). The aggregation process leads to presumptions that the majority of rural people are an undifferentiated peasantry lacking in capital, technology, and investment strategies. It ignores the presence of stratification, of significant differences between households in access to the means of production, in differential levels of consumption, and differences in investment strategy. The persistence by economists of holding to aggregate statistics as a measure of individual well-being needs to be replaced with statistics that account for landholdings by households, that do not carelessly bundle all land owners, say, with less than five hectares into one class, when that class may lump a majority of rural peoples and when differences within that class may be significant to understanding individual well-being. Nor should such statistics leave out the significant role of trader/merchants, the landless, and other nonfarmers within rural communities (ibid., 15). This problem occurs not only in Third World countries but in the First World as well. Errors in forecasting GNP change have fluctuated between 28 and 56 percent (Lee 1967:638). Estimates of current GNP are often found to be in error. Rosanne Cole of the National Bureau of Economic Research in Washington estimates that about 20 to 25 percent of the GNP forecast errors result from data errors (ibid.).

> One cannot help developing a certain amount of uneasiness about the proportion of time which has been devoted to aggregate analysis over this span of years. The work done has been generally first-rate work, but it has tended to produce a preoccupation with aggregate analysis and a tendency to seek solutions to economic fluctuation problems in terms of aggregates. The current preoccupation with aggregate analysis has induced relatively little theoretical or analytical work with the kinds of facts the [National] Bureau has gathered and published . . . what is needed and, hopefully, what is about to happen, is an approach to the study of economic fluctuations and

growth which incorporates the detail of information typified by the Bureau. (450–51).

But, having criticized GNP, and especially per capita GNP, as a measure of social welfare, what might anthropology suggest be put in its place?

Anthropological Approaches to Development

Anthropology has clearly stood apart in the social sciences in defending the importance of local institutions as representations of a society's moral order. While modernization and loss of local autonomy has undermined many of the moral systems of so-called traditional societies, many of them have survived and still stand in counterpoint to the homogenizing forces of economic development based upon simplistic indices of welfare. One of their valuable features as moral orders is that they frequently are made up of multiple moral systems that coexist and litigate with one another for supremacy with regard to their moral authority. An important potential area for unique anthropological contributions could very well be the exploration of culturally specific systems of moral preference and human welfare embedded in local institutions. Their ethical valuation of what constitutes welfare would be a starting point in developing indices that are morally appropriate to different societies. DeWalt has suggested that anthropology, and especially that branch of it associated with ecological approaches, has identified some of the fundamental problems with recent development approaches:

1. Models of economic growth run counter to ecological processes, making economic growth unsustainable in the long run. The growth of economies has been at the expense of the physical environment, thereby undermining their long-term productive capacity.
2. Development models place too great an emphasis on growth rather than on its purpose—what the growth is for. This leads inevitably to an abuse of resources and to lack of attention to moral ends.
3. Growth inevitably leads to greater hierarchy and greater losses in system maintenance. As greater proportions of the population must devote themselves to regulation of the system, controls become so complex and interconnected that there is a loss of

control, and efforts at control have counterintuitive consequences leading to system disorder.
4. The loss of cultural diversity implied by development leads to the loss of a pool of available solutions, which further destabilizes the system and reorders it along new lines (DeWalt 1988).

While human populations always surprise us with their resiliency, the rate of change is such that the periods of destabilization are severe and frequent enough to entail high mortality and morbidity, before stability is reestablished.

These disorders of development call for amelioration, and anthropological findings suggest positive ways to proceed in dealing with the four disorders above.

1. It is not uncommon for economic development activities to destroy native habitats. This is the result of the compartmentalization of decision making in organizations, the lack of specificity of development processes, and an uncritical emphasis on growth in economics that cannot even conceive as desirable a period of stable relations in the exploitation of resources. This is a deep cause of modern humanity's disorders, since it fails to couple our use of resources with their sustainability or renewability, with the relative impact of different technologies on different ecosystems, and ignores local-level expertise. The latter results not only in cultural loss and marginalization of local peoples but also in costly mistakes that waste capital and degrade the physical environment (cf. Johnston and Kilby 1975).

2. The emphasis on growth of capital and the lack of moral ends of such growth results in profound disorders in human society. While it is acknowledged that the goal of development is a "better living standard," some economists have managed to keep their attention not on these ultimate ends but, instead, on intermediate ends and on their achievement, measured purely in terms of capital growth. The problem is that intermediate ends can never be satisfied. If "a better life" is the goal, then indices of development based on stratified data measuring improved nutritional status, birth weight of neonates, infant mortality rates, life expectancy at birth and at age twenty, growth rates of prepubertal children, rates of morbidity and mortality, prevalence of parasitic and infectious diseases, calorie and protein availability per household, water availability per household, death rates from violence, and disaggregated stratified income statistics and occupational structure

would be better than those emphasizing growth in aggregate product. No perfect measure of living standards is likely to be attained, but one that emphasizes human freedom is closer to it than one that is purely based on total output or per capita access to material goods.

The accuracy of the infant mortality rate (IMR) as an index of level of literacy, income level, nutrition, standard of living, housing, and health care availability has been recently noted (Wallace and Taha 1988:158) and deserves some comment here. The IMR is a useful index not only of the health status of infants but also of the socioeconomic conditions under which they live (WHO 1981). Data on the IMR is available in most countries at the national level and by region, permitting at least the same level of aggregate analysis currently dominated by GNP. IMR has an inverse relationship with GNP per capita: countries with a GNP of $1,000+ showed an IMR in the range of 28–95, while the $500–999 group had a range of 75–115, that of $250–499 had a range of 65–180, and the group of less than $249 had a range of 105–180 per 1,000 births (Wallace and Taha 1988:160). The advantage of IMR over GNP is also its weakness; i.e., it is a composite index that includes a variety of factors relevant to the evaluation of the socioeconomic well-being of a population and not simply the degree to which their activities have become monetized—as is the case with GNP. It also means that the causes of its changes may be difficult to tease out; i.e., is an increase in IMR due to worsening water supplies, higher fertility, an economic downturn, or something else. Thus, while IMR may be better than GNP as an index of "general socioeconomic well-being," it requires supplementary indices to target direct policy interventions. (See table 7.1.)

3. The growth of hierarchy and system maintenance resulting from economic development leads to system disorders due to the counter-intuitive system responses, resulting from attempts to control them. This is a well-known general systems' problem (Rappaport 1982). Solutions may or may not be developed someday to cope with this situation. Until then the prudent course ought to be to reduce interdependence, promote local autonomy, and design local/regional development with full use of local knowledge as part of the design. "The present scale of world trade is another of the entropic trends brought on by centralization and concentration" (DeWalt 1988:117). While this might reduce rates of growth of capital in the aggregate, it may very well level off the current inequalities between groups in developing societies. "All individuals constantly scan their environment to determine how successfully they

TABLE 7.1. Infant Mortality Rate and Child Death Rate according to GNP per capita

GNP per capita	Country	IMR	Child Death Rate
$249 or less	Chad	140	37
	Ethiopia	155	25
	Mali	180	27
	Zaire	105	20
	Burkina Fasso	150	36
	Malawi	165	29
	Niger	145	27
Range		105–80	18–37
Median		140	27
$250–499	Somalia	155	47
	Rwanda	130	25
	Togo	100	25
	Ghana	95	15
	Madagascar	65	23
	Sierra Leone	180	50
	Kenya	80	13
	Sudan	120	23
	Liberia	110	17
Range		65–180	7–50
Median		125	24
$500–999	Zambia	90	20
	Egypt	100	14
	Zimbabwe	80	14
	Morocco	95	22
	Cameroon	100	16
	Botswana	75	13
Range		75–115	13–22
Median		97.5	18
$1000+	Mauritius	28	3
	Congo	80	10
	Tunisia	85	6
	Libya	95	11
Range		28–95	3–11
Median		85	10

Source: Adapted from Wallace and Taha 1988:160.

are coping and where they rank with others in their social field. Self-esteem is the emotive summation of this scan. It is constructed from, among other factors, the success or failure in occupying roles and the degree of acceptance or rejection of one's social identity. . . . Loss of self-esteem can produce health and behavioral impairments" (Appell 1988:57). Among these are more frequent visits to the medical dispensary and even political violence (Aberle 1962; Rasl and French 1962; Gurr 1970). These impairments are exacerbated by the erosion of social support mechanisms, such as networks of friends and kin, who provide access to emotional and material resources in times of need. Modernization has been found to erode these mechanisms, such as the system of exchanges, kin networks, and obligations of reciprocity. There is growing evidence of the role of social support in reducing stress-related syndromes in First World settings (Raplan et al. 1977; Balshem 1985; Fleming-Moran 1988).

4. The loss of cultural solutions to local problems resulting from the homogenization promoted by development and the erosion of moral ends is behind many of our current disorders. "Decentralization, local autonomy and contextual development could help to reverse the process of cultural wastage. A reemphasis on local culture will encourage the kind of cultural diversity that we should recognize as important in evolutionary terms" (DeWalt 1988:118). The growing conflict between north and south is but a representation of a deeper conflict between those who advocate centralization of capital and those who see the process as a form of neocolonialism rather than a way to achieve the alleged goal of development—a better living standard.

The need to move away from the trajectories of development of the past forty years is evident all around us. Resources have become more unevenly distributed, and scarcities are created through export of local resources to the centers of capital. If systems are to be adaptive in the long run, higher orders of control in hierarchical systems must keep their ordering functions at a high level of abstraction or aggregation (Rappaport 1982:154). Thus, "compatibility between people and the physical environment" seems a moral goal appropriate to development and change. Specifics will have to be left to lower-level orders of the system that take into account both past history and current status. This also means that higher levels in the hierarchy of social systems stop mandating details, as they do in current national economies, or meddle with instrumental values (155). These values are left to lower-level orders, in which case locally based moral ends in economic behavior can return to play a more important role in organizing the production and distribution of local resources. Growth of capital consistent with this compatibility with the physical environment and with instrumentalities left to lower-level system orders (i.e., decentralization) might remain an objective, but it would now be subordinated to questions of long-term survival and well-being—a higher moral end than simply capital growth. Capital has no moral content, but, in the absence of effective moral ends, capital growth has proven to subvert the values of many a society and undermined local systems of resource sharing and access.

The current high standards of living of the First World nations belie distortions in distribution that are as serious as those one finds in the Third World. There is evidence that, despite enormously higher GNP and GNP per capita in First and Second World nations, these nations have also experienced a decline in living standards and a growing gap between households experiencing growth of income and those experiencing decline. The destruction and pollution of the environment that has accompanied economic development in First and Second World nations has led to a growing concern with environmental impact. Despite the evidence that such a process is not unilineal or marked by obligatory stages and experiences, efforts to take environmental impact into account is being resisted by developing nations, who interpret this effort as an attempt to restrain their development. Those who stand to benefit from the individualistic paradigm of classical economics in the Third World oppose efforts to introduce social system and global system considerations in their economic behavior.

Anthropological findings would suggest that a less aggregative, more community-centered approach to development must be given priority. The moral goals of communities need to become part of the goals of development, and such goals are best seen as long-run in nature. Long-run goals, in turn, imply a recognition that economic growth cannot take place at the expense of the destruction of the physical environment or be built on the backs of a majority of the population, which sees its well-being diminished despite per capita GNP increases.

Efforts to decentralize decision making for development and to disaggregate the measurement of development projects have been undertaken on and off in the past forty years. Yet, they have not been sustained for long, nor have political groups benefiting from maintaining centralized control supported local level development. Recent efforts to emphasize basic human needs and mandates to focus on the poorest of the poor are consistent with the kinds of goals development should have. These efforts have been subverted, however, by the recent rise of monetarist, supply-side economics in policy circles of First World nations. The return of this kind of economics has been associated with greater income disparities in First World nations as well as Third World nations. That this has been the case is not surprising, the economic policy built as it is on the primacy of individual satisfaction, without acknowledging disparities in power. The presumed goal of individuals—to maximize utility—is not necessarily the proper goal for nations.

Anthropology takes a moral position that economic growth is justified only if the results are enhanced well-being for a majority of the population, if it occurs with consultation and participation with local peoples and if the physical environment's long-term productive capacity and nonproductive value is assured. To know if that is the case, indices that are capable of measuring changes in well-being of society's strata are necessary. Income alone is an insufficient index. It must be supplemented by other indices known to reflect the well-being of individuals and populations: normal rates of growth of children; a low incidence of infant mortality; low parasite loads; low incidence of malnutrition; and normal neonate birth weight. None of these should be used in the aggregate but, rather, stratified on the basis of criteria such as geographic region, ethnicity, and income decile. The disaggregation of data must be a fundamental starting point for reindexing the measures of development. The disorders of the modern world come from an increasing interdependence of the world's economies without an accompanying effort to deal with the misinformation communicated by aggregate data such as per capita GNP and other bad statistics that are fed to the Food and Agriculture Organization (FAO) of the United Nations and other international organizations demanding to know the state of the world.

Indices will also have to reflect sensitivity to the special conditions of the populations whose welfare concerns us. The impact of development is different in India than it may be among relatively isolated Amazonian Indians. In societies experiencing their first contact with the modern world the indices that are most important to monitor are epidemiological indicators, given the impact made by the epidemiological transition on these populations. Great pandemics of measles, the common cold, influenza, chickenpox, and tuberculosis tend to follow the initial period of contact with diseases from more densely populated areas, and high rates of mortality result where permanent medical services are not provided. Many areas of the world's tropical forests today are experiencing just such a change as a result of development activities of nations, as they seek to integrate their forested lands into the national drive toward development. Economic planning has not given adequate attention to the changes in welfare that accompany these initial contacts between relatively isolated native populations and the state (cf. Wagley 1951; Ribeiro 1957; Salzano and Callegari-Jacques 1988; Coimbra Jr. 1989).

Simultaneous with this severe depopulation accompanying cultural contact are a severe erosion of the capacity of these populations to produce enough food and a host of nutritional deficiencies accompanying disruption of their traditional access to resources. The lack of food, when addressed through imports, can lead gradually to an erosion in the food habits of the population which, in turn, can lead to a number of nutritional deficiencies arising from a diet with an excess of carbohydrates, salt, and fat. Thus, epidemiological indicators must be supplemented with nutritional indices of adequacy.

Development activities, such as road building, often promote the creation of malaria-breeding sites through poor drainage and impounding of seasonal streams (N. Smith 1981). Monitoring changes in morbidity and mortality can help identify areas for necessary intervention to reduce greater losses if the problem goes unaddressed. Malaria, throughout much of the tropical Third World, is the major scourge of populations. Also important are trypanosomiasis, schistosomiasis, filariasis (including onchocerciasis), leishmaniasis, and leprosy (Shimkin 1989).

In more densely populated areas, especially in cities, the scourges tend to be different and are related to poverty, crowding, and poor sanitation (especially clean water supplies). Tetanus, pneumonia, diarrhea, whooping cough, measles, and polio are the most important (ibid.).

With achievement of a modicum of development the population enters into a different set of problems associated with sedentarism, high-fat diets, more salt and alcohol, and greater psychological stress. Hypertension is the end result, especially among the urban elite (ibid.).

The first need of Third World nations is to increase production of food staples. This is a political objective, with important welfare consequences for members of a nation. Food reduces the vulnerability of a nation politically and provides a degree of financial discipline (Robinson 1979:132). Food production is the most effective form of import-saving investment. To import food means to borrow to eat, and the debt incurred remains after the food has been eaten—and no goods and services have been produced to pay for the principal or interest. Many countries fell into the trap of believing those who preached "comparative advantage" as a principle that applied to all economic activities, even staple food production. For some nations, indeed, food self-sufficiency is out of the question, but it is possible to develop more resilient social and political systems by strengthening the agricultural sector. The priority assigned to industrial development has paid off handsomely for First World economies, with their abundance of capital and technology, but less often for many Third World nations.

Correction of the disorders brought about by misapplied indices of development will require that items of real welfare become the indices and that policies seek to bring about positive changes in those dimensions: health, education, and nutrition. The disparities in consumption present today are intolerable—all the more so because through the media we are all too aware of the injustice of famine alongside conspicuous consumption.

When the indices begin to utilize disaggregated data and, by consequence, to value distributional questions, then it may be possible to see policies that favor security of land tenure over aggregate output increases. This, in turn, will lead to a lessened emphasis on export crops and greater emphasis on staple crops—thereby enhancing food security, the diet of the farming households, the fabric of social and cultural life in rural areas, and other positive values of system maintenance and gradual evolution. This does not mean that the agricultural sector be given an entirely free hand. A tax structure that resists land concentration and encourages intensity of land use needs to be implemented to increase the burden to those who reduce the welfare of others through less intensive food staple production. To find the pattern of prices that will induce the required pattern of cropping is a complex matter with no easy answers. Each country will have to experiment and adjust its indices until it finds the point that succeeds in increasing welfare to the majority of its people.

Conclusions

Economics developed as a discipline from the powerful concepts generated by Adam Smith. To him the market was a powerful mechanism that aggregated individual wants into social outcomes. The hidden hand of supply and demand—i.e., the market—permitted prices to represent the optimal flow of goods and services at a given time. The ideal conditions of free markets are, in fact, rarely present, and this has become increasingly clear in the past four decades. Governments have always interfered in the operation of markets: by providing public services, by facilitating the flow of some goods but not others, and by implementing preferential tax policies. Public goods can generate negative incentives, too, by encouraging free riders, who would opt to obtain goods for free, or undersupply public goods (Bates 1983b:373).

In addition, even economists have begun to question the validity of the equilibrium price-auction model of microeconomics (Thurow 1983). In the basic model of microeconomics it is impossible to find over- and underemployed resources. By the same model inflation either cannot exist, or it makes little difference. The price-auction, or neoclassical, model bears little resemblance to the real economies we observe today, and, unfortunately, the tide of economics has been to become increasingly distanced from real economies in favor of abstract ideal models of how economies ought to work given the assumptions of a price-auction model.

It behooves anthropology to work with those economists who have begun to acknowledge the contradictions of current economic theory and practice—and to work toward new theories in which the real behavior of individuals, and the real behavior of regional and national economies, is taken into account. They will be without a doubt less elegant models, but perhaps they will better represent the behavior of real systems. One such effort is represented by the work of the so-called socioeconomists, led by A. Etzioni (1988), who have proposed a reconceptualization of economics that takes into account the social responsibilities of *Homo economicus* (1988). Also notable is the work of many agricultural economists, welfare economists, the new institutional economists, ecological economists and political economists, whose work shares anthropology's concern for the majority of the world's population and the importance of local variation and resource distribution.

Many current practices in international economic development seem to encourage that national elites collude with international organizations in order to obtain capital—by agreeing to megaprojects that put Third World nations in debt, the projects benefiting a small number of construction companies and elite groups capable of obtaining the large contracts. Less often do multilateral development banks encourage decentralization of capital, control of information by local populations, participatory approaches to decision making, and self-help. This has been left largely to the NGOs and other grassroots organizations, which, in so doing, have in many cases collided with Third World states over political and social policy. Left out of this whole effort at development are the populations in greatest need, those rarely, if ever, favored by development efforts. The continual emphasis on aggregate measures to evaluate the success of development projects leads to counterintuitive results: aggregate development and individual underdevelopment. Clear examples of these outcomes can be seen in Brazil, where GNP rose from about $270 in 1965 to more than $1,840 in 1986, while the share of GNP by the 50 percent poorest went in that same period from 17.71 of the total to 11.81 percent. During the same period the share of the richest 5 percent went from 27.69 percent of the total wealth to 39 percent of the total (Malan 1979:39). This trend toward concentration of wealth continued unabetted throughout the 1980s.

The only way to turn this situation around is to explicitly de-emphasize the use of aggregate indices and to develop stratified indices that reflect the situation of the majority of the population. Thus, in a country in which 80 percent of farmers own less than ten hectares of land, indices may need to account for the majority of categories in the range from zero to ten hectares, using as many as five intervals in this range instead of "standard" intervals that swamp the important variability within the majority group. Categories such as landless, craftsman, merchant, etc., should not be left out of the accounting in the rural sector, since the individuals who fill these categories are responsible for marketing output, supplying inputs, and making technology available in rural areas. In other words, the indices need to be able to account for the local-level differentiation present in national economies.

On each of these strata data on measures of health and nutrition are among the most sensitive to well-being. It is presumed that the greater the income, the better the health and nutrition of a population. If that is the case, why not use these measures to establish the success of development projects? It is more difficult and time-consuming but, in the light of what we have said earlier, can one trust aggregate income figures as indices? In the task of generating these indices on a country-to-country basis and in monitoring the success of this kind of individual-level development, anthropology has an important and necessary role to play. Not to engage these thorny issues simply guarantees that a certain kind of economics will continue to be the sole judge of what development is and how it should proceed. It is clear that anthropology disagrees with current practices and that it has alternatives to offer.

REFERENCES

Aberle, D. F.
    1962   A Note on Relative Deprivation Theory as Applied to Millenarian and Other Cult Movements. In *Millennial Dreams in Actions: Essays in Comparative Study*, ed. S. L. Thrupp. The Hague: Mouton.

Adelman I., and C. T. Morris
    1973   *Economic Growth and Social Equity in Developing Countries.* Stanford, Calif.: Stanford University Press.

Appell, George
    1988   The Health Consequences of Development. *Sarawak Museum Journal* 36:43–74.

Arrow, K. J.
    1983   *Social Choice and Justice: Collected Papers of K. J. Arrow*, vol. 1. Cambridge, Mass.: Harvard University Press.

Balshem, M.
    1985   Job Stress and Health among Women Clerical Workers. Ph.D. diss., Department of Anthropology, Indiana University at Bloomington.

Barraclough, S.
    1973   *Agrarian Structure in Latin America.* Lexington, Mass.: Lexington Books.

Bates, Robert
    1983a   *Essays on the Political Economy of Rural Africa.* Cambridge: Cambridge University Press.
    1983b   Some Core Assumptions in Development Economics. In *Economic Anthropology*, ed. S. Ortiz. Washington, D.C.: University Press of America.

Bennett, J. W., and J. Bowen, eds.
    1988   *Production and Autonomy: Anthropological Studies and Critiques of Development.* Washington, D.C.: University Press of America.

Bernstein, B. B.
    1981   Ecology and Economics: Complex Systems in Changing Environments. *Annual Review of Ecology and Systematics* 12:309–30.

Berry, R. A., and W. F. Cline
    1979   *Agrarian Structure and Productivity in Developing Countries.* Baltimore: Johns Hopkins University Press.

Boeke, J. H.
    1953   *Economics and Economic Policy of Dual Societies as Exemplified by Indonesia.* New York: Institute of Pacific Relations.

Brokenshaw, D. W., and P. D. Little, eds.
    1988   *Anthropology of Development and Change in East Africa.* Institute for Development Anthropology Monographs. Boulder, Colo.: Westview Press.

Cernea, Michael
    1987   *Putting People First.* 2d ed. New York: Oxford University Press/World Bank.

Chenery, H. B.
: 1979 Structural Change and Development Policy. New York: Oxford University Press/World Bank.

Chenery, H. B., et al.
: 1974 Redistribution with Growth. London: Oxford University Press.

Coimbra, Carlos, Jr.
: 1989 From Shifting Cultivation to Coffee Farming: The Impact of Change on the Health and Ecology of the Surui Indians in the Brazilian Amazon. Ph.D. diss., Department of Anthropology, Indiana University at Bloomington.

Colson, Elizabeth
: 1982 Planned Change: The Creation of a New Community. Berkeley: Institute of International Studies.

Daly, H. E., and J. B, Cobb Jr.
: 1989 For the Common Good: Redirecting the Economy toward Community, the Environment, and a Sustainable Future. Boston: Beacon Press.

de Janvry, A.
: 1981 The Agrarian Question and Reformism in Latin America. Baltimore: Johns Hopkins University Press.

DeWalt, Billie
: 1988 The Cultural Ecology of Development. Agriculture and Human Values (winter–spring): 112–23.

Domar, D. J.
: 1946 Capital Expansion, Rate of Growth and Employment. Econometrica 4:137–47.

Dorner, P., and D. Ranel
: 1971 The Economic Case for Land Reform: Employment, Income Distribution, and Productivity. In Land Reform in Latin America, ed. P. Dorner. Madison: University of Wisconsin Land Tenure Center.

Eicher, C., and J. Staatz, eds.
: 1984 Agricultural Development in the Third World. Baltimore: Johns Hopkins University Press.

Etzioni, A.
: 1988 The Moral Dimension: Toward a New Economics. New York: Free Press.

Fei, J. C. H., G. Ranis, and S. Ruo
: 1979 Growth with Equity: The Taiwan Case. New York: Oxford University Press/World Bank.

Fleming-Moran, Millicent
: 1988 Women, Job-Stress, and Heading a Household: An Epidemiological Study of Psychosocial Determinants of Systolic Blood Pressure in Employed Women. Ph.D. Dissertation, University of North Carolina at Chapel Hill, Dept. of Epidemiology.

Frank, A. G.
: 1966 "The Development of Underdevelopment." Monthly Review 18 (4): 17–31.

Gill
　1967　*Economic Development: Theory and Practice.* Englewood Cliffs, N.J.: Prentice Hall.
Gurr, T. R.
　1970　*Why Men Rebel.* Princeton: Princeton University Press.
Hanslukwa, H. E.
　1985　Measuring the Health of Populations: Indicators and Interpretations. *Social Science and Medicine* 20(12):1207–24.
Harrod, R. F.
　1952　*Towards a Dynamic Economics.* London: Macmillan
Hayami, Y., and V. Ruttan.
　1972　*Agricultural Development: An International Perspective.* Baltimore: Johns Hopkins University Press.
Hill, Polly
　1986　*Development Economics on Trial.* Cambridge: Cambridge University Press.
Hirschman, A. O.
　1958　*The Strategy of Economic Development.* New Haven: Yale Univ. Press.
　1981　"The Rise and Fall of Development Economics." In *Essays in Trespassing: Economics to Politics and Beyond.* New York: Cambridge Univ. Press.
Hoselitz, B. F.
　1960　Theories of Stages of Economic Growth. In *Theories of Economic Growth,* ed. B. F. Hoselitz, Glencoe, Ill.: Free Press.
Johnston, B. B., and W. C. Clark
　1982　*Redesigning Rural Development: A Strategic Perspective.* Baltimore: Johns Hopkins University Press.
Johnston, B. F., and P. Kilby
　1975　*Agriculture and Structural Transformation: Economic Strategies in Late-Developing Countries.* New York: Oxford University Press.
Jorgenson, D. W.
　1961　The Development of a Dual Economy. *Economic Journal* 66:25–48.
　1969　The Role of Agriculture in Economic Development: Classical versus Neoclassical Models of Growth. In *Subsistence Agriculture and Economic Development,* ed. C. Wharton Jr., 320–48. Chicago: Aldine.
Kamarck, A. M.
　1976　*The Tropics and Economic Development: A Provocative Inquiry into the Poverty of Nations.* Baltimore: Johns Hopkins University Press/ World Bank.
Kaplan, B. H., J. C. Cassel, S. Gore
　1977　Social Support and Health. *Medical Care* 15:47–58.
Kasl, S., and J. French
　1962　The Effects of Occupational Status on Physical and Mental Health. *Journal of Social Issues* 18:67–89.

Lee, M. W.
  1967 *Macroeconomics: Fluctuation, Growth and Stability,* 4th ed. Homewood, Ill.: Irwin.
Lewis, W. A.
  1954 Economic Development with Unlimited Supplies of Labor. *Manchester School of Economic and Social Studies* 22(2):139–91.
  1955 *The Theory of Economic Growth.* London: George Allen and Unwin.
List, Friedrich
  1966 (orig. 1885) *The National System of Political Economy.* New York: A. M. Relley.
Little, P. D., and M. M. Horowitz, eds.
  1985 *Lands at Risk in the Third World: Local-Level Perspectives.* Boulder, Colo.: Westview Press/Institute for Development Anthropology Monographs.
Lloyd, C., ed.
  1983 *Social Theory and Political Practice.* Oxford: Clarendon Press.
Malan, P. S.
  1979 Distribuição da Renda e Desenvolvimento: Novas Evidencias e Uma Tentativa de Clarifição da Controversia no Brasil. *Dados* 21:39.
Marshall, A.
  1920 *Principles of Economics,* 8th ed. New York: Macmillan.
Marx, Rarl
  1918 *A Contribution to the Critique of Political Economy.* Trans. N. I. Stone. Chicago: Charles H. Kerr.
McKenzie, G. W.
  1983 *Measuring Economic Welfare: New Methods.* Cambridge: Cambridge University Press.
Mellor, John
  1966 *The Economics of Agricultural Development.* Ithaca, N.Y.: Cornell University Press.
  1976 *The New Economics of Growth: A Strategy for India and the Developing World.* Ithaca, N.Y.: Cornell University Press.
Popkin, S. L.
  1979 *The Rational Peasant.* Berkeley: University of California Press.
Ranis. G., and J. Fei
  1961 A Theory of Economic Development. *American Economic Review* 51(4): 533–65.
  1963 Innovation, Capital Accumulation, and Economic Development. *American Economic Review* 53(3): 283–313.
  1964 *Development of the Labor Surplus Economy: Theory and Policy.* Homewood, Ill.: Irwin.
Rappaport, R.
  1982 *Ecology, Meaning, and Religion.* Richmond, Calif.: North Atlantic Books.
Rapport, D. J., and J. E. Turner
  1977 Economic Models in Ecology. *Science* 195:367–73.

Ribeiro, Darcy
    1957   Convivio e Contaminação: Efeitos Dissociativos da Depopulação Provocada por Epidemias em Grupos Indigenas. *Sociologia* (São Paulo) 18:3–50.

Robinson, J.
    1979   *Aspects of Development and Underdevelopment.* Cambridge: Cambridge University Press.

Rostow, W. W.
    1956   The Take-Off into Self-Sustained Growth. *Economic Journal* 66:25–48.
    1961   *The Stages of Economic Growth: A Non-Communist Manifesto.* Cambridge: Cambridge University Press.

Salzano, F. M., and S. M. Callegari-Jacques
    1988   *South American Indians: A Case Study in Evolution.* New York: Oxford University Press.

Schultz, T. W.
    1964   *Transforming Traditional Agriculture.* New Haven, Conn.: Yale University Press.

Schumpeter, J. A.
    1954   *History of Economic Analysis.* New York: Oxford University Press.

Scitovsky, T.
    1986   *Human Desire and Economic Satisfaction.* New York: New York University Press.

Seers, D.
    1970   *The Meaning of Development.* New York: Agricultural Development Council Reprint.

Sen, Amartya
    1981   *The Standard of Living.* Cambridge: Cambridge University Press.
    1982   *Choice, Welfare and Measurement.* Cambridge, Mass.: MIT Press.

Shimkin, Demitri
    1989   Africa's Health Problems: How Can Anthropology Help? Paper presented at Society for Applied Anthropology annual meeting,

Sirkin, G.
    1965   *Introduction to Macroeconomic Theory,* rev. ed. Homewood, Ill.: Irwin.

Smith, J., I. Wallerstein, and H. Evers, eds.
    1984   *Households and the World Economy.* vol. 3 of *Explorations in the World Economy.* Beverly Hills, Calif.: Sage Publications.

Smith, N.
    1981   Colonization Lessons from a Tropical Forest. *Science* 214:755–61.

Streeten, P., et al.
    1981   *First Things First: Meeting Basic Needs in Developing Countries.* New York: Oxford University Press.

Tata, R. J., and R. R. Schultz
    1988   World Variation in Human Welfare: A New Index of Development Status. *Annals of the Association of American Geographers* 78:580–93.

Thurow, Lester
    1983 *Dangerous Currents: The State of Economics*. New York: Random House/Vintage Books.
Tinker, I., and M. B. Bramsen, eds.
    1976 *Women and World Development*. Washington, D.C.: Overseas Development Council.
United Nations (U.N.)
    1951 *Measures for the Economic Development of Underdeveloped Countries*. New York: Department of Economic and Social Affairs, U.N.
Wagley, C.
    1951 Cultural Influences on Population: A Comparison of Two Tupi Tribes. *Revista do Museu Paulista,* n.s. 5:95–104.
Wallace, H. M., and T. E. Tahir Taha
    1988 Indicators for Monitoring Progress in Maternal and Child Health Care in Africa. *Journal of Tropical Pediatrics* 34:158–64.
Waring, M.
    1989 *If Women Counted: New Feminist Economics*. San Francisco: Harper and Row.
Wharton, C. R., ed.
    1969 *Subsistence Agriculture and Economic Development*. Chicago: Aldine.
Wilber, C. R., and R. P. Jameson
    1983 *An Inquiry into the Poverty of Nations*. Notre Dame, Ind.: Notre Dame University Press.

Chapter 8

Hunger Vulnerability from an Anthropologist's Food Systems Perspective

Ellen Messer

Since 1985 the American Anthropological Association Task Force on African Hunger, Famine, and Food Security has been organizing anthropologists to provide information to diagnose, redress, and prevent famine in Africa (Huss-Ashmore, Curry, and Hitchcock 1989; Huss-Ashmore and Katz 1989, 1990; Shipton 1990; Downs, Kerner, and Reyna 1991). The premise behind providing rosters of anthropologists knowledgeable about Africa and hunger problems and symposia and publications on their ideas and methods is that anthropologists offer unique perspectives and capabilities that might improve performance of intergovernment (IGO) and nongovernment organizations (NGOs) that monitor and respond to hunger problems.

At the same time that some anthropologists promote anthropological perspectives, we also find ourselves employed in interdisciplinary enterprises that address hunger problems, whether academic research and outreach programs such as the Alan Shawn Feinstein World Hunger Program at Brown University, privately funded think tanks such as Resources for the Future, or international agencies such as the International Food Policy Research Institute or the World Bank. These interdisciplinary efforts offer distinctive frameworks for assessing, monitoring, and overcoming hunger problems. They benefit from anthropological inputs but rarely cover ground in precisely the terms that anthropologists might, as they seek to incorporate also the viewpoints and values of geographers, economists, and people in other disciplines who, coincidentally, also direct them.

In this chapter, I share some of the advances of our World Hunger

Program interdisciplinary research on hunger vulnerability and compare our typology with anthropology's food systems analysis. I then examine some recent work on food commodity choices and hunger presented principally by food economists (D'Agostino and Staatz 1989; Reardon 1989). These efforts enjoyed substantial inputs by anthropologists and are being used as background documents to conceptualize improvements in famine early warning systems (FEWS) and food price and trade policies. But in at least three aspects they fall short in their utilization of anthropological perspectives. First, they fail to take full advantage of anthropological analyses of the relationships between international organizations, states, NGOs, and local communities (see C. A. Smith, chap. 2; Fisher, chap. 3). Second, they miss central elements of the anthropological analysis of food habits and food systems. Third, they do not address the values and political-economic interests that lead key institutional or government actors to monitor, respond, and act in cases of famine or hunger. These three areas of anthropological concern constitute an ongoing agenda for anthropological research and interdisciplinary studies of hunger.

Hunger Vulnerability

The World Hunger Program's Hunger Typology
In July 1986 the World Hunger Program faculty at Brown University, directed by geographer Robert Kates, began formulating a conceptual framework for analyzing hunger and hunger-related policy making.[1] Based on a three-tiered paradigm of hunger causation and consequences that draws on methods of famine research, entitlement theory, and nutrition/nutritional anthropology, the concept brings together the disparate disciplines and data sets on hunger into an easily manageable form. Using some analogies from risk analysis in geography, we argue that people may be *food short, food poor,* or *food deprived.* At a regional or national level a food shortage may be due to political, climatic, or other socioeconomic forces. We distinguish such food short famine conditions from food poverty at the household level, in which people go hungry because they lack the resources to acquire food even when the regional food supply is sufficient. Ultimately, however, even if households have sufficient resources to command and access food, individuals go hungry if distribution rules militate against their getting an adequate share, if cultural rules of consumption prejudice them from consuming an adequate mix of nutrients, or if individuals are ill and unable to ingest,

metabolize, and benefit from the nutrients potentially available. This third context, which we term food deprivation, includes situations of malnutrition among the so-called vulnerable groups: infants and young children, pregnant and lactating women, and others who are deprived of food in situations of social powerlessness or illness.

An additional component of this hunger framework is the notion of sequencing in hunger causation and social response. A climatic or social disaster that leads to localized food shortage may create situations of resource poverty that set the stage for chronic food poverty and periodic food shortage later. Alternatively, where markets and food relief penetrate relatively isolated local systems, as in many parts of Africa, people may be exchanging periodic food shortage for more chronic food poverty (Messer 1989a,b). Using this framework, it is possible to profile the incidence of different types of hunger in any single year (Kates et al. 1988) or across years—to arrive at a history of hunger through the ages (Newman 1994).

In 1989–90 the World Hunger Program tested the utility of this model for diagnosing hunger vulnerability in famine-prone areas. Thomas Downing (1991) wrote a document that drew on our common discussions. This stage of the work was developed specifically for USAID Famine Early Warning Systems, to see how our three-part hunger typology might help identify vulnerable populations, households, or individuals in a more timely and efficient manner. Here it is useful to compare this three-part hunger typology with the anthropological food systems model, for the purpose of discussing their relative strengths and weaknesses and their possible combination.

Anthropology's Food Systems Analysis

Food systems research addresses potentially all aspects of food procurement and consumption strategies: ecology of food production and marketing; food classification and social rules for food distribution; nutritional and health consequences of particular uses and classifications of the food environment; and political-economic contexts of food production and consumption strategies.

Ecology of Food Production

Classic anthropological investigations, such as Audrey Richard's (1939) study of politics, agriculture, and malnutrition among the Bemba of Northern Rhodesia (now Zambia), are usually community studies, set in the context of the colonial or national political economy. They explicate the local ecosystem as it is managed by local agricultural customs and locate the factor that, if undermined, might damage food production, reduce household food availability, and induce hunger. A first factor is the availability of adequate cultivable land, which may be reduced as a result of erosion, pollution, pests, or non-food-productive uses of the land. Rules of land tenure, intergenerational fragmentation of plots, and competing uses for land all can undermine household food (production) security.

A second factor is labor. Competing markets that draw off workers, or cultural rules for division of labor that limit participation in certain tasks, may undermine the household's ability to produce and earn income. Poor nutrition or illness, particularly at essential production seasons, may enmesh individuals and households in ongoing cycles of undernutrition (Richards 1939; Haswell 1953; Brieger and Guyer 1990; Scrimshaw and Cosminsky 1991). Whole communities may be at risk, or risk may be distributed according to household structure, skills at managing resources, or illness (Sharman 1970; Brieger and Guyer 1990).

A third factor, related to the first, is ecology. Attrition of traditional seedstock occurs through the demise of traditional risk-averse planting strategies that emphasized food security rather than possible maximum yields of single crops. Political or market pressure for monocropping or cash cropping can reduce risk-averting crop diversification, and in some cases, leads to the abandonment of such traditional crops as sorghum and finger millet that are drought-resistant or less nutrient demanding. Pressure to produce intensively may also undermine soil and water regimes and threaten future cropping stability. Communities may lose their traditional knowledge of practices that had enabled them to avert or cope with climatic and biological stressors (weeds, insects, or diseases) that interfere with crop production at critical levels and at critical times in the cultivation cycle. A fourth factor is the requisition of crops by local interests, the state, or insurgents. Social instability or warfare that interfere in any way with agriculture and market processes are additional factors. All these elements can indicate impending famine for a local population or for particular households.

Many anthropological studies of traditional societies now stressed by war, drought, changes in settlement patterns, and famine describe also the ways people deal with the privations of lean seasons or years. These coping mechanisms include foraging; consuming less preferred, bulky foods that might be processed so as to increase bulk and fillingness; and food rationing, especially the reduction in the numbers of meals per day. Other coping mechanisms widen the sources of income for the household: people might try to expand nonagricultural economic activities, such as crafts production and trade, or sell household animals or other valuables. Some members of the household might migrate in search of work and to reduce the number of mouths to feed at home. Eventually, weaker members of the household might be sent out or, if they are children, sold. And, finally, the remaining members of the household, in some cases groups or communities, might move (Colson 1979).

Population growth, changes in land-use patterns that reduce forageable areas, and famine relief policies that keep people in a fixed location, where they cannot support themselves in a bad year or bad season—often themselves responses to food insecurity at some earlier time—become unworkable and stressors themselves. Moreover, populations who suffer endemic seasonal hunger with progressive debilitation prove highly vulnerable to drought and other sources of acute food shortages. Specific dimensions of pastoral, agricultural, and mixed farming and nonfarming strategies shape the ways households or communities cope with food stress. For example, the particular range of products that a pastoral group has to sell determines its viability under varying climatic conditions. Monitoring areas in which farmers and herders suffer seasonal hunger should provide a rough indicator of those areas and groups most likely to suffer in the case of major drought as their coping mechanisms are exhausted (Messer 1989a,b).

Classification and Social Distribution of Food

Additional components of the food systems analysis include cultural rules of food classification that determine preferred foods and combinations of foods, the timing and spacing of meals, the sharing of meals and snacks, and nutrition and health consequences, especially for the poor. Farming systems and the choices of dietary staples may be critical to a group's weathering of a bad year. Within an area groups growing exclusively or mainly maize, for example, may be more vulnerable to drought than those that have continued to grow sorghum or other more drought-tolerant grains, plus a variety of root crops and vegetables. Dietary structure, particularly the ratio of grains or starches to leaf or protein-based relishes and condiments, provides an indicator of normal times versus times of stress, as people cut back on the number and content of meals according to the availability of staple and other foods. In the past increased foraging during lean times was the way the disadvantaged survived, but that wild food resource base is shrinking as terrains are cultivated, inhabited, or otherwise reduced by alternative utilization (Moris 1989).

Rules for social distribution of food trace the pathways by which the less entitled receive food during normal times. These provide an additional set of indicators for times of stress versus normal times, as the networks of food hospitality shrink as resources are depleted. Mary Douglas suggested that it should be possible to program by computer the rules of food classification and food distribution and then to run the rules for "normal" and "extreme" conditions. This would allow investigators to identify which social categories might be malnourished in all and which only in extreme circumstances (Douglas and Gross 1981). To our knowledge, however, no one has attempted this task.

Health and Nutritional Consequences
Illness, particularly during planting and weeding times, can critically set back household production (e.g., Haswell 1953; Chambers 1981). Poor nutritional status during production seasons can embed whole societies in ongoing cycles of undernutrition (Richards 1939). Epidemic illnesses, including potentially AIDS, are also implicated in famine and, therefore, a factor to monitor. Notions of what constitutes adequate food, adequate nutrition, and food- and nutrition-related health disorders are furthermore related to feeding and consumption behaviors and may have significant consequences on what types of food are fed to very young children or others who are nutritionally vulnerable and less able to fend for their food.

Comparing and Combining the Hunger Typology with Food Systems Analysis

Food systems analysis challenges the linkages and levels of the hunger typology. Although food systems analysis generally is carried out at the local level, it can be expanded to consider how localities interact and connect with administrative units in the regional or larger context. For instance, food poverty might be construed at a regional or community level, not just a household level, since food may be available but shipped out for reasons of political-economic powerlessness or lack of entitlement. Food deprivation, particularly micronutrient imbalances, the third hunger type, might be considered not just an individual but also a community or regional phenomenon. Such types of malnutrition as iodine insufficiency or vitamin A deficiency in young boys may be broadly endemic to whole communities or even regions (see, e.g., Greene 1977; van Veen 1971). Thus, the food systems model encourages a more careful assessment of social linkages and levels of hunger problems. For this reason food systems analysis can also provide insights into the best social directions for interventions. A more general challenge is to incorporate anthropological findings on seasonal hunger, detailed analysis of community characteristics, and superior descriptions of food habits and nutritional specifics of communities into the hunger typology.

Reciprocally, the hunger typology has lessons for food systems analysts. It encourages them to deal seriously with time and space issues, including the sequencing of causation and response at different levels in identifying, quantifying, and intervening in contexts of hunger vulnerability. It also involves examining in some detail the overlap in spatial referents: How does scale affect diagnosis and intervention in hunger problems?

Hunger Typology, Social Units, and Levels of Analysis

Assessment of hunger vulnerability raises the question of level of analysis, social classification within levels, and counting. The hunger typology is conceptualized at regional (food shortage), household (food poverty), and individual (food deprivation) levels. At the regional level, Downing (1991) sorts his social units by agroclimatic, occupational, and market access zones. Another dimension of hunger vulnerability is the political stability of the region. The challenge is to go beyond a simplistic matrix described in terms of gross spatial factors, such as agroclimatic zones, to create a more accurate and sensitive set of spatial indicators for hunger vulnerability.[2] From a food systems perspective, can anthropologists describe where agroclimatic zones are good surrogates for population density, infrastructure, and hunger vulnerability; and, where they are not, what other units might be superior, such as market access or political stability?

Below the regional level, anthropologists have an advantage in describing local groupings by peoples or communities within regions, which may be more accurate than other methods and units for following populations and their vulnerability to hunger. Downing tries, in a preliminary fashion, to move beyond the tripartite framework of the hunger typology to include an "institutional" or "community" dimension. Can anthropologists use their analyses and frameworks for describing community/state, community/international agency, and community/ NGO relations, to provide better indicators of which communities are most likely to miss state or nonstate aid in times of environmental or political crisis? Can we identify stressors in the political as well as natural climate that render particular local populations vulnerable to periodic food insecurity? Can we pinpoint and monitor populations that are dependent for ongoing food security on particular government or NGO programs, which, if interrupted, render them vulnerable to famine (see McMillan 1989; and discussion in Messer 1989b)? As another point, is it possible to inject a time dimension to measure the stability of populations over time, in response to environmental, market, and political challenges/ stressors? All the model life tables used by demographers relate to stable populations (DeWaal 1989a:9). In sum, how relevant is the community as a unit to assess food shortage? Since most interventions, including many grain programs, are aimed at the community level, this would seem to be an important but neglected unit.

Another community-level dimension to observe and use for predicting hunger vulnerability is food habits. Data on staple foods, including cultural food preferences and consumption patterns, can document changes in well-being and hunger vulnerability. Food preferences are based more in the community than in the region. Moreover, food patterns appear to be quite flexible, changing with the changing market, political, and production conditions for different crops, and provide good indices of changing food security, as people change food production, marketing, and consumption practices according to market information, prices, and availability.[3]

Findings on seasonal hunger should be incorporated into a hunger vulnerability analysis. Anthropological studies seem to indicate that, in many instances, market mechanisms have been removing the burden of seasonal food insecurity only to replace it with chronic food insecurity. Does anthropologists' documentation of this process provide insights into possible interventions? What are the gaps in knowledge? Along these lines we need to deal seriously with Scudder's (1962) and Colson's

(1979) observations (based on Zambian data) that state relief boards make survival possible through food allocations in zones that do not support sustained food production. In former times people would have been forced to move out of such zones; today they are maintained there in impoverished and underproductive fashion. Thus, anthropologists, as they examine how to build on local coping mechanisms, are also discovering the limits of those mechanisms. To document these social units and levels of analysis, anthropologists need to collect case studies detailing the mechanisms of vulnerability for particular communities, socioeconomic groups, or peoples. This will give them content and substance and perhaps clarify their existence as salient units for famine analysis. As we look at institutional structures of response, we might also experiment with nonhierarchical structures to describe what goes on. It is not self-evident that monitoring and response to food shortages are strictly top-down phenomena, and it is probably time we tried to show some alternative structures, such as web connections among social units, that allow for lateral communication of information and materials.

Finally, we might look more systematically at the local organizations that characterize the African countryside in various settings. The political science literature is weak in that it offers some vague terms such as *economy of affection* that subsume a variety of forms (including nepotism!) but no systematic account of how national level aspirations of "food self-sufficiency" articulate with household, community, or local organizational designs of ensuring adequate food (e.g., Hyden 1980). Anthropologists can provide background historical and conceptual information on types and levels of articulation of food security through a series of community-national case studies.

Thresholds of Suffering and Mortality

A related task is to examine population studies of mortality for specific cultural and analytical factors or biases. For example, DeWaal's (1989a, b) detailed reports on famine mortality in Darfur, Sudan, during 1984–85, tease out the seasonal, occupational, and locational factors that influenced who died and the overall levels of mortality during those drought years. Simple factors of vulnerability, such as resource base, occupations, socioeconomic status, age, and sex, were not sufficient to predict mortality. More sensitive knowledge of local conditions indicates additional factors are often relevant. The key factor in the Darfur case appears to have been a source of clean water. Contamination provided a conduit for infection. A lack of water in itself meant that starvation foods were improperly prepared and sometimes poisonous.

DeWaal also found that ownership of livestock provided a buffer against mortality. Households with a milk-providing animal, being less hungry and probably less susceptible to disease, were less at risk of mortality, although who consumed the milk (i.e., intrahousehold distribution of resources) was also important in determining who died. Competent health care as well as where people moved in case of food insufficiency were also significant. An additional factor—social disruption—also had consequences but was not adequately specified. All of these factors, which pinpointed household location in relation to sources of, and responses to, infection, proved to be significant in explaining differential mortality and why simpler agroclimatic and socioeconomic indicators did not suffice. DeWaal (1989a) concludes that it is disease, not starvation, that drives famine mortality. His findings suggest that medical anthropologists might be contributing more to helping donors structure their reponse to the health crisis model, supplementing the typical emergency food response, to minimize mortality in situations of famine.

Who are the Poor? Refining Socioeconomic Screening for Hunger Vulnerability
Another dimension is clarifying who are the poor. In drought-stricken communities in India, as a case in point, Martha Chen (1991) has shown that the very poor have very different coping strategies—and perceptions and responses to risk—than the less poor or the better off. How might a more fine-grained typology of poverty improve design and targeting of intervention programs? A related issue is describing varying strategies for diversification of income. Curry (1989) has provided an excellent case study from a Hausa village in Niger. It shows that those who cope better with seasonal hunger are those with more diversified sources of income. But we lack systematic studies that detail how modes of saving or of buffering risks change with changes in occupational and sociopolitical structure or which food, nonfood, or monetary instruments provide superior buffers in specific situations. The stability and range of food prices in particular localities affect decisions on savings, marketing, and other occupational choices and should be monitored over the seasons in order to understand how households perceive and respond to risk.[4]

Anthropologists might also look more carefully at the temporal dimensions of savings and investment under different social and economic resource regimes; for example, what are the social and economic incentives and deterrents for household investments in schooling for male and female children of particular ages? Such anthropological, ethnographically based studies move social science inquiry beyond the dehumanizing notion of household, social, or donor investments in "human capital."

Political Contexts and Access to Aid
Finally, anthropologists might also be combining hunger vulnerability and food systems analysis and adding to this combined analysis factors of political power and access to markets (e.g., Barraclough 1991). How likely is it that a group will be in a position to command food relief, from either the government or an international organization? Which communities are most vulnerable to neglect, or least able to respond by diversifying income, should there be programs of relief, such as food for work, as a response to climatic or political crisis? Is there a typology of ethnic, religious, or social discrimination that can be drawn, by nation, to identify such groups? Within communities which households are likely to be left out because of social, ethnic, or religious affiliation? Finally, which communities will suffer more severely, and be least likely to recover rapidly, in cases of civil disturbance or outright war?[5]

Analogously, access to markets for labor and products, in the context of cultural food preferences and social rules for food and labor sharing, will greatly shape food strategies and household and community vulnerability to local climatic or political hazards (Guyer 1989). These additional political and economic dimensions become increasingly important in the modern world, where isolation should no longer be a factor inducing famine. But political and market connections shape the resistance and resilience to stressors. They also influence the food choices that are integral components of food security.

Diet and Commodity Choices

Anthropologists undertake diet and nutrition studies in relation to cultural patterns of production and consumption, but these have not been well integrated into famine or food security studies. The food habits literature of the 1960s (e.g., Mead 1964) atrophied in the 1970s and was replaced by literature on the "domestic economy" and "decision making" in the 1980s (Sharman, Theophano, Curtis, and Messer 1991). Both provide precedent and background for anthropologists to quantify and qualify dietary indicators for food security and to understand how households respond to food policy initiatives on price and trade in staple foods.

Commodity Choices
Commodity choice is a prominent issue confronting food policy makers. The production, price, and trade policies surrounding basic staple foods (cereal grains and root and tuber crops) usually finesse the complex issues of cultural preference, population, and productive and market ecology. Such international agencies as the International Food Policy Research Institute try to monitor consumer demand for different grains and track commodity flows and pricing policies. The importation of rice, in Africa not widely grown but widely consumed, may draw down precious monetary reserves. Economists examining the grain trade in West Africa often conclude that it is in everyone's best interest that these nations continue to import large quantities of rice (e.g., D'Agostino and Staatz 1989; Reardon 1989), but they do not bolster their argument with data from what should be comparative case studies of nations that restrict trade to promote food self-reliance. Nor do they justify their conclusions with careful examination of the food systems dimensions that might indicate historically why a particular pattern developed and why it should be continued. What was the impact on urban consumption and rural production of grains, for instance, of Nigeria's import-restricting policies in the early 1990s?

The historical and cultural factors leading so many West Africans to prefer rice over traditional staples demand greater investigation in the quest for culturally and economically justifiable commodity mixes. Is there a threshold price for cereal grain or root crop substitution? Reardon indicates that rice is significant as the major component of the purchased midday meal of poor, urban Sahelian consumers. But what is the history of this practice? We need a clarification also of whether the midday meal is the main meal of the day or simply a meal purchased outside of the household consumption unit. Why do food vendors prepare rice rather than some other staple?

The most important gap in knowledge about such changes and choices is the dynamics of coarse grain production relative to urban demand. Reardon (1989) presents a twenty-year (1968–88) survey of rice consumption without indicating how the population might have changed during that period of increasing urbanization. Might it be that coarse grain production in the countryside just did not keep up with demand? Ethnohistorical studies, like Guyer's for cassava in Nigeria (see n. 3), might fill this gap, but we also need to understand why maize should be on the upswing as the preferred grain in much of Africa. This includes looking not only at productivity and price but also transport costs and storage and marketing losses, by grain and location. Is maize intrinsically superior, or are there compelling factors for its lower price relative to the other coarse grains, other than that governments, and by extension, commercial interests, have created a market for it? Ethnographic studies suggest that on good lands, in good rainfall years, maize yields are higher than those of coarse grains. People prefer its lesser bulk, and, since its seeds are not exposed, it also resists bird damage, which is extensive particularly in areas that are short of school-age labor. But we still do not have good information about how decisions on production and consumption might be made if government-controlled market opportunities, such as grain marketing boards, and production incentives, including extension services, were commensurate for traditional coarse grains and maize.

Nor do we have much good information on pest-resistant qualities of new species or varieties of grains or on how changing methods of grain storage may reinforce or disrupt traditional community power structures as well as food relationships among households and between genders (Donahaye and Messer 1991). In some settings grain banks traditionally were administered by local committees. The grain banks were designed to dampen price fluctuations and provide the committees with profits that could be used for educational and other purposes. How might food aid, as in Mali, be used to restructure the cereal market and improve village-level storage? What has been the experience of local self-help groups, such as exist in Kenya, in stabilizing grain supply for their local peoples? What kinds of lessons in the areas of local grassroots organization and control over production, storage, and supply, might be used by local, regional, or national governments or NGOs to replicate positive outcomes?

In other instances, new grain storage structures, although they may promise superior grain supplies for local communities, threaten to upset existing gender-based power relations and thereby their impact on inter- and intra-household food distribution (e.g., McCann 1989; Maguire 1989). Is *women's* participation and power assured? What happens to the relative vulnerability of different classes of households (i.e., what are the differential impacts on hunger)? Again, these are the kinds of analyses anthropologists undertake in small-scale societies.

Food Security, Hunger, and Development

Other issues for evaluating hunger vulnerability include: closer examination of development activities, including the possibly negative impact of development aid on different types of hunger; the possibly positive impact of innovative uses of food aid; and the politics of different actors in counting the numbers hungry, providing food and information, and enabling communities or households to recover rapidly from the stress of hunger.

Hunger Vulnerability and Development Aid
One of the key challenges of development policy is to avoid marginalizing further vulnerable communities and social categories. Impact evaluation involves identifying and monitoring conditions of the poorest of the poor, or other groups who will have their entitlements threatened by particular projects, such as large dams, and then, if necessary, targeting programs specifically at them. In her paper, *The Social Dimensions of Adjustment in Africa,* Nancy Farmer (1990) summarized certain World Bank concerns with the impact of their policies on people. Challenged with the spectre of "adjustment with a human face" and to develop economic programs "as if people mattered," the World Bank has been investigating how to monitor and develop compensation programs for those who are marginalized further by development policies at higher levels of social organization; to protect them during the transition phase or, better yet, incorporate them into plans for development (Cernea 1991).

Beyond opposing projects that marginalize vulnerable groups, such concerns about impacts suggest two roles for anthropologists. First, anthropologists might work with local groups and national governments to design special programs for those dislocated due to changes in infrastructure and national economic strategies. Second, anthropologists might provide more realistic assessments of conditions in the informal economic sector, to which the displaced often flee when other lines of production are disrupted. Recent U.S. newspaper business page estimates of the scale of the informal sector in the economies of developing countries such as Mexico indicate that informal economic activities, were they counted, might raise the GDP figures by as much as 40 percent. Certainly, those planning and evaluating projects need to have better understandings of the possibly important role of informal economic activities in transforming local economies, integrating local economies into growing national economies, and providing transitional income.

Innovative Uses of Food and Aid
Outside of the contexts of disaster aid, food aid can be redirected to help end long-term poverty and hunger, if not short-term hunger (see, e.g., Reutlinger 1988; Anderson and Woodrow 1989; Lakes 1990). But to create reasonable objectives for food aid programs, and to improve effectiveness, aid administrators also need to have superior understandings of community or household skills and capacity for organization and self-administration. They need to be able to assess the possibilities of building on traditional coping strategies as well as to identify where traditional responses are themselves stressors that need to be overcome. They also need to be able to articulate the *demand* side of aid: How do communities and households assess their own vulnerability, in contrast to the ways in which Famine Early Warning Systems, the World Food Program, or other respondents assess vulnerability? Two types of anthropological data are relevant. First are detailed analyses of ecological and economic conditions as well as thresholds of hardship and response. Second are efforts to give potential aid recipients greater voice in assessing their needs, recommending or demanding particular categories of response (see, e.g., Torry 1988; 1993).

As a corollary, it is also useful for the community and donors offering and delivering food aid programs, or development programs more generally, to have better understandings of the objectives of the aid community, so that they can negotiate program design, delivery, and criteria for evaluation. Although economists and nutritionists very recently have attempted to consider such objectives more carefully as they attempt to understand why nutrition planning programs have failed, they tend to consider more political-economic than sociocultural issues and leave out entirely an anthropological perspective. Even when investigating issues such as the political economy of communities and households as these affect intrahousehold allocation of (nutritional) goods, they tend to neglect references to anthropological findings (e.g.,

Pinstrup-Anderson 1993). What are the different perceptions of nutritional needs within households and communities, and how do these differ still further from those of government planners? What kinds of translations need to be made from the bottom up (the household and the grassroots to policy makers) as well as from the top down (planners and service providers to communities and households) for effective nutrition planning? Anthropologists are beginning to answer such questions in a more straightforward fashion through rapid assessment and other formal methods specifically designed to assist nutrition planners and communities (see Scrimshaw and Gleason 1992). Such findings add to a growing anthropological corpus indicating what cultural factors facilitate or block program success at provider and institutional as well as recipient community levels.

Institutional Considerations: The Politics of NGOs and Other Aid Organizations

Institutional analyses of the objectives, strategies, and operations of organizations responsible for warning and responding to famines are beginning to emerge (e.g., Harrell-Bond 1986), but more are needed. Aid organizations might invite anthropologists to analyze what they do and to provide clues for improving the effectiveness of aid. All of the summaries of FEWS and other warning systems, as cases in point, tend to be technical, asking, for instance, what are reliable diagnostics, be they climatic, price, or behavioral indicators? But they leave out important sociopolitical dimensions. Warning systems, for example, are often designed to diagnose and respond to hunger vulnerability on the basis of some percentage of the people in a community appearing to be hungry or at risk for hunger. The task of reading warning signs might seem to be routine, but in fact there exist differences in technical expertise and evaluation and, perhaps more important, among political interests, to see that the food and income benefits of food aid reach certain communities and regions and not others. Assessment of risk, therefore, may differ among NGO, international agency, and government actors, as may corresponding recommendations for intervention. In order for any aid to flow there must be a careful negotiation of which regions or communities qualify for aid that satisfies both the donor and national recipient.

Such sociopolitical dimensions demand closer examination, so that the linkages between perception of need and responsive action can be sorted out. Where response is insufficient, is it because there was insufficient knowledge (clearly, some people had the information) or, more insidiously, insufficient institutional (including national) will or capacity to respond?[6] A task for anthropologists would seem to be to understand these political connections of vulnerable communities and regions to state and aid communities and to use this information to contribute to more timely and appropriate response. A corollary would be an explication of the political and cultural motivations for diagnosing and defining hunger and hunger numbers in particular ways as these conditions and numbers influence response.

Throughout the 1980s, for example, international agency and national food institute and program nutritionists and economists debated the validity of a "protein gap," the accuracy of recommended energy allowances, and the requirements for particular micronutrients (Messer 1989c,d). Anthropological studies of the culture and politics of the decision makers should be able to make a special contribution to clarifying the extent of the problem as perceived "on the ground" and according to the varying biases of the bureaucracies. Such political subtleties are not easily captured in statistics or data bases. Anthropological analyses of information systems and information flows, including investigations of how the news and advertising media handle timely issues ranging from environment to food and nutrition, provide another dimension of analysis (see, e.g., Kottak 1989).

The Hunger Typology and an Anthropological Analysis of Stress

Additionally, it may be possible to model hunger vulnerability in new ways. As the flip side of adaptation and coping studies, anthropologists, among others, have worked with conceptual models of stress. These hold some promise for conceptually modeling stressors, stress perception, stress response, and the breakdown of coping mechanisms. Selye (1955) many years ago proposed a tripartite model of stress response, which for animal and human models he termed the "general adaptation syndrome." He noted that an organism responding to stress passes through three stages: first, an alarm reaction, in which the unit shows change characteristic of first exposure to a stressor. At the same time resistance is diminished, and, if the stress is sufficiently severe, it can lead to destruction and death. Barring that, the organism passes into a second stage of resistance, in which the alarm signs disappear, and adaptive resistance rises above normal. This enables the organism to withstand the stressor, although, following prolonged exposure to the stressor, the organism reaches the (third) stage of exhaustion, bereft of further energy to adapt, such that the alarm signs reappear irreversibly, and the organism expires. Variations on this stress model have proposed that it is also important to study how organisms maintain health and avoid helplessness, who recovers most rapidly and why, and what the continuum of health might be (e.g., Antonovsky 1979).

Most anthropological writings on stress and adaptation have focused on illness and disease (e.g., Alland 1970; Levine and Scotch 1970; Monat and Lazarus 1977). They make little attempt to link this model to ecological models of the response of local cultural systems and ecosystems that can also be discussed as homeostatic systems subject to stressors and perturbations. Yet, in cases of famine, there might be a diagnostic sequencing of adaptive responses that might be labeled alarm, response, and exhaustion and might help identify better the stages at which communities, households, and individuals become vulnerable to famine that kills (DeWaal 1989b). This is not to say that an improved food security conceptual model can be easily extrapolated from a human security (health care) conceptual model. Prerequisites are good measures of adaptation or adjustment, the resources for which can be conceptualized as finite or exhaustible but also subject to restructuring.

The stress model also provides a framework through which to study the severity and duration of individual, household, or community responses to stressors and how such units manage to maintain health and avoid helplessness. An analogy might be drawn to hunger stressors and type and timing of response by individuals, households, or communities. The severity of famine impact on various communities and households varies. Most studies of vulnerability focus on who is at risk of hunger but then stop. They do not return to ask: Who recovers most quickly? Inability to recover from famine may constitute a different set of risk factors, with far-reaching implications. Yet there has been no concentrated examination of this issue. A stress model offers one way to conceptualize and explore such dimensions of vulnerability.

Targeting a Development Community Audience

Anthropologists have a comparative advantage in describing social units of analysis and their integration within states. As a relative newcomer to African studies, I am struck by the lack of any coherent and convincing analysis of what these units are and how they articulate with higher-level social units. Utilizing a superior typology and set of descriptive factors for analyzing local- through national-level social units in interaction, anthropologists could help resolve the problem of defining who is vulnerable to hunger (in what social units they are located) and the processes of response to hunger within and between social levels. We also have a comparative advantage in analyzing local food systems and their linkages to the national and international political economies.

Nevertheless, working in the interdisciplinary context of the World Hunger Program, I note that anthropologists also have several lessons to learn. First, we must simplify. In spite of the complexities of food systems, we must figure out how to define manageable problems and conceptual schemes in terms that development agency task forces can understand and use. Second, we must be open to the reality that geographers, economists, or other disciplines may be asked to take the lead in development work. But that should not stop us from trying to inject the best of anthropological theory and practice into such interdisciplinary efforts. Third, we have to be thinking continually about the mix between concept- and action-oriented anthropology as well as about ways to monitor whether we are making a difference. Downing's (1991) essay began as a communal exercise in which we at the Brown University World Hunger Program responded to a FEWS request for guidance in assessing hunger vulnerability and indicators. For us it became an opportunity to adapt the food-short, food-poor, food-deprived paradigm to an action-oriented context. Certainly, anthropologists can identify similar opportunities to apply methods and models as we explore the processes at various social levels that contribute to food security.

NOTES

This chapter was originally prepared for a special meeting of the Task Force on African Famine and Food Systems in June 1989, Binghamton, New York. A shortened version of the chapter was published previously in *Development Anthropology Network* 8(2) (1990): 8–15.

1. Other participants were me, a cultural and nutritional anthropologist; Nora Groce, a cultural and medical anthropologist; and Sara Millman, a sociologist-demographer.

2. Geographers are also approaching this issue through the concept of "criticality" (see Bohle et al. 1993).

3. Jane Guyer (pers. comm.) has been documenting changing staple crop production and consumption for Cameroon and Nigeria, to try to represent more adequately the dynamic spectra of farming systems that are not "maize" or other staple crop based but, rather, respond to market or other political incentives.

4. William Torry (in progress) has been trying to formulate and compare notions of risk among different donor or nongovernment aid organizations and recipient populations.

5. Geographers concerned with pinpointing hunger vulnerability are also exploring the critical dimensions in terms of spatial, temporal, and personal position (see, e.g., Bohle et al. 1993).

6. An interview with the head of Geographic Information Early Warning System (GIEWS [FAO]) in 1988 suggested that they really have enough information; what they lack is the capacity to respond.

REFERENCES

Alland, A.
    1970 *Adaptation in Cultural Evolution: An Approach to Medical Anthropology*. New York: Columbia University Press.

Anderson, M., and P. Woodrow
    1989 *Rising from the Ashes: Development Strategies in Times of Disaster*. Boulder, Colo.: Westview Press.

Antonovsky, A.
    1979 *Health, Stress, and Coping*. San Francisco: Jossey-Bass.

Barraclough, S. L.
    1991 *An End to Hunger? The Social Origins of Food Strategies*. London: Zed Books Ltd.

Bohle, H. G., T. E. Downing, J. O. Field, and F. N. Ibrahim, eds.
    1993 *Coping with Vulnerability and Criticality*. Fort Lauderdale, Fla.: Verlag Breitenbach Publishers.

Brieger, W. R. and J. Guyer
    1990 Farmers' Loss Due to Guinea Worm Disease: A Pilot Study. *Journal of Tropical Medicine and Hygiene* 93:103–11.

Cernea, M.
    1991 Involuntary Resettlement: Social Research, Policy, and Planning. In *Putting People First: Sociological Variables in Development,* ed. M. Cernea, 188–215. New York: Oxford University Press.

Chambers, R.
    1981 Introduction. In *Seasonal Dimensions to Rural Poverty,* ed. R. Chambers, R. Longhurst, and A. Pacey, 1–8. London: Frances Pinter.

Chen, Martha A.
    1991 *Coping with Seasonality and Drought*. New Delhi: Sage Publications India Private Ltd.

Colson, E.
   1979   In Good Years and Bad: Food Strategies of Self-Reliant Societies. *Journal of Anthropological Research* 35:18–29.
Curry, J.
   1989   Seasonality, Monetization, and Occupational Diversity in a Hausa Village in Niger. In *Coping with Seasonal Constraints,* ed. R. Huss-Ashmore, with J. Curry and R. Hitchcock, 5:121–30. MASCA Research Papers in Science and Archaeology. Philadelphia: University Museum, University of Pennsylvania.
D'Agostino, V. C., and J. M. Staatz
   1989   *Food Security and Economic Growth in the Sahel: A Summary of the September 1989 Sahel Cereals Workshop.* East Lansing: Michigan State University Department of Agricultural Economics.
DeWaal, A.
   1989a Famine Mortality: A Case Study of Darfur, Sudan 1984–85. *Population Studies* 43:5–24.
   1989b *Famine That Kills.* New York: Oxford University Press.
Donahaye, E., and E. Messer
   1991   *Reduction in Grain Storage Losses of Small-Scale Farmers in Tropical Countries.* Providence, R.I.: World Hunger Program, Brown University, Research Report 91–7.
Douglas, M., and J. Gross
   1981   Food and Culture: Measuring the Intricacy of Rule Systems. *Social Science Information* 20:1–35.
Downing, T.
   1991   *Assessing Socioeconomic Vulnerability to Famine: Frameworks, Concepts, and Applications.* Providence, R.I.: World Hunger Program, Brown University, Research Report, 91-1.
Downs, R. E., D. O. Kerner, and S. P. Reyna, eds.
   1991   *The Political Economy of African Famine.* New York: Gordon and Breach.
Farmer, N.
   1990   *The Social Dimensions of Adjustment in Africa.* Washington, D.C.: World Bank. Paper prepared for the Third Annual World Hunger Briefing, Providence, R.I., World Hunger Program, Brown University, April 1990.
Greene, L.
   1977   *Malnutrition, Behavior, and Social Organization.* New York: Academic Press.
Guyer, J.
   1989   From Seasonal Income to Daily Diet in a Partially Commercialized Rural Economy (Cameroon). In *Seasonal Variability in Third World Agriculture: The Consequences for Food Security,* ed. D. Sahn, 137–50. Baltimore: Johns Hopkins University Press.
Harrell-Bond, B.
   1986   *Imposing Aid: Emergency Assistance for African Refugees.* Oxford: Oxford University Press.

Haswell, M.
   1953   *Economics of Agriculture in a Savannah Village.* Colonial Research Study no. 8. London: MHSO.
Huss-Ashmore, R., with J. Curry and R. Hitchcock, eds.
   1989   *Coping with Seasonal Constraints.* MASCA Research Papers in Science and Archaeology, vol. 5. Philadelphia: University Museum, University of Pennsylvania.
Huss-Ashmore, R., and S. Katz, eds.
   1989   *African Food Systems in Crisis,* part 1: *Microperspectives.* New York: Gordon and Breach.
   1990   *African Food Systems in Crisis,* part 2: *Contending with Change.* New York: Gordon and Breach.
Hyden, G.
   1980   *Beyond Ujamaa in Tanzania: Underdevelópment and an Uncaptured Peasantry.* London: Heinemann.
Kates, R., R. Chen, T. Downing, J. Kasperson, E. Messer, and S. Millman
   1988   *The Hunger Report: 1988.* Providence, R.I.: World Hunger Program, Brown University.
Kottak, C.
   1989   *Prime Time Society: An Anthropological Analysis of Television and Culture.* Belmont, Calif.: Wadsworth Publishing.
Lakes, Anthony, ed.
   1990   *After the Wars.* New Brunswick, N.J.: Transaction Publishers.
Levine, S., and N. A. Scotch, eds.
   1970   *Social Stress.* Chicago: Aldine.
Maguire, R. E.
   1989   Control beyond the Farm Gate: Peasants, Poverty, and Power in Haiti. Barbados, W.I.: XIV Annual Conference, Caribbean Studies Association.
McCann, J. C.
   1989   The Socio-Economic Context of Food Storage in Highland Ethiopia: Gera Wereda. Draft of report prepared for American Jewish World Service, with the Cooperation of Redd Barna Ethiopia. Boston, Mass.
McMillan, D.
   1989   Seasonality, Planned Settlements, and River Blindness Control in Burkina Faso. In *Coping with Seasonal Constraints. MASCA Research Papers in Science and Archaeology,* ed. R. Huss-Ashmore, with John Curry and R. Hitchcock, 5:131–41. University Museum, University of Pennsylvania. 96–120. Baltimore: Johns Hopkins University Press.
Mead, M.
   1964   *Food Habits Research: Problems of the 1960s.* Publication no. 1225. Washington, D.C.: United States National Academy of Sciences.
Messer, E.
   1989a Seasonality in Food Systems: An Anthropological Perspective on

Household Food Security. In *Seasonal Variability in Third World Agriculture: The Consequences for Food Security,* ed. D. Sahn, 151–75. Baltimore: Johns Hopkins University Press.

1989b Seasonal Hunger and Coping Strategies: An Anthropological Discussion. In *Coping with Seasonal Constraints. MASCA Research Papers in Science and Archaeology,* ed. R. Huss-Ashmore, with John Curry and R. Hitchcock, 5:131–41. University Museum, University of Pennsylvania.

1989c Small but Healthy? Some Cultural Considerations. *Human Organization* 48(1): 39–52.

1989d Indian Nutritionists and International Nutritional Standards. *Social Science and Medicine* 29(12): 1393–99.

Monat, A., and R. Lazarus, eds.
  1977 *Stress and Coping.* New York: Columbia University Press.

Moris, J.
  1989 Indigenous versus Introduced Solutions to Food Stress in Africa. In *Seasonal Variability in Third World Agriculture: The Consequences for Food Security,* ed. D. Sahn, 209–34. Baltimore: Johns Hopkins University Press.

Newman, L., gen. ed.
  1994 *Hunger in History,* 2d ed. Cambridge, Mass.: Basil Blackwell.

Pinstrup-Anderson, P., ed.
  1993 *The Political Economy of Food and Nutrition Policies.* Baltimore: Johns Hopkins University Press.

Reardon, T.
  1989 *Cereal Demand in West Africa: Implications for Sahelian Regional Protection.* SL89/23, October. Washington, D.C.: International Food Policy Research Institute (IFPRI).

Reutlinger, S.
  1988 Efficient Alleviation of Poverty and Hunger. *Food Policy* 13(1): 56–66.

Richards, A.
  1939 *Land, Labour, and Diet in Northern Rhodesia: An Economic Study of the Bemba Tribe.* London: G. Routledge.

Scrimshaw, Mary, and Sheila Cosminsky
  1991 Impact of Health on Women's Food-Procurement Strategies on a Guatemalan Plantation. In *Diet and Domestic Life in Society,* ed. A. Sharman, J. Theophano, K. Curtis, and E. Messer, 61–89. Philadelphia: Temple University Press.

Scrimshaw, N., and G. Gleason, eds.
  1992 *Rapid Assessment Procedures, Qualitative Methodologies for Planning and Evaluation of Health-Related Programs.* Boston: International Nutrition Foundation for Developing Countries.

Scudder, T.
  1962 *The Ecology of the Gwembe Tonga.* Manchester: Manchester University Press.

Selye, H.
    1955 Stress and Disease. *Science* 122:625–31.
Sharman, A.
    1970 Social and Economic Aspects of Nutrition in Padhola, Bukedi District, Uganda. Ph.D. diss., University of London.
Sharman, A., J. Theophano, K. Curtis, and E. Messer, eds.
    1991 *Diet and Domestic Life in Society.* Philadelphia: Temple University Press.
Shipton, P.
    1990 African Famines and Food Security: Anthropological Perspectives. *Annual Review of Anthropology* 19:353–94.
Torry, W. I.
    1988 FEWS: The Need for an Anthropological Dimension. *Human Organization* 47:1–14.
    1993 Information for Food. In *The Challenge of Famine,* ed. J. O. Field, 209–38. W. Hartford, Conn.: Kumarian Press.
Van Veen, M. S.
    1971 Some Ecological Considerations of Nutritional Problems on Java. *Ecology of Food and Nutrition* 1:25–38.

Chapter 9

Culture Change and Health: Third World Perspectives

Demitri B. Shimkin, assisted by Denise Roth,
with an addendum by Dennis A. Frate

A systematic exposition of the determinants of health in Third World countries is an undertaking of great scope and complexity. This discussion is more limited, seeking to delineate patterns and trends. It will deal with health in tropical countries (Shimkin 1988) and examine more thoroughly developments in tropical Africa and patterns, trends, problems, and plans in Tanzanian health. Finally, questions of foreign technical aid, with special reference to anthropology, are addressed.

Two considerations are fundamental in this discussion. First, world health is a technical problem that has advanced since World War II but that is encountering new levels of difficulty and cost with rising life expectancies. Apart from a few African areas plagued by severe environmental conditions and long-term conflicts, life expectancies everywhere have, in recent years, been exceeding forty years at birth. In other words, even very poor countries are surpassing British life expectancies of the nineteenth century. This tremendous achievement has been realized through the eradication of smallpox, the limitation of major epidemic diseases such as plague, cholera, yellow fever, syphilis, and tuberculosis, immunization for major infectious diseases of childhood, and other advances in primary health care. This achievement has also been realized despite the growing pantropical burden of malaria and the worldwide threat of AIDS.

Further advances in longevity involve structural changes corresponding to the demographic effects of prolonged better health. With life expectancies at birth of thirty-five to fifty years, the basic causes of death are infectious diseases intensified by malnutrition. Up to half of all deaths are of children under age five. These deaths usually are overshadowed by high fertility, so that vital rates may run 3 percent or more annually.

With life expectancies of fifty to seventy years at birth, infectious diseases and malnutrition are largely controlled, while the aging population is more subject to morbidity and mortality from cardiovascular diseases and cancer. A growing population of young adults generates behavioral problems, including alcoholism and other drug addictions, sexually transmitted diseases, and accidents. The costs of health care multiply several times over as more complex procedures become essential (Bicknell and Parks 1989).

When life expectancies run in the mid- or high seventies, the medical care of the aged becomes a major problem. The primary and secondary prevention of major chronic diseases, adequate medical coverage for the poor, and the maintenance of social and even economic functionality of the aged become basic issues. Costs per capita again rise five- or even tenfold (Anderson 1989; Plath 1988a, b; Roghmann 1989; Scheuch 1989; Shimkin 1983).

World health is also a psychosocial and political problem. Because they affect fundamental values, health maintenance resources and health care are never fully surrendered even by the very poor. Some level of pluralism (faith healers vis-à-vis physicians, midwives vis-à-vis obstetricians) appears to be universal; correspondingly, folk and cosmopolitan theories of illness compete everywhere. Tensions over the control of health resources are also active at regional, national, and international levels. Drugs and other medical technology and the domination of health policies are often at issue (Davis 1987; van der Geest 1987; Wolfson 1982).

Throughout the spectrum of health there is an inherent conflict between efficacy and autonomy. This conflict is intensified by the frequently arbitrary identification of health problems. Health also is an environmentally conditioned phenomenon: in Nigeria, for example, the cognitive losses of schizophrenia are far less disabling, particularly in villages, than in the United States (Hoban 1985). Conversely, facilities for the severely disabled permit the functional survival of many in the United States who would be helpless in Africa.

Everywhere health is today at once a personal, family, community, regional, national, even world problem. It is integrated by modern communications and fragmented by conflicts of power that generate medical pluralism.

Issues in Tropical Health

The concept of "Third World" is truly ambiguous from the standpoints of epidemiology and health statuses. A more restricted concept, in large part coincident with Third World, is "the tropics." Tropical environments permit continuity of life processes and hence of disease processes markedly different from the seasonality of temperate lands. Moreover, tropical populations are, with few exceptions, predominantly agricultural and poor. Urbanization, when it occurs, is generally supported by inadequate housing, water supplies, food processing, and other facilities. In consequence, the diseases of poverty as well as endemic tropical diseases are prevalent (on the latter, see TDR et al. 1988). Finally, because of past exploitative and often racist colonial or quasicolonial policies, health services and research are still generally inadequate.

Within the tropics the epidemiology of Africa and India are very similar. In both areas malaria, respiratory diseases, dysentery and diarrhea, leprosy, leishmaniasis, and filariasis are widespread. Malnutrition, especially among weanlings, is ubiquitous. The importance of trypanosomiasis in Africa and of lathyrus toxin poisoning in India, both phenomena limiting usable protein supplies, are among the few differences. At the same time, national unity and health policies have permitted more consistent progress in health levels in India than on the African continent. Such differences in development, even more than those in environment, have led to major differences in life expectancies and other health indicators. The Americas and insular Southeast Asia have done particularly well in controlling infectious diseases. In such countries as Jamaica, Venezuela, Sri Lanka (prior to its devastating civil war), and Singapore life expectancies at birth have been well over sixty years (Shimkin 1988).

Experts from more successful tropical countries far more than consultants from remote areas can provide the leadership needed for improvement of tropical health. The World Health Organization (WHO) should be lauded for helping develop centers of excellence in tropical countries (TDR et al. 1988). But material assistance remains very inadequate, despite long continued support from Western European countries and the recent emergence of Japan as a major donor.

Health in Africa

Our review will consider four aspects: (1) disease patterns; (2) fertility, birth control, and maternal mortality; (3) health services; and (4) health improvements. It also needs to be noted that, judging from Nigerian data, urbanization, with all its costs in bad housing, pollution, motor vehicle accidents, hypertension and behavioral problems, is nevertheless a major force for health improvement (Adegbola 1987; Olugbile and Oyemode 1981). These confirm earlier materials from Nairobi (Mugo 1974).

Disease Patterns: A Selective Review
Of the many disease problems prevalent in Africa eight are noteworthy. First, nutritional deficiencies affect all African populations. The basic problems are not those of inadequate total food supply. Even agricultural populations with minimal consumptions of animal products have satisfactory food supplies (Kimati 1986). But problems of weaning by overworked mothers lacking proper baby foods are ubiquitous in rural areas. The consequences are growth retardation and sometimes marasmus and kwashiorkor (Kingamkono et al. 1987; Latham 1979). Iron deficiency anemia is widespread. It reflects dietary lacks and the synergic effects of malaria, schistosomiasis, and hookworm. This is a particularly serious problem for women (Winikoff 1988). In mountain areas, and wherever cassava is a major food, iodine deficiency diseases are prevalent (Kavishe and Maletnlema 1984). Vitamin A deficiencies also are common, and in combination with measles and trachoma they contribute to high levels of blindness.

Second, endemic, infectious diseases are of major importance. Over the last forty years smallpox has been eradicated, while cholera, plague, and yellow fever are either partially controlled or territorially restricted. But a number of other severe infectious diseases remain as major burdens in Africa, India, and other tropical areas. These are targets for WHO's Programme for Research and Training in Tropical Diseases and include malaria, the world's most prevalent disease, African and American trypanosomiasis, schistosomiasis, filariasis (including onchocerciasis), leishmaniasis, and leprosy. All kill or debilitate millions of people (Addy, Minami and Agadzi 1986; Bruce-Chwatt 1980; Fivawo 1986).

Third, diseases of poverty, crowding, and poor sanitation are major killers of infants and children. Some are largely preventable through immunization. Tetanus, pneumonia, diarrhea, measles, whooping cough, and poliomyelitis are the most important. These diseases cause over half of all deaths in young children. Substantial progress is taking place in tackling these problems, in important part from excellent aid by Scandinavian countries (Hull, Williams, and Oldfield 1983; Pigman 1987).

Fourth, gonorrhea, nonspecific pelvic inflammation, and syphilis are highly prevalent in East and Central Africa (Cooper-Poole 1986; Podgore and Omar 1986). Prostitution is a widely accepted occupation, and condoms are only sporadically used. A number of studies show that venereal infections abet the heterosexual transmission of AIDS (Simonson et al. 1988). The role of female genital mutilation is unclear. Moreover, while intravenous heroin addiction appears to be rare in tropical Africa, neotraditional healers widely use injections—e.g., chloroquine and quinine against malaria—in their therapy. Such injections and births to infected mothers constitute significant avenues for the transmission of AIDS.

In Tanzania, according to a recent comprehensive review (Mwaluko et al., in press), the AIDS problem, which has developed since 1985, corresponds proportionately to that in the United States. More than half of all cases are in Dar es Salaam and along the highway leading to Central Africa. Prostitutes and truck drivers are particularly at risk.

Fifth, tuberculosis, a disease largely introduced since World War I and particularly prevalent in South African mines, appears to be an increasing problem despite the widespread use of the BCG vaccine as a preventative. The disease is a common opportunistic infection in African AIDS. With rapid urbanization tuberculosis threatens to become a major health problem. Its current prevalence is estimated at three cases per thousand persons (Gottschalk 1988; Ndeki 1979; Quinn 1986; Ndeki 1979).

Sixth, motor vehicle accidents though not diseases, do constitute a serious health problem in Africa. Over the past thirty years motor vehicle ownership and use have increased greatly in Africa. Today highways are crowded with vehicles ranging from large trucks, often with trailers, to buses, passenger cars, and motorcycles. Pedestrians often share the roads. Road surfaces may be very poor and traffic regulation all but lacking. In consequence, injuries and fatalities are rising. At present they still constitute a small fraction, generally under 1 percent, of total deaths, but rates are much higher in large cities: in Nairobi in 1972 they accounted for 6 percent of all deaths (Mugo 1974:166); in Lagos in 1977 such accidents accounted for 14 percent of all deaths (Ayeni 1980). They are significant as sources of devastating injury (Asogwa 1978).

Seventh is substance abuse. Traditionally, native beers were the essential elements of ritual life in much of Africa, while their consumption was largely limited to elders. Although heavy drinking was characteristic of chiefs, shortages of materials generally held down consumption. Colonialism and independence have brought about major changes (described in Carlson 1989) for the Bahaya of Tanzania. The introduction of a money economy and the decline of customary controls stimulated, first, domestic alcohol production and, second, the purchase of strong commercial beers and liquors. Economic expansion was funneled appreciably into increased drinking, including that of women and youths. Bars, with attendant problems of alcoholism, disruptive behavior, prostitution, and venereal diseases, became the centers of consumption. Evangelical Christian sects in particular promoted a counter trend of strict abstinence.

Concern with drinking as a social and medical problem was widely manifested by colonial administrators (Carlson 1985). Since independence, however, much less attention has been devoted to drinking. Surveys of drinking in Nigeria and Kenya date to the late 1970s. In Tanzania the sole systematic, quantitative study of drinking, in Dodoma City, has been by Singavo (1984). This investigation determined that, in a stratified random sample of 384 adults, 58 percent were drinkers who consumed an average of four to six half-liter bottles of commercial beer or local *pombe* at least twice a week. A typical drinker was married, male, aged forty to forty-nine, Christian, and a worker or peasant with secondary or higher education. At the same time, 48 percent of the women compared to 66 percent of the men drank, as did 37 percent of the Muslims compared to 66 percent of the Christians. The site of drinking was a *pombe* shop or bar for 70 percent of the drinkers.

In Nigeria, Obembe and Fagbayi (1988) found, in hospital research in Kaduma, that among those involved in serious traffic accidents 9.5 percent of the drivers and 24.3 percent of the nondrivers were alcohol intoxicated; for cannabis or amphetamine intoxication the corresponding figures were 20.5 percent and 21.7 percent, respectively.

Eighth is cardiovascular diseases. Studies of African rural populations have generally found them to have low blood pressure lifelong and little evidence of cardiovascular disease. Yet in the Usari area of Kilimanjaro District, at higher altitudes, a different picture has been found. Blood pressures rose steadily with age; 14 percent of the males and 12 percent of the females over fourteen were hypertensive. By ages fifty-five to sixty-four, the proportions rose to 33 percent and 27 percent, respectively. The causes for this anomaly are unclear, although hypertension and diabetes are closely associated in African rural populations (Lutalo and Mabonga 1985).

Seedat, Seedat, and Hackland (1982) discovered substantial prevalences of hypertension among Zulus. In a rural Zulu study of 987 persons the prevalences of hypertension (as defined by the WHO) were 8.7 percent for men and 10 percent for women. In a house-to-house study of 994 urban Zulus the prevalence of hypertension was 23 percent for men and 27 percent for women. The mean number of years of residence of Zulus in Durban was significantly greater in both male and female hypertensive subjects than in those normotensive. There was no difference in the prevalence of hypertension among urban men who resided in the hostels and the "subeconomic" houses. That urbanization per se was probably not a major risk factor is indicated by a study of blood pressures in Benin City, Nigeria, in which Alakija (1979) found very low hypertension rates: 4 percent for males and 3.4 percent for females. These findings correspond to those for rural Benin (Oviasu 1978).

A great deal of concern surrounds cardiovascular diseases in Africa today. While extensive epidemiological research is just under way, rheumatic heart disease, primary and secondary hypertension, and stroke are of general clinical concern. For urban people, especially men, more sedentary lives, high-fat diets, more salt, more alcohol, and job- and family-related sociopsychological stresses are manifest risk factors, especially in combination with obesity.

Fertility, Birth Control, and Maternal Mortality
Pro-natalism is a major force in African societies. Bleek's (1978) study of a town in Ghana reveals ideal family sizes of 5.4 children, while completed fertilities in a small sample ran from 5 to 7 live births. In Kenya older males and extended families are strongly pro-natalist (Sindiga 1985). Almost everywhere childlessness is deplored. At the

same time, traditional birth limitation is basically limited to prolonged nursing and concurrent sexual abstention, particularly in polygamous families (Delvoye and Robyn 1980; Orbuloye 1981). Modern contraception is still limited. In Kenya 9.6 percent of sexually active women used "equipment supported" methods; in the catchment zone of Chogoria Hospital, east of Mt. Kenya, a special family planning program raised this statistic to 34 percent (DeBoer and McNeil 1989). In Tanzania reported contraceptive use in 1989 was reported as "about 7 percent."

Nevertheless, birthrates vary considerably, from perhaps forty-five to fifty per one thousand persons down to fifteen to twenty; in some populations as many as 40 percent of the women may be infertile, compared to an expected 5 to 6 percent (Lesthaeghe et al. 1981). It is believed that high levels of gonorrheal and other pelvic inflammations plus heavy fetal mortality from malaria and other sources of anemia are major causes (Patel 1980). Lapido and Osoba (1978) have also noted the significance of infections by the fungus *Ureaplasma urealyticum* in reducing sperm counts.

Very young mothers, often physically overworked, unsupported by prenatal care, and delivering babies, in large part, aided only by midwives all contribute to high rates of maternal as well as neonatal mortality. In many instances the very small size of mothers generates problems of cephalo-pelvic nonconformity requiring competent surgical intervention. In general Royston and Lopez (1987) estimate an average maternal mortality of 640 per 100,000 live births for Africa. The lifetime risk of dying from pregnancy-related causes is at least 1 in 15 (ibid., 220). Even at such a competent facility as Muhimbili Medical Centre in Tanzania, 224 maternal deaths took place in 1974–77 out of a total of 105,311 deliveries. Deaths from toxemia or associated with cesarean section, anemia, sepsis, and hemorrhage predominated. In many instances the patients were admitted in obstructed labor, exhausted and dehydrated. In Lagos, Nigeria, 6 percent of all female mortality was attributable to complications of pregnancy, childbirth, and the puerperium (Ayeni 1980:144).

Data on induced abortions in tropical Africa are largely limited to hospital information in which governmental or religious pressures may produce serious distortions. There is no doubt that abortions are grossly underreported and that abortions, particularly those induced clandestinely, are a significant cause of maternal death (Boerma 1987; Coeytaux 1988; Lamptey et al. 1985; and Mtimavalye, Lisasi and Ntuyabaliwe

1980). In general the rate of maternal mortality reported by the last authors, one-tenth of the pregnancies, is a conservative minimum for urban Africa. The risk is maximum for unmarried school girls who, in many countries, are expelled from school upon evidence of pregnancy. In Tanzania, between 1970 and 1982, 24,977 primary and secondary schoolgirls were expelled for pregnancy. An important contributory factor has been the absence of sexual education and consequent sexual ignorance, even among high-status, secondary school students (Fundikora 1985).

In general, while birth control has been a favorite subject of foreign donor agencies, particularly from the United States, family planning has made little headway in Africa. Programs poorly related to broader issues of women's health and status, and often distorted by donor constraint in regard to abortion and various forms or contraception, have been ineffective.

Health Services

Throughout tropical Africa health services are pluralistic. They offer varying admixtures of free governmental services of a cosmopolitan type and paid services offered by missionary institutions, private practioners, pharmacists, and traditional and neotraditional healers. In some areas, such as Mali (Hielcher and Sommerfield 1985), traditional views and practices prevail. In others, notably Kenya (Mwabu 1986), consumers select from alternatives—cosmopolitan to traditional—on the basis of self-diagnosis and propinquity.

The supply of physicians, nurses, other trained health personnel, and medical facilities varies widely in tropical Africa, both between and within countries. Kenya, Tanzania, Ghana, Botswana, and, in some states, Nigeria appear to have the most extensive resources, including tertiary care hospitals and research establishments. Uganda's modern services are reviving. These are public or financed by religious institutions. But even here the number of physicians is less than one per 10,000 persons, and the facilities are concentrated in a few cities. In spite of vigorous efforts, especially in Tanzania, rural areas must depend on paraprofessionals and traditional healers. In countries such as Mali and the Central African Republic modern medicine is all but unavailable (Orubuloye and Oyenoye 1982, for Nigeria; Onyango 1974, for Kenya; Gish 1983, and Heggenhougen et al 1987, Jonsson 1986, for Tanzania; Dodge 1986 and Turaya 1985, for Uganda; Hogh and Peterson 1984, for

Botswana; MacCormack 1984, for Sierra Leone; Hielcher and Sommerfield 1985, for Mali).

In large part medical strategies in Africa are still legacies of colonial policies and missionary undertakings. In particular large-scale research has been dominated by foreign initiatives, direction, and personnel. This has included not only the great program of smallpox eradication but also Buck's (1970) investigations of disease ecology in Chad, Cunningham's (1978) work on "under 5's," the Garki effort to control malaria in the savanna (Molineaux and Gramiccia 1980), and recent interventions to control onchocerciasis (Dodzie, Remne, and Thylefos 1986). It is to the great credit of WHO that its important program on tropical diseases has emphasized building indigenous research capacities since its start in 1977 and that the guiding concept now is a "global research partnership" (TDR et al. 1988). Also, indigenous innovations have not been lacking—for example, Nigeria's highly successful colonies for the mentally ill (Erinosha 1978).

Yet the buildup of service, training, and modest research capacities in major cities has been clearly inadequate to meet the needs of rural populations. Consequently, in 1978 a drastically new approach was promoted by an international conference at Alma Ata in the USSR. It advocated universal health coverage based on village health workers with limited training who would emphasize prevention and who would be supported, in part, by their own efforts as subsistence workers, in part by small payments from fellow villagers. Backing these workers would be a hierarchy of care up to major hospitals (Muhondwa 1986).

This program of primary health care has developed with varying success in Africa and other tropical regions. It has been successful in many aspects of health promotion, such as latrine building. In association with village health councils it has also helped to articulate villagers with dispensary-level care, especially for birthing, immunization, and nutritional education. Most important, this system has been reinforced by measures such as the provision of Essential Drug Kits by Scandinavian donors.

At the same time, primary health care, at least in Tanzania, has suffered from several major deficiencies. Limited training and limited rewards have discouraged workers. More than this, poor transportation, poor communications, and limited knowledge have minimized referral to more skilled care. And the hierarchical system as a whole has proven to be slow and cumbersome. It is often bypassed, with sick patients coming to dreadfully overcrowded urban hospitals. Hasty diagnoses, often inappropriate therapy, and breaks in the continuity of care have been frequent consequences (Jonsson 1986; Heggenhougen et al. 1987).

One experimental program in Bagamoyo District, Tanzania, has shown far greater potentialities in Primary Health Care. Relatively well funded, it has greatly improved the health of children under five by providing direct medical supervision facilitated by adequate transportation. It has greatly improved the diagnostic capacities of village health and dispensary workers, so that pneumonia, for example, can be diagnosed with good reliability. It has expanded the drugs available to the workers to include antibiotics. And it has emphasized the continuing training of workers, including new areas such as family planning. The essential weakness of this innovative effort is its dependence upon external funding from Germany (Neuvians, Mtango, and Kielman 1988).

Enhanced primary health care on the Bagamoyo model is clearly a basic strategy for African health. It needs expansion to a wider range of health problems, an expansion based upon systematic epidemiological and health care research. It requires expanded domestic funding and external technical assistance. It faces extremely large, unsolved problems, particularly malaria and the growing menace of AIDS.

Despite the successes of the past generation, severe pessimism prevails in some assessments of Africa's future health. The neo-Malthusian viewpoint of King (1987) is particularly at issue. Other analysts have approached this problem more hopefully. Cumper (1987) has calculated the inputs for construction (including safe water supplies), manpower development, and recurrent expenditures on health and education that would make possible infant mortality rates of 50 per 1,000 or lower in developing countries. The aggregate estimates are under $100 billion, a modest level for developed countries as an aggregate but an enormous effort for the poorest ones. Weak tax systems and inflexible expenditures intensify these difficulties. Enormous levels of foreign debt impose crippling payments and onerous conditions, including reduced health budgets, upon almost all African countries.

Nevertheless, this impression or extreme financial incapacity is in large part illusory. Central government health expenditures constitute only a quarter to half of the total expenditures, which include individual private expenditures on traditional healers, pharmacists, missionary hospitals, and other health services providers that are substantially supported (Dunlop 1983:2020). In contrast to Latin America, private health insurance is limited largely to Kenya, which also has developed rural prepayment and community financing programs. Elsewhere few mechanisms for prosperous populations to initiate autonomous health services can be found.

Structural limitations also have hampered African health services. As Foege and Henderson (1986) have stressed, these programs overemphasize therapy over prevention. This deficiency is intensified by the scarcity of the epidemiological and clinical research essential to define problems, determine optimal solutions, and monitor progress. Lacks in management training, system organization, and data management underlie these weaknesses. But it is clear that answers to these problems need to come not from external expeditions but, rather, by systematic upgrading of indigenous human and technical resources, tasks that have become increasingly feasible with educational expansion in many African countries.

Of fundamental importance in health improvement is far better knowledge of community values and behavior. Sindiga (1985:81) has brought out the severe pressures from clan lineage elders in Kenya against using contraceptives. These inhibitions intensified rational calculations of the need for high fertility to offset heavy child mortality. It must also be emphasized that much other health behavior is fully rational and empirically based. Fivawo (1986) established that mothers' resistance to chloroquine prophylaxis for malaria in children was based on observations of side effects rather than social pressures or prejudices. MacCormack's (1987) evaluation of bed net use to reduce mosquito exposure in Gambia is also relevant.

Emphasis must also be placed on the increasing importance of national self-reliance in health and other major programs. Many African countries, such as Nigeria, Kenya, and Tanzania, now have trained and experienced scientific and administrative cadres. They are urged by leaders such as Dr. Gottfried Monekosso "to use [African] university departments for technical advisory services instead of depending on foreign experts who charge exorbitantly for their services" (*Dar es Salaam Daily News*, 28 August 1989).

Finally, in looking to the future, the experience of many tropical countries and Indian states such as Kerala in escaping the burdens of high mortality and fertility needs to be kept in mind. In general, such transitions have taken place in areas with different sociopolitical orientation, both socialist and capitalist (Shimkin 1988). Their association with general economic development and urbanization has been asymmetrical: better health is essential to development, but development, as in Kenya, may be coincident with persistent poor health. The most important common factor has been the level of literacy and education among women. This has been indispensable both to self-esteem and to the effective use of media for health education. Functional communities with stable leadership have also been significant. These have been the foundations upon which new facilities, trained staff, and improvements in sanitation have accumulated, often over decades, as in the case of Jamaica (Cumper 1983).

Patterns, Trends, Problems, and Plans in Tanzanian Health

Patterns of Health Services
At the present time Tanzania's health services are made up of four components: the national health system, services affiliated with religious bodies, other private medical practitioners, and traditional and neotraditional healers (Heggenhougen el al. 1987; Jonsson 1986; Shimkin 1983, 1988; van Etten 1976).

The national system has, from the 1920s, been heavily based on paraprofessional workers, especially in rural areas. This orientation was intensified by the Titmuss report of 1964, which urged the development of health centers and dispensaries in rural areas. By 1978, the entire system employed 32,000 workers. In 1984, 1,065 physicians, 3,974 medical and rural medical assistants, and other workers provided services to about 20.5 million people.

Today the system includes central facilities and a hierarchy of service units. The major central facilities are four consultant (tertiary care) hospitals, the most important being the 1,700-bed Muhimbili Medical Centre, which is also the site of the country's medical, dental, nursing, pharmacy, and other faculties and a major center for health research. Also important are the National Institute for Medical Research, particularly involved in vector-borne and parasitic diseases; the Tanzania Food and Nutrition Centre, which monitors the nation's food supply and undertakes field and laboratory studies of nutritional problems; and the Health Education Unit of the Ministry of Health, the activities of which will be described later.

The hierarchy of service units includes nearly two hundred regional and district hospitals in urban places and nearly three thousand rural health centers and rural dispensaries. Perhaps half of Tanzania's eight thousand villages have one or two village health workers employed and minimally compensated by village health committees.

Religious bodies—Catholic, Protestant, and Islamic—run more than sixty-six hospitals and a substantial number of rural dispensaries. Unlike the facilities of the national health system, these charge for services performed. They may perform 20 to 25 percent of the inpatient health services of the country as well as a lower fraction of the outpatient work.

As in many African countries, most health care, certainly for adults, is administered by twenty-five to thirty thousand traditional and neotraditional healers, including birth attendants. They have considerable diagnostic, pharmacological, and psychotherapeutic skills. Characteristically, they maintain herbal gardens; over six thousand useful herbs are known. Moreover, many traditional healers use equipment and medications from modern medicine. Some are very affluent; in 1978 one had "a female and male ward, a dispensing room, and a preparation room for drugs. The total number of inpatients was 68 and, including floor cases, numbered up to over 150 patients" (Nyamka 1979:48).

Trends, 1977–85
Between 1977–78 and 1983–84, as part of an intensifying national economic crisis, budget allocations to health fell in real terms by 43 percent. At the rural health centers transportation, equipment, and medicinal supplies fell sharply. Poor communications and transportation as well as cursory patient examinations contributed to inadequate referrals to other facilities: "of the 36% of patients who should have been referred only 3% actually were. The others were given drugs which could not help them" (Jonsson 1986:750). Similar inadequacies have been reported by Heggenhougen et al. (1987). In consequence, while Tanzanian life expectancy at birth had risen from thirty-seven years in 1960 to forty-eight years in 1977, it only attained fifty years by 1986. It must be noted, however, that infant mortality fell from 190 per 1,000 births to 152 per 1,000 births between 1966 and 1977 and again to 103 per 1,000 births in 1986 (Barry and Bia 1986; Kingamkomo et al. 1986). Partially offsetting these unfortunate trends was the initiation of important, externally funded intervention projects.

Since 1983 a Tanzanian–West German team, led by F. D. E. Mtango and D. Neuvians, has sought to maximize the effectiveness of primary health care in the Bagamoyo District's seventy-two villages. Three physicians and nine medical assistants and nurses provided with ample transportation, and supported by requisite supplies of medicine and basic equipment, have trained and supervised the staffs and village health workers serving over 100,000 rural people. The training for village health workers has included an initial period of basic instruction in general symptomology, disease prevention and health education, simple therapy, and diagnostic criteria. This has been reinforced by annual training of a month's duration adding skills in the control of key diseases and, most recently, family planning. Much attention has been devoted to improving supervision, including operations research methods to identify decision points, alternatives, and consequences. Administrative problems, including recruitment, remuneration, and employee relations, have received much attention (Mtango and Neuvians 1987; and personal observation). (For Bagamoyo prior to 1983, see Heggenhougen et al. 1987; 116–19.)

The entire effort has concentrated on reducing mortality in the nineteen thousand children under five years of age. In four years, 1983–84 to 1986–87, mortality in this population has fallen from 38.5 to 28.3 per 1,000. In 1983–85 the average level was 34.1 per 1,000, including an infant mortality of about 78 per 1,000 births and a mortality at age one through four of 21.5 per 1,000 children (calculated from Mtango 1987).

Mortality reduction in Bagamoyo has reached different levels of success with different diseases. Measles mortality dropped from 5.0 to 1.3 per 1,000, or by 74 percent; that for pneumonia fell from 13.1 to 8.9 per 1,000, or by 32 percent. Diarrhea deaths declined from 6.6 to 4.8 per 1,000, or by 26 percent; those from malnutrition, from 6.0 to 5.0 per 1,000, or by 17 percent. In contrast, the toll of malaria actually rose by 5 percent, or from 7.9 to 8.3 deaths per 1,000 children. Improved immunization, active intervention including oral rehydration and the administration of antibiotics, and extensive health education were among the measures taken by primary health care workers. It must also be stressed that, in 1983–85, village health workers, dispensaries, and health centers together treated only 65 percent of the children dying. The remainder were treated at home or by traditional healers (Mtango and Neuvians 1987:854).

Since 1984 WHO, UNICEF, and the Italian government have helped a major program for improving child nutrition and health in Iringa Region, an area of high mortality. The program has embraced forty-six thousand children under five. It has emphasized disease control, including oral rehydration; immunization, growth monitoring, and health education. Men are encouraged to participate. Associated with these efforts has been a reduction in infant mortality from 152 to 107 per 1,000 births and of malnutrition from 56 to 40 percent of the children (*Dar es Salaam Daily News*, 21 January 1988). As at Bagamoyo, the gains have been real but modest. Clearly, malnutrition in young children is a massive problem necessitating such technical innovations as a calorific "power flour" weaning food (TFNC 1987:5). Also, since half the pregnant women have static or even dropping weights, measures such as the reduction of women's workloads as well as increased food intake are much needed in rural areas (ibid., 5, 12).

Developments, 1986–89
Since 1986 important changes have taken place. Major economic reforms such as privatizing agriculture stimulated all sectors. From 1986 on, economic growth exceeded population growth, albeit modestly. The severe recession of the early 1980s was reversed. Food shortages largely vanished. Improved veterinary support permitted a large increase in cattle herds, especially in coastal areas previously lethal to domestic animals. Urban activities, including construction, trade, and transportation, increased sharply. Few of the numerous beggars of 1983–84 were still visible. Foreign aid, including extensive assistance to health service and research projects, increased sharply. The Japanese, former West Germans, British, Danes, and Italians, in addition to international agencies, undertook large commitments.

Nevertheless, the financing of health institutions remained meager. As J. M. Tembe, the assistant chief medical officer for preventive services, noted that mother and child health facilities suffered from inadequate funds. Even Muhimbili Medical Centre suffered from acute shortages of soap, gloves for nurses, and other essentials, according to Tauby Shimkin, R.N.

Despite these constraints, rural dispensaries in Bagamoyo, Morogoro, and Iringa Regions were operating well, according to the field observations of F. D. E. Mtango, M.D., Tauby Shimkin, and D. B. Shimkin. Specifically, they had satisfactory levels of essential equipment and supplies, including kerosene-powered refrigerators and essential drug kits, patient records, sanitation, and patient education. With few exceptions workers were knowledgeable and clearly committed to their responsibilities. The felt problems were many. They ranged from schistosomiasis to a lack of water supply at one dispensary to severe inadequacies of housing for the workers in another. For the village health worker transportation and irregular drug supplies were real difficulties. Interactions with village health councils appeared to be functional, while staff from the region and the district appeared to be cognizant of village operations.

A number of general limitations were evident to us from the report of dispensary workers. About half of all births are attended by traditional midwives who may or may not have basic instruction in sanitation. While immunization levels are generally good, tetanus coverage, particularly prenatal, was only 50 percent of pregnancies in one good dispensary. No evidence was seen of microscopes for the reliable diagnosis of malaria, and, except for pregnant women, adult medicine was given little attention. The frequent lack of blood pressure measuring equipment precluded adequate diagnosis of hypertension.

Another significant development has been in health education. The Health Education Unit Division of Preventive Services, Ministry of Health, now directs a national effort. It prepares and produces health posters and pamphlets in Swahili. It also develops appropriate radio broadcasts, especially by local people speaking their dialects. Twenty nurse-educators maintain outreach to every region, assessing local problems, conducting workshops, especially in rural areas, and eliciting grassroots participation in health promotion.

Because Tanzania has a rather high literacy rate—80 percent for adult males and 70 percent for adult females (Kingamkono 1986:15)—posters and pamphlets combining vivid cartooning with simple texts are major educational tools. Basic poster topics include immunization in the first year of life; proper infant nutrition from birth to age nine months; wearing foot gear (including rubber boots for high and wet grass); clearing house surroundings of grass and brush harboring insects, ticks, and snakes; building covered latrines; protecting eyes; and spraying house interiors against malaria-carrying mosquitoes. The danger of AIDS, *ukimwi*, is stressed.

The pamphlets cover similar health needs but in more detail. Explicit discussions and graphic drawings aid communication. All emphasize prevention. One deals with eleven rules for good health; another sets an immunization schedule for infants, beginning with prenatal inoculation of the mother against tetanus and ending with measles immunization at nine months. Five approaches to child health are discussed in still another pamphlet. Noteworthy here are injunctions to monitor weight status, instructions for rehydration in case of diarrhea, and illustrations of fathers as well as mothers engaged in child feeding.

Two pamphlets on providing safe water and building proper latrines are reinforced by others on gastrointestinal diseases—hookworm, schistosomiasis, diarrhea, and dysentery. One pamphlet discusses in some detail the nutritional diseases all too common in Tanzania: kwashiorkor, rickets, vitamin deficiencies, anemia, goiter, marasmus, and obesity. There is also a grim warning against sexual immorality, stressing the risks of gonorrhea, syphilis, and septic sores. Finally, the dangers of AIDS are well stated.

These national educational efforts are reinforced by the staffs of dispensaries and by village health workers. Sometimes dispensaries produce their own posters. One at Melila village in Morogoro Region was a very fine summary of kwashiorkor and marasmus symptoms. Most generally, dispensary staffs utilize the waiting periods of patients for oral instruction. In addition and in contrast to past neglect, many village health workers are active health educators, stressing latrine building, water boiling, immunization, and other themes.

Family planning is a new theme, being developed particularly in the Bagamoyo District, which has an almost totally Muslim population. The training materials are still externally produced, either by international agencies or by the English Collier Macmillan Company. They discuss contraceptive techniques, including contraceptive injections, in explicit detail. The pill and the condom, which also provides protection against AIDS, have had limited acceptance. Sterilization and abortion have very negative connotations.

As mentioned earlier, Tanzania has, since 1986, developed a national program for monitoring, preventing, and providing palliative help to victims of AIDS. The program integrates the best technical resources of the country with outreach at the village level. This indirectly helps the integration of primary health care as a whole. Health education with emphasis on compassion for those at risk as well as victims is the main vehicle of prevention. In Dar es Salaam, an area of high AIDS prevalence, a volunteer society to help AIDS victims has been formed.

Problems

The net effect of changes since 1986 has been small. As G. F. Mbowe, the chairman of the University Council, has observed: "our country is still underdeveloped. The per capita income of our people is around

270 US Dollars compared with 13,000 US Dollars in the United States of America. Our life expectancy is still staggering around 54–55 years whereas in advanced countries it is between 75–80 years. Our real growth rate in GDP is 4% when our population is growing at 3%" (Mbowe 1989). Tanzania is a vast country and endowed with all the natural resources such as arable land, rivers, lakes, minerals, and human resources. Nonetheless, over 26 to 30 percent of our people suffer from malnutrition; the crude index of death rate in the rural areas is hovering between 18 and 20 percent; maternal death rate is 3 for every 1,000; prenatal death rate is around 60 for every 1,000; infant mortality is between 134 and 135 for every 1,000, whereas in advanced countries it is less than 20. "Our deepening problem in the country is how to deal with preventable diseases such as whooping cough, measles, diarrhea and the like. All these diseases are within the control of our human power."

Particularly troubling today is the steady rise in illness from malaria, which, according to Prime Minister Joseph Warioba, accounted for 30 percent of hospitalizations in 1988 (*Dar es Salaam Daily News*, 12 August 1989). Malaria was also a factor in the recent rise of infant mortality. Also adverse was the continued high level of malnutrition (as evidenced by growth and weight retardation), to which 50 percent of the children under five were subject in 1988.

Malnutrition in children is an exceedingly difficult problem. Despite a favorable situation overall and prompt intervention in case of serious local food shortages, the nutrition of small children remains poor. A recent study of Morogoro Region, an area of considerable food surplus (Kingamkono et al. 1986), examined the nutritional status of 3,256 rural children aged two to five. Birth weights for 534 children averaged slightly under 2.9 kilograms, compared to 3.4 kilograms for U.S. children (ibid., 5). For 1,986 children up to thirty-six months of age infant mortality came to 112 per 1,000 births, and average mortality in the second and third years was 60 per 1,000 (9). Of 628 children from birth to thirty-six months that were assessed, only 37 percent were normal in weight and size. This proportion fell with increasing age, being 73 percent at ages zero to six months, 46 percent at seven to eleven months, 25 percent at twelve to thirty-six months, and 22 percent at over thirty-six months (7). The others were underweight, stunted, or both. Severe malnutrition characterized 6.4 percent of this population. It rose with increasing age: 1.9 percent at ages zero to six months, 3.4 percent at seven to eleven months, 8.5 percent at twelve to thirty-six months, and 15.6 percent at over thirty-six months.

The dismal findings at Morogoro, which are paralleled in many places in Tanzania, are explicable, according to Kingamkono et al. (1986), by the synergetic effects of disease, especially fevers, diarrhea, and coughing, and bad nutritional practices, notwithstanding exposures to appropriate knowledge. High illiteracy—30 percent to 48 percent of the females—was an impediment to learning (ibid., 14). The poor health statuses of mothers, many of whom were undernourished and overworked, were also factors.

Only a minority of the mothers fed children separately from the adults; a substantial fraction of the mothers had food taboos, and they began weaning at 4 to 6 months of age (ibid., 19). The children received, apart from breast feeding, two to three meals per day, primarily of gruel. This was supplemented, in diminishing frequencies, by green vegetables, sugar, vegetable protein, fruits, fats and oils, and animal protein.

Plans

At meetings in Dar es Salaam on 21–26 August 1989 it became clear that Tanzanian leaders are deeply concerned with their country's continuing difficulties. They are searching for a strategy based on indigenous resources and particularly the growing numbers of young, well-educated people.

In the words of Kitwana Kondo, the mayor of Dar es Salaam, at a planning meeting, a true social transformation will be needed. The basis of that transformation is not a specific ideology, let alone a detailed blueprint for the future. Rather, it is faith in discovery. As Mbowe (1989) has stated:

> Scientific knowledge can be acquired and technology can be bought. But if they are taken as layers superimposed over old thoughts, we shall merely reflect other countries. The mixture of science and society cannot be physical. It must be organic. We have to understand the dynamics of change. The nation looks to our intellectuals to guide us through intellectual perplexity and to build a new nation to live. . . . The development of human capital is the key to the future prosperity of our country. The real strength lies in the capacity of our people for disciplined work. Only hard work can produce wealth for us to rid us of our poverty. We did not invest in education

in our young men and women in order that they can rest afterwards but in order they can work harder to hold and strengthen our human resources. Our labours as educated men and women will lay a firm foundation for a great future and our labor of love for our country and her people will endure, so will the fact that we shall all be building brick [by brick] the great mountain [*roshani*] to Tanzania.

The Role of Foreign Aid and of Anthropology in Improving African Health

Many African countries are seeking to be self-reliant, in spite of grave health problems, economic weaknesses including rising foreign debts, and a paucity of health services resources. Certainly, they wish to determine their own priorities and strategies. From the wealthy nations they seek not patronage but partnership.

The pattern of foreign aid to date has been far from optimal. A major difficulty is that each donor is concerned with his or her own priorities and ways of doing business, often including the mandatory use of perhaps inappropriate equipment from a particular source. Cooperation between foreign donors and between external and domestic projects is generally poor. In consequence, there is often little feedback, and the long-term improvement of health facilities and capacities is often slight.

There are important exceptions to these generalizations. WHO is deeply concerned with permanent gains, as are such small nations as the Scandinavian countries and the Netherlands. Above all, the small company of long-term expatriate workers, such as D. Neuvians, from Germany, and D. McLarty, from Scotland, have played exemplary roles.

These remarks suggest a pattern for the future. But, more than this, a great need exists for the development and low-cost distribution of appropriate technology, which is often no longer produced in sophisticated countries. Simple microscopes, re-agent kits, sphygmomanometers (blood pressure meters), and reusable surgical gloves are cases in point. Textbooks and training manuals are also in great demand. Transportation and communications including record-keeping equipment are systemic needs. Furthermore, while much fundamental research is needed, a compelling urgency attaches to introducing a large inventory of successful health experiments, such as Cunningham's (1978) and Mtango and Neuvians's (1986), into general, routine practice. A major need is improved health systems integration, both within and between African nations. The multinational role of the School of Dentistry in Muhimbili Medical Centre is a case in point.

In this context the social and behavioral sciences are of exceptional importance. Their proper use is indispensable for sound epidemiology and the design of effective health services. They are as yet poorly developed almost everywhere in Africa. Biosocial anthropology, with its strong commitment to field investigations and to community involvement, has particular promise. Among the meritorious research conducted to date the following may be mentioned: Bleek (1978) on sexuality, Buck et al. (1970) on community health assessment, Carlson (1989) on alcoholism, Devlieger (1989) on disability, Etkin and Ross (1982) on nutrition and traditional medicine, Fivawo (1986) on community reactions to malaria, Bibeau et al. (1980) on traditional medicine, and van der Geest (1987) on pluralism in health behavior.

Such basic research constitutes only a small element of the potential contributions of anthropology to medical social sciences. Most important would be the training of indigenous workers in a wide range of technical skills in the field, in the analysis of findings, and in their integration into assessments and plans.

ADDENDUM

Health Behavior Change and Community Institutions
in Rural Mississippi
Dennis A. Frate

The following section serves as an addendum to the preceding article by Demitri B. Shimkin, who passed away in 1992. The article below demonstrates both the cross-cultural and applied aspects of Professor Shimkin's theoretical perspective on communities, empowerment, and change. Professor Shimkin's involvement with this basic and applied research in Mississippi dates back to 1965.

Historical Context
The history of systematic social and health research in rural Mississippi dates back to early 1965 and the emergence of the International Biological Program (Shimkin and Golde 1983). This international effort was

interested in investigating and theoretically mapping the human ecosystem, especially those in high-risk environments, and in identifying the adaptive mechanisms of such populations. It was felt that any directed change in a high-risk population could only develop out of a thorough understanding of the social, economic, political, and health systems operative in a community. Such a participant community would have to be studied over a long period of time, with any quantitative measures preceded by systematic observations on the population. This approach led researchers in the United States to central Mississippi and resulted in a five-year biosocial assessment funded by the U.S. Public Health Service (ibid., 1983). The basic quantitative research included population enumeration, a residential dwelling survey, a nutritional assessment, and a focused study on the epidemiology of hypertension. These investigations were all conducted in one particular geographic area, Holmes County, Mississippi. Prior to the conduct of these quantitative measures the basic research protocol centered on more qualitative approaches, such as observation on community social institutions. In this regard participant observation, focus group meetings, and key informant techniques were used for a three-year period. All of these basic quantitative and qualitative research activities contributed to the development of a foundation for the eventual design of applied models centered on directed change. The basic research efforts and the development of applied models of directed change paved the way for the two community-based health intervention activities to be described here.

Community Health Workers
The concept of community health workers or lay health advisors is not necessarily new (Farguhar 1978; Salber et al. 1976). In the United States use of such health workers has been promoted to address the health needs of minority communities, especially those in which chronic, noninfectious conditions dominate (Whitehead et al. 1984). Such diseases demand repetitive care and, generally, modifications of high-risk behaviors. These disease characteristics can result in compliance problems and/or problems in making the lifestyle changes required (e.g., weight loss). At times these populations also experience problems associated with access to health care. These problems with access center not only on availability of care but also on economic, social, and/or educational deprivation. Consequently, in central Mississippi there was a population with chronic disorders residing in an area with few clinical

resources. Health care professionals in areas such as central Mississippi, when available, are overburdened and have little time, and possibly not the necessary training or sociocultural background, to address the health behavior changes needed to manage and/or prevent these diseases.

To address these complex issues of access and the need for culturally sensitive health intervention approaches, there has been an increase in the promotion and use of community health workers and peer counselors during the past ten years (Greenberg et al. 1985). In rural Mississippi the specific model developed for community health workers was based on systematic observations conducted in 1971 on the African American "granny" midwives, a perinatal care worker widespread in the rural South prior to 1976 (Frate et al. 1980). This addendum examines a quantitative outcome evaluation of such community health workers. These community health workers were recruited to function as high blood pressure management counselors in one study and as weight loss counselors in a separate study conducted in rural, central Mississippi.

Research Area

The geographic area utilized for this study was located in rural central Mississippi. The area covered over three thousand square miles and was composed of five counties: Attala, Carroll, Grenada, Holmes, and Montgomery. According to the 1990 U.S. census, over eighty-three thousand individuals resided in the project area, which can be characterized as: biracial (approximately 50 percent were African American), rural (over 68 percent of the population resided in rural settings), undereducated (approximately 47 percent of persons twenty-five years of age and older had less than twelve years of education), and poor (approximately 36 percent of household incomes were less than ten thousand dollars per year), resulting in over 34 percent of all residents living below the poverty level (Bureau of the Census 1991). One of the dominant sociocultural themes of the African American population here has been the form and function of the multihousehold extended family. As contrasted with the white population, this familial unit has influenced behaviors in all areas of life (Shimkin et al. 1978). Also, the church and the interrelatedness of the sacred aspects of life are a dominating influence on the residents. Concerning health status, this area had one of the highest rates of essential hypertension and one of the highest rates of obesity ever documented in a defined population in this country (Storer and Frate 1990). The 1990 mortality rates for diseases of the heart (defined as ICD codes 390–398, 402, 404, 410–429) were officially reported as 393.9 per 100,000 population and 356.8 per 100,000 population, respectively (Mississippi State Department of Health 1991). Nationally, the mortality rate for diseases of the heart (defined comparatively as ICD codes 390–398, 402, 404–429) was 155.9 per 100,000 population (National Center for Health Statistics 1992).

The dominance of both the prevalence of chronic diseases here, including obesity, the familial and sacred nature of society, and the model of the "granny" midwife were all features incorporated into the development of the particular model of the community health workers implemented and evaluated in this geographic setting.

The Use of Community Health Workers
The health and cost effectiveness of community health workers were evaluated both for disease (hypertension or high blood pressure) management and for disease prevention—i.e., weight loss, functions. For the disease management activities self-help networks were established in thirteen white and African American extended families and nineteen white and African American churches. Consequently, thirty-two community health workers were recruited and trained in the management of hypertension; these community health workers were unpaid volunteer health workers. Their training took approximately five hours. The actual training was conducted by allied health professionals. These volunteers were to function as network leaders and were designed to be involved in the clinical measurement of blood pressure and the modification of high-risk behaviors, such as dietary changes. For the disease prevention activities, or weight loss, self-help networks were established in eighteen different African American churches. Consequently, eighteen additional volunteer community health workers were trained in weight loss techniques, including menu planning, behavior modification, and exercise. The training for these volunteers was also approximately five hours, and they were trained by the same allied health professionals.

The project evaluating the effectiveness of the role of community health workers in controlling hypertension was conducted in 1982. In hypertension, or high blood pressure, management the goal is to achieve a "controlled" blood pressure or a blood pressure below a particular numeric level. The level of control is defined statistically and is that particular level at which the occurrence of co-morbid events is reduced or lower than events at a higher level of blood pressure. Based on six months of outcome data, thirty-two self-help networks were in operation in white and African American churches and extended families. These groups contained 211 hypertensives, or individuals diagnosed as having high blood pressure. At the time of initiating the program, 101, or 47.9 percent, of these participating had already achieved a controlled blood pressure. At the end of six months 177, or 83.9 percent, had achieved a controlled blood pressure; this change in proportion with a controlled blood pressure was statistically significant using a chi-square test at the $p < 0.001$ level (Whitehead et al. 1984).

Based on this initial success in using community health workers to enhance the management of a chronic disease, in this case therapy compliance to antihypertensives, it was decided to test this community-based, culturally sensitive model for disease prevention, in this case weight loss. The weight loss program was initiated in 1988. For reasons related to the evaluation and different from the effort centering on blood pressure control, the weight loss activity was designed to include a control population. Individuals in both the experimental and control populations for this research activity had to have a weight > 130 pounds of ideal for inclusion into the study.

For purposes of evaluation eighteen experimental and sixteen control African American churches were randomly selected from the area. In this sample 123 obese individuals in the experimental cohort and 115 obese individuals in the control cohort completed the nine-month evaluation period. Eighteen community health workers or self-help network leaders, volunteers, from the experimental churches, were trained by allied health professionals in weight loss techniques, which included increasing physical activity, and were equipped with a standard mechanical scale to measure weight and a packet of culturally sensitive dietary materials. Monthly contact by the allied health professionals with these volunteer leaders was maintained during the initial nine months of the weight loss intervention. During these contacts new recipes were transmitted, problems discussed, outcome data checked, and overall motivation and program enthusiasm reestablished. As designed, none of these programmatic activities took place in any of the sixteen control churches.

During the nine-month intervention period weight measurement data were officially collected at two different times. Time 1 was the first measurement, or the measurement at entry into the study, and the second measurement, or time 2, was the final assessment in this phase of the study for determination of program outcomes; this exit measurement occurred nine months after entry into the study. As originally proposed, the allied health professional staff remained in close contact with the volunteers during this nine-month intervention period, providing suggestions and written materials related to changes in diet and physical activity.

The primary outcome measure evaluated in this study was changes in body weight. Secondary outcome measures included estimates of caloric intake, total dietary fat intake, and dietary fiber intake (determined by a computerized nutrient analysis of twenty-four-hour food intake recalls). Outcome data were collected by the allied health professional staff, electronically processed, and analyzed. Appropriate statistical tests of significance ($p < 0.05$), including analysis of variance, t-test, chi-square test, and Fisher's Exact Tests, were used for the analysis.

A breakdown of the demographic and socioeconomic characteristics of the experimental and control populations indicates that there were no statistically significant differences between the two cohorts in age, gender, education, marital status, and income. The only significant difference ($p < 0.001$) found was with employment status, in that a greater proportion of the control population was unemployed. In addition, the two groups did not have any significant differences in self-reported health status, smoking behavior, alcohol consumption, classification of obesity levels, family history of cancer, usual source of medical care, and number of physician visits during the past year.

The mean weight change and percentage who lost weight in both the experimental and control cohorts for the intervention period, one to nine months, shows that there was a significant difference ($p = 0.010$) in weight change between the experimental cohort and the control cohort during this time, with the experimental population losing an average of 4 pounds from entry to nine months, while the control population lost an average of only 0.4 pounds in this same time period. Upon examination of the percentage of each cohort who lost weight, it can be seen that a significantly higher proportion ($p = 0.007$) of the experimental cohort lost weight during the first intervention period, 67.5 percent, as compared to the control cohort, 50.4 percent.

Upon analyzing the demographic, socioeconomic, and health-related factors associated with weight change in the experimental cohort during the intervention, it was found that being older ($p = 0.049$), not drinking alcoholic beverages ($p = -0.006$), having a usual source of medical care

($p = 0.019$), and going to a doctor more often ($p = 0.028$) were statistically associated with weight loss during the intervention period.

Changes in dietary behaviors, explanations for relative weight loss, related health changes, weight loss continuity, perceived health status changes, and program satisfaction were also explored for those individuals in the experimental population who lost weight compared to those who did not lose weight during the intervention period. The statistically significant findings indicated that those individuals who did not lose weight were still more aware of the proper ways to prepare foods ($p = 0.045$), while those who did lose weight were more likely to exercise ($p = 0.010$), spend more time relaxing ($p = 0.007$), have a better perceived change in health status ($p = 0.004$), and be more satisfied with the program ($p = 0.001$).

Discussion

Based on years of preliminary ethnographic and other qualitative data gathering, it was determined that any health behavior changes needed in this high-risk population in rural central Mississippi could only be made if culturally sensitive and appropriate models were employed. Utilizing the familial and sacred orientation of the local community, the social institutions of the extended family and the church were used as the settings in which modifications of high-risk health behaviors were to occur. The use of community health workers as change agents also fit into the normative social structure in both the white and African American communities here (as the granny midwife performed a similar health behavior change role for years). Social support through the expansion of available resources is commonly found in rural Mississippi (Shimkin et al. 1978). The health intervention model based on the community health workers did just that, as this model expanded the access to health professional care and increased culturally sensitive health information to the high-risk cohort. Consequently, by understanding the community, real changes in measurable health outcomes occurred. Directed change based on a thorough understanding of community institutions is not limited to the health arena. The two demonstration studies described here, however, document the effectiveness of such community-based models for health behavior change, an area receiving more attention both within the United States and beyond as chronic diseases continue to be a dominant force contributing to the health status of contemporary people. This model of community-based service owes a great debt to Demitri Shimkin's work both in Mississippi and Africa.

REFERENCES

Addy, P. A. K., K. Minami, and V. K. Agadzi
    1986   Recent Yellow Fever Epidemics in Ghana (1969–1983). *East African Medical Journal* (June): 422–33.

Adegbola, O.
    1987   The Impact of Urbanization and Industrialization on Health Conditions: The Case of Nigeria. *World Health Statistics Quarterly* 40:74–83.

Anderson, J. G.
    1989   The U.S. Health Care System in the 21st Century. In *Health and Illness in America and Germany*, ed. G. Luschen, W. C. Cockerham, and G. Kunz, 167–76. Munich: R. Oldenbuurg Verlag.

Asogwa, S. E.
    1978   Road Traffic Accidents: The Doctors' Point of View. *African Journal of Medicine and Medical Science* 7:29–36.
    1980   Some Characteristics of Drivers and Riders Involved in Road Traffic Accidents in Nigeria. *East African Journal of Medicine* 57(6): 399–404.

Ayeni, O.
    1980   Causes of Mortality in an African City. *African Journal of Medicine and Medical Science* 9:139–49.

Barry, M., and F. Bia
    1986   Socialist Health Care in Tanzania: A View from Kilimanjaro Christian Medical Center. *Annals of Internal Medicine* 104:438–40.

Bibeau, G., et al.
    1980   *Traditional Medicine in Zaire: Present and Potential Contribution to the Health Services*. Ottawa: International Development Research Center. Revised and abridged by R. Ahluwalia and B. Mecin.

Bicknell, W. J., and C. L. Parks
    1989   As Children Survive: Dilemmas of Aging in the Developing World. *Social Science and Medicine* 28(1): 59–67.

Bleek, W.
    1978   *Sexual Relationships and Birth Control in Ghana: A Case Study of a Rural Town*. Uitage 10. Afdeling Culturele Antropologie, Antropologisch Sociologisch Centrum, Universiteit van Amsterdam.

Boemma, T.
    1987   The Magnitude of the Maternal Mortality Problem in Sub-Saharan Africa. *Social Science and Medicine* 24(6): 551–58.

Bruce-Chawtt, L. J.
    1980   *Essential Malaria*. London: William Heinemann Medical Books, Bureau of the Census.

1991   *Census of Population and Housing, 1990.* Summary tape files 1A and 3A (Miss.), Washington, D.C.: U.S. Department of Commerce.

Carlson, R. G.
- 1985   Alcohol in Africa: Historical Perspectives with a Focus on Tanzania. Unpublished manuscript. Anthropology Department, University of Illinois, Urbana-Champaign.
- 1989   Bahaya Worldview and Ethos: An Ethnography of Alcohol Use in Bukoba, Tanzania. Ph.D. diss. Department of Anthropology, University of Illinois, Urbana-Champaign.

Coeytaux, F. M.
- 1988   Induced Abortion in Sub-Saharan Africa: What We Do and Do Not Know. *Studies in Family Planning* 19(3): 186–90.

Colson, E., and T. Scudder
- 1988   *For Prayer and Profit: The Ritual, Economic, and Social Importance of Beer in Gwembe District, Zambia, 1950–1982.* Stanford, Calif: Stanford University Press.

Cooper-Poole, B.
- 1986   Prevalence of Syphilis in Mbeya, Tanzania—The Validity of the VDRL as a Screening Test. *East African Medical Journal* 63(10): 646–51.

Cox, J. L.
- 1983   Postnatal Depression: A Comparison of African and Scottish Women. *Social Psychiatry* 18:25–28.

Cumper, G. E.
- 1983   Jamaica: A Case Study in Health Development. *Social Science and Medicine* 17:1983–93.
- 1987   The Resource Requirements of Basic Health Care in Developing Countries with Special Reference to Africa. *Journal of Tropical Pediatrics* 33 (supp. 1): 18–25.

Cunningham, N.
- 1978   The Under Fives Clinic: What Difference Does It Make? *Journal of Tropical Pediatrics and Environmental Child Health* 24(6): 237–76, 281–322.

Dadzie, K. Y., J. Remme, A. Roland and B. Thylefors
- 1986   The Effect of Seven to Eight Years of Vector Control on the Evolution of Occular Onchocerciasis in West African Savana. *Tropical Medicine and Parasitology* 37:263–70.

Davis, A.
- 1987   Drug and Vaccine Development. *Tropical Medicine and Parasitology* 38:215–21.

DeBoer, C. N., and M. McNeil
- 1989   Hospital Outreach Community-Based Health Care: The Case of Chogoria, Kenya. *Social Science and Medicine* 28(10): 1007–17.

Delvoye, P., and C. Robyn
- 1980   Breastfeeding and Post-Partum Amenorrhea in Central Africa. *Journal of Tropical Pediatrics* 26:184–89.

Devlieger, P.
  1989 The Cultural Significance of Physical Disability in Africa. Paper presented at the annual meeting of the Society for Applied Anthropology, Santa Fe, 5–9 April 1989.
Dodge, C. P.
  1986 Uganda—Rehabilitation or Redefinition of Heath Services. *Social Science and Medicine* 22(7): 755–61.
Dunlop, D. W.
  1983 Health Care Financing: Recent Experience in Africa. *Social Science and Medicine* 17(24): 2017–25.
Erinosho, O. A.
  1978 Nigeria's ARO Community Psychiatric Care in Action: An Appraisal. *African Urban Studies*, no. 1 (spring): 19–25.
Etkin, N. L., and P. J. Ross
  1982 Food as Medicine and Medicine as Food. *Social Science and Medicine* 16:1559–73.
Farguhar, J. W.
  1978 The Community-Based Model of Life Style Intervention: Trials. *American Journal of Epidemiology* 108:103–11.
Fivawo, M.
  1986 Community Response to Malaria: Muheza District, Tanzania, 1983–1984. Ph.D. diss., Department of Anthropology, University of Illinois, Urbana-Champaign.
Foege, W. H., and D. A. Henderson
  1986 Selective Primary Health Care. XXV Management Priorities. *Reviews of Infectious Diseases* 8(3): 467–75.
Frate, D. A., T. L Whitehead, and S. A. Johnson
  1984 The Use of Traditional Social Settings in the Management of Contemporary Health Problems. *Journal of Voluntary Action Research* 13:42–48.
Fundikora, S. R.
  1985 Sexuality, Fertility and Contraception: Knowledge and Attitudes among Secondary School Girls in Dar es Salaam. Ph.D. diss., Diploma in Public Health, Muhimbili Medical Center.
Gish, O.
  1983 Some Observations about Health Development in Three African Socialist Countries: Ethiopia, Mozambique and Tanzania. *Social Science and Medicine* 17(24): 1961–69.
Gottshalk, K.
  1988 The Political Economy of Health Care: Colonial Nambia, 1915–1961. *Social Science and Medicine* 26(6): 577–82.
Greenberg, A. M., D. A. Frate, and D. B. Shimkin
  1985 Extended Families and the Control of Hypertension in Central Mississippi. *Central Issues in Anthropology* 6:19–26.
Heggenhougen, K., P. Vaughn, E. P. Muhondwa, and J. Rutabanzibwa-Ngaiza
  1987 *Community Health Workers: The Tanzanian Experience*. Oxford: Oxford University Press.

Hielcher, S., and J. Sommerfield
  1985 Concepts of Illness and the Utilization of Health Care Services in a Rural Malian Village. *Social Science and Medicine* 21(4): 469–81.
Hoban, S.
  1985 *Mental Health in the Third World: An Unexpected Success.* Urbana-Champaign: Anthropology Department, University of Illinois.
Hogh, B., and E. Peterson
  1984 The Basic Health Care System in Botswana: A Study of the Distribution and Cost in the Period 1973–1979. *Social Science and Medicine* 19(8): 783–92.
Hull, F., P. J. Williams, and F. Oldfield
  1983 Measles, Mortality and Vaccine Efficacy in Rural West Africa. *Lancet* (30 April): 972–75.
Jacobs, G. D., and P. R. Fouracre
  1977 Further Research on Road Accidents in Developing Countries. MS. Transport and Road Research Laboratory, Department of the Environment, Department of Transport, Crowthorne, Berkshire, Eng.
Jonsson, U.
  1986 Ideological Framework and Health Development in Tanzania, 1961–2000. *Social Science and Medicine* 22(7): 745–53.
Kavishe, F. P., and T. N. Maltenlema
  1984 The Control of Iodine Deficiency Disorders in Tanzania. *Tanzania Food and Nutrition Centre Report*, no. 891.
Kimati, V. P.
  1986 Who Is Ignorant? Rural Mothers Who Feed Their Well-Nourished Children or the Nutrition Experts? The Tanzania Story. *Journal of Tropical Pediatrics* 32:130–36.
King, M.
  1987 The Present State of Health in Africa. *Journal of Tropical Pediatrics* 33(1): 6–8.
Kingamkono, R. P., et al.
  1986 Baseline Survey on Nutritional Status and Weaning Practices in Morogoro Region. *Tanzania Food and Nutrition Centre Report*, no. 1047.
Lamptey, P., et al.
  1985 Abortion Experience among Obstetric Patients at Korle-Bu Hospital, Accra, Ghana. *Journal of Biosocial Science* 17:195–203.
Lapido, O. A., and A. O. Osoba
  1978 *Ureaplasma urealyticum* (T. mycoplasma) and Male Infertility in Tropical Countries. *African Journal of Medicine and Medical Science* 7:187–90.
Last, M., and G. L. Chavunduka, eds.
  1986 *The Professionalization of African Medicine.* Manchester: Manchester University Press.
Latham, M. C.
  1979 *Human Nutrition in Tropical Africa.* Rome: FAO.

Lesthaeghe, R., et al.
  1981 Child-Spacing and Fertility in Sub-Saharan Africa: An Overview of Issues. In *Child-Spacing in Tropical Africa: Tradition and Change,* ed. H. J. Page and R. Lesthaeghe, 3–23. London: Academic Press.
MacCormack, C.
  1986 The Articulation of Western and Traditional Systems of Health Care. In *The Professionalization of African Medicine,* ed. M. Last and G. L. Chavundaka. Manchester: Manchester University Press.
  1987 The Human Host as Active Agent in Malaria Epidemiology. *Tropical Medicine and Parasitology* 38:233–35.
Makanyuola, J. D. A., and O. Okubanjo
  1986 Pattern and Management of Substance Abuse at ARO Neuropsychiatric Hospital (1980–1982): A Study in Advance of the Establishment of a Special Unit. *East African Medical Journal* 63(4): 269–80.
Mbowe, G. F.
  1989 Graduation speech, University of Dar es Salaam, 26 August (official English trans.).
McLarty, D., et al.
  N.d. Comparative Investigation of Hypertension and Diabetes in Tanzanian Villages. Unpublished manuscript.
Mississippi State Department of Health
  1991 *Vital Statistics, Mississippi, 1990.* Jackson.
Molineaux, L., and G. Gramiccia
  1980 Practical Conclusions for the Future of Malaria Control. In *The Gorki Project. Research on the Epidemiology and Control of Malaria in the Sudan Savana of West Africa,* ed. L. Molineaux and G. Gramiccia. Geneva: World Health Organization.
Mtango, F. D. E.
  1987 Community-Based Recording and Reporting of Mortality and Verbal Autopsy in Bagamoyo PHC Project. Paper Presented at Child Mortality Workshop. Arusha Muhimbili Medical Center, Dar es Salaam, 17–20 August.
Mtango, F. D. E., and D. Neuvians
  1986 Acute Respiratory Infection in Children under Five Years: Control Project in Bagamoyo District, Tanzania. *Transactions of the Royal Society of Tropical Medicine and Hygiene* 80:851–58.
Mtimavalye, L. A. R., D. Lisai, and W. K. Ntuyabaliwe
  1980 Maternal Mortality in Dar es Salaam, Tanzania, 1974–1977. *East African Medical Journal* 57(2): 111–17.
Mugo, W.
  1974 Health Problems in Urban Areas. In *Health and Disease in Kenya,* ed. L. C. Vogel et al., 161–68. Nairobi: East African Literature Bureau.
Muhondwa, E. P. Y.
  1986 Rural Development and Primary Health Care in Less Developed Countries. *Social Science and Medicine* 22(11): 1247–56.

Mwabu, G. M.
  1986   Health Care Decision at the Household Level: Results of a Rural Health Survey in Kenya. *Social Science and Medicine* 22(3): 315–19.
Mwaluko, G. M. P., et al.
  In press   Combating AIDS through Health Education: A Strategy for Tanzania. Proceedings of the National Medical Seminar. Muhimbili Medical Center, Dar es Salaam.
National Center for Health Statistics
  1992   *Health, United States, 1991.* Hyattsville, Md.: Public Health Service.
Ndeki, S. S.
  1979   The Tuberculosis Infection Rate and BCG Coverage: The Effect of BCG Vaccination on Tuberculosis Allergy in Bagamoyo School Children. Ph.D. diss., Diploma in Public Health, Muhimbili Medical Center, Dar es Salaam.
Neuvians, D. F. D., E. Mtango, and A. A. Kielman
  1988   The Burden of Disease among Preschool Children from Rural Tanzania. *Tropical Medicine and Parasitology* 39:9–13.
Nyamka, R.
  1979   A Report on the Activity of the Muhimbili Medical Center for the Year 1978. MS. Muhimbili Medical Center, Dar es Salaam.
Obembe, A., and A. Fagbayi
  1988   Road Traffic Accidents in Kaduna Metropolis: A Three-Month Survey. *East African Medical Journal* 65(9): 572–77.
Olugbile, A. O. B., and A. Oyemade
  1981   Health and the Environment—A Comparative Study of Agricultural and Industrial Workers in Nigeria. *African Journal of Medicine and Medical Science* 10:107–12.
Onyango, Z.
  1974   Health Facilities and Services in Kenya. In *Health and Disease in Kenya,* ed. L. C. Vogel et al. Nairobi: East African Literature Bureau.
Orubuloye, I. O.
  1981   Child-Spacing among Rural Yoruba Women: Ekiti and Ibadan Divisions in Nigeria. In *Child-Spacing in Tropical Africa: Tradition and Change,* ed. H. J. Page and R. Lesthaeghe, 225–36. London: Academic Press.
Orubuloye, I. O., and O. Y. Oyeneye
  1982   Primary Health Care in Developing Countries: The Case of Nigeria, Sri Lanka and Tanzania. *Social Science and Medicine* 16:675–86.
Oviasu, V. O.
  1978   Arterial Blood Pressure and Hypertension in a Rural Nigerian Community. *African Journal of Medicine and Medical Science* 7:137–43.
Page, H. J., and R. Lesthaeghe, eds.
  1981   *Child-Spacing in Tropical Africa: Tradition and Change.* London: Academic Press.

Patel, S. R.
   1980   The Practice of Medicine in East Africa, 1970–1979 and Future Prospects. *Obstetrics and Gynecology* 57(11): 729–33.
Pigman, H. A.
   1987   Polio Plus: Racing the Clock against Disease. *Rotarian* (April): 16–19.
Plath, D. W.
   1988a Aging in Japan. *Culture Crossroads*. Part 1. (March): 505–13.
   1988b Aging in Japan. *Culture Crossroads*. Part 2. (May): 464–71.
Podgore, J. K., and M. A. Omar
   1986   A Survey of Sexually Transmitted Diseases in the Democratic Republic of Somalia. *East African Medical Journal* 63(10): 640–45.
Quinn, T. C., et al.
   1986   An Epidemiological Paradigm. *Science* 234:955–63.
Raval, S. K.
   1974   Traffic Accidents and Casualties. In *Health and Disease in Kenya*, ed. L. C. Vogel et al., 523–29. Nairobi: East African Literature Bureau.
Roghmann, K.
   1989   The Evolution of the U.S. and West German Health Care Systems: Contracts and Challenges. In *Health and Illness in America and Germany*, ed. G. Lushcen, W. Cockerman, and G. Kunz, 121–32. Munich: Oldenbourg Verlag.
Royston, E., and A. O. Lopez
   1987   On the Assessment of Maternal Mortality. *World Health Statistical Quarterly* 40:214–24.
Salber, E. J., W. L. Berry, and E. J. Jackson
   1976   The Role of the Health Facilitator in Community Health Education. *Journal of Community Health* 2:5–20.
Scheuch, E. K.
   1989   Recent Social Changes and Their Consequences for the Health Care System in the Federal Republic of Germany. In *Health and Illness in America and Germany*, ed. G. Lushcen, W. Cockerman, and G. Kunz, 147–66. Munich: Oldenbourg Verlag.
Seedat, Y. K., M. A. Seedat, and D. B. T. Hackland
   1982   Prevalence of Hypertension in the Urban and Rural Zulu. *Journal of Epidemiology and Community Health* 36:256–61.
Shimkin, D. B.
   1983   Health and Social Research in Tanzania: The Results of an Exploratory Visit. Unpublished manuscript. Department of Anthropology, University of Illinois, Urbana-Champaign.
   1988   Community Health and Socio-Economic Development: A Tropical Perspective. *South Asian Anthropologist* 9(1): 5–24.
   N.d.   Longevity, Aging and the Aged in the United States Today. MS.
Shimkin, D. B., and P. Golde, eds.
   1983   *Clinical Anthropology*. New York: University Press of America.

Shimkin, D. B., E. M. Shimkin, and D. A. Frate, eds.
　1978　*The Extended Family in Black Societies.* The Hague: Mouton.
Simonsen, J. N., et al.
　1988　Human Immunodeficiency Virus Infection among Men with Sexually Transmitted Diseases. *New England Journal of Medicine* 319(5): 274–78.
Sindiga, I.
　1985　The Persistence of High Fertility in Kenya. *Social Science and Medicine* 20(1): 71–84.
Singano, B. J.
　1984　The Prevalence and Patterns of Alcohol Consumption in Urban Communities of Dodoma Municipality. Ph.D. diss., Diploma in Public Health, Muhimbili Medical Center, Dar es Salaam.
Storer, J. H., and D. A. Frate
　1990　Hunger, Poverty, and Malnutrition in Rural Mississippi: Developing Culturally Sensitive Nutritional Interventions. *Human Services in the Rural Environment* 14:25–30.
TDR/UNDP/World Bank/WHO
　1988　Tropical Disease Research, A Global Partnership at Work: New Approaches to Research Capability Strengthening. Special program for Research and Training in Tropical Diseases.
Tanzania Food and Nutrition Centre (TFNC)
　1987　*Annual Report, 1986–87* (September). Tanzania Food and Nutrition Centre: Dar es Salaam.
Turaya, E. B.
　1985　Practical Therapeutics: Lessons for Primary Health Care from Experience with Medical Assistance in Uganda. *East African Medical Journal* 62(7): 523–29.
van der Geest, S.
　1987　Self-Care and the Informal Sale of Drugs in South Cameroon. *Social Science and Medicine* 25(3): 293–305.
van Etten, G. M.
　1976　*Rural Health Development in Tanzania.* Amsterdam: Van Gorcum.
Vennema, A.
　1974　Tuberculosis in the Coastal Area of Tanzania. *East African Medical Journal* 51(3): 262–69.
Whitehead, T. L., D. A. Frate, and S. A. Johnson
　1984　Control of High Blood Pressure from Two Community-Based Perspectives. *Human Organization* 43:163–67.
Winikoff, B.
　1988　Women's Health: An Alternative Perspective for Choosing Intervention. *Studies in Family Planning* 19(4): 197–214.
Wolfson, A. B.
　1982　The Problems with Inappropriate Drugs Donated for Refugees. *Cultural Survival Quarterly* 6(1): 3–31.

Chapter 10

Anthropological Research Methods in a Changing World

Timothy J. Finan

The preparation of anthropologists in American universities has traditionally been built around an extended fieldwork experience. Within the Malinowskian paradigm the isolated year (or more) in the field is regarded as a personal rite of passage and an existential self-exploration as much as an information-gathering exercise. As Roger Keesing writes:

> For the anthropologist, fieldwork has been a kind of vision quest. By immersing oneself in another way of life, one comes to view oneself, one's own way of life, and humanity in a new perspective. Fieldwork is a profound experience, uncomfortable and sometimes shattering, but richly rewarding as well. (1976:8)

Thus, the temporal dimension of fieldwork is determined as much by time needed for the researcher to find an appropriate structural niche in the community as by the actual research itself. Following this logic, the required term of fieldwork increases in a direct proportion to the initial cultural distance between researcher and local community (Whyte 1984:28).

Associated with the profoundly human fieldwork experience in anthropological research is participant observation, the major technique used both to gain acceptance and gather information. In terms of time demands Bernard suggests that at the very minimum three months of residence are needed to even begin effective participant observation (Bernard 1988:159). As a participant, the researcher adopts a lifestyle similar to that of the community under study and assumes an often implicit set of rights and responsibilities associated with a unique structural position. As an observer, however, the anthropologist maintains an objective, almost detached, aloofness in order to record and document the social and cultural life of the community. The ethnographic mission always carries the double objective of, first, gaining access to the thickest strands of meaning that organize and orient the community (Geertz 1973) and, second, of "translating" that system of meaning into terms that scholars can appreciate and debate. In its traditional application, participant observation involves a strong reliance on "key-informant interviewing," which provides, among other things, insider interpretations of the events witnessed in the course of fieldwork. In more recent formulations anthropologists have complemented participant observation with other, more formal data-gathering techniques such as village censuses and surveys as well as with historical and archival information where available (e.g., Netting 1981).

In the traditional mold, anthropological methodology is by definition time-consuming and restricted in its focus of inquiry. Especially in the latter regard, participant observation has tended to be an effective research tool when applied to the internal workings of the community but less appropriate when analyzing forms of integration into wider regional, national, and international systems. The rapid postwar expansion of the world economic system and the increasing technical sophistication of communication networks have reduced the isolation of communities often targeted for anthropological research. Regular economic and political contact as well as the expansion of public services such as education have all stimulated processes of diversification within communities, as local groups articulate differently with the outside world (see Colson and Kottak, chap. 4). Thus, to the standard territorial scope of anthropological study must be added the theoretical and applied issues that focus on the complexities of these external relationships.

In response to this emerging diversification within local communities, anthropologists have increasingly turned their theoretical research interests to questions of articulation (e.g., Wolf 1982; DeWalt and Pelto 1983; C. A. Smith 1984). In the applied realm anthropologists have also been recruited into the change process, particularly in development anthropology. Policy analysis (Finan 1991), project evaluation (Scudder, Colson, and Scudder 1982), "social engineering" (Kottak 1985), and farming systems analysis (DeWalt 1985) are but a few of the areas that have called upon anthropological expertise. The involvement of anthropologists in applied, nonacademic activities requires, however, a modification in methods, since both time and resources are seldom available for traditional ethnographic fieldwork. In effect, anthropologists are now asked to acquire important sociocultural information relevant to specific problems of change but within a more limited time frame. The issue at hand, then, is both theoretical and methodological. Can anthropology, under time and resource constraints, make a positive contribution to the understanding of communities undergoing a process of fundamental change? Will anthropological insights inform enlightened policy makers, steer project planners from damaging designs, and help mitigate the negative consequences of economic integration?

This chapter explores the methodological alternatives and suggests possible strategies for anthropological research that meet the demands of a changing world. Then two case studies are presented to exemplify the possibilities of these strategies. In a concluding section implications for the training of anthropologists are considered.

Research in Contemporary Societies: The Learning Curve

I assume that the goal of anthropological research is the acquisition of social knowledge. Any local community organizes and expresses itself around sets of social facts (in a Durkheimian sense) and systems of interpretations or "local explanations" of those facts. In development studies, for example, social facts might include household structure, tenure relationships, levels of production technology, patterns of credit, and local medical and health care practices. Local explanations of these facts may be expressed in terms of intracommunity power relationships, class structures, myth, and religion. The combination of social facts and their interpretations constitutes the social knowledge of the community. This knowledge is encoded in a local idiom with unique categories and classifications, which anthropologists are trained to recognize. The researcher thus faces a challenge of discovering this social knowledge in terms of its own internal logic then decoding this knowledge into more standardized categories that academics or change agents can mull over.

I further assume that social knowledge is divisible and can be accumulated. From a research perspective this assumption implies that one can acquire more (or less) knowledge, given the influence of certain variables (e.g., time, choice of method). Furthermore, since social knowledge is an essential human characteristic, it is dynamic and processual, evolving in the context of constant human interaction. Thus, the research endeavor is an evolving quest toward a moving target.

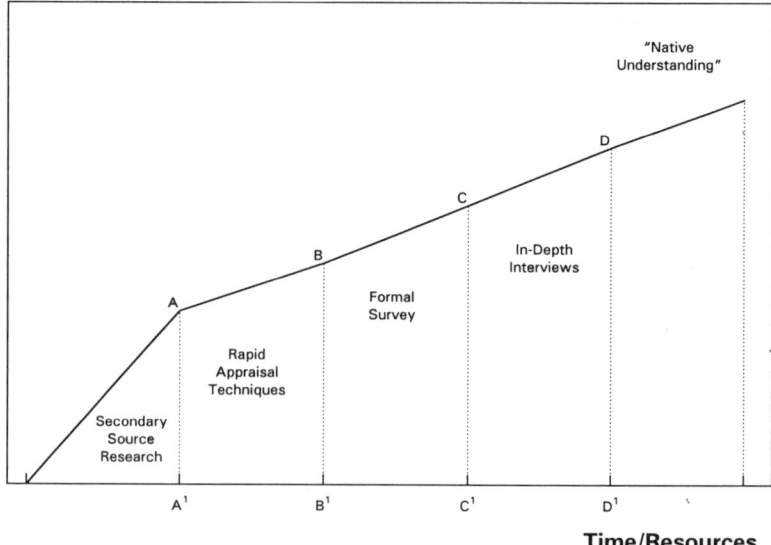

Fig. 10.1. The learning curve

For heuristic purposes, the pursuit of social knowledge might be illustrated as an upward bending "learning curve" (fig. 10.1). To best frame the methodological argument, access to social knowledge is seen as a function of time and resources, expressed on the horizontal axis (x). The quantity of social knowledge is illustrated on the vertical axis (y). Conceptually, a researcher can invest no time or resources and acquire next to nothing (somewhere near the origin O). Alternatively, the curve indicates that with the maximum of effort and resources the researcher can approach (but probably never reach) the elusive maximum. In situations typical of contemporary society, anthropologists find themselves located near point O, faced with an important problem-solving task yet under definite time and resource limitations.

The curve suggests that the acquisition of social knowledge follows a logical pattern in which certain research strategies are associated with different levels of resource investment. In most cases, with little prior experience, the anthropological researcher will begin with a prefieldwork review of published materials including public documents, reports, and academic books and articles. This information provides access, albeit limited, to social knowledge. In figure 10.1, for example, point A on the learning curve represents the amount of pre-fieldwork progress that corresponds to an investment of A^1 in research time and resources.

In most cases firsthand experience, or fieldwork, is the superior alternative to secondary review, but it is also more costly. An investment in fieldwork provides the researcher access to a greater level of social knowledge, i.e., to a higher point on the learning curve. Two critical observations are relevant at this point. First, the fieldwork experience builds upon and is enhanced by the complementary use of secondary materials, which can help determine the line of inquiry, identify the appropriate key informants, and facilitate fieldwork logistics. Second, the rate of progress up the learning curve is a function of time available for fieldwork. The greater the investment in time, the more social knowledge a researcher can expect to obtain.

Conceptually, shorter periods of fieldwork may be necessary because of resource constraints. I assume a hypothetical point B on the learning curve attainable by expending B^1, the corresponding amount of time and resources. The methods employed under the constraints represented by B^1 are commonly known as rapid appraisal techniques (Hildebrand 1981; Rhoades 1985; McCracken, Conway, and Pretty 1988; Molnar 1990), which have gained increasing popularity among social science researchers.

With rapid appraisal the researcher relies on observational skills, focus groups, and informal interviews to achieve research goals. Almost always this research activity seeks some critical amount of social knowledge that will determine subsequent action, usually in the context of a development project or other public intervention (see McCracken 1988). Rapid appraisals tend to be short in duration (from three to six weeks) but intense in application. Typically, although not necessarily, they are carried out by multidisciplinary teams (an issue addressed in subsequent sections) bolstered by carefully prepared topic outlines. The topic outline is a framework for systematic information gathering and imposes a sense of order on an otherwise highly informal activity. Researchers have also developed data organizational techniques (e.g., the land-use transect [McCracken, Conway, and Pretty 1988]; see also Whyte [1984]) to increase the efficient use of time.

The product of the rapid appraisal depends on the nature of the research problem. In farming systems research the rapid rural appraisal identifies representative farms (in Hildebrand's terminology [1981], "recommendation domains"); in other contexts the rapid appraisal may assess the local perspective on a proposed policy intervention, document local land tenure categories, provide the background information for a drug treatment center, and so on. While the specific information domain varies with the research problem, the researcher is always in pursuit of social knowledge. Frequently, research situations place the anthropologist in two arenas, in which access to the local community is combined with an understanding of the policy-making process, health provisioning system, the educational system, or whatever. In these cases the researcher procures social knowledge in both groups and then assumes the role of cultural interpreter, working to make indigenous social knowledge understandable and relevant to the intervention agent, and vice versa.

Anthropologists—working in rural development, health, and education—have made instrumental contributions to the development of these techniques (Van Willigen and Finan 1991). The anthropological emphasis on a holistic perspective in research is an invaluable approach for both observation and informal interviewing, because no variables are ignored *ex ante*. Moreover, our methodological tradition insists on the identification of native (emic) categories of knowledge and avoids the imposition of researcher categories on local phenomena. To the extent that an artful anthropologist can relate these indigenous funds of knowledge to the problem at hand, much learning can be obtained in a relatively short period of time.

Rapid appraisal methods often involve interdisciplinary teamwork in which the anthropologist has a specific and defined role. The advantage of a team approach (given fruitful group dynamics) derives from the cross-fertilization of ideas, especially in the identification of crucial variables that condition the articulation of the local community into larger physical, economic, and social systems. In short, the interaction of the disciplines supports the anthropological emphasis on holistic analysis.

There are, however, basic weaknesses in these rapid research techniques, and they can be dangerous in the hands of the naive and unaware. Time limitations often impose a severe schedule on the research routine, and it is difficult to develop among local community representatives the bonds of trust upon which successful communication is built. Similarly, the researcher has less time to assess the representativeness of those who participate in the interviews and, consequently, to evaluate the structural variation in the community. Thus, while the rapid appraisal in trained hands can provide great amounts of information, it often does not solve the issue of variation within and between communities. Moreover, the limited length of stay restricts access to the deep explanations normally sought by anthropologists.

When more time and resources are available, other research methods can be employed. In terms of our conceptual model an expenditure of C^1 in time and resources advances the researcher to point C on the learning curve. The additional social knowledge obtained from this investment can help solve the problem of variation, because a more systematic survey is possible. Structured surveys (Casley and Kumar 1988) use statistically representative sampling techniques to estimate variation in the specific community (or population). Also referred to as the "formal" survey, this method relies on a standardized instrument, or schedule, to which all participants respond, and the responses are then analyzed using quantitative statistical techniques, most of which are available in some easily managed microcomputer statistical package.

The well-implemented formal survey produces estimates of systematic variation in a given population. The quality of information, or the validity of the results (H. W. Smith 1981:333–48; Cook and Campbell 1979), depends upon the adequacy of the sampling design, the logical construction of the survey questionnaire, and the training of the enumerators, among other things. As highly sophisticated opinion polls demonstrate, these factors can be accurately controlled where good background knowledge is readily available. When not available, as in many anthropological research situations, the formal survey requires much more of the researcher's artistic touch.

The creative challenges of survey research loom large when, for example, little information can be obtained on the size or composition of the population to be studied, questionnaires are administered by primary schoolers in an indigenous language translated into an official language with the results reported in English, and the sampled households are dispersed over a wide geographical extension with poor transportation access. All these conditions are realistic problems in anthropological research. Sampling decisions must be made judgmentally by researchers based on the best available information. The questionnaire has to be structured to include the emic categories for local institutions (e.g., work groups, diseases, land classes), weights and measures, kinship, and so on. Since enumerators are often of varied background and training, the danger of "interviewer effect" (Webb et al. 1966:21) is great. That is, the questionnaire responses may actually measure the differential abilities of the enumerators rather than the actual variation in the sample (Feinstein 1988).

When such problems are addressed, the survey can become a powerful research tool, especially effective for determining internal heterogeneity due to processes of differential articulation with external forces. In development anthropology, for example, the survey can usefully establish classes of landowners, wealth distinctions by ethnic group, sexual division of labor patterns, and market integration levels. This type of social knowledge requires the breadth of coverage that only a survey can capture.

Certain methodological difficulties are inherent to the formal survey. As a research activity, it is time and resource intensive. Furthermore, random sampling, a basic component of survey research, means that each household (or person) in the population has an equal probability of inclusion in the sample. For a typical anthropological population random sampling does not exclude the illiterate respondent, persons unsure of researcher motives, as well as those who do not articulate well in cross-cultural (or social hierarchical) interaction. To restrict the sample to the literate and articulate introduces a possible bias into the results. An alternative strategy, however, is to structure the survey instrument in such a way that the maximum number of possible respondents can in fact answer the questions. In practice, then, the questionnaire limits inquiry to knowledge domains that most people can discuss, such as family size and other demographic information (including migration histories), land and land-use patterns, labor allocation, formal and informal employment, disease remedies, education, and so on. In most anthropological (particularly rural) populations open-ended questions that seek attitudes and opinions—such as a farmer's assessment of the extension service—are best left to other methodological strategies or more prolonged field stays.

In the formal survey applied to anthropological communities breadth of coverage necessarily sacrifices depth. While patterns of variation can emerge from the analysis of survey data, the responses will seldom suggest why those patterns exist or provide the community's perspective on those patterns. For example, the survey documents the proportion of landowners and sharecroppers in a rural community but offers little information on the nature of that relationship, how it emerges, and how it is maintained. Once, however, the categories of landowner and sharecropper have been established, key informants for each of those can be sought out for more in-depth interviews.

If our anthropological researcher can invest D^1 in terms of time and resources, point D along the learning curve can be reached. This advance implies the use of traditional ethnographic methods, such as key informant interviews and focus group encounters, but in the model presented here the sampling procedure is purposive. Once the formal survey has identified the heterogeneity of the community by discriminating significant social groups (whose particular version of local social knowledge would probably vary), the researcher can approach the literate or articulate member of each group (identified in the survey) as its representative "spokesperson," who can provide the missing insights and local interpretations. With these in-depth techniques and the appropriate allocation of time, the researcher progresses up the learning curve toward a conceptual optimum (D) that approximates a "native" level of social knowledge, or the local "funds of knowledge" (cf. Goodenough 1956; Frake 1961; Vélez-Ibañez 1988:38).

The methodological literature recognizes the complementary nature of mixed methods approaches to research (e.g., Pelto and Pelto 1978; Brewer and Hunter 1989). The research strategy of "triangulation," for example, employs different types of methods that seek reconfirmation of original results, thus enhancing the validity of the research. Here, however, the learning curve model adds a further dimension in that it emphasizes the interactive and the cumulative relationships of multimethod research. Rapid appraisal techniques build in an essential way on the information obtained by a review of secondary sources. The construction of a formal questionnaire necessarily requires the firsthand knowledge that a rapid appraisal (or some adaptation of it, such as summer fieldwork reconnaissance common in anthropology) can provide. For its part the formal survey often serves to define the classes from which key informants (or focus groups) will be chosen for in-depth interviewing. The logical progression of knowledge acquisition implicit in the learning curve thus argues that one research method is intrinsically related to another in a definite temporal and interactive sequence.

The learning curve model also imposes a sense of humility on the researcher. To traverse cultural boundaries and thereby share social knowledge is a quintessential human experience, but even when most successful, it is an approximation toward some ideal goal. The development anthropologist, for example, can describe or even explain patterns of land and labor use in a community but not reach a point of total empathy or full understanding of land and labor strategies. In this imperfect way research involves the progressive application of complementary techniques, each of which provides marginal increments of understanding. The ultimate research ideal is indeed elusive and humbling but also encouraging, in the sense that there is always another enticing level of understanding to reward our efforts.

Practical Constraints to Application

The learning curve model of knowledge acquisition directly addresses what is the essential problem of social science research: the need to achieve both representativeness and insight. In scholarly eras past, when anthropologists were self-styled voices for their "people," standard reporting format accommodated such declarations as, "The Kuru do . . . or the Dinka believe. . . ." In other words, either little variation actually existed within these groups, or it was not deemed worthy of revelation—there simply were *no* Balinese of interest not obsessed with cockfighting.

Given the complexities of contemporary societies, most problem-oriented anthropological research has adopted a more stochastic approach based on the theoretical assumption that human process will by its nature generate variation in practices and beliefs (expressed so well in the work of Barth [1966] and Bailey [1969]). Such variation is especially evident in communities in which structural power is unequally distributed among groups (see Wolf 1990) and in which articulation with outside forces has historical depth (Roseberry 1989). For the development anthropologist the explicit research charge is, in fact, to document and explain this variation.

To capture systematically the existing variation in a cultural community requires methodological tools that assess the representativeness of results. Formal statistical methods, based on probability theory, provide quantitative estimates of the likelihood of measured events, if certain conditions are met. But the application of formal methods in a cultural community also poses rather unique problems. Our discipline has a long theoretical history of applying the litmus test of cultural context to purportedly universal theories and methods. The formalist-substantivist debate revolved around non-Western applications of neoclassical economic theory (Frankenberg 1967); Margaret Mead's classic Samoan research evaluated the cross-cultural usefulness of established psychoanalytic theory (Mead 1928). In just such a vein the cross-cultural application of statistical techniques that measure representativeness constitutes another anthropological challenge (Bernard 1978). The requirements of formal survey methods, from sampling to measurement to analysis and interpretation, need cultural contextualization. In the absence of prior information on the population and with all the problems associated with cross-linguistic and cross-cultural communication, the pursuit of representativeness within acceptable confidence intervals demands well-developed anthropological skills and methodological innovation.

As the multimethod approach suggests, the acquisition of social knowledge is only partially satisfied when variation has been characterized, since explanation, or insight into that variation, is a tandem goal. While different tools of quantitative analysis provide for the testing of hypotheses and the estimation of causal explanations, the anthropologist tends to rely on the perspective provided by the community itself. Deep knowledge is best communicated in local categories by local representatives, and the artful interviewer can achieve great insights.

In the real world of field research passage to the deep levels of social knowledge is limited primarily by time. Particularly in development anthropology, the nature of contract research is problem oriented and short term; however, even academic anthropologists often find their post-dissertation field time restricted to occasional visits. Can an anthropologist ever hope to achieve adequate understanding without the conventional one-year fieldwork period, or can the multimethod approach and team-based field studies be executed so that changing contemporary societies are better appreciated in terms of breadth and depth?

In practice, the time/resource efficiency of fieldwork can be significantly improved by both the application of well-known anthropological principles and a reliance on practical, realistic research designs. *The first principle is to intensify non-fieldwork preparation.* Most cultural communities, if not already studied by anthropologists, have at least been the object of some development intervention or a little-known government report. These documents serve the researcher by indicating what sources of variation are to be expected. *The second principle is to adopt the holistic perspective systematically.* Even during the first fieldwork endeavor, the researcher should enter the community with professional sensitivities honed to systemic relationships among different spheres of activities, especially those that direct the internal and external distribution of power. *The third principle is to treat interviewing as an intimate act of human communication rather than a data-gathering enterprise.* As scientific as we would like our research to be, the basic foundation of the quest for knowledge is the ability to communicate fellowship and humanity. The quality of fieldwork improves geometrically when local people begin to show interest in the research goals of the fieldworker. At this point respondents become research partners willing and even anxious to participate in the discovery process, and movement up the learning curve is rapid. The artful researcher and interviewer seem to achieve this level of communication during even short periods of fieldwork, although the art of interviewing itself is seldom part of the formal anthropological training curriculum.

These principles form the basis for research strategies that maximize the efficiency of field time. One such strategy I call the "stepwise" research design. While development anthropologists seldom can have the luxury of extended fieldwork contact (even when assigned "in-country"), they sometimes can revisit a community several times over a specified period. In this case a systematic stepwise design redraws the learning curve more as a stairway. Each visit contributes increments of social knowledge through the application of a multimethod approach. Moreover, the time between field visits allows for a greater period for preparation based on the firsthand results of the previous visit. The stepwise strategy also effectively captures intra-annual variation in certain variables (see Colson and Kottak, chap. 4, for an approach like this).

Even when multiple visits are not possible, an interactive research strategy can be adopted. Under this strategy the researcher treats the field situation as an emergent process in which each data-gathering activity constitutes the basis for a subsequent one. For example, the questionnaire for the formal survey is prepared and tested only after the rapid appraisal has identified the appropriate local terminology for agricultural tasks. In turn, in-depth interviewing occurs only after specific patterns of variation have been established by the formal survey results. With the interactive strategy time constraints do not curtail or preclude the application of one or another of the methods but may be reflected in sample size limits, variations in the survey instrument, or an expanded use of hired enumerators. In these cases the design decisions of the researchers should reflect the underlying trade-offs in terms of breadth and depth of coverage.

Anthropologists increasingly participate in teams, often composed along multidisciplinary lines. Many are the stories of the Sir George or Madam Georgina anthropologist who slew the ethnocentric dragons on the project team. I have found, on the other hand, that a less royal approach to teamwork renders far more positive results. In accordance with the holistic principle, the anthropologist more often than not will find that technical scientists and agricultural economists contribute information that complements his or her knowledge areas of the household or social system. Harmonious teamwork based on consensus building often proves a more insightful and time-saving experience, particularly when the anthropologist is versed in the technical language of other team members.

A final strategy to increase the time effectiveness of fieldwork is participatory research, which sports two dimensions. First, there is the dimension of local counterpart relationships. Increasingly, anthropological research in the development context involves collaboration between counterparts and the outside fieldworker. The ability to create a true collegial and cooperative relationship can vastly improve the quality of the research, since counterparts begin much further up the learning curve than the outside fieldworker. The key to successful cooperation is to communicate effectively the research objectives to local colleagues so that they can recognize the importance of their contribution and the value of their interpretation. The second dimension of participatory research is the integration of the target community in the research process. Anthropology has long stressed the importance of the key informant, but participatory research goes further—by allowing the community to share in the responsibility for the success of the research project (see Reason 1988, on the "cooperative inquiry group"). To paraphrase Reason, research is not on people but, rather, with people. Both these dimensions of participatory research represent highly innovative and relatively recent strategies that have yet to be developed to their full potential.

Two Case Studies: Northwest Portugal and Cape Verde

Every research project has its unique needs and individual challenges. The following case studies seek to demonstrate the application of multimethod research strategies under differing field conditions and different resource availabilities. Both have provided the empirical basis for the methodological ideas presented here. The study in northwest Portugal was more constrained by time (about three months for the fieldwork phase), more experimental in design, and involved the intense collaboration of counterparts, but the researchers had the benefit of previous experience in-country and spoke Portuguese. Also, the research was designed to answer a specific problem with immediate implications for policy making. The Cape Verdean example was designed as a stepwise strategy with short visits spread over a longer period of time, and the researchers began near zero on the learning curve and had to employ interpreters. In contrast to the Portuguese example, the initial objective of the study was to develop a database of information on rural society.

Northwest Portugal: Agricultural Policy and Land Structure Study

The Northwest of Portugal is particularly noted for its smallholder, intensive agriculture. The average farm size in the region is 2.2 hectares of cropland, fragmented into six noncontiguous parcels. Three agroclimatic zones are commonly distinguished in the northwest. A narrow 30-kilometer coastal strip in relatively flat and densely populated. Toward the east the terrain rises through an intermediate zone (to about 300 m. in altitude) then becomes a more sparsely populated mountain zone with a distinctly colder and wetter climate.

In 1987 a multidisciplinary team of social scientists (agricultural economists and anthropologists) published the results of a five-year study that estimated the impacts of Portuguese agricultural policy on representative farming systems and predicted the medium-run consequences of Portugal's accession to the European Economic Community (EEC) for these same farms (Pearson et al. 1987). The analysis suggested that under the Common Agricultural Policy of the EEC the small-farm sector of northwest Portugal, the major producing region of milk, corn, and wine (*vinho verde*), would suffer significant negative impacts as measured by decreases in farm income. These economic pressures were anticipated to provoke agricultural change in the northwest, either through a restructuring of landholdings to larger, more viable units or through technical change that increased output or decreased production costs.

Portuguese negotiators to the EEC were able to use these dire predictions for its small farm sector to obtain favorable access to community funds for structural investment in agriculture. In effect, Portuguese policy makers ceded control over such direct intervention measures as price policy in return for control over the allocation of substantial investment funds. The use of investment monies became Portugal's principal food policy instrument on the production side.

How a country makes an investment plan for its agriculture is never a trivial question. And how a member country taps available funds from various EEC programs is exceedingly complex. In this regard the specific challenge facing Portuguese policy makers was to apply the available investment resources in such a way that technical or structural change could increase small farmer income. The investment resources would thus help the adjustment process for small dairy, corn, and wine producers in the northwest region who lose under the pricing regulations of the Common Agricultural Policy.

With the problem so defined, a research strategy was designed to estimate the impacts of different investment strategies and to identify the socioeconomic constraints to change. In the case of northwest Portugal initial research hypotheses had identified small size and fragmentation of landholdings, the inadequacy of local, traditional irrigation systems, and poor machine access to fields as major constraints to technical change. Investment funds under different community programs could be mobilized as policy instruments that address these constraints. But, since the northwest has such wide intraregional variation, a research method was needed to relate resource availability to specific regional situations. In this context, a formal survey emerged as a methodological solution.

The basic geopolitical unit in Portugal is the *freguesia* (often translated as "parish"), which has a local governing board, a church (and priest), and usually a small concentration of petty merchants. At the methodological level our sampling frame was the *freguesia*, and we chose eight *freguesias* that represent specific, known sources of variation within the region. Three *freguesias* were from the mountain zone where dairy activities predominate; two were from the intermediate zone, where wine production predominates; and one was from the coastal zone.

The research team was composed of the outside research team together with counterparts from the agricultural university and the regional offices of the Ministry of Agriculture. Although the Portuguese counterparts had designed the overall research problem and developed the analytical framework, they had little or no experience in fieldwork. In many ways the outside researchers enjoyed a learning advantage due to their previous work with small farmers in the region (although not in the chosen *freguesias*). The entire fieldwork phase lasted about two months.

Teams of two or three researchers were assigned to each *freguesia*, and they began by seeking out available published materials (e.g., census data) on their adopted study site. The first fieldwork phase (application of rapid appraisal techniques in fig. 10.1) identified in each *freguesia* several key members who either were official representatives or were locally recognized as "funds of knowledge" experts. Since the research questions focused primarily on farmers and their use of land and labor, the research team relied significantly on the insights of the local real estate assessor (*louvado*), usually an old, respected farmer called in to divide up a land patrimony equally among the heirs. Another community guardian of local funds of knowledge was the retired emigrant. Virtually every *freguesia* could claim a once-poor man who had sought fortune in France, returned after twenty years with a steady retirement pension, and now practiced a sort of hobby gardening. These individuals tended to be structural parts of the *freguesia* but at the same time a bit detached and able to reflect objectively.

From these local informants the research teams identified constraints and problems as they were perceived by the community. The team also used aerial maps of chosen *freguesias* to locate traditional irrigation systems, residential concentrations, and road (and path) systems. The local orientation phase also revealed patterns of historical change in the *freguesia*, the history of emigration, rates and sources of off-farm employment, marketing channels, land ownership patterns and rental customs, inheritance practices, and other factors relevant to the research.

The rapid appraisal phase lasted about three days in each *freguesia* and was followed by preparations for the formal survey. Local residents from each *freguesia* were selected to serve as guides and to make introductions. The sampling of intra-*freguesia* variation presented an immediate challenge. As a general pattern, households are clustered into defined groups called *aldeias*, which are surrounded by the agricultural fields. Since several kinds of investment, such as irrigation improvement, are area specific, the sampling strategy began with the random selection of a clearly delineated agricultural area, normally a valley outside the *freguesia*. The guides helped to identify the respective landowners and renters of these lands and indicated their residences in the neighboring *aldeias*. The basic survey unit itself was the household.

The household questionnaire requested information on each specific parcel of cropland and forested area, including tenure relationships, the history of acquisition, source of irrigation, degree of access, and crop rotations. Since off-farm employment alternatives are important factors determining household income, the allocation of household labor was recorded. Also, the interview determined differences in technology as reflected in the level of mechanization, the use of improved seeds and breeds, the application of purchased inputs, and so forth. During the questionnaire process it was relatively straightforward to classify the households into types that would be eligible for different investment programs.

During the survey phase researchers identified those farmers who seemed especially knowledgeable or articulate and, in team terminology, referred to them as "expert informants." In each *freguesia* the teams returned to spend more time with these households in an attempt to procure greater insight into the research problem. The expert interview phase began after team members had the opportunity to discern intuitively patterns of response to certain key questions in the survey instrument. This phase focused on issues and sought value statements and opinions. For example, several EEC programs offer incentives for early retirement from agriculture (in order to stimulate increases in farm size), subsidy payments to young farmers, and direct payments to uproot vineyards. On the assumption that selected households represented the range of typical situations, the team researchers used this interview format to elicit responses from farmers to these different alternatives. Thus, one representative farmer might explain that land was the household's only patrimony and that divestment of one's land would be tantamount to a rejection of one's children. Another household might express distaste for the rigors of farm life and prefer that its children not follow in the profession. The expert interviews were meant to capture relationships between attitude sets and the household's place in the socioeconomic fabric of the society.

The interplay between quantitative (or etic) data and qualitative (or emic) data permitted a rapid advance up the learning curve. With the specific land information from the survey, for example, it was possible to estimate what an improved irrigation or road system would bring in terms of increased farm income. The qualitative data from the interviews, however, sprinkles a flavor of reality over the range of changes that public investment might bring and farmers might accept. Upon completion of the fieldwork the analysis and report writing were carried out by the entire research team (Monke and Avillez 1989).

Cape Verde: Food Crops Research Project
The Food Crops Research Project began in 1984 and represents a good example of stepwise research. As part of a U.S. foreign aid program designed to increase food production on Cape Verde, this project provided support to the National Agrarian Research Institute (INIA) and its Department of Social Sciences and Agricultural Economics. Not only is INIA a recent institution (inaugurated in 1984), but Cape Verde itself has been independent (from Portugal) only since 1975. Cape Verde does not yet have a resident anthropologist, and, since there are no universities on the archipelago, nearly all social science research is coordinated through INIA.

In the design of the project an economic anthropologist and an agricultural economist were responsible for designing and implementing a rural survey of the principal agricultural islands. The original purpose of this research was to provide INIA's research staff—all trained abroad—with a set of baseline data on rural society, patterns of resource use, and current agricultural practices, and this information would be used to establish research priorities for the institute. Hence, the problem statement was formulated in general rather than specific terms.

Cape Verde, composed of nine inhabited islands located 453 miles west of Senegal, is a very poor country especially bereft of natural resources. Agriculture is the major activity of over two-thirds of the population, but Cape Verde produces only about 10 percent of staple food needs. Many rural households live at a subsistence margin, surviving on international donor aid or emigration remittances. There is a strong sense that many Cape Verdeans are engaged in agriculture for lack of alternative opportunities off-farm, and the high incidence of out-migration and public work front employment supports this hypothesis. Thus, rural Cape Verde, in general terms, can be characterized along several dimensions. There is a large proportion of subsistence households that depend on public subsidies (through food aid or work front employment)—some commercial farmers, some large landholders with various off-farm activities, and female-headed households, which tend to be the poorest of the poor.

An initial review of the existing literature identified a previous agricultural sector report prepared by a multidisciplinary team, and that document provided the informational basis for initiating the research design (Freeman et al. 1978). Following up on the secondary resource phase, the social scientists (the anthropologist and economist) conducted a three-week rapid rural appraisal during the first year of the project. The appraisal team (which had virtually no previous experience in the country) was joined by local INIA counterparts, including an experienced survey specialist and two enumerators/interpreters. During this phase the researchers visited two of the main agricultural islands, met informally with farmers, and prepared the design of the subsequent surveys. The most effective element of the rapid appraisal was to identify the counterparts' expertise and to recruit their interest and participation in the design of the project.

During two subsequent six-week visits (1984 and 1985) three major agricultural islands were surveyed—Santiago (Finan and Belknap 1985), Santo Antão (Langworthy, Finan, Varela, and Rodrigues 1986), and São Nicolau (Langworthy, Finan, and Varela 1986). Stratified random sampling techniques were used in order to incorporate known differences between rain-fed and irrigated farms. Access to irrigated farmland distinguishes major differences in rural society, and the sample was chosen so as to reflect relative proportions published in the 1979 agricultural census.

The survey questionnaires were applied by the professional enumerators from INIA (at times with the assistance of local extension agents). These survey instruments were designed to capture expected variations in household demographics, household labor allocations, use of nonfamily wage labor, access to agricultural land, animal inventories, and levels of input use (the latter a measure of technology). With sample sizes of approximately two hundred each for Santiago and Santo Antão and one hundred for São Nicolau, the surveys required from four to six weeks of fieldwork time.

The individual island surveys generated a working typology of households and permitted the socioeconomic mapping of a rural society previously thought to be largely homogeneous. This characterization compared the living standards of female-headed households with jointly headed households, rain-fed with irrigated agriculture, small farmers with large farmers, and diversified farms with more commercialized farms. The analysis further associated a coefficient of representativeness with each type. This information was incorporated into the five-year national development plan of the Cape Verdean government.

If the surveys acquired much usable knowledge, however, they were equally remarkable for what was not achieved: the underlying logic of resource use. The surveys uncovered representative patterns of variation in labor exchange, a high incidence of sharecropping (despite its official prohibition), a striking poverty among female-headed households, and a strong market orientation among irrigated farmers. The dynamics of rural society, especially strategies for change within the socioeconomic and cultural environment, were not particularly illuminated. There remained several puzzles regarding the persistence of sharecropping institutions, the survival strategies of female managers, and the potential for technical change in agriculture. In sum the representativeness of the survey exercise lacked depth of insight. For this the team returned on subsequent trips to apply ethnographic interviewing techniques to the specific issues.

The project focussed ethnographic interviews on the largest and principal agricultural island, Santiago. The island has nearly 150,000 inhabitants, about half the population of the country. Two-thirds of Santiago's households are engaged in agricultural activity. Volcanic in origin, the island has a central mountainous region from which valleys wind toward the ocean. It is in these valleys, called *ribeiras,* that most farming occurs, irrigated near the valley floor (usually several hundred meters wide) and rain-fed on neighboring slopes. Cape Verde suffers extended periods of drought punctuated by highly isolated torrential rainstorms that result in severe erosion of agricultural lands.

The ethnographic stage of the research selected a sample from four of the island's *ribeiras*. The professional enumerators from INIA, together with the anthropologist and agricultural economist, visited each *ribeira* and asked for meetings with local farmers. At these meetings, the enumerators explained (in native *crioulo*) the research project and its aims, then introduced the notion of a research partnership, thus encouraging local farmers to become participant observers in an agricultural research project. Rather than base our analysis on elicited information, we sought shared information.

From these introductory orientations a group of forty households were selected to begin the research. This sample, ten from each *ribeira*, was selected according to the categories of the typology from the formal survey. In some cases a female manager or a small farmer was actively sought out to ensure one representative minimally for each type. The INIA researchers did not elicit information but collected it, since the farmer became the principal data gatherer. This phase of the research was organized during a four-week visit by the outside research team then carried out by the local INIA counterparts. Both case studies illustrate the effort to apply a multimethod approach in the quest for both representativeness and insight. The time constraints varied between projects, but the fieldwork episodes were always short, intense, and well prepared for. Both multidisciplinary and counterpart teams were used, and various degrees of participatory research strategies were attempted. In each example critical research decisions had to be made in the field, and, as expected, research progress often yielded to the vicissitudes of logistical realities. Nonetheless, for both Cape Verde and Portugal these research strategies resulted in significant amounts of useful learning.

Conclusions: Implications for Training

This chapter has presented a conceptual model of social knowledge acquisition that has significant implications for anthropological research in a changing, complex world. It argues that anthropologists commonly encounter research situations in which time constraints limit the amount of fieldwork and suggests a multimethod approach that builds on anthropological strengths that combine representativeness and insight.

The learning curve model of approximating social knowledge requires a rethinking of graduate training priorities for anthropologists. In the contemporary world, in which local communities define and redefine themselves in response to external influences, the research mission depends on a broader range of methods and techniques for both quantitative and qualitative analysis. Unfortunately, the theoretical gap between empirical and interpretive anthropology has resulted in methodological specialization and dogmatism, when complementarity might be better recommended.

The training of anthropological graduate students could be reoriented in two important ways. The first, and most critical, emphasis would be the inclusion of research methodology courses based on mixed methods. The essential argument here is that in contemporary communities the important explanatory variables have changed, as have the conditions under which research is undertaken. Research methodology in anthropology has to respond to such changing circumstances. Second, to the extent that the research focus shifts toward macro-micro linkages, anthropologists should be encouraged to develop multidisciplinary skills. Those interested in economic development should be versed in the language of the relevant sister disciplines; those interested in environmental anthropology should understand ecology; those interested in nutritional anthropology need a firm basis in biological systems. Anthropologists have always been avid borrowers of useful concepts, and the argument here is that multidisciplinary interests be promulgated explicitly in the graduate programs.

In sum, to meet the changing demands on anthropological research, students must be able to count both quantitative and qualitative techniques in their methodological armamentarium. And their ability to work in the context of multidisciplinary teams can also be honed through formal training. But it is wise to remember that all the methodological solutions have not been identified. Anthropologists face much broader challenges in their enterprise. The variables of interest have changed, the constraints to research are greater, and some retooling will be necessary.

REFERENCES

Bailey, F. G.
    1969 *Stratagems and Spoils: A Social Anthropology of Politics.* New York: Schocken Books.

Barth, Fredrik
    1966   *Models of Social Organization.* Royal Anthropological Institute: Occasional Paper no. 23.
Bernard, H. Russell
    1988   *Research Methods in Cultural Anthropology.* Newbury Park, Calif.: Sage Publications.
Brewer, John, and Albert Hunter
    1989   *Multi-Method Research: A Synthesis of Styles.* Newbury Park, Calif.: Sage Publications.
Casley, Dennis J., and Krishna Kumar
    1988   *The Collection, Analysis, and Use of Monitoring and Evaluation Data.* Baltimore: Johns Hopkins University Press, for the World Bank.
Cook, Thomas D., and Donald T. Campbell
    1979   *Quasi-Experimentation Design and Analysis Issues for Field Settings.* Boston: Houghton Mifflin.
DeWalt, Billie R.
    1985   Anthropology, Sociology, and Farming Systems Research. *Human Organization* 44(2): 106–13.
DeWalt, Billie R., and Pertti J. Pelto, eds.
    1985   *Micro and Macro Levels of Analysis in Anthropology: Issues in Theory and Research.* Boulder, Colo.: Westview Press.
Feinstein, Oswaldo N.
    1988   Guidelines for the Design and Conduct of Baseline and Follow-Up Studies to Assess Effects and Impact on Project Beneficiaries Disaggregated by Gender and Socio-Economic Groups. Unpublished manuscript. International Fund for Agricultural Development, Rome.
Finan, Timothy J.
    1991   Macro-Micro Linkages in Northwest Portuguese Agriculture: An Application of the Policy Analysis Matrix (PAM). *American Anthropologist* 93(1): 137–48.
Finan, Timothy J., and John Belknap
    1985   Characteristics of Santiago Agriculture. Report presented to the National Institute of Agrarian Research, São Jorge, Cape Verde.
Frake, Charles O.
    1961   The Diagnosis of Disease among the Subanun of Mindanao. *American Anthropologist* 63:113–32.
Frankenberg, Ronald
    1967   Economic Anthropology: One Anthropologist's View. In *Themes in Economic Anthropology,* ed. R. Firth, 47–89. London: Tavistock Publications.
Freeman, Peter H., et al.
    1978   Cape Verde: Assessment of the Agricultural Sector. MS. U.S. Agency for International Development, Praia, Cape Verde.
Geertz, Clifford
    1973   *The Interpretation of Cultures.* New York: Basic Books.

Goodenough, Ward H.
    1956   Componential Analysis and the Study of Meaning. *Language* 32:195–216.

Hildebrand, Peter E.
    1981   Combining Disciplines in Rapid Appraisal: The Sondeo Approach. *Agricultural Administration* 8:423–32.

Keesing, Roger M.
    1976   *Cultural Anthropology: A Contemporary Perspective.* New York: Holt, Rinehart and Winston.

Kottak, Conrad Phillip
    1985   When People Don't Come First: Some Sociological Lessons from Completed Projects. In *Putting People First: Sociological Variables in Rural Development,* ed. Michael Cernea, 325–56. New York: Oxford University Press.

Langworthy, M., T. Finan, and R. Varela
    1986   Characteristics of São Nicolau Agriculture. Report presented to the National Institute of Agrarian Research, São Jorge, Cape Verde.

Langworthy, M., T. Finan, R. Varela, and E. Rodrigues
    1986   Characteristics of Santo Antão Agriculture. Report presented to the National Institute of Agrarian Research, São Jorge, Cape Verde.

McCracken, Jennifer A.
    1988   Participatory Rapid Rural Appraisal in Guarajat: A Trail Model for the Aga Khan Rural Support Programme (India). London: IIED.

McCracken, Jennifer A., J. N. Pretty, and G. R. Conway
    1988   *An Introduction to Rapid Rural Appraisal for Agricultural Development.* London: IIED.

Mead, Margaret
    1928   *Coming of Age in Samoa.* New York: William Morrow.

Molnar, Augusta
    1989   *Community Forestry: Rapid Appraisal.* Rome: Food and Agriculture Organization.

Monke, Eric, and Francisco Avillez, eds.
    1989   Government Policy and the Development of Small-Farm Agriculture in Northwest Portugal. Report presented to the Luso-American Development Foundation, Lisbon.

Netting, Robert McC.
    1981   *Balancing on an Alp: Ecological Change and Continuity in a Swiss Mountain Village.* Cambridge: Cambridge University Press.

Pearson, Scott R., et al.
    1987   *Portuguese Agriculture in Transition.* Ithaca, N.Y.: Cornell University Press.

Pelto, Pertti J., and Grettel H. Pelto
    1978   *Anthropological Research: The Structure of Inquiry.* Cambridge: Cambridge University Press.

Reason, Peter
    1988   The Cooperative Inquiry Group. In *Human Inquiry in Action: Devel-*

opments in *New Paradigm Research,* ed. P. Reason, 18–39. London: Sage Publications.

Rhoades, Robert E.
    1985 Informal Survey Methods for Farming Systems Research. *Human Organization* 44(3): 215–18.

Roseberry, William
    1989 Peasants and the World. In *Economic Anthropology,* ed. S. Plattner, 108–26. Stanford, Calif.: Stanford University Press.

Scudder, Thayer, E. Colson, and M. B. D. Scudder
    1982 An Evaluation of the Gwembe South Development Project, Gambia. Institute for Development Anthropology Working Paper no. 5, Binghamton, N.Y.

Smith, Carol A.
    1984 Local History in Global Context: Social and Economic Transitions in Western Guatemala. *Comparative Studies in Society and History* 26(2): 193–228.

Smith, H. W.
    1981 *Strategies of Social Research: The Methodological Imagination.* Englewood Cliffs, N.J.: Prentice Hall.

Van Willigen, John, and Timothy J. Finan, eds.
    1991 *Soundings: Rapid and Reliable Research Methods for Practicing Anthropologists.* NAPA Bulletin no. 10. Washington, D.C.: American Anthropological Association.

Vélez-Ibañez, Carlos G.
    1988 Networks of Exchange among Mexicans in the U.S. and Mexico: Local Level Mediating Responses to National and International Transformations. *Urban Anthropology* 17(1): 27–52.

Webb, Eugene J., D. T. Campbell, R. D. Schwartz, and L. Sechrest
    1966 *Unobtrusive Measures: Nonreactive Research in Social Sciences.* Chicago: Rand McNally.

Wolf, Eric R.
    1982 *Europe and the People without History.* Berkeley: University of California Press.
    1990 Distinguished Lecture: Facing Power—Old Insights, New Questions. *American Anthropologist* 92(3): 586–96.

Whyte, William Foote
    1984 *Learning from the Field: A Guide from Experience.* Beverly Hills, Calif.: Sage Publications.

Chapter 11

Thoughts on Development Anthropology after Twenty Years

Michael M. Horowitz

A principal transformation of anthropology during the last two decades has been its increasing involvement with the process of accelerated incorporation of African, Asian, Middle Eastern, Pacific, and Latin American agrarian and urban communities into the world economic system. Commonly referred to as "development," this process frequently involves the transfer to poor, usually former colonial nations, of technology, funding, and expertise from countries of the industrial north through multinational, governmental, and nongovernmental organizations (NGOs). Since the early 1970s anthropologists have figured prominently among the experts involved in development's design, implementation, and assessment.

At the inauguration several years ago of its section on Development Anthropology, the German Ethnological Society asked me to assess the status of the field in the United States. I said then that, while the legitimacy of anthropologists working in development had been largely accepted by the development establishment—with the prominent exception of some economists—substantial challenges to that legitimacy are posed by other anthropologists. These economists, claiming universal validity for the paradigm based on scarcity and competition, find the local expertise and alternative models suggested by anthropologists to be unnecessarily complex. Anthropologists are accused of methodological fuzziness and statistical imprecision; of manifesting negative attitudes toward change and of supporting traditional practice rather than identifying tradition as an obstacle to be overcome; of insisting on unreasonably long field research, unduly delaying the project design and implementation cycle; of being arcane, esoteric, and academic; and of not being team players, of being "unresponsive to the requirements of the host country and donor organization to move rapidly from design to implementation" (Horowitz 1990a:190). The economists' attack was understood as a defense of territory, as anthropologists challenged their monopoly over social science in development—or quasimonopoly that tolerates the occasional participation of some political scientists and public administration specialists.[1] But the assault on development from academic anthropologists appeared rather to be based on ideology:

> While economists challenged the entry of anthropologists into development with the claim, among others, that the latter were too protective of the people and too resisting of change, academic anthropologists—who long scorned the "application" or "policy relevance" of their studies—mounted the opposite attack, claiming that development anthropology violates two traditionally dominant precepts in the discipline: moral neutrality and the preference for the pristine. (Horowitz 1990a:191)

At that time I was reflecting personal experiences in a large university department in which the faculty was deeply riven into pro- and antidevelopment anthropology camps yet in which most of the social anthropology graduate students studied development. Some in the department, uncomfortable with Elizabeth Colson's charge for anthropologists to consider the "policy environments that lead to the impoverishment both of other countries and of our own people" (1989:3), found it hard to acknowledge that students committed to methodological and theoretical rigor would reject relativism and moral neutrality to assume postures of engagement and seek to create of anthropology a scientific instrument for just social change.

These students know that the subjects of anthropological investigation are, for the most part, the rural and urban poor of agrarian societies incorporated into the peripheries of the world political economic system. The process of incorporation did not, of course, begin in the twentieth century. On the contrary, as Eric Wolf (1982) so powerfully reminds us, it long predates the emergence of anthropology, despite most anthropologists' having until recently ignored it.[2] Nonetheless, there remain anthropologists whose preference for the pristine disposes them to write *as if* modern tribal and peasant peoples lived in Edenic isolation from the rest of the world, pelagic Tasadays who know neither colonial and postcolonial domination and exploitation nor violent death, hunger, and environmental degradation. Of course, anthropologists who today task themselves with ethnographic descriptions of self-contained, "primitive" peoples are few, although they continue to provide the public image of the discipline. Far more numerous are those who may acknowledge the centrality of hegemonic core-periphery relationships yet object to using anthropology in ways that might contribute to the empowerment of the oppressed. Perhaps because it is politically incorrect to disdain a concern for empowerment, some of these critics cover their objections to an engaged science by accusing development anthropologists of accelerating the process of incorporation or, worse, of seeking to legitimize it (Escobar 1991; for a critique of Escobar's position, see Little and Painter 1993; for another informed and critical discussion of anthropologists in development, with emphasis on a European perspective, see Hobart 1993).

Despite the protestations of those who elevate nonengagement to the status of scientific and moral imperative, many anthropologists are moving the discipline to a more policy-relevant stance. Of the nineteen largest U.S. departments of anthropology, measured by the awarding of at least seven Ph.D.s in 1993–94 (*1994–1995 Guide to Departments of Anthropology*), all but two list at least one staff member interested in the application of anthropology to issues of socioeconomic development,[3] and their work is widely ventilated in professional fora. Recent meetings of the American Anthropological Association include dozens of sessions exploring findings that give shape to policies dealing with economic development, the environment, health, refugees, ethnicity and conflict,[4] and indigenous peoples, and the association has established official task forces to consider anthropological concerns with resettlement, the environment, human rights, and African hunger. The Washington locale for many of these meetings (e.g., 1993 and 1995) is apt, as Washington houses the World Bank, the Agency for International Development, the Inter-American Development Bank, the World Wildlife Fund, and various other nongovernmental organizations and development consulting groups in which anthropologists have been appointed to career and consultant positions.

Rather than speculate about why the field has moved so markedly in a direction nearly unimaginable twenty years ago when, coincident with the congressional "New Directions" in U.S. foreign economic assistance and the "McNamara Doctrine" at the World Bank, a handful of professionals began labeling themselves *development anthropologists*,[5] I will focus on its importance and on some of its current developments, its shortcomings as well as successes. As will become clearer, I share the sentiments of Paul Sillitoe (1993:597–98), who wrote:

> An important direction that [anthropology] should take is to move more emphatically towards so-called development. . . . While there is an honourable tradition in the subject for the study of development issues . . . , practical engagement with the problems of assisting those we study has never been a fundamental part of the discipline's practice. . . . It is time . . . that the profession actively promoted practical concern for the frequently dire problems facing the human beings taken as anthropology's subject matter.

I read this to mean that it is morally necessary for anthropology to become centrally engaged in today's critical issues—poverty, powerlessness, environmental degradation, and national, class, caste, gender, ethnic, religious, and racial oppression—and that anthropology has important contributions yet to make to debates about the kinds of formations that will characterize human social life in the twenty-first century.

This question is not being raised uniquely in the industrial north. An appeal for a policy-relevant anthropology was made by Abdalla Bujra (1991:20–21), addressing the 1991 meetings of the Council for the Development of Economic and Social Research in Africa (CODESRIA) on "Anthropology and the African Crises":

> [The research of development anthropologists in Africa] is generally linked to projects, dealing directly with contemporary problems affecting people, especially in rural areas. Apart from the scale of research in development anthropology, it is in my opinion substantive, relevant and more likely to yield theoretical tools useful for a better analysis and understanding of contemporary African societies. African anthropologists in their present search for a return or a new start in anthropology should carefully consider development anthropology as an area of entrée.

While anthropologists were prominent in development work in the immediate post–World War II period, when the International Cooperation Agency employed more American anthropologists than any university (Hoben 1982; see also Arensberg and Niehoff 1964), the current receptivity of anthropologists to working in development, and of development professionals to the inclusion of anthropology, can be dated from the early 1970s, coincident with a paradigm shift in the discipline away from cultural relativism, structural-functionalism, and evolutionism toward models informed by political ecology and the political economy of French Marxist sociology.

> The anthropology of the 1970s was better prepared than its predecessors to deal with the dynamism and complexity of rural communities, and with the effects on rural systems of the political economies in which they were enmeshed. While much earlier anthropology emphasized the uniqueness of each cultural situation and its structural stability, anthropologists trained in the 1960s and 1970s were more disposed to see both cross-cultural regularities, allowing for comparison, and internal heterogeneity, conflict, and creativity leading to social change. The ecological perspective in anthropology directed students to explore relations between productive technologies and the environment, and the social, economic, political, and ideological institutions of society. It also facilitated sectoral studies and comparisons, and new specializations became prominent in anthropology, such as river basin development, resettlement, pastoral production systems, artisanal fisheries, and natural resource management. (Horowitz and Painter 1986:2)

As anthropological paradigms were changing, mainstream development thinking also changed. Despite two decades of resource transfers from rich industrial countries to poor agrarian ones, the gap between rich and poor was increasing both between and within countries, and the economies of many poor countries, especially in Africa, but also in Latin America and in Asia, had actually deteriorated. The so-called modernization hypothesis, associated most prominently with economist Walter Rostow (1960), that underdevelopment is an evolutionary stage through which all countries pass on their way to development (which absolves the affluent north from responsibility for the impoverishment of the south), became increasingly suspect,[6] and even some liberal economists became persuaded that a more equitable distribution of income and assets both within and between countries was not only morally desirable but also a necessary condition for sustainable economic health. The notion of equity became enshrined in U.S. law in 1973, when Congress rewrote the Foreign Assistance Act. These "New Directions," as they came to be known, shifted the foreign aid emphasis from the urban industrial sector to the rural agrarian sector and, in the process, created a niche within which the special skills and perspectives of anthropology were sought. Since then the relationship between anthropologists and the other development specialists has hardly been smooth, but it has shown a fairly steady evolution, in which anthropology has become a recurrent component of the development enterprise.

Among the most remarkable changes in the last few years, indeed, largely since my address to the German Ethnological Society in 1989, has been the substantial increase in both the number and, more important, the influence of development anthropologists at that bastion of laissez-faire economics and free market thinking, the World Bank, whose "goals are, as a financial institution, to increase profitability and to promote economic growth in developing countries" (Kardam 1993:1776).

> Sociological issues do not naturally fit into the goals and procedures of the World Bank. Neither have the major donors pressured the Bank to incorporate sociological issues into their operations. Increased profitability as a financial institution and increased economic growth for developing countries (with reliance on the market mechanism) put constraints on the consideration of nonquantifiable issues that do not directly promote "efficiency" and cannot be transformed into cost-benefit ratios. (1777)

In large part the expanded presence of social scientists at the World Bank is due to the persuasive contributions to development debates of Michael Cernea, the Bank's senior advisor for social policy and sociology. While many at the Bank remain skeptical at best and indeed hostile to challenges to what Cernea has termed the centrality of technocratic/ econocratic development, social scientists there are now generally treated as "respected and desirable (although sometimes troublesome!) professionals" (Cernea 1993:1).

> Development is not about commodities. It is not even about new technologies. It is about people and institutions. That is why I think that non-economic social scientists must be present, hand in hand with economists, in the core teams that prepare and design *the*

content of development policies and programs, and that actually manage and monitor the implementation of development projects. (ibid., 2)[7]

The increasing number of anthropologists involved in development activities within major donor organizations may be a cause for celebration, though, given the need for development interventions to be *socially* as well as *environmentally* sustainable, that number remains far too small. In part because the relative number of anthropologists is low compared with that of other development practitioners, it is not at all clear that anthropological participation has made much of a difference on the ground to date;[8] that is, it is often difficult to establish that some measurable portion of sustainable improvements in the well-being of the poor majorities of developing countries is attributable to social scientists, whether at the major multilateral development organization, the World Bank, or at a large bilateral donor such as USAID.[9] Although both have recruited staff with social science training, the two organizations differ in how these persons are employed. Anthropological responsibility at the World Bank is focused *primarily* on social analysis. At AID, which for years had the largest absolute number of anthropologists on its staff, few of them since the 1970s have actually functioned as social scientists, and there is no career track at AID for social science advisors, as there is for economists. On the other hand, through its contracting, grant, and cooperative agreement procedures, AID has been far more supportive than the World Bank of external anthropological research.[10] The critical issue, however, is whether the appointment of anthropologists in a development agency makes much difference in that agency's operations. In what ways have anthropologists working for development organizations helped to empower or otherwise benefit the impoverished and oppressed? Is the action commensurate with the rhetoric?

A systematic assessment of the contributions of anthropologists to development theory, practice, and effectiveness would require substantial financial support and the full cooperation of the scientists and the organizations that employ them. Above all, it would need a rigorous methodology that could disaggregate development activities in which anthropologists played key parts from those in which their contributions were negligible or nonexistent. This chapter merely suggests some of the things that such an assessment might consider.

While the number of anthropologists concerned with development has increased during the twenty years since the congressional New Directions (and the parallel McNamara doctrine at the World Bank) turned development attention toward the rural poor majorities of agrarian countries and thereby widened the niche for anthropological participation, more significant are changes in anthropologists' development roles and in the quality of the contributions many of them have made to anthropological and development understanding. I will outline the most salient of these here, not necessarily in order of importance. The examples cited are merely illustrative; no attempt is made to be comprehensive.

1. Anthropologists provide critical understanding of the nature of development. During the past two decades anthropologists have been prominent among those who have elaborated a systematic critique of the development process, exposing conventional top-down interventions as serving the interests of national and international elites and as further impoverishing the rural majorities of poor countries and degrading their habitats. A number of these critiques were brought together in *Lands at Risk in the Third World* (Little and Horowitz 1987), in which anthropologists with long experience in development reveal the too often socioeconomically and environmentally adverse impacts of externally imposed change in Asia, Africa, and South America. In that collection Jane Collins (1987) demonstrates that, contrary to establishment development opinion, rural households frequently lack sufficient labor properly to use their land. This lack accelerates the cycle of out-migration in search of off-farm employment, furthering resource degradation and impoverishment. The process that Collins terms "semiproletarianization" of the rural poor, in which wage labor is required because of insufficient returns from farming yet does not itself generate enough income for household reproduction, is confirmed by several other contributors to the volume (Little 1987; Horowitz and Salem-Murdock 1987).

Dealing with livestock sector interventions among pastoralists on semiarid rangelands in another collection, I demonstrated the fundamental contradictions between the environmentally sound practices of herders and the destructive interventions imposed by national governments and international donor agencies (Horowitz 1986). I pursued the accusation that "major lenders finance and . . . many African governments accept financing for environmentally and socioeconomically destructive interventions" (1990b:3) by adding the case of tropical river basin development to that of pastoral production systems. In both areas of intervention the interests of remote elites—consumers of cheap meat and cheap electricity—run havoc over the interests of the rural populations and jeopardize their very survival. Thayer Scudder (1981) had long before made the same argument. More recently, Scudder (1990) and I (1989, 1991), looking at instances of river development in the Senegal, Tana, Mahaweli, and Nile basins, showed that the number of stakeholders who are victimized by development may exceed the number of supposed beneficiaries. Our critiques are from outside the development establishment. Working from *inside* the World Bank, Michael Cernea, who authored the Bank's resettlement policy and guidelines (World Bank 1994), led a Bank-wide effort that powerfully exposed that major development organization's involvement in involuntary resettlement.[11] Responding, in part, to the uproar over the Bank's long support for Narmada River Basin Development, including the controversial Sardar Sarovar Dam (Morse and Berger 1992), the Cernea-led effort was perhaps the most comprehensive and useful self-critique ever carried out by a development organization.

Anthropology's principal contributions to development understanding have been to reveal to economists and technical specialists the *expertise* of local peoples, who are the targets and supposedly the beneficiaries of development actions,[12] and to demonstrate the internal complexity and socioeconomic differentiation of local communities that were typically assumed by planners to be homogeneous. Anthropologists have repeatedly demonstrated that pastoral herders are extraordinarily knowledgeable about husbanding livestock on semiarid rangelands, that flood recession cultivators on riverine wetlands are extraordinarily skillful farmers, and so on. This does not mean, of course that there are no improvements to be made; on the contrary, plant genetics and veterinary medicine have a great deal to offer. But their proponents must demonstrate, not merely assume, that what is being introduced is more productive, more income generating, and more sustainable than are the local practices that are being replaced. This is rarely done.

By locating themselves in mediating positions, and by electing to facilitate communication between local communities and outside experts rather than identifying themselves unequivocally with the intervening planners and experts, anthropologists risk being labeled as non–team players whose commitment to the proposed intervention lacks enthusiasm and even belief. But they clearly have going for them the abysmal record of most rural development actions (targeted at the poorest people) that were not based on sound social or ecological understanding.

2. Anthropologists have demonstrated the need for in-depth research and won support for it from development organizations and host governments. Although the typical anthropological association with development involves a relatively brief appraisal or evaluation mission, using methodologies aimed at obtaining a good deal of information in a short time—techniques called "rapid rural appraisal" by those who favor them and "quick and dirty" or "rural development tourism" (Chambers 1983)[13] or even "drive-by anthropology" by those uncomfortable with their tempo—donor agencies are increasingly receptive to supporting long-term social research. AID has been especially supportive of creative research, such as the multiyear studies of floodplain production in Senegal, involuntary resettlement in Mali, periurban agriculture throughout Africa, and potable water use in Tunisia, carried out by the Institute for Development Anthropology (IDA).[14] These research endeavors are multidisciplinary, involving agronomists, hydrologists, engineers, economists, geographers, remote sensing specialists, and others, but they are all directed by anthropologists. The World Bank and United Nations Development Programme (UNDP) supported IDA's study of settlement and land use in the eleven West African countries that participated in the Onchocerciasis (river blindness) Control Programme (OCP). A number of consulting groups were invited to apply, but the award went to a group of anthropologists directed at various stages by David Brokensha and Thayer Scudder. United Nations Development Fund for Women (UNIFEM) and UNDP jointly supported the institute's study of gender relations of pastoral production (Horowitz and Jowkar 1992). A National Science Foundation program director, concerned with why the organization received relatively few proposals for development-oriented research, speculated that development anthropologists have alternative arenas for research funding not enjoyed by other sociocultural anthropologists and so did not need to pursue the long, tedious review process the foundation imposed on proposals.[15]

3. This long-term research has yielded new understanding leading to clear recommendations for development action. Horowitz and Salem-Murdock (1993) have explained how anthropological research in the Middle Senegal Valley generated recommendations for more effective management of the flood regime from the Manantali Dam, recommendations that have been accepted by the Senegal government (Gersar et al. 1991) and the World Bank (Tractebel et al. 1991) and are being considered by the Senegal River Basin Development Authority, the three-

country consortium responsible for managing the dam. According to a representative of German aid (Frechen 1994), "There is already a general consensus about the importance of maintaining artificial floods." Since no hydropower dam anywhere in the world is managed with an augmented flood for the benefit of the downstream ecosystem and smallholder productivity, this is potentially a monumental contribution of anthropology to sustainable and equitable development, and it has clear implications for development in other tropical river basins where flood regimes have been interrupted by dam construction (Hollis et al. 1993:4–5).

In Tunisia, where a study of water use argued that user associations be established at each of a USAID project's thirty new water points, the recommendation was picked up by the Tunisia government, and with support from the German Kreditanstalt für Wiederaufbau (KfW) Tunisia now has more than 1,400 officially recognized potable water user associations. Confronting the government over such issues as financial autonomy, these water user associations are being transformed into instruments of rural democratization (Huxley 1991). Thayer Scudder's long research on involuntary relocation influenced the adoption of resettlement guidelines by the World Bank (Cernea 1988). Long-term research by anthropologists on pastoral management of dry rangelands—combined, to be fair, with unusually unsuccessful development agency interventions in the pastoral livestock sector—largely gave the quietus to "tragedy of the commons" attempts to divide and privatize pastures, sedentarize herders, and force mandatory stock reductions (Horowitz and Little 1987). The Land Settlement Review (McMillan et al. 1990) yielded clear recommendations for sustainable settlement and land use in the OCP areas, which the UNDP presented to a ministerial meeting in Paris in April 1994.

4. Anthropologists are increasingly assuming team leadership (chief of party/task manager) positions on multi-disciplinary teams. When the niche opened for anthropologists twenty years ago, our involvement was largely restricted to preparing project social analysis appendices to reports written by other specialists. These appendices, cosmetic responses to requirements, rarely influenced implementation, which was shaped, rather, by the work of economists and such technical specialists as agronomists and veterinarians. In the 1960s, 1970s, and 1980s, when anthropologists were occasionally chiefs of party on project implementation—Jon Moris in Tanzania, David Gow in Zaire, and Max Goldensohn in Mauritania—where their assumed cultural and linguistic

expertise was considered important, they almost never led appraisal or evaluation missions. Today it is not at all uncommon for an anthropologist to lead a team composed of economists and other technical specialists, because not only is cultural expertise desired, but it is increasingly recognized that anthropologists, by virtue of the holistic focus of their discipline, are often best able to *integrate* the various specialist reports into a coherent set of recommendations for action. Thayer Scudder, for example, recently led a World Conservation Union (IUCN) team assessing land and water management in the Okavango Delta, Botswana, and that work is influencing development policies in this unique wetland. The IDA activities in Tunisia and Senegal, noted earlier, called for inputs from hydrologists, hydrogeologists, agronomists, soil scientists, and remote sensing specialists, who reported to the anthropologists directing the work. In 1993 anthropologist Stephen Reyna was the leader of an International Fund for Agricultural Development team, consisting also of an entomologist, hydrogeologist, and economist, that evaluated a Food and Agriculture Organization of the United Nations (FAO) Oasis Rehabilitation project in Mauritania. This centrality of anthropology at various points in the project cycle may be a step toward the achievement of a people-focused development that is rare in traditional econocratic and technocratic efforts.

5. The recent sensitivity to environmental issues and sustainability has created an active alliance between anthropologists and some biophysical ecologists. One consequence is that such major environmental NGOs as the World Wildlife Fund and IUCN (van den Oever 1993) have begun to appoint *social* scientists to their core staffs. Linking poverty alleviation and environmental sustainability is potentially an enormously powerful and productive collaboration, because "both poverty and resource abuse are caused by policies and actions that seek rapid returns on investments. . . . No solution to the environmental crises will be forthcoming . . . if . . . projects exclude local populations in their identification, design, implementation, and evaluation" (Horowitz 1987:2), and it is exactly the task of the anthropologist to ensure that the political ecological realities facing local populations effectively inform every stage of the project cycle. At the World Bank the most persuasive arguments for a socially just development that repudiates supply-side and trickle-down economics are articulated by its senior environmental advisors, who conclude:

Political will is the scarcest resource. It is very difficult to face up to the need for income redistribution and population stability. If the concept of environmental sustainability becomes a verbal formula for glossing over these harsh realities, then its very conception will have been a big step backwards. Markets, for example, will have to learn to function without expansion, without wars, without wastes, and without advertising that encourages waste. . . . Reduction of poverty and inequality is essential to environmental sustainability— to saving our global life support systems. (Goodland and Daly 1993:29)

It would be imprudent to exaggerate the impact on World Bank lending, but it is interesting to see how far the rhetoric has shifted from the days when its President A. W. Clausen saw poverty as the independent variable causing environmental degradation rather than both being consequences of exploitative economies.

If growth was the buzzword of the 1960s and equity that of the 1970s and early 1980s, today's development liturgy invokes above all the notion of "sustainability." Perhaps the most important contribution now being made by anthropologists is the recurrent demonstration that environmental sustainability in development cannot be achieved independently of or in opposition to the interests of the rural poor. Environmentally sound development must be predicated on increased real income for small producers. Anthropologists can help plan, design, implement, and assess programs and projects that sustainably enhance *both* the habitat and the economic status of the largest number of persons. So long as wealth continues to be appropriated from the poor in as gross disproportion as it is in most parts of the world today, they will be unable to make the investments in land, labor, and capital that will help reverse the rapid deterioration of environmental conditions: watershed degradation, soil loss, deforestation, overgrazing, and overfishing. On the other hand, given the new global centrality of environmental thinking caused by fears of the greenhouse effect and ozone depletion, anthropologists need to remind listeners that the bulk of such massive degradation finds its origin in the practices and policies of the industrial north, in both market and former socialist economies, and not in the agrarian economies of the south.

Sustainable improvements in the environmental health of the earth require prior and parallel improvements in the economic health of the poor, especially the agrarian proletariat and smallholder farmers, fishers, and herders. Most senior development officials still do not understand that environmental degradation is not a problem of the relationship between people and their habitats but, rather, of relationships *among* peoples competing for access to productive resources. This competition will not be resolved by introducing specific *environmental* projects, such as biodiversity reserves from which people are excluded, any more than so-called *women's* projects, like teaching mothers to sew at home, resolved gender inequities in income distribution. The greening of the development establishment will require special efforts from anthropologists to contribute to understanding the causes of, and therefore the solutions to, the declining capacity of earth to sustain life. Since that declining capacity is vested in the acquisitive behavior of the powerful, in greed, the task is not at all easy. But no task is more worthwhile for our discipline.

6. Anthropological inputs, until recently limited to appraisal and evaluation, are increasingly being sought across the full project cycle, although the process of full participation is slow and often awkward. When anthropological inputs were locked uniquely into *ex post* or *ex ante* assessments, the social analyst, often recruited from outside the funding organization, was almost inevitably forced into an adversarial relationship with the proposed or completed activity. Cernea (1993:14–15) provides a view from the optic of the World Bank:

> The conventional entry points into development planning for sociologists and anthropologists have traditionally been very narrow, constraining, and Procrustean-like. We have learned in our daily work at the World Bank that the range of entry points for sociology clearly can and must be broadened. This is probably true for bilateral agencies as well, and for the work of in-house sociologists in various government agencies. But such broadening and multiplication of "entry points" is not a gift that will be graciously handed over to sociologists in a neatly tied package. . . . [D]emand will probably increase, gradually, as frustrated development practitioners seek new approaches and ideas. But social scientists could do a lot more than we are doing now by adopting a pro-active rather than an expectant stand, taking initiative, expanding the supply of knowledge, and putting forward our analytical and social-construction

skills. This way, a *supply driven strategy* can accelerate the use of social science in planning induced development.

Cernea answers those who suggest that sociological input is a luxury unaffordable in times of declining funding for foreign aid, by pointing out that World Bank interventions that had significant social analyses achieved an average 18.5 percent rate of return, whereas those without such inputs achieved an average less than half that rate (15–16). This is a key point at the World Bank, because it and the other multilateral development lending organizations—such as the Inter-American, African, and Asian Development Banks and the new European Bank for Reconstruction and Development—are first and foremost *banks,* and their success is measured by positive returns on investment. These returns, positive or negative, go to the borrowing country. The bank's return is fixed: it is the interest on the loan.[16]

The proactive stance that Cernea implores us to take, it seems to me, implies the need to provide policy makers with relevant recommendations for action based on scientifically sound analyses and to celebrate our successes not only through fora that preach to the already saved but also at meetings and seminars and in publications aimed at nonanthropological audiences. *World Development* is one of the most progressive journals read by the development community. In recent months articles have appeared dealing with such heartland anthropological issues as the conditions for pastoral transhumance and floodplain production systems in Nigeria and in Bangladesh. These were very good articles. Yet they were not written by anthropologists. In *Foreign Affairs* a debate raged over the political implications of ethnicity, yet anthropologists, who are supposed to be expert, were singularly absent in the discussions. On the other hand, our own journals, interesting as they may be, too often reaffirm rather than falsify the stereotypic image of the anthropologist as self-indulgent manipulator of ethnographic trivia or ego-tripper in other people's communities.

Of course, anthropological input in policy debates does not automatically ensure a more enlightened discussion. A peculiarly unfortunate intrusion of some anthropologists is in the debate on U.S. immigration policy. An organization called Population-Environment Balance (P-EB), whose journal is edited by an anthropologist, claims "a national commitment to a population policy that will foster a stable population, a strong economy, sustainable resource use, and an ecologically healthful environment for all Americans." It proposes to reverse domestic environmental degradation by an ecologically justified closed-door policy:

> a *Fremdenfeindlichkeit* that echoes some of the ugliest ethnocentrism of the twentieth century. The group lobbies against legislation allowing immigrants to settle in the United States, and it opposes the entry even of those who are the innocent targets of ethnic violence in other parts of the world, unless they are balanced by a commensurate emigration. "With unemployment already a serious problem in this country, and with recession impending, it does not make sense to continue to import even more competition for our own citizens, who are already unemployed or underemployed" (*Balance Report* 68:7, December 1990). Beyond its indictment of immigration for creating economic competition, P-EB points to immigration as the principal element in population growth in the United States: "While the U.S. contains only about 5% of the world's population, it uses disproportionately large amounts of the world's resources. . . . Thus, stopping population growth in the United States is essential if we are to protect both the United States' and the world's environment" (*Balance Data* 27:2, May 1990). (Brokensha et al. 1992:2–3)

By naively dividing resource use by total population, P-EB ignores the fact that consumption in the United States is driven by affluent greed rather than by the meager demands of the poor and unemployed—that is, the classes in which recent immigrants to the United States are overwhelmingly located. P-EB acknowledges with regret that its anti–immigrant stand could be interpreted as racist. And indeed it is. "By ignoring the relevance of equitable access as the key to sustainable resource use, and targeting immigrants few of whom are western Europeans, P-EB does appear to adopt a racist perspective, blaming the poor, who are far more the victims of environmental abuse than they are its cause" (ibid., 3).

The effectiveness of anthropology's contributions to development is being made even more difficult by the shift in the development agenda once again to macroeconomics. While the GNP has not (yet?) resumed its centrality as *the* measure of economic development, the current "policy-based lending" dialogue espoused by various macroeconomists at multilateral and bilateral development funding institutions is shored up by "cross-conditionality," in which recipient countries must, for example, agree to a World Bank–imposed structural adjustment austerity program to remain eligible for grants and loans from other donors. This austerity program invariably calls for decreases in public sector investment, subsidies, and employment, accompanied by currency devaluation, "privatization" across a variety of sectors, trade "liberalization"—providing, for example, for the expatriation of profits by foreign firms—and program, rather than project, funding. This is unfamiliar ground to many anthropologists. At just the time when we are most critically needed, when modest though increasing numbers of anthropologists in many countries are appropriately trained to work in development, the shift back to top-down planning and trickle-down economics threatens once again to marginalize us.

The threat is more explicitly made in the report of the Bretton Woods Commission (1994), also known as the "Volker report" after its convener, Paul A. Volker. Seeking a new orientation for the International Monetary Fund and the World Bank as they face their second half-century, the report recommends that the bank reduce its activities that involve lending to developing *countries:* "The Bank Group must change the way it does business, emphasizing its role as a mobilizer of resources—private and public, intellectual and financial—and not as a lender of money to governments."

> The World Bank should shift much more of its activity toward its private sector-oriented subsidiaries, the IFC [International Finance Corporation] and MIGA [Multilateral Investment Guarantee Agency], encourage investments through greater use of co-financing guarantees and innovative financing techniques, and consistently support private sector development with assistance strategies that encourage privatization, financial sector reform and creation of appropriate institutional and regulatory frameworks. (Bretton Woods Commission 1994:2)

Those areas of the World Bank that are not specifically focused on the "private sector" should "significantly cut staff." Since neither the IFC nor the MIGA has shown much enthusiasm for the imposition of environmental, gender, indigenous peoples, poverty, governance, or human rights criteria in lending, and neither has shown much inclination to add social and environmental scientists to its staff, the shift recommended by the Bretton Woods Commission risks reversing such progress in these areas as has been achieved by the World Bank during the last decade.

Again I do not mean to exaggerate the World Bank's commitment to operationalizing these issues. As far as human rights are concerned, they command at best an ambivalent interest among the major development organizations and the Western industrial economies whose governments support them. Referring to constraints in its *Articles of Agreement*, the bank is loath to interfere with the "internal affairs" of borrowing states unless it can be shown that their policies are economically counterproductive (Shihata 1993a, b). Gender oppression did not become a matter of mainstream concern until the economic costs of denying women full social participation were demonstrated. Since few other development professionals seem to be focusing broadly on human rights, it is the obligation of anthropologists to seize these issues and move them from the margins to the center of development discussion. Retreats from human rights in international affairs by the past three U.S. administrations reverberate in international organizations, in which human rights matters risk being even further marginalized.[17] Anthropology, which (perhaps more than any other discipline) displays both scientific and moral obligations to protest human rights violations, has a strong contribution to make in advocating a more proactive adoption of human rights criteria by development organizations (see Messer, chapter 6, this volume).

Anthropologists can help ensure that a new development agenda will be based on respect for human as well as for natural resources, that it will not contribute to the degradation of human beings through poverty and oppression, any more than it will contribute to a degradation of natural resources. A critical focus for anthropologists is to continue to work toward the empowerment of local communities, including women, men, and children who are economically, socially, and politically deprived. As I have argued:

> empowerment is not inherently more expensive, even in the short run, than the approach now ventilated in the halls of major multilateral financing institutions, an approach that seems to be based on a kind of weariness with the poor and with poverty's claim on the development dollar. . . . Anthropologists can demonstrate that because it leads to sustainability, [empowerment] is less expensive.
> In any case, it is urgent that we confront the issue. The risk is not

only a declining participation of anthropology in development, but, and more importantly, a reduced voice of advocacy for a development that is cost beneficial, sustainable, and promotes genuine growth with social justice. (Horowitz 1988:3)

In this chapter I have looked uniquely at American anthropology. That focus, as the quotation from Abdalla Bujra clearly indicates, is much too narrow. To achieve the goal of sustainable, cost beneficial, and socially just development, we can no longer afford the luxury of being nationally bounded social scientists. We need to form global alliances in the search for collaborative actions that transcend geographic, cultural, and linguistic frontiers as we are learning to transcend conventional disciplinary boundaries in the universities. As development anthropologists, we need especially to encourage the expansion of the field in developing countries and to be ready to withdraw where local people's capacities emerge to assume responsibility and ownership over their own development programs. In such a way anthropology will become, as Claude Meillassoux has challenged it to do, an instrument of justice and freedom (1981:x).

NOTES

Parts of this chapter were drawn from an address to the German Ethnological Society in Marburg, October 1989; most of the ideas emerged from conversations with colleagues at the Institute for Development Anthropology and at the World Bank, where I held a Visiting Research Fellowship, January–July 1994, and with graduate students at Binghamton University. I am especially grateful to Michael Cernea, Sarah Forster, Nicole Glineur, David Gow, Forouz Jowkar, Shem Migot-Adholla, Emilio Moran, Tjaart Schillhorn Van Veen, and David Steeds for their critical comments on the chapter in draft. A version of this chapter was published in *Development Anthropology Network* 12(1–2) (1994):1–14, under the title "Development Anthropology in the Mid-1990s."

1. For the first thirty years or so since their founding, action and discourse especially at the International Monetary Fund and the multilateral development banks and at some of the major bilateral official development aid organizations such as the Japanese International Cooperation Agency was controlled by economists. Some organizations within the United Nations system (UNIFEM, UNICEF, UNESCO, ILO, and, more recently, UNDP itself) were more receptive than the banks to including "noneconomic" criteria in their programs, despite what Kardam (1993:1774) refers to as the "wide circle of accountability" that constrains their ability to act autonomously. That is, they are governed by the principle of one member equals one vote, unlike the banks, where voting is

proportional to the member states' contributions. Among bilateral development agencies the Canadian, Scandinavian, and Dutch appear to be particularly sensitive to social factors.

2. While Boasian anthropologists who studied Native Americans during the twentieth century, such as Lowie (1935), ignored the colonial context of the reservations on which they worked, their nineteenth-century predecessors, such as James Mooney (1965), were very much involved in analyzing that context.

3. Boston and Colorado each count three development anthropologists, Michigan lists four, Florida and City University of New York list five each, Harvard lists six, and Binghamton University (SUNY) claims seven.

4. Consideration by anthropologists of the salience of ethnicity in organizing political action in postcolonial and post-Soviet states is welcome and overdue, and Nancie Gonzalez, who organized the session at the 1993 meetings, does an important service by confronting a major lacuna in the contribution of anthropology to public policy concerns. Curiously, there has been relatively little anthropological exploration of our central concepts of "culture" and "ethnicity" as they relate to the political arena, and most recent work has been carried out by practitioners of other disciplines. Political scientist Samuel Huntington quotes Jacques Delors, president of the European Economic Community: "future conflicts will be sparked by cultural factors rather than economics or ideology" (1993:194). One does not have to embrace Huntington's politics to acknowledge the theoretical centrality that he and many other political scientists accord to notions of culture and ethnicity, and one might well query the recurrent anthropological imperviousness to appreciating that ethnicity may have territorial dimensions and aspirations.

5. To give liberal economics its due, I suspect that a good deal of the growth in university offerings in development anthropology is demand driven by students, many of whom have Peace Corps, NGO, or developing country experience and seek training in development anthropology to qualify for positions with nonacademic institutions prepared to employ them.

6. Parts of the hypothesis, wedded to a resuscitation of McClelland's (1961) concept of "achievement motivation," have been revived by Lawrence Harrison, a former USAID mission director with a good deal of Latin American experience, who privileges an inherent predisposition to entrepreneurial behavior as *the* critical causal factor explaining relative levels of development: "the cultural pathology of underdevelopment is a vital backdrop for this book, in which the principal objectives are to develop a better appreciation of the array of factors that have contributed to national and ethnic group *success;* the relative importance of cultural factors, traditional or recent; what those cultural factors are; the way they may have changed; and the way they have promoted progress or stood in its way" (1992:21).

7. Cernea's bracketing of *social scientist* with *noneconomic* is a shorthand usage in the context of the World Bank. Much of what anthropologists do in development is indeed economic—that is, analyses of the allocation of land, labor, and capital to commodity production, distribution, and consumption but

in areas largely ignored by economists. The Institute for Development Anthropology's Senegal River Basin Monitoring Activity was persuasive in large part because it provided hard field data on economic decision making at the level of the rural production unit (Horowitz and Salem-Murdock 1990; Salem-Murdock and Niasse 1993). These data on yields per unit capital and per unit labor, in addition to those per unit land, were absent in earlier economic appraisals of irrigation projects in the region carried out by various bilateral and multilateral development financing agencies.

8. "Social analysis may be included in the Bank operations manual but that does not necessarily mean that implementation will take place with attention to its stipulations. . . . The emphasis on the timely delivery of projects and the pressure on staff members to get a certain number of projects approved in a given amount of time also both act as disincentives for the consideration of sociocultural issues" (Kardam 1993:1778).

9. According to the *Economist*, "AID and the World Bank are unusual (although their critics rarely admit as much) in their openness and in the rigor with which they try to evaluate what they do" (7 May 1994, 19). Surely the social scientists within each of these agencies are at least partly responsible for both the internal critiques and the rigor with which they are carried out.

10. An interesting arena for anthropological involvement is in the various international agricultural research institutes focused on improving on-farm productivity primarily in developing countries, where "social scientists [doubtless including economists] comprise close to 15 percent of the senior staff" (Collinson and Platais 1994:xi). These centers, supported by the Consultative Group on International Agricultural Research (CGIAR), which provided the basic research in plant genetics that led to the Green Revolution, became active in what used to be called "farming systems research." One of the contributors to the report noted that social scientists have so "broad a canvas on which to work . . . [that] it is thus not surprising that they have contributed so strongly—and perhaps increasingly—within the agricultural research community. The main surprise is that it took as long as it did for their potential contributions to be recognized and implemented" (Anderson 1994:88).

11. In a widely circulated letter to U.S. treasury secretary Lloyd Bentsen (22 April 1994) on the occasion of this report's publication, sixteen policy NGOs in the environmental and human rights fields, including Friends of the Earth, Greenpeace-U.S., and the Sierra Club, indicate their fear that, rather than limiting bank support for involuntary relocation, this document will lead to more forced movements of people and to the possible creation of a "resettlement industry." In a separate statement *International Rivers Network* issued a "Manibel Declaration" calling for a total cessation of World Bank funding of large dams: "The Bank's own 1994 Resettlement and Development review admits that the vast majority of women, men and children evicted by Bank-funded projects never regained their former incomes nor received any direct benefits from the dams for which they were forced to sacrifice their homes and land. The Bank has consistently failed to implement and enforce its own policy on forced

resettlement" (1 June 1994). For a powerful critique of the World Bank's adverse actions on the environment and its failure to achieve poverty alleviation, see Rich 1994.

12. An excellent periodical source of information on local expertise is *Indigenous Knowledge and Development Monitor,* published three times a year in the Netherlands.

13. Chambers enthusiastically embraces the approach known as "participatory rural appraisal," which emerges from rapid rural appraisal but differs from it in that "more of the activities previously appropriated by outsiders are instead carried out by local rural or urban people themselves" (1994:953).

14. Repeated references to work carried out by persons associated with the Institute for Development Anthropology (IDA) in this essay reflect only the author's familiarity. No comparison with other organizations is implied. Many other groups—university, nonprofit, and commercial—have also undertaken long-term anthropological field research with support from AID and other development financing organizations.

15. This is not quite sufficient an explanation, as funders of development research often impose review procedures that are at least as cumbersome as those of scientific foundations. Baba doubts that NSF is at all receptive to proposals from practitioners: "An additional barrier to the theoretical contribution of applied research . . . may be the lack of support for [it] by traditional anthropological funding agencies (e.g., National Science Foundation, Wenner-Gren Foundation). Such agencies are in a good position to encourage and promote a productive relationship between theory and application. The fact that they generally do not do so means that applied anthropologists must turn to other sponsors" (1994:182).

16. While the International Development Association, the World Bank's "soft-loan window," open to its poorest borrowers, is funded by contributions from high-income member countries, the bulk of the bank's funding is raised through the sale of bonds in international capital markets.

17. According to Nüket Kardam, "The World Bank would be more likely to respond to new issues if major donors recommended that the Bank pay attention to them" (1993:1777). It seems that the bank is reluctant to lead on issues that its principal shareholders themselves eschew.

REFERENCES

Anderson, Jock
    1994   Social Science in Agricultural Research: Implications and Issues for IARCs. In *Social Science in the CGIAR,* ed. Michael P. Collinson and Kerri Wright Platais, 88–104. Proceedings of a Meeting of CGIAR Social Scientists, International Service for National Agricultural Research (ISNAR), The Hague, August 1992. CGIAR Study Paper no. 28. Washington, D.C.: World Bank.

Arensberg, Conrad M., and Arthur Niehoff
  1964 *Introducing Social Change.* Chicago: Aldine.
Baba, Marietta L.
  1994 The Fifth Subdiscipline: Anthropological Practice and the Future of Anthropology. *Human Organization* 53(2): 174–86.
Bretton Woods Commission
  1994 Bretton Woods: Looking to the Future. Commission Report, Staff Review, and Background Papers. Bretton Woods Commission, Washington, D.C.
Brokensha, David, Michael Horowitz, and Thayer Scudder
  1992 Antipastoralism, Ethnic Cleansing, and Wearing the Green: An Editorial. *Development Anthropology Network* 10(2): 1–3.
Bujra, Abdalla S.
  1991 Anthropology and the African Crises: Challenging the Dilemma. Paper presented at the "Anthropology in Africa: Past, Present and Emerging Visions" workshop, Council for the Development of Economic and Social Research in Africa, Dakar, Senegal, 11–13 November.
Cernea, Michael M.
  1988 *Involuntary Resettlement in Development Projects: Policy Guidelines in World Bank Financed Projects.* Washington, D.C.: World Bank.
  1993 Sociological Work within a Development Agency: Experiences in the World Bank. Unpublished manuscript.
Chambers, Robert
  1983 *Rural Development: Putting the Last First.* Harlow: Longman.
  1994 The Origins and Practice of Participatory Rural Appraisal. *World Development* 22(7): 953–69.
Collins, Jane L.
  1987 Labor Scarcity and Ecological Change. In *Lands at Risk in the Third World: Local-Level Perspectives,* ed. P. D. Little and M. M. Horowitz, 19–37. Boulder, Colo.: Westview Press.
Collinson, Michael P., and Kerri Wright Platais, eds.
  1994 *Social Science in the CGIAR.* Proceedings of a meeting of CGIAR Social Scientists, International Service for National Agricultural Research (ISNAR), The Hague, August 1992. CGIAR Study Paper no. 28. Washington, D.C.: World Bank.
Colson, Elizabeth
  1989 Overview. In *Annual Review of Anthropology,* ed. B. J. Siegel, 1–16. Palo Alto, Calif.: Annual Reviews.
Economist
  1994 Foreign Aid: The Kindness of Strangers. 7 May, 19–22.
Escobar, Arturo
  1991 Anthropology and the Development Encounter: The Making and Marketing of Development Anthropology. *American Ethnologist* 18(4): 658–82.

Frechen, Dr.
   1994 Communication to the World Bank. In response to a draft Mauritania Country Environmental Strategy Paper from German Kreditanstalt für Wiederaufbau (KfW). 24 March.
Gersar/CACG, Euroconsult, Sir Alexander Gibb and Partners, and SONED-Afrique
   1991 Plan Directeur de Développement Integré pour la Rive Gauche de la Vallée du Fleuve Sénégal. Final report. Dakar, Ministry of Planning and Cooperation, Senegal.
Goodland, Robert, and Herman Daly
   1993 Poverty Alleviation Is Essential for Environmental Sustainability. Divisional Working Paper no. 1993–42. Environment Department, Environmental Economics and Pollution Division, World Bank, Washington, D.C.
Harrison, Lawrence E.
   1992 *Who Prospers? How Cultural Values Shape Economic and Political Success.* New York: Basic Books.
Hobart, Mark, ed.
   1993 *An Anthropological Critique of Development: The Growth of Ignorance.* London and New York: Routledge.
Hoben, Allen
   1982 Anthropologists and Development. In *Annual Review of Anthropology*, vol. 11, ed. B. J. Siegel, A. R. Beals, and S. A. Tyler, 349–75. Palo Alto, Calif.: Annual Reviews.
Hollis, G. E., W. M. Adams, and M. Aminu-Kano
   1993 The Hadejia-Nguru Wetlands: Environment, Economy and Sustainable Development of a Sahelian Floodplain Wetland. Gland, Switz.: International Union for the Conservation of Nature and Natural Resources.
Horowitz, Michael M.
   1986 Ideology, Policy, and Praxis in Pastoral Livestock Development. In *Anthropology and Rural Development in West Africa*, ed. M. M. Horowitz and T. M. Painter, 251–72. Boulder, Colo.: Westview Press.
   1987 Destructive Development. *Development Anthropology Network* 5(1): 1–3.
   1988 Anthropology and the New Development Agenda. *Development Anthropology Network* 6(1): 1–4.
   1989 Victims of Development. *Development Anthropology Network* 7(2): 1–8.
   1990a Development Anthropology in the United States. In *Ethnologische Beiträge zur Entwicklungspolitik 2*, ed. Frank Bliss and Michael Schönhuth, 189–204. Bonn: Beiträge zur Kulturkunde 14.
   1990b Donors and Deserts: The Political Ecology of Destructive Development in the Sahel. In *African Food Systems in Crisis, part 2: Contend-*

ing with Change, ed. R. Huss-Ashmore and S. H. Katz, 3–28. New York: Gordon and Breach.
1991 Victims Upstream and Down: The 1991 Elizabeth Colson Lecture. *Journal of Refugee Studies* 4(2): 164–81.

Horowitz, Michael M., and Forouz Jowkar
1992 Pastoral Women and Change in Africa, the Middle East, and Central Asia. Working Paper no. 91, Institute for Development Anthropology, Binghamton, N.Y.

Horowitz, Michael M., and Peter D. Little
1987 African Pastoralism and Poverty: Some Implications for Drought and Famine. In *Drought and Hunger in Africa: Denying Famine a Future,* ed. M. Glantz, 52–82. Cambridge: Cambridge University Press.

Horowitz, Michael M., and Thomas M. Painter
1986 Introduction: Anthropology and Development. In *Anthropology and Rural Development in West Africa,* ed. Michael M. Horowitz and Thomas M. Painter, 1–8. Boulder, Colo.: Westview Press.

Horowitz, Michael M., and Munecra Salem-Murdock
1987 The Political Economy of Desertification in White Nile Province, Sudan. In *Lands at Risk in the Third World: Local-Level Perspectives,* ed. P. D. Little and M. M Horowitz, 95–111. Boulder, Colo.: Westview Press.
1990 The Senegal River Basin Monitoring Activity: Phase I Synthesis. Binghamton, N.Y.: Institute for Development Anthropology.
1993 Development-Induced Food Insecurity in the Middle Senegal Valley. *GeoJournal* 30(2): 179–84.

Huntington, Samuel P.
1993 If Not Civilizations, What? Paradigms of the Post–Cold War World. *Foreign Affairs* 72(5): 186–94.

Huxley, Frederick C.
1991 Drinking-Water Projects in Rural Tunisia: More Democratic Control of a Local Resource? Unpublished manuscript.

Kardam, Nüket
1993 Development Approaches and the Role of Policy Advocacy: The Case of the World Bank. *World Development* 21(11): 1773–86.

Little, Peter D.
1987 Land Use Conflicts in the Agricultural/Pastoral Borderlands: The Case of Kenya. In *Lands at Risk in the Third World: Local-Level Perspectives,* ed. Peter D. Little and Michael M Horowitz, 195–212. Boulder, Colo.: Westview Press.

Little, Peter D., and Michael M. Horowitz, eds.
1987 *Lands at Risk in the Third World: Local-Level Perspectives.* Boulder, Colo.: Westview Press.

Little, Peter D., and Michael Painter
1993 Discourse, Politics, and the Development Process: Reflections on

"Anthropology and the Development Encounter" by Arturo Escobar. Paper presented at the Panel on Development Anthropology, Discourses and Praxis, American Anthropological Association 1993 annual meeting, Washington, D.C.

Lowie, Robert
    1935   *The Crow Indians.* New York: Farrar and Rinehart.

McClelland, David
    1961   *The Achieving Society.* Princeton, N.J.: Van Nostrand.

McMillan, Della, Thomas Painter, and Thayer Scudder
    1990   Settlement and Development in the River Blindness Control Zone. World Bank Technical Paper no. 192. Washington, D.C.: World Bank.

Meillassoux, Claude
    1981   *Maidens, Meal, and Money.* Cambridge: Cambridge University Press.

Mooney, James
    1965   *The Ghost Dance Religion and the Sioux Outbreak of 1890.* Chicago: University of Chicago Press.

Morse, Bradford, and Thomas R. Berger
    1992   Sardar Sarovar: The Report of the Independent Review. Ottawa: Resource Futures International.

Rich, Bruce
    1994   *Mortgaging the Earth: The World Bank, Environmental Impoverishment, and the Crisis of Development.* Boston: Beacon Press.

Rostow, Walter
    1960   *The Stages of Economic Growth: A Non-Communist Manifesto.* Cambridge: Cambridge University Press.

Salem-Murdock, Muneera, and Madiodio Niasse
    1993   *Senegal River Basin Monitoring Activity II: Final Report.* Binghamton, N.Y.: Institute for Development Anthropology.

Scudder, Thayer
    1981   What It Means to Be Dammed: The Anthropology of Large-Scale Development Projects in the Tropics and Subtropics. *Engineering and Science* 54(4): 9–15.
    1990   Victims of Development Revisited: The Political Costs of River Basin Development. *Development Anthropology Network* 8(1): 1–5.

Shihata, Ibrahim F. I.
    1993a   Legal Aspects of Involuntary Population Resettlement. In *Anthropological Approaches to Resettlement: Policy, Practice, and Theory,* ed. Michael M. Cernea and Scott E. Guggenheim, 39–54. Boulder, Colo.: Westview Press.
    1993b   The World Bank and the Promotion of Human Rights. Paper presented at the World Human Rights Conference, Vienna, 14–25 June.

Sillitoe, Paul
    1993   Comment: The Development of Anthropology. *Man,* n.s. 28(3): 597–98.

Tractebel, Hydro-Québec International, Dessau, and Electricité de France
  1991 Projet Manantali Energie: Etude Economique Complémentaire du Réseau 225 kV Associé à la Centrale. Rapport de Phase 3, vol. 1. Washington, D.C.: Industry and Energy Department, World Bank.

van den Oever, Pietronella
  1993 Women's Roles, Population Issues, Poverty, and Environmental Degradation. In *Women and Children First: Environment, Poverty, and Sustainable Development,* ed. F. C. Steady, 111–27. Rochester, Vt.: Schenkman Books.

Wolf, Eric
  1982 *Europe and the People without History.* Berkeley: University of California Press.

World Bank
  1994 *Resettlement and Development: Bankwide Review of Projects Involving Involuntary Resettlement, 1986–1993.* Washington, D.C.: World Bank.

Contributors

Elizabeth Colson is Professor Emeritus, University of California–Berkeley. Her major research involvement over the past forty years has been with the longitudinal study of social change centering on Gwembe District, Zambia, shared with Thayer Scudder of the California Institute of Technology. Recent publications include *For Prayer and Profit* (1988); *The History of Nampeyo* (1992); "Reflections on Fifty Years of Social Anthropology and the Role of the Wenner-Gren Foundation," report of the Wenner-Gren Foundation, fiftieth anniversary issue (1991); "Conflict and Violence," in *The Paths to Domination, Resistance and Terror*, ed. C. Nordstrom and J. Martin (1992).

Timothy J. Finan is Director of the Bureau of Applied Research in Anthropology at the University of Arizona. He has worked extensively in Africa and Latin America, where his interests include the impacts of structural adjustment policy reform on traditional communities, food policy analysis, food security systems, markets, natural resource use, and farming systems research. He has recently completed a book on agriculture and natural resource management on the Cape Verde Islands.

Julie Fisher is Visiting Professor at the Program on Non-Profit Organizations, Yale University, and the author of *The Road to Rio: Sustainable Development and Non-Governmental Movement in the Third World* (1993). She is also an independent development consultant who has worked for UNICEF, Save the Children, Interaction, World Vision, Lutheran World Relief, Technoserve, and CARE. She received her doctorate in comparative politics from Johns Hopkins School of Advanced International Studies.

Michael M. Horowitz is Professor of Anthropology, State University of New York–Binghamton and Director of the Institute for Development Anthropology. Focused on the intersection of environment, development, and human rights, his research deals with the social organization of resource management, in association with World Bank, the United Nations Development Programme, the U.N. Development Fund for Women, the U.N. Environmental Program, the International Fund for Agricultural Development, the Food and Agricultural Organization, and the Agency for International Development. He is the author, coauthor, or coeditor of the following: *Morne-Paysan: Peasant Village in Martinique*, *Peoples and Cultures of the Caribbean*, *Manga of Niger*, *Anthropology and Rural Development in West Africa*, *Lands at Risk in the Third World*, *Anthropology and Rural Development in North Africa and the Middle East,* and *Pastoral Women and Change in Africa, the Middle East, and Central Asia*. He wrote and directed the documentary film *Large Dams and Small People: Management of an African River*.

Conrad Phillip Kottak is Professor of Anthropology at the University of Michigan, where he has taught since 1968. He has conducted fieldwork in cultural anthropology in Brazil, Madagascar, and the United States. His general interests are in processes by which local cultures are incorporated into larger systems. This interest links earlier work on ecology and state formation in Africa and Madagascar to his more recent research on global change, economic development, national and international culture, and mass media. Currently he is directing research projects investigating "The Emergence of Ecological Awareness in Brazil," "Deforestation in Relation to Variant Land-Use Patterns in Madagascar," and "Strategies for Participatory Development in Northern Brazil." He was chair of the General Anthropology Division of the American Anthropological Association from 1990 to 1992.

Ellen Messer is Director of the World Hunger Program at Brown University. Her interests are in anthropology and human rights, the future of food and hunger, religions and complex societies, and the history of nutrition policy. Her recent publications include "Overview," "Food Wars: Hunger as a Weapon of War in 1993," "The International Conference on Nutrition: Historical Perspectives and Prospects," *The Hunger Report: 1993*; and "Anthropology and Human Rights," *Annual Review of Anthropology: 1993*.

Emilio F. Moran is the Rudy Professor of Anthropology and Director of the Anthropological Center for Training and Research on Global Environmental Change (ACT) at Indiana University, Bloomington. He is a specialist in ecological anthropology, resource management, and agricultural systems in the humid and dry tropics. He is author of *Human Adaptability: An Introduction to Ecological Anthropology*, *Developing the Amazon*, and *Through Amazonian Eyes: The Human Ecology of Amazonian Populations*. He chaired the Panel on Social Transformations and is currently chair of the American Anthropological Association's Task Force on the Environment.

Demitri B. Shimkin was Professor Emeritus in the Department of Anthropology at the University of Illinois at Urbana until his death in 1992. He had been a student of A. L. Kroeber and R. Lowie at the University of California–Berkeley, where he received the Ph.D. degree in 1939. Over the years he studied the Wind River Shoshone, rural populations of Alaska, Central Mississippi, and Tanzania. He was a pioneer in the study of human ecology and political economy and a committed medical and applied anthropologist. He was an advocate of grassroots ownership of research findings and funding—before "empowerment" became fashionable. He was the embodiment of an engaged anthropologist. At a daylong symposium held in his honor at the annual meeting of the Society for Applied Anthropology, he said: "Eighty percent of the world is in desperate need. . . . There is no such thing as theoretical applied anthropology any more than there is theoretical surgery. You have got to get in there, get dirty, and do it. It is not an activity which is purely writing eloquent essays and so on. It is basically a personal commitment to tackle real problems with the best knowledge that you have." His students, his colleagues, the discipline, and the authors in this volume with whom he shared his thoughts were enriched by his vision of an anthropology that tried to make a difference in the condition of fellow human beings. We dedicate this volume to his memory.

Carol A. Smith is Professor of Anthropology at the University of California–Davis. Her research interests are in political economy, nations and nationalism, Third World intellectuals, and race/class/gender systems in Central America. Her publications include *Regional Analysis: vols. 1–2* (1976); "Beyond Dependency Theory: National and Regional Patterns of Underdevelopment in Guatemala," *American Ethnologist* (1978); "Local History in Global Context: Social and Economic

Transitions in Western Guatemala," *Comparative Studies in Society and History* (1984); "Culture and Community: The Language of Class in Guatemala," *Year Left 2: An American Socialist Yearbook* (1987); and *Guatemalan Indians and the State: 1540–1988* (1990). She has served as the President of the Society for Latin American Anthropology.

Index

Africa, 1, 14, 62, 64, 136, 137, 171, 202 n. 4, 241, 267, 268–77, 328
Agricultural development, 216–17
AIDS, 269, 275, 282
Ayllu, 59–60, 66–67, 84
Amazon Basin, 1
American Anthropological Association (AAA), 166, 173, 174, 327
  Task Force on African Hunger, Famine, and Food Security, 241
Amnesty International, 33, 193–94
Angra dos Reis (Rio de Janeiro), 150–52, 160 n. 14
Anthropology
  contributions in, 322–40, 344 n. 4, 344 n. 6, 345 n. 10, 346 n. 15
  cultural, 10–11
  development and its transformations, 18–20
  development and the state, 25–53
  and problems transforming societies, 3–12
  and research methods, 11, 301–21
Anthropology and Human Rights, 166
Apartheid, 176
Asia, 1, 192–93
Asian Cultural Forum on Development (ACFOD), 87
Association of Development Agencies in Bangladesh (ADAB), 79

Bangladesh Rural Advancement Committee (BRAC), 70, 84, 185
Boas, Franz, 2
Brazil, 111–18, 135–36, 138–39, 140–42, 143–52, 154–55, 160 n. 12, 234

Brazilian Association of Canoeing and Ecology (ABRACE), 78
Bretton Woods Commission, 341–42

Capital development and growth, 37–38, 219–20, 225–26, 228–29
Cardiovascular disease, 271
Center of Indigenous Peoples and Communities in Eastern Bolivia (CIDOB), 75
Children, 187–88, 269, 275, 279–80, 283–84
Commodity Choices, 252–54
Community health workers, 287–88, 289–92
Cooperatives (and Precooperatives), 71–73, 74, 92 n. 7, 93 n. 16, 93 n. 20
Coordinating Council for Local Development Associations, 74
Cultural imperialism, 152–53
Cultural relativism, 174–76, 179–80

Displacement studies, 17
Dominican Republic, 60, 66

Economic development, 4, 5–6, 30, 37, 38, 42–43, 47, 90, 142–43, 340–41, 344 n. 7
  anthropological approaches to, 224–32
  and epidemiological indicators, 231–32
  goals and indices, 211–34
  theory and disorders, 214–19
  troubles with GNP, 219–24

357

358   Index

Economic Social, and Cultural Rights, 170
Education, 47, 111, 121, 183, 281–82
Elderly populations, 186–87
Environment, 9, 78, 93 n. 21, 116–18, 149–53, 160 n. 11, 160 n. 12, 337–38
Ethnography, 106–8
European Economic Community (EEC), 314
Evolutionary studies, 182–83

Famine, 16, 64, 186, 187–88, 190, 194, 244–45, 246, 258
Famine Early Warning Systems (FEWS), 242, 243, 255, 256
Federal Land Development Authority (FDLA), 43, 44
First International Conference on Indian Life, 59–60
Fishery development projects, 40–41
Food and Agriculture Organization (FAO), 170, 202 n. 5, 230
Food production and supply, 15–16, 231–32
  classification and social distribution of, 245–46
  ecology of, 243–45
  health and nutritional consequences, 246
Fundación del Centavo, 89–90

Geneva Convention, 184
Genocide, 16, 176, 181–82, 184
Global culture, 8
Globo network, 112, 113, 115, 136, 138, 140–41, 157
Grameen Bank, 70, 72, 86
Grassroots organizations (GROs), 57–59, 94 n. 34
  classification by origin, 61–63
  empowerment and development of, 81–82
  facts and figures, 59–61
  federations and horizontal networking, 73–76, 93 n. 20, 93 n. 22, 93 n. 23
  and government connections, 65
  growth since 1970, 64–67
  and linkages with GRSOs, 82–88, 94 n. 30
  and religious groups, 63
  and support organizations (GRSOs), 76–81
  types of, 67–73
  and women, 64–65
Greenbelt Movement, 78
Gross National Product (GNP), 18, 44, 212, 213–14, 216, 217–18, 219–24
Guatemala, 31, 37, 45–48, 51–52
Gwembe District, Zambia, 118–23, 126 n. 4

Haiti, 34–35, 39–40, 50
Health and disease, 122–23, 265–93
  in Africa, 268–86
  changes in the study of, 12–15
  fertility, birth control, and maternal mortality, 271–73, 282
  patterns of, 268–71
  and role of foreign aid, 285–86
  in rural Mississippi, 286–93
  services for, 14–15, 273–77
  sexual transmission, 269, 272
  in Tanzania, 277–85
  and the tropics, 267–68
Holocaust, 170, 173
Hometown Associations, 70–71
Honduran Women's Peasant Federation (FEMUC), 68
Horizontal networking, 73–76, 93 n. 20, 93 n. 22, 93 n. 23
  amorphous grassroots movements, 73–74, 75–76
  informal economic networks, 73–74
  regional, 73
Human classification, 172–73
  and deprivation by age, 186–88
  and deprivation by gender, 185–86

ethnicity and pluralism, 180–81
ingroup-outgroup, 178–80
and policy implications, 182–85
violence and genocide, 181–82
Human Rights, 5, 45, 342–43
and anthropologists, 166–67
civil and political, 170, 171
contributions to, 167–70, 176–77
and cultural relativism, 174–76, 179–80
economic, social, and cultural, 170, 171, 188–89
and human classification, 172–73, 177–88, 202 n. 4, 202 n. 5, 202 n. 6, 203 n. 10
and indigenous rights, 171
institutions and linkages, 189–90
and international law, 172–73
and special human development issues, 170, 171
and the state, 190–95
studying, 15–18
transformations in, 195–99, 203 n. 14, 203 n. 15
and the United Nations, 170–73, 201 n. 1, 202 n. 2
Human Rights Watch Committees, 193–94
Hunger vulnerability, 241–60
and development aid, 254–55
diet and commodity choices, 251–54
food systems analysis, 243–47, 251
and hunger typology, 247–49, 257–58, 260 n. 3
innovative uses of food and aid, 255–56
institutional considerations of, 256–57
and the poor, 250–51
suffering and mortality, 249–50

Ibirama (Santa Catarina), 150–52, 160 n. 14
Immigration policy, 339–40

Independent Commission on International Humanitarian Issues (ICIHI), 194
India, 267
Indigenous rights, 168, 171–72, 199
Infant Mortality Rate (IMR), 226, 227
Infectious disease. *See* Health and disease
Inter-American Foundation, 66, 67, 82
Interest associations (IAs), 67, 68–70, 74, 92 n. 10
Inter-Ethnic Association for the Development of the Peruvian Jungle (AIDESEP), 75–76
Intergovernmental organizations (IGOs), 193, 241
International Covenant on Economic, Social and Cultural Rights, 192
International Covenants on Civil and Political Rights, 170
International Development Research Council, 137
International Labor Organization (ILO), 170, 192, 198, 217
International Monetary Fund (IMF), 29, 121, 341, 343 n. 1
International Planned Parenthood Federation, 79
International Women's Tribune Center, 69
Iringa Rural Nutrition Program, 79

Keynes, J. M., 214
Kottar Social Service Agency, 84

Life expectancies, 265–66, 267, 278
Linkages Methodology
definition of, 103–4
from isolate to world system, 106–11
multisite and multitime research in Brazil, 111–18
questions to consider, 123–25
and research, 104–5

Linkages Methodology *(continued)*
  social transformation in Gwembe District, 118–23, 126 n. 4
List, Friedrich, 215
Literacy, 141–42, 159 n. 3, 159 n. 4, 281
Local Development Associations (LDAs), 67–68, 74, 86, 88

Madres Educadores, 74
Maison Familles Ruraux Centers, 74
Malaria, 267, 268, 272, 275, 283
Malaysia, 43–45, 48, 49, 50–51
Malnutrition, 13, 79, 242–43, 247, 265–66, 267, 268, 280, 283–84
Marshall Plan, 27–28
Marx, Karl, 214–15
Mead, Margaret, 168, 310
Media, 2, 7–8, 9, 110, 111–16, 118, 126 n. 3, 127 n. 7, 127 n. 8, 127 n. 9. *See also* Print media
  and censorship, 137–38
  and cultural imperialism, 152–53
  and cultural resistance, 154–55
  and demographic transition, 146–48, 160 n. 8, 160 n. 9
  and the environment, 149–53, 160 n. 11, 160 n. 12, 160 n. 13, 160 n. 14
  and information transmitted by, 139–40
  and literacy, 141–42, 159 n. 3, 159 n. 4
  and national identity, 135–36
  and measuring the cultivation effect, 144–46, 159 n. 7
  and participation in the cash economy, 142–44, 159 n. 5
  and questions remaining, 157–58
  sex and gender attitudes, 148–49
  social navigation and migration, 140–41
  in a translocal world, 156–57
Microenterprise development, 78–79, 94 n. 27

Mortality, 1, 4, 9–10, 13, 231, 249–50, 272, 278, 279–80, 283

Naams, 83–84, 85
National Alliance of Environmental Groups, 78
National Bureau of Economic Research, 223–24
National Council of Kenyan Women, 78
National Peasant Association, 85
National Union of Peasants, 68
Nicaragua, 42–43
Nicaraguan Central Bank, 42
Nigeria, 136, 202 n. 4
Nongovernmental Organizations (NGOs), 2, 6–7, 9, 11, 17, 29, 46, 58, 59, 65, 66, 69, 86, 167, 193–95, 241, 336, 345 n. 11
Nutrition, 12–14, 246, 255–56, 282

Organization for Economic Cooperation (OECD), 6

Palawan Center for Appropriate Rural Technology, 85
Pan American Development Foundation, 66
Peasantries, 6, 30–31, 35, 92 n. 4
Population-Environment Balance (P-EB), 339–40
Poverty, 64, 78–79, 80, 81–82, 217, 243, 246–47, 250–51, 267, 269, 337
Print media, 141–42, 151, 159 n. 3, 159 n. 4, 160 n. 13, 281–82
Prostitution, 269, 270

Research Methods
  in Cape Verde, 317–20
  constraints to, 309–13
  interviewing, 308–9, 316–17, 319
  and the learning curve, 303–10
  in Northwest Portugal, 314–17
  rapid appraisal, 305–6, 309, 315–16, 318, 334
  and stepwise design, 312, 317

structured surveys, 306–8, 309, 316–17, 319
  training of, 321
Rostow, Walter, 215, 329
Rural Reconstruction Movement, 63, 65
Russia, 137, 274

Save the Children, 65, 93 n. 12
Six S Association, 77, 78, 79, 83–84, 85, 94 n. 26
Smith, Adam, 232
Social welfare, 220, 221, 222
Sociedad de Profesionales para el Desarrollo Rural (SOPRODER), 84
Sri Lanka, 39, 50, 89, 181
Staple food production, 6, 231–32, 248, 252, 260 n. 3
State development, 25–33
  current institutional models, 32–38
  and debt, 28–29, 37–38
  and future research and experimentation, 49–52
  in Guatemala, 45–48, 51–52
  and ideologies, 31–32
  in Malaysia, 43–45, 48, 49, 50–51
  in Nicaragua, 42–43
  and state autonomy and power, 33–38, 39–40, 52 n. 3
  and treatment in the Third World, 38–49
Stress, 257–58
Substance abuse, 121, 270
Supply-side economics, 217–18, 229–30

Taller de Estudios Rurales (TER), 84
Tanzania (Africa), 277–85
Telenovelas, 113, 115, 136, 140–41, 142–43, 144, 147, 148, 149
Television, 111–16, 118, 126 n. 3, 127 n. 7, 127 n. 8, 135–49, 151–52, 154–55, 156, 159 n. 4, 159 n. 5, 159 n. 6, 160 n. 13, 160 n. 14
  contraceptive effects of, 146–48
  and sex-gender attitudes, 148–49
Transportation, 107–8, 118
Trickle Up Program, 72

UN Economic, Social, and Cultural Organization (UNESCO), 166, 170, 176, 198
UNICEF, 65–66, 73, 187, 202 n. 5, 279
United Nations, 5, 165, 166, 167, 170–73, 197, 198
  Conference on the Environment and Development (UNCED), 117
Universal Declaration of Human Rights (1948), 168, 170, 174, 175–76, 192, 196–97, 201 n. 1, 202 n. 2, 202 n. 4
USAID, 28, 31, 46, 243, 331, 334
U.S. Peace Corps, 27

Violence, 16, 181–82, 184

Working Women's Forum, 70
Workshop for Andean Oral History, 66
World Bank, 2, 17, 29, 31, 43, 50, 66, 78, 81, 85, 121, 217, 241, 254, 330, 331, 333, 336–37, 338–39, 341–42, 345 n. 11, 346 n. 16, 346 n. 17
World Food Programme (WFP), 170, 202 n. 5, 255
World Health Organization (WHO), 170, 202 n. 5, 267, 268, 274, 279, 285
World Hunger Program, 241–42, 243
Women, 64–65, 67, 69–70, 72, 77–78, 87–88, 93 n. 12, 143–44, 145, 159 n. 6, 159 n. 8, 185–86, 268, 280

YMCA, 63